414467

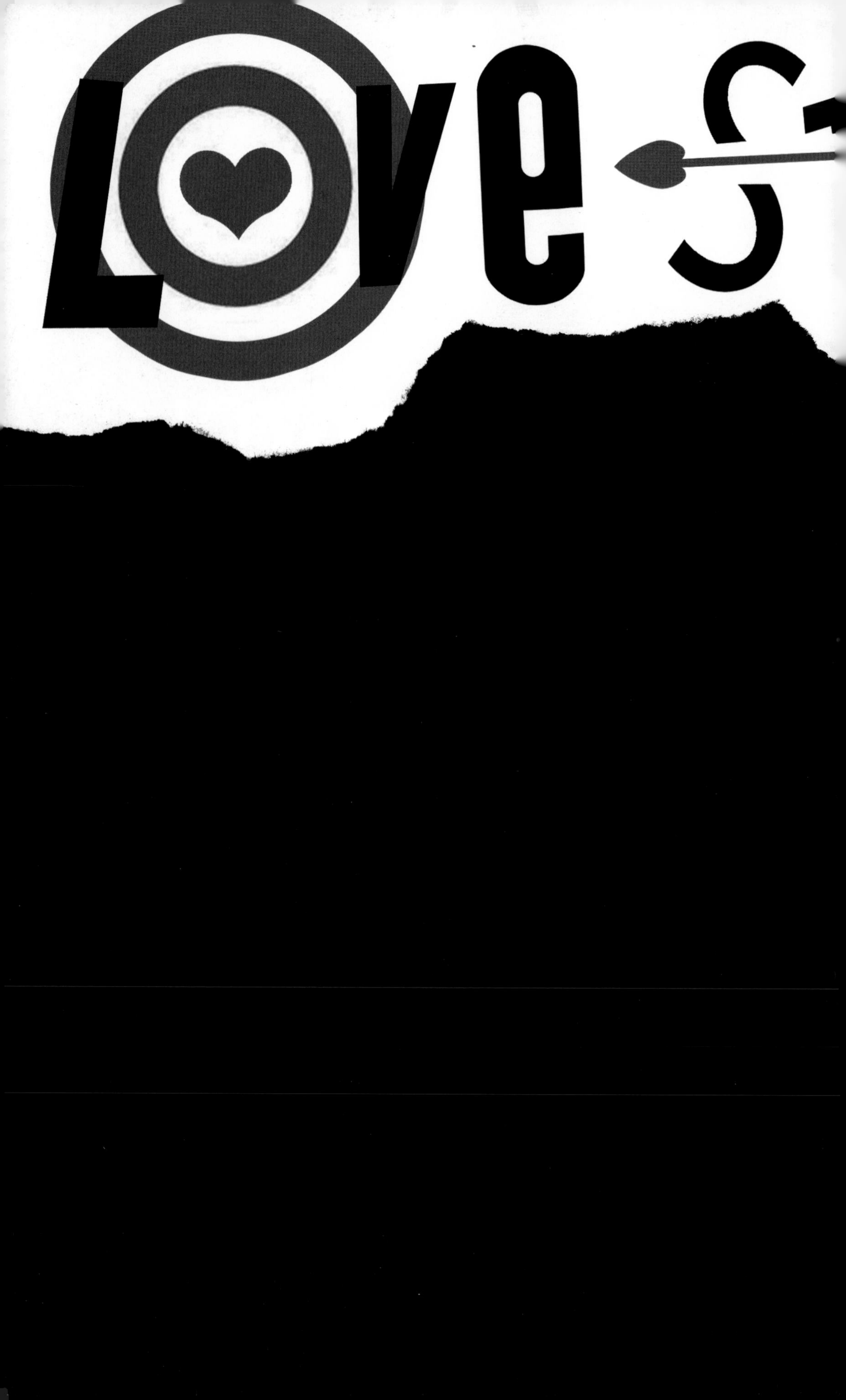
Love S

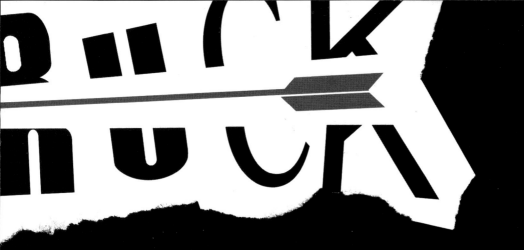

WORDS BY DENNIS
HOPELESS

ART BY KEVIN
MELLON

IMAGE COMICS, INC.

Robert Kirkman - chief operating officer
Erik Larsen - chief financial officer
Todd McFarlane - president
Marc Silvestri - chief executive officer
Jim Valentino - vice-president

Eric Stephenson - publisher
Todd Martinez - sales & licensing coordinator
Sarah deLaine - pr & marketing coordinator
Branwyn Bigglestone - accounts manager
Emily Miller - administrative assistant
Jamie Parreno - marketing assistant
Kevin Yuen - digital rights coordinator
Tyler Shainline - production manager
Drew Gill - art director
Jonathan Chan - senior production artist
Monica Garcia - production artist
Vincent Kukua - production artist
Jana Cook - production artist

www.imagecomics.com

LOVESTRUCK. First Printing. Published by Image Comics, Inc. Office of publication: 2134 Allston Way, 2nd Floor, Berkeley, CA 94704. Copyright © 2011 Dennis Hopeless. All rights reserved. LOVESTRUCK™ (including all prominent characters featured herein), its logo and all character likenesses are trademarks of Dennis Hopeless, unless otherwise noted. Image Comics® and its logos are registered trademarks of Image Comics, Inc. No part of this publication may be reproduced or transmitted, in any form or by any means (except for short excerpts for review purposes) without the express written permission of Image Comics, Inc. All names, characters, events and locales in this publication are entirely fictional. Any resemblance to actual persons (living or dead), events or places, without satiric intent, is coincidental. International Rights Representative: Christine Meyer (christine@gfloystudio.com). PRINTED IN KOREA. ISBN: 978-1-60706-447-3.

CHAPTER 1

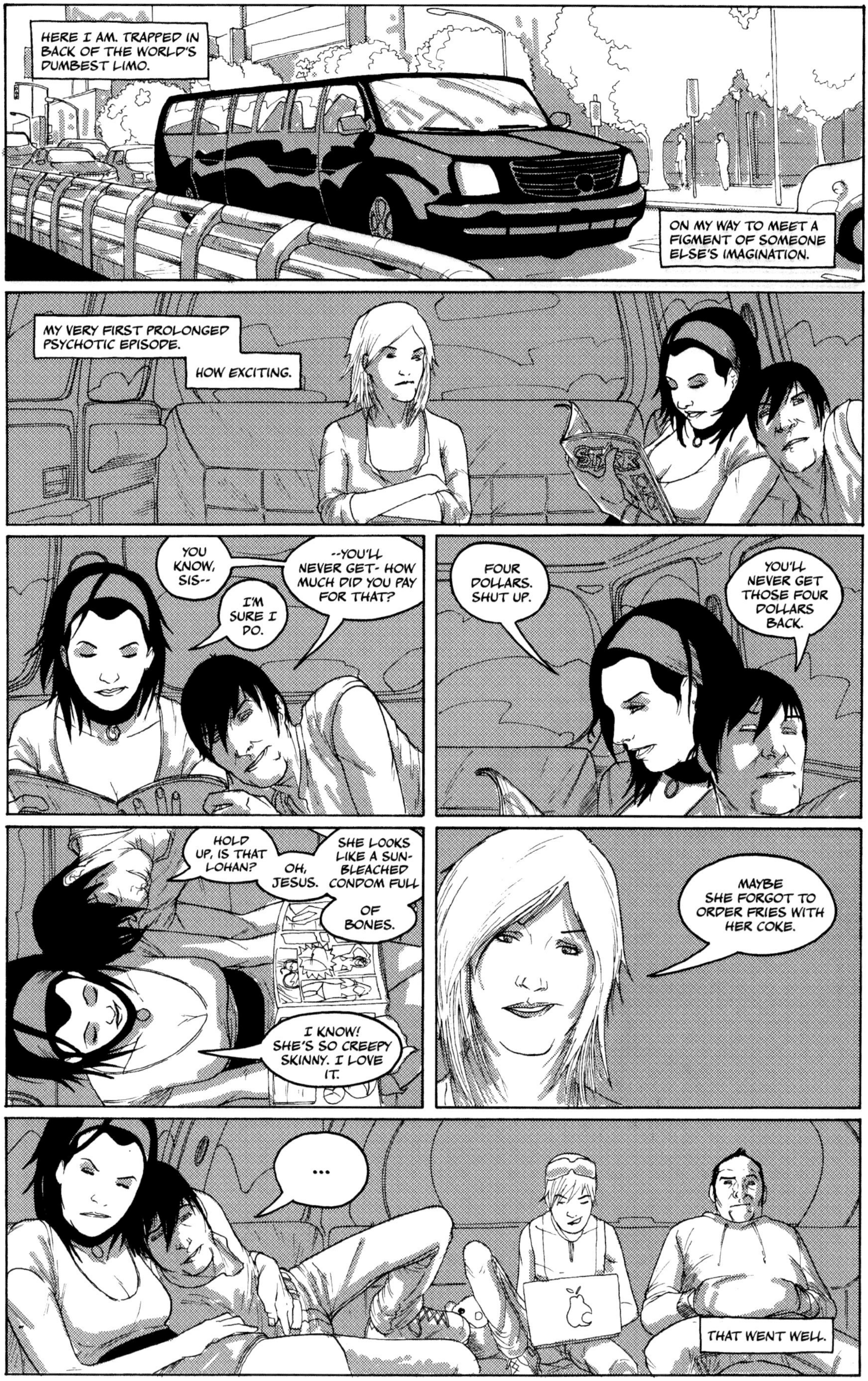
HERE I AM. TRAPPED IN BACK OF THE WORLD'S DUMBEST LIMO.
ON MY WAY TO MEET A FIGMENT OF SOMEONE ELSE'S IMAGINATION.
MY VERY FIRST PROLONGED PSYCHOTIC EPISODE.
HOW EXCITING.
YOU KNOW, SIS--
I'M SURE I DO.
--YOU'LL NEVER GET- HOW MUCH DID YOU PAY FOR THAT?
FOUR DOLLARS. SHUT UP.
YOU'LL NEVER GET THOSE FOUR DOLLARS BACK.
HOLD UP, IS THAT LOHAN?
OH, JESUS.
SHE LOOKS LIKE A SUN-BLEACHED CONDOM FULL OF BONES.
I KNOW! SHE'S SO CREEPY SKINNY. I LOVE IT.
MAYBE SHE FORGOT TO ORDER FRIES WITH HER COKE.
...
THAT WENT WELL.

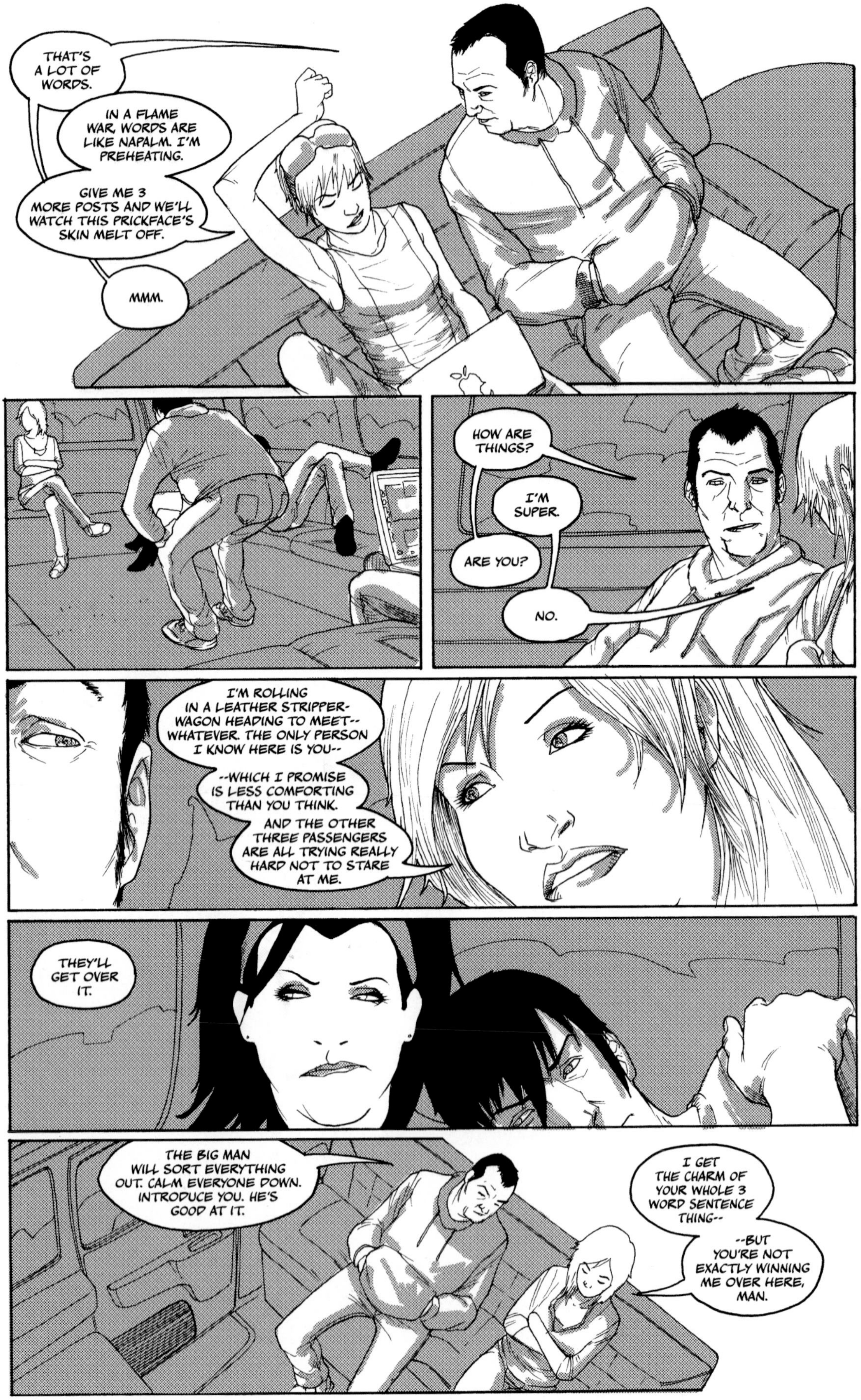
THAT'S A LOT OF WORDS.
IN A FLAME WAR, WORDS ARE LIKE NAPALM. I'M PREHEATING.
GIVE ME 3 MORE POSTS AND WE'LL WATCH THIS PRICKFACE'S SKIN MELT OFF.
MMM.
HOW ARE THINGS?
I'M SUPER.
ARE YOU?
NO.
I'M ROLLING IN A LEATHER STRIPPER-WAGON HEADING TO MEET--WHATEVER. THE ONLY PERSON I KNOW HERE IS YOU--
--WHICH I PROMISE IS LESS COMFORTING THAN YOU THINK.
AND THE OTHER THREE PASSENGERS ARE ALL TRYING REALLY HARD NOT TO STARE AT ME.
THEY'LL GET OVER IT.
THE BIG MAN WILL SORT EVERYTHING OUT. CALM EVERYONE DOWN. INTRODUCE YOU. HE'S GOOD AT IT.
I GET THE CHARM OF YOUR WHOLE 3 WORD SENTENCE THING--
--BUT YOU'RE NOT EXACTLY WINNING ME OVER HERE, MAN.

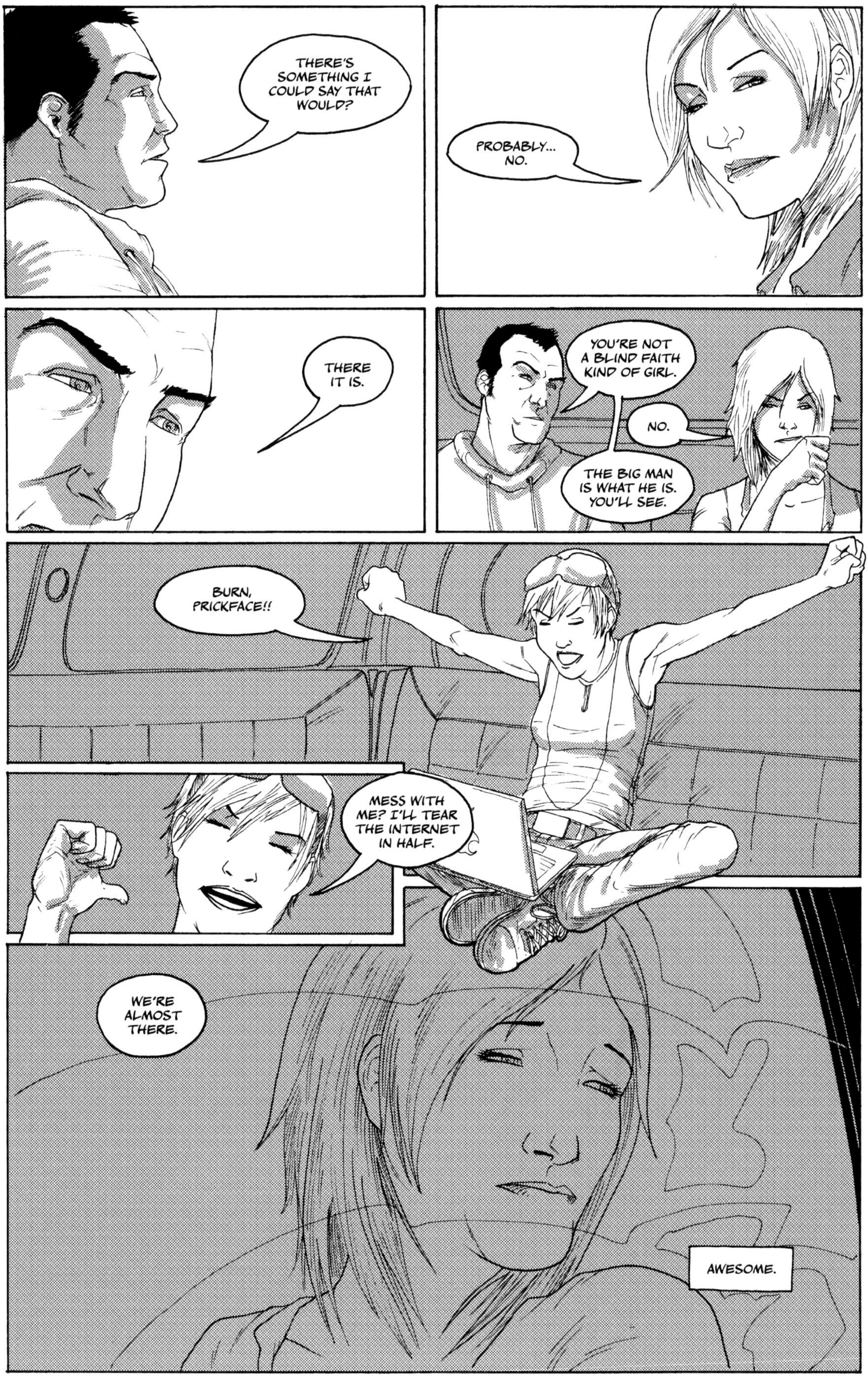
THERE'S SOMETHING I COULD SAY THAT WOULD?
PROBABLY... NO.
THERE IT IS.
YOU'RE NOT A BLIND FAITH KIND OF GIRL.
NO.
THE BIG MAN IS WHAT HE IS. YOU'LL SEE.
BURN, PRICKFACE!!
MESS WITH ME? I'LL TEAR THE INTERNET IN HALF.
WE'RE ALMOST THERE.
AWESOME.

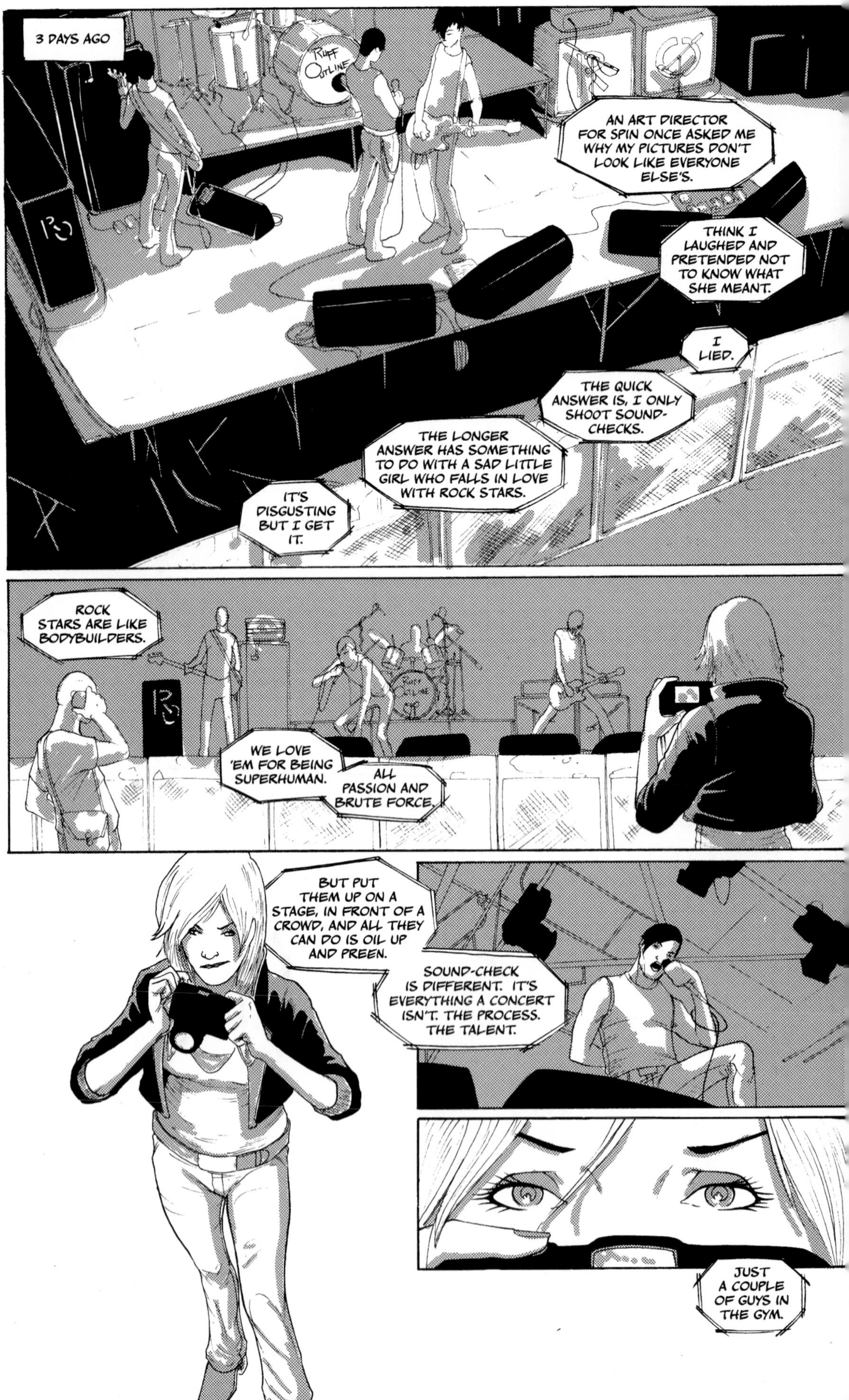
3 DAYS AGO
RUFF OUTLINE
AN ART DIRECTOR FOR SPIN ONCE ASKED ME WHY MY PICTURES DON'T LOOK LIKE EVERYONE ELSE'S.
THINK I LAUGHED AND PRETENDED NOT TO KNOW WHAT SHE MEANT.
I LIED.
THE QUICK ANSWER IS, I ONLY SHOOT SOUND-CHECKS.
THE LONGER ANSWER HAS SOMETHING TO DO WITH A SAD LITTLE GIRL WHO FALLS IN LOVE WITH ROCK STARS.
IT'S DISGUSTING BUT I GET IT.
ROCK STARS ARE LIKE BODYBUILDERS.
WE LOVE 'EM FOR BEING SUPERHUMAN.
ALL PASSION AND BRUTE FORCE.
BUT PUT THEM UP ON A STAGE, IN FRONT OF A CROWD, AND ALL THEY CAN DO IS OIL UP AND PREEN.
SOUND-CHECK IS DIFFERENT. IT'S EVERYTHING A CONCERT ISN'T. THE PROCESS. THE TALENT.
JUST A COUPLE OF GUYS IN THE GYM.

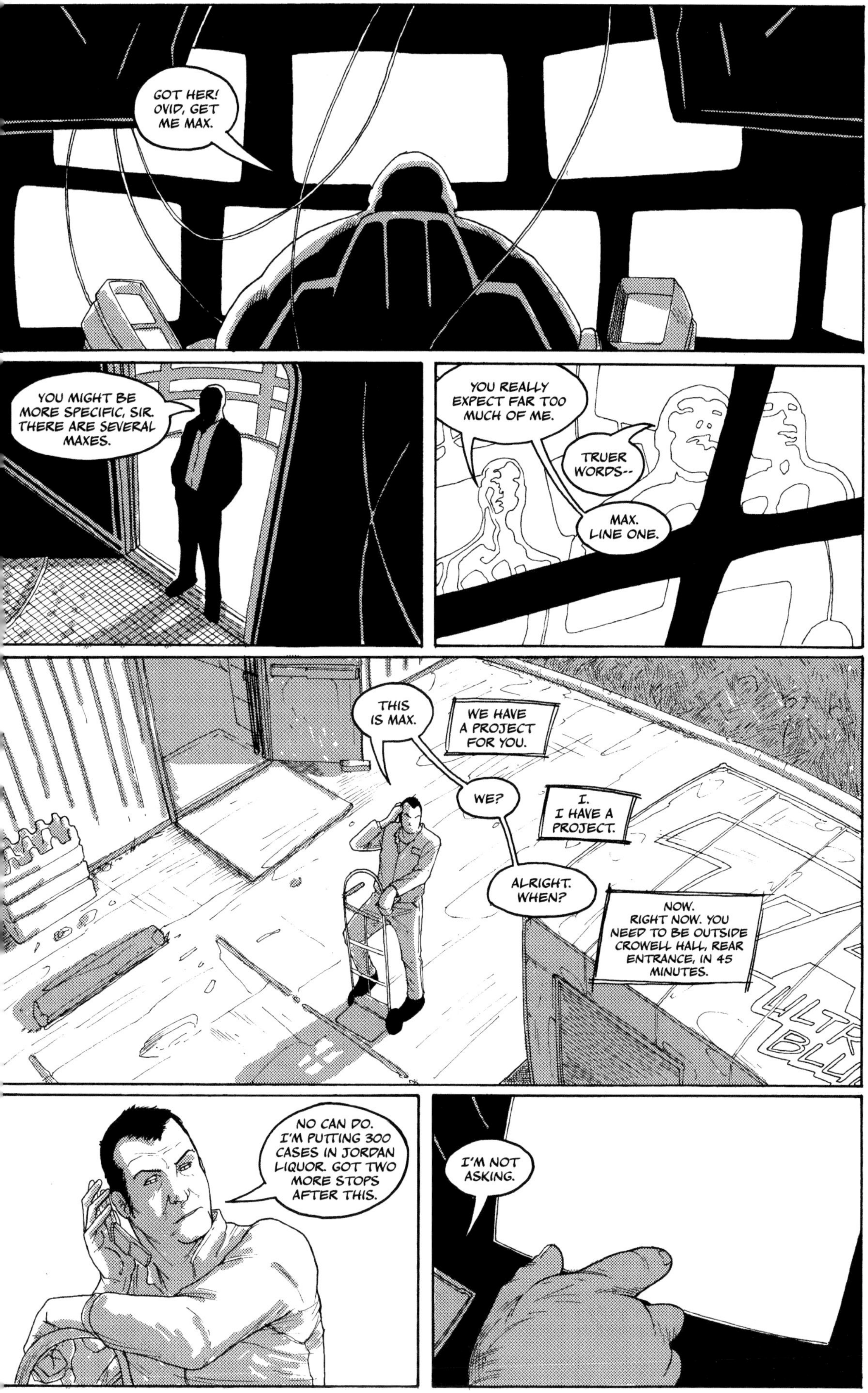
GOT HER! OVID, GET ME MAX.
YOU MIGHT BE MORE SPECIFIC, SIR. THERE ARE SEVERAL MAXES.
YOU REALLY EXPECT FAR TOO MUCH OF ME.
TRUER WORDS--
MAX. LINE ONE.
THIS IS MAX.
WE HAVE A PROJECT FOR YOU.
WE?
I. I HAVE A PROJECT.
ALRIGHT. WHEN?
NOW. RIGHT NOW. YOU NEED TO BE OUTSIDE CROWELL HALL, REAR ENTRANCE, IN 45 MINUTES.
NO CAN DO. I'M PUTTING 300 CASES IN JORDAN LIQUOR. GOT TWO MORE STOPS AFTER THIS.
I'M NOT ASKING.

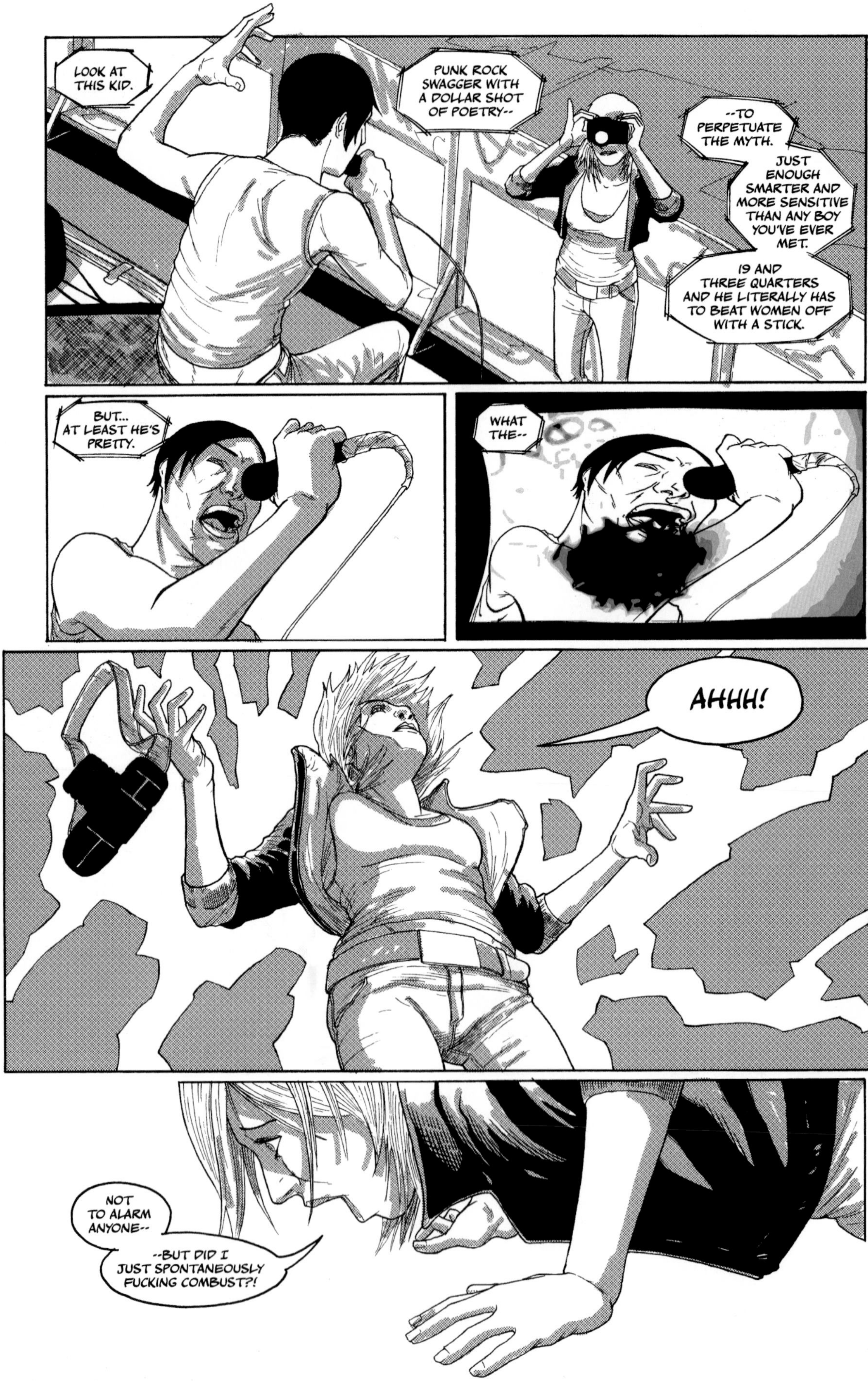

LOOK AT THIS KID.
PUNK ROCK SWAGGER WITH A DOLLAR SHOT OF POETRY--
--TO PERPETUATE THE MYTH.
JUST ENOUGH SMARTER AND MORE SENSITIVE THAN ANY BOY YOU'VE EVER MET.
19 AND THREE QUARTERS AND HE LITERALLY HAS TO BEAT WOMEN OFF WITH A STICK.
BUT... AT LEAST HE'S PRETTY.
WHAT THE--
AHHH!
NOT TO ALARM ANYONE--
--BUT DID I JUST SPONTANEOUSLY FUCKING COMBUST?!

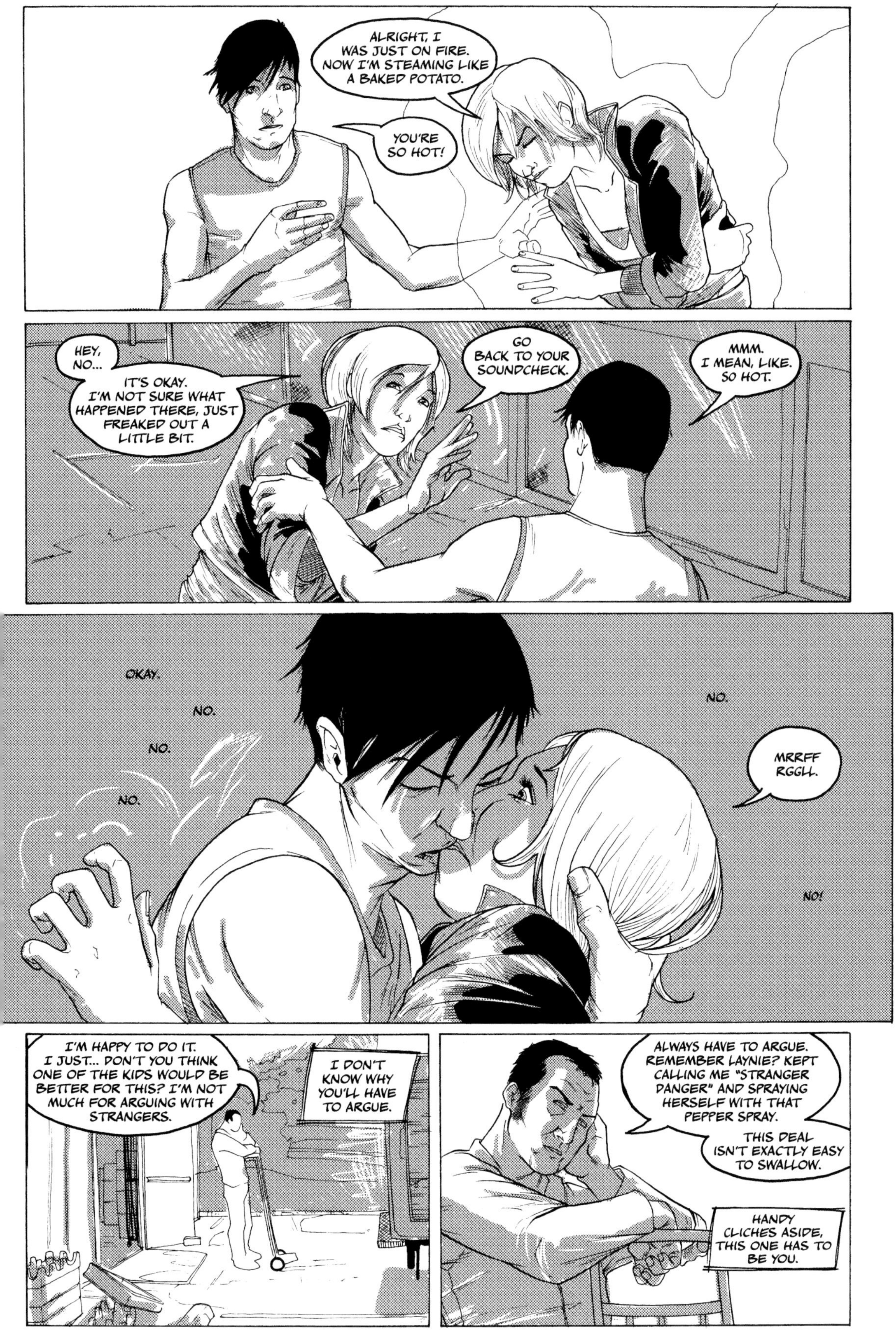
ALRIGHT, I WAS JUST ON FIRE. NOW I'M STEAMING LIKE A BAKED POTATO.
YOU'RE SO HOT!
HEY, NO...
IT'S OKAY. I'M NOT SURE WHAT HAPPENED THERE, JUST FREAKED OUT A LITTLE BIT.
GO BACK TO YOUR SOUNDCHECK.
MMM. I MEAN, LIKE. SO HOT.
OKAY.
NO.
NO.
NO.
NO.
MRRFF RGGLL.
NO!
I'M HAPPY TO DO IT. I JUST... DON'T YOU THINK ONE OF THE KIDS WOULD BE BETTER FOR THIS? I'M NOT MUCH FOR ARGUING WITH STRANGERS.
I DON'T KNOW WHY YOU'LL HAVE TO ARGUE.
ALWAYS HAVE TO ARGUE. REMEMBER LAYNIE? KEPT CALLING ME "STRANGER DANGER" AND SPRAYING HERSELF WITH THAT PEPPER SPRAY.
THIS DEAL ISN'T EXACTLY EASY TO SWALLOW.
HANDY CLICHES ASIDE, THIS ONE HAS TO BE YOU.

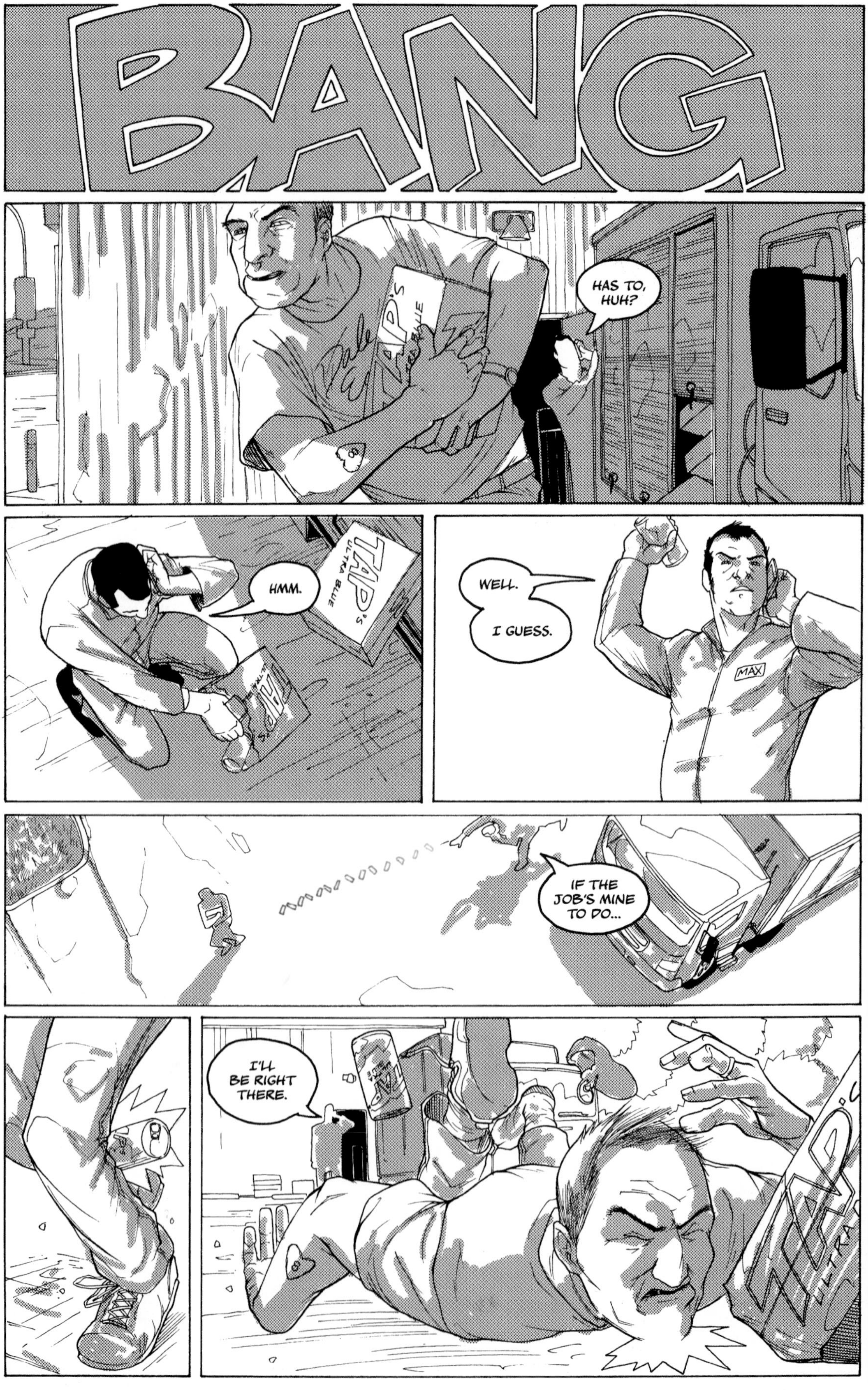
BANG
HAS TO, HUH?
TAP'S
HMM.
TAP'S ULTRA BLUE
WELL.
I GUESS.
MAX
IF THE JOB'S MINE TO DO...
I'LL BE RIGHT THERE.

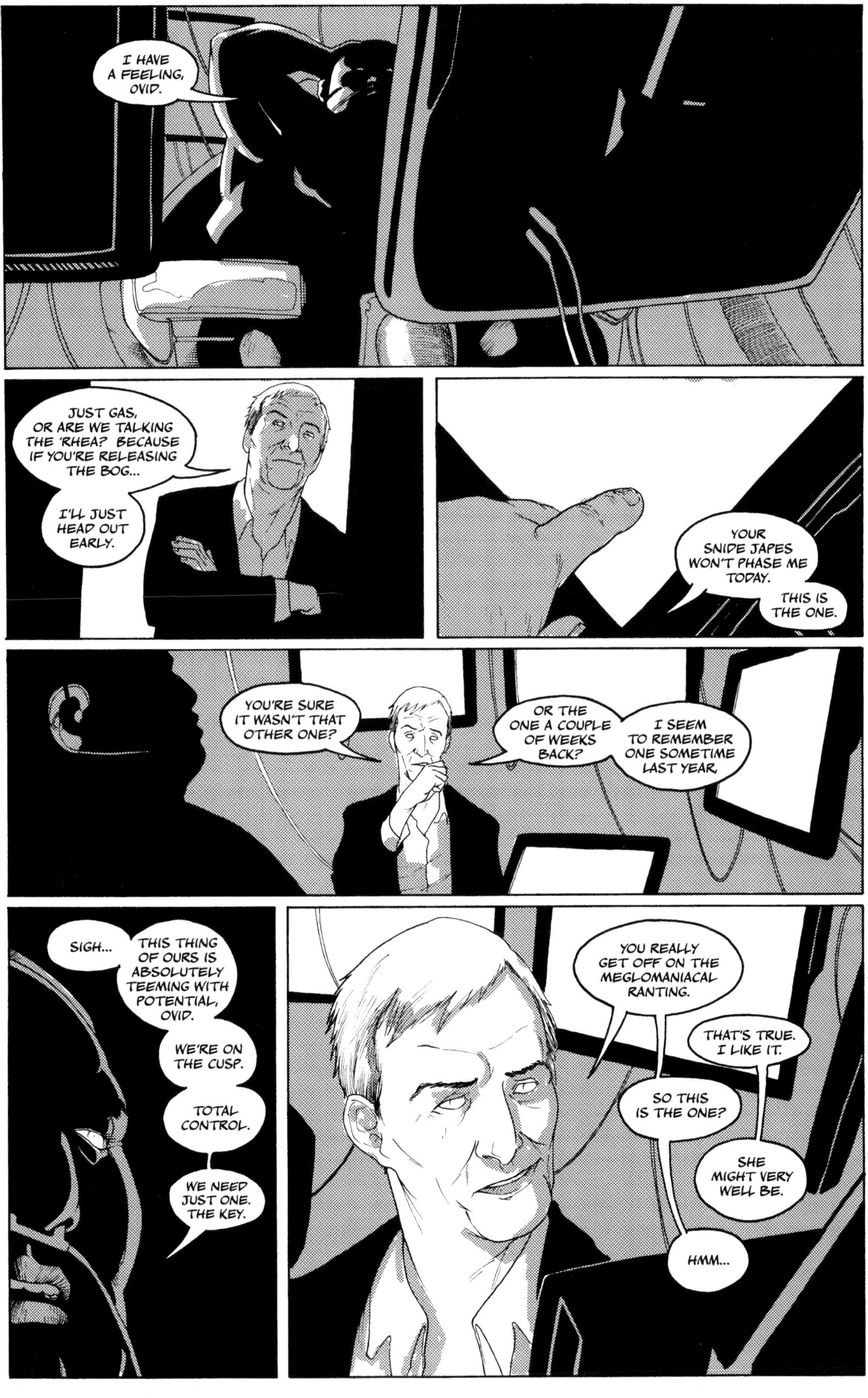
I HAVE A FEELING, OVID.
JUST GAS, OR ARE WE TALKING THE 'RHEA? BECAUSE IF YOU'RE RELEASING THE BOG...
I'LL JUST HEAD OUT EARLY.
YOUR SNIDE JAPES WON'T PHASE ME TODAY.
THIS IS THE ONE.
YOU'RE SURE IT WASN'T THAT OTHER ONE?
OR THE ONE A COUPLE OF WEEKS BACK?
I SEEM TO REMEMBER ONE SOMETIME LAST YEAR.
SIGH...
THIS THING OF OURS IS ABSOLUTELY TEEMING WITH POTENTIAL, OVID.
WE'RE ON THE CUSP.
TOTAL CONTROL.
WE NEED JUST ONE. THE KEY.
YOU REALLY GET OFF ON THE MEGLOMANIACAL RANTING.
THAT'S TRUE. I LIKE IT.
SO THIS IS THE ONE?
SHE MIGHT VERY WELL BE.
HMM...

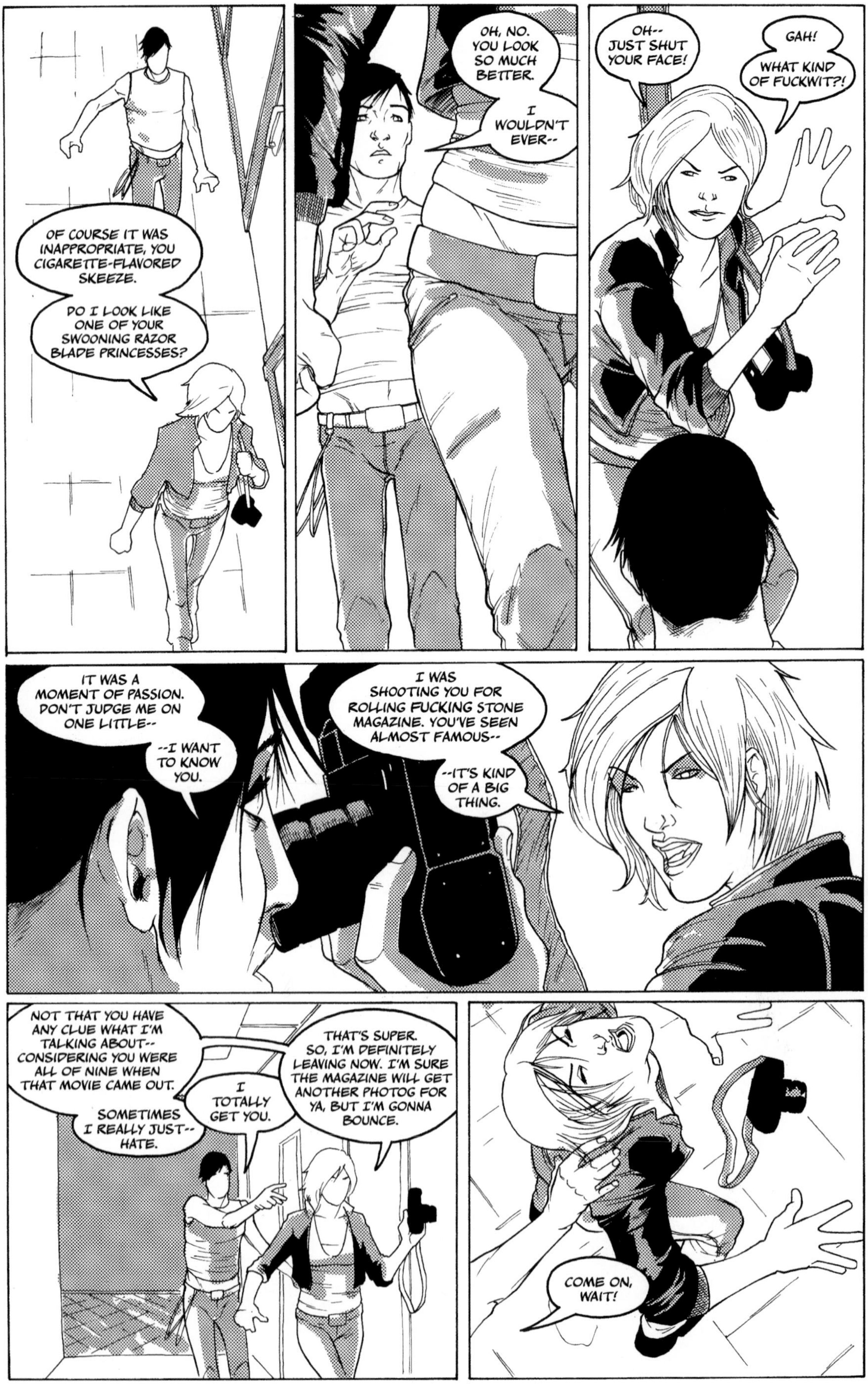

OF COURSE IT WAS INAPPROPRIATE, YOU CIGARETTE-FLAVORED SKEEZE.
DO I LOOK LIKE ONE OF YOUR SWOONING RAZOR BLADE PRINCESSES?
OH, NO. YOU LOOK SO MUCH BETTER.
I WOULDN'T EVER--
OH-- JUST SHUT YOUR FACE!
GAH!
WHAT KIND OF FUCKWIT?!
IT WAS A MOMENT OF PASSION. DON'T JUDGE ME ON ONE LITTLE--
--I WANT TO KNOW YOU.
I WAS SHOOTING YOU FOR ROLLING FUCKING STONE MAGAZINE. YOU'VE SEEN ALMOST FAMOUS--
--IT'S KIND OF A BIG THING.
NOT THAT YOU HAVE ANY CLUE WHAT I'M TALKING ABOUT-- CONSIDERING YOU WERE ALL OF NINE WHEN THAT MOVIE CAME OUT.
SOMETIMES I REALLY JUST-- HATE.
I TOTALLY GET YOU.
THAT'S SUPER. SO, I'M DEFINITELY LEAVING NOW. I'M SURE THE MAGAZINE WILL GET ANOTHER PHOTOG FOR YA, BUT I'M GONNA BOUNCE.
COME ON, WAIT!

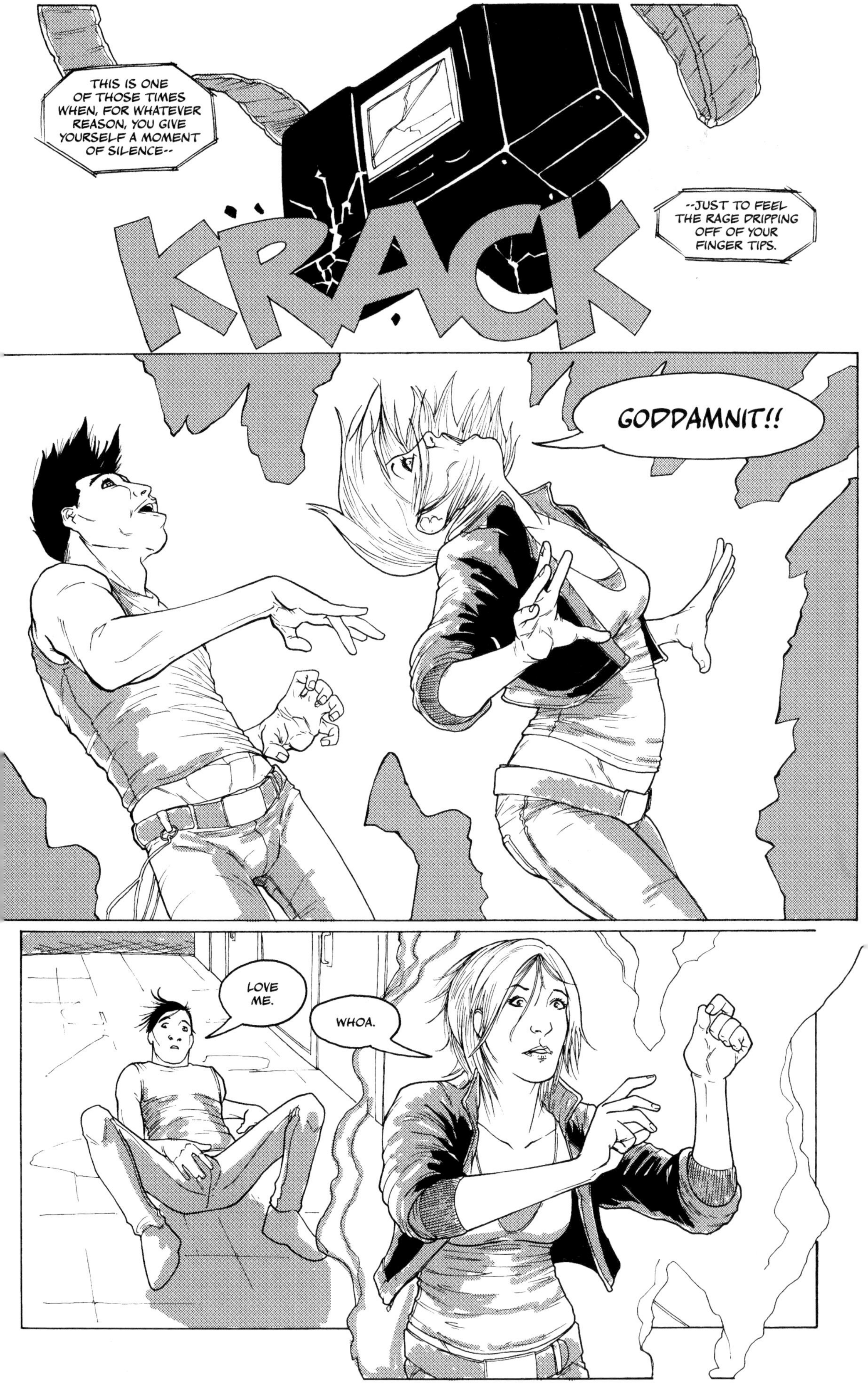
THIS IS ONE OF THOSE TIMES WHEN, FOR WHATEVER REASON, YOU GIVE YOURSELF A MOMENT OF SILENCE--
KRACK
--JUST TO FEEL THE RAGE DRIPPING OFF OF YOUR FINGER TIPS.
GODDAMNIT!!
LOVE ME.
WHOA.

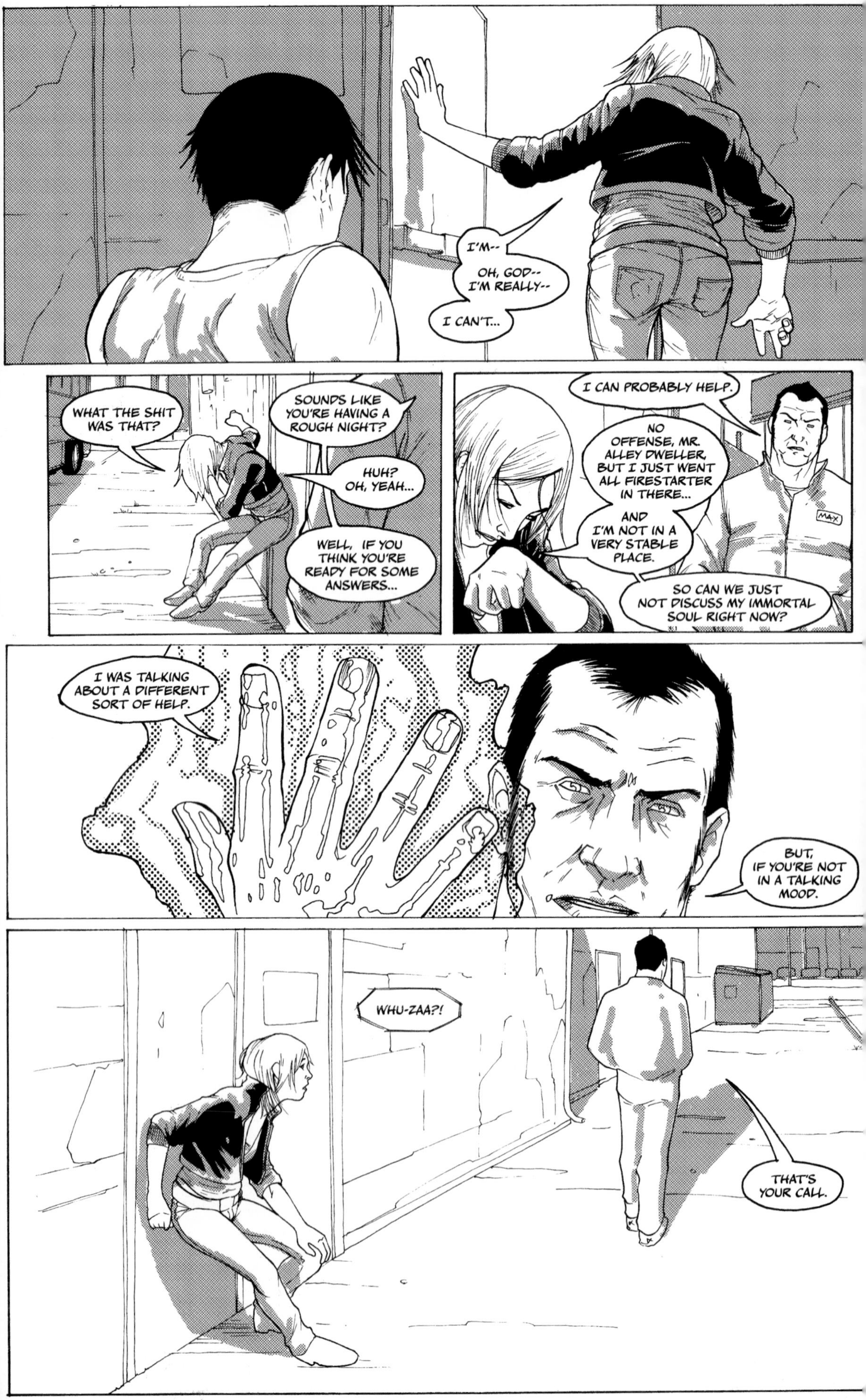
I'M--
OH, GOD-- I'M REALLY--
I CAN'T...
WHAT THE SHIT WAS THAT?
SOUNDS LIKE YOU'RE HAVING A ROUGH NIGHT?
HUH? OH, YEAH...
WELL, IF YOU THINK YOU'RE READY FOR SOME ANSWERS...
I CAN PROBABLY HELP.
NO OFFENSE, MR. ALLEY DWELLER, BUT I JUST WENT ALL FIRESTARTER IN THERE...
AND I'M NOT IN A VERY STABLE PLACE.
SO CAN WE JUST NOT DISCUSS MY IMMORTAL SOUL RIGHT NOW?
MAX
I WAS TALKING ABOUT A DIFFERENT SORT OF HELP.
BUT, IF YOU'RE NOT IN A TALKING MOOD.
WHU-ZAA?!
THAT'S YOUR CALL.

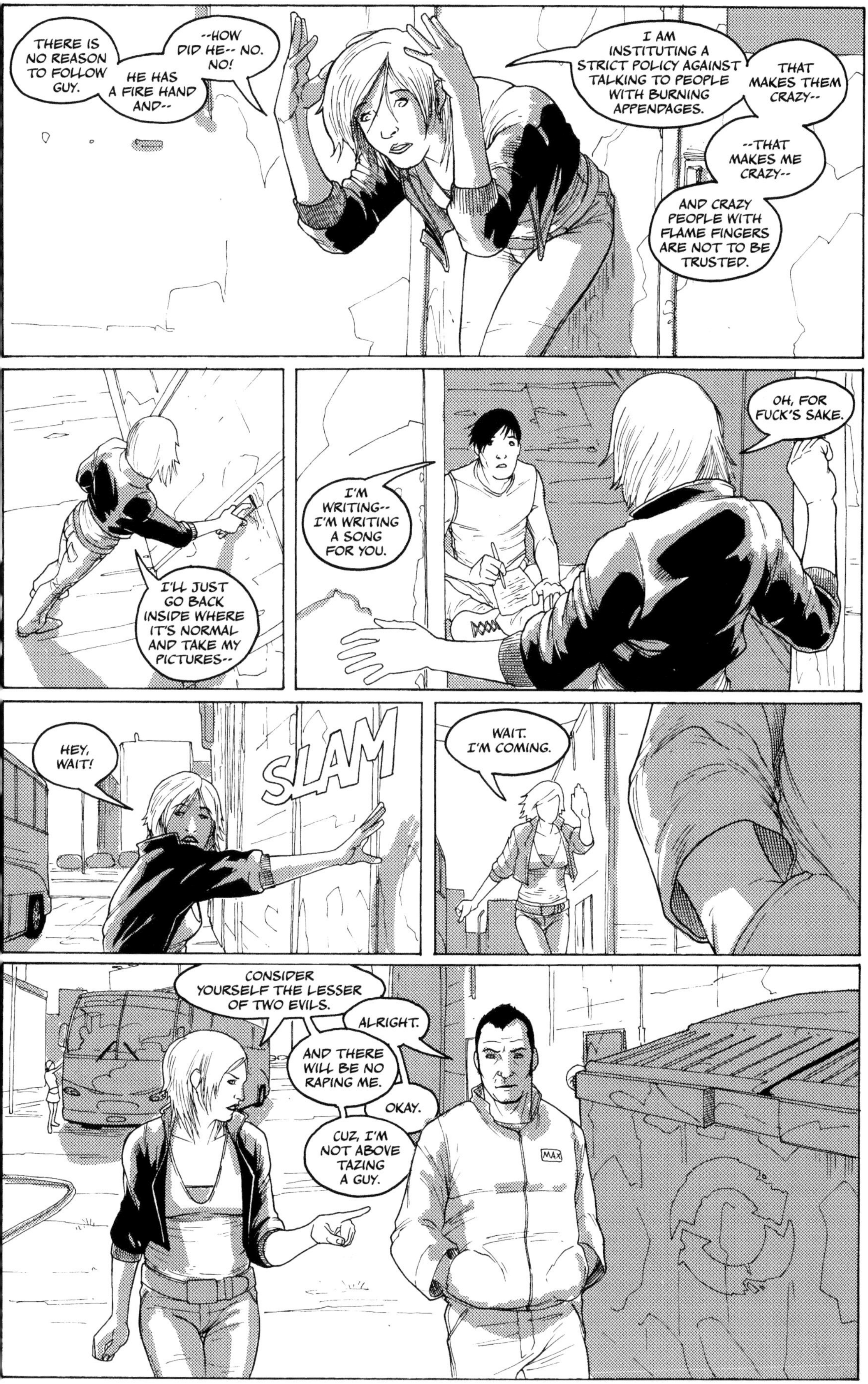
THERE IS NO REASON TO FOLLOW GUY.
HE HAS A FIRE HAND AND--
--HOW DID HE-- NO. NO!
I AM INSTITUTING A STRICT POLICY AGAINST TALKING TO PEOPLE WITH BURNING APPENDAGES.
THAT MAKES THEM CRAZY--
--THAT MAKES ME CRAZY--
AND CRAZY PEOPLE WITH FLAME FINGERS ARE NOT TO BE TRUSTED.
I'LL JUST GO BACK INSIDE WHERE IT'S NORMAL AND TAKE MY PICTURES--
I'M WRITING-- I'M WRITING A SONG FOR YOU.
OH, FOR FUCK'S SAKE.
HEY, WAIT!
SLAM
WAIT. I'M COMING.
CONSIDER YOURSELF THE LESSER OF TWO EVILS.
ALRIGHT.
AND THERE WILL BE NO RAPING ME.
OKAY.
CUZ, I'M NOT ABOVE TAZING A GUY.
MAX

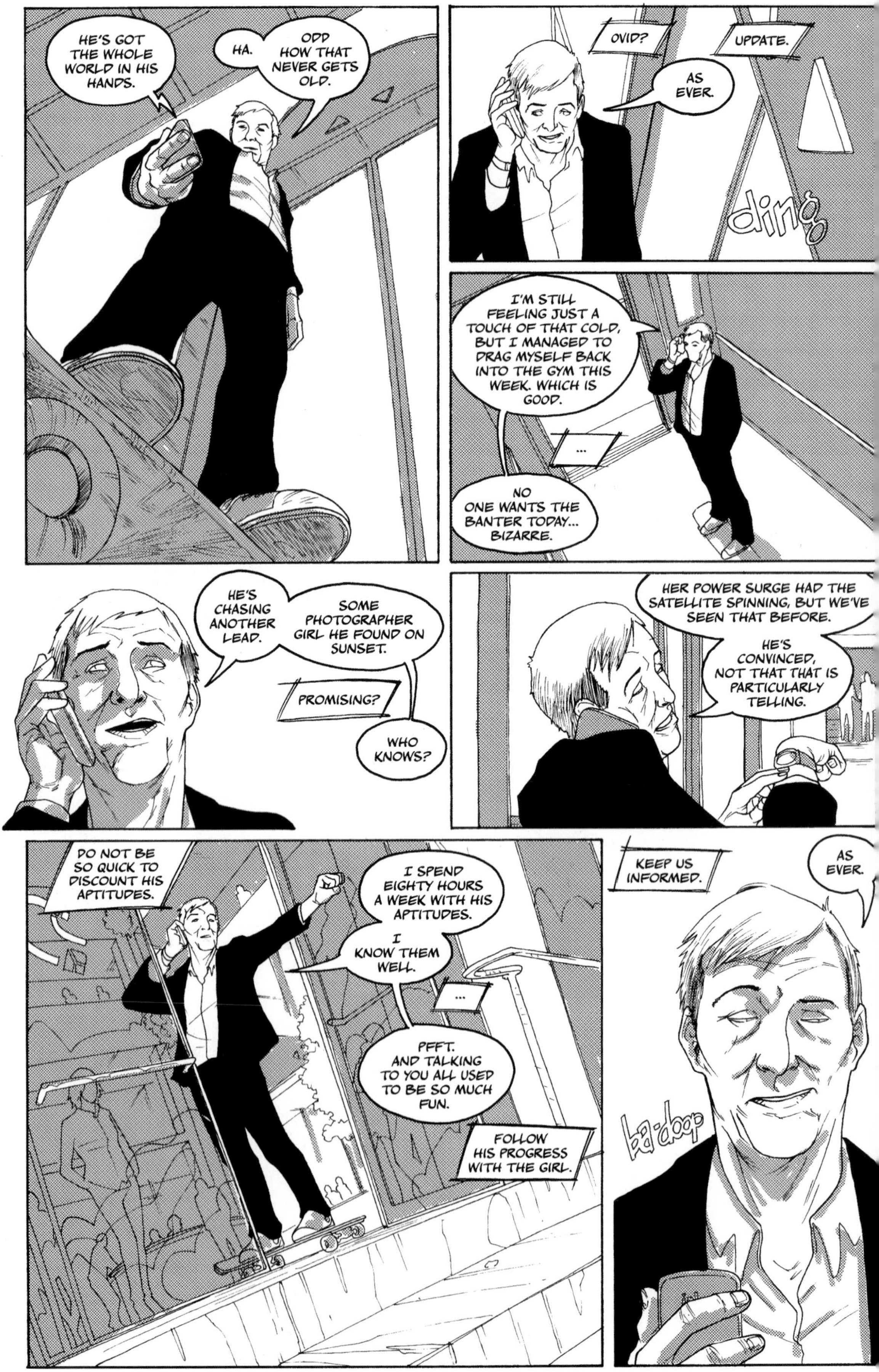

HE'S GOT THE WHOLE WORLD IN HIS HANDS.
HA.
ODD HOW THAT NEVER GETS OLD.
OVID?
UPDATE.
AS EVER.
ding
I'M STILL FEELING JUST A TOUCH OF THAT COLD, BUT I MANAGED TO DRAG MYSELF BACK INTO THE GYM THIS WEEK. WHICH IS GOOD.
...
NO ONE WANTS THE BANTER TODAY... BIZARRE.
HE'S CHASING ANOTHER LEAD.
SOME PHOTOGRAPHER GIRL HE FOUND ON SUNSET.
PROMISING?
WHO KNOWS?
HER POWER SURGE HAD THE SATELLITE SPINNING, BUT WE'VE SEEN THAT BEFORE.
HE'S CONVINCED, NOT THAT THAT IS PARTICULARLY TELLING.
DO NOT BE SO QUICK TO DISCOUNT HIS APTITUDES.
I SPEND EIGHTY HOURS A WEEK WITH HIS APTITUDES.
I KNOW THEM WELL.
...
PFFT. AND TALKING TO YOU ALL USED TO BE SO MUCH FUN.
FOLLOW HIS PROGRESS WITH THE GIRL.
KEEP US INFORMED.
AS EVER.
ba-doop

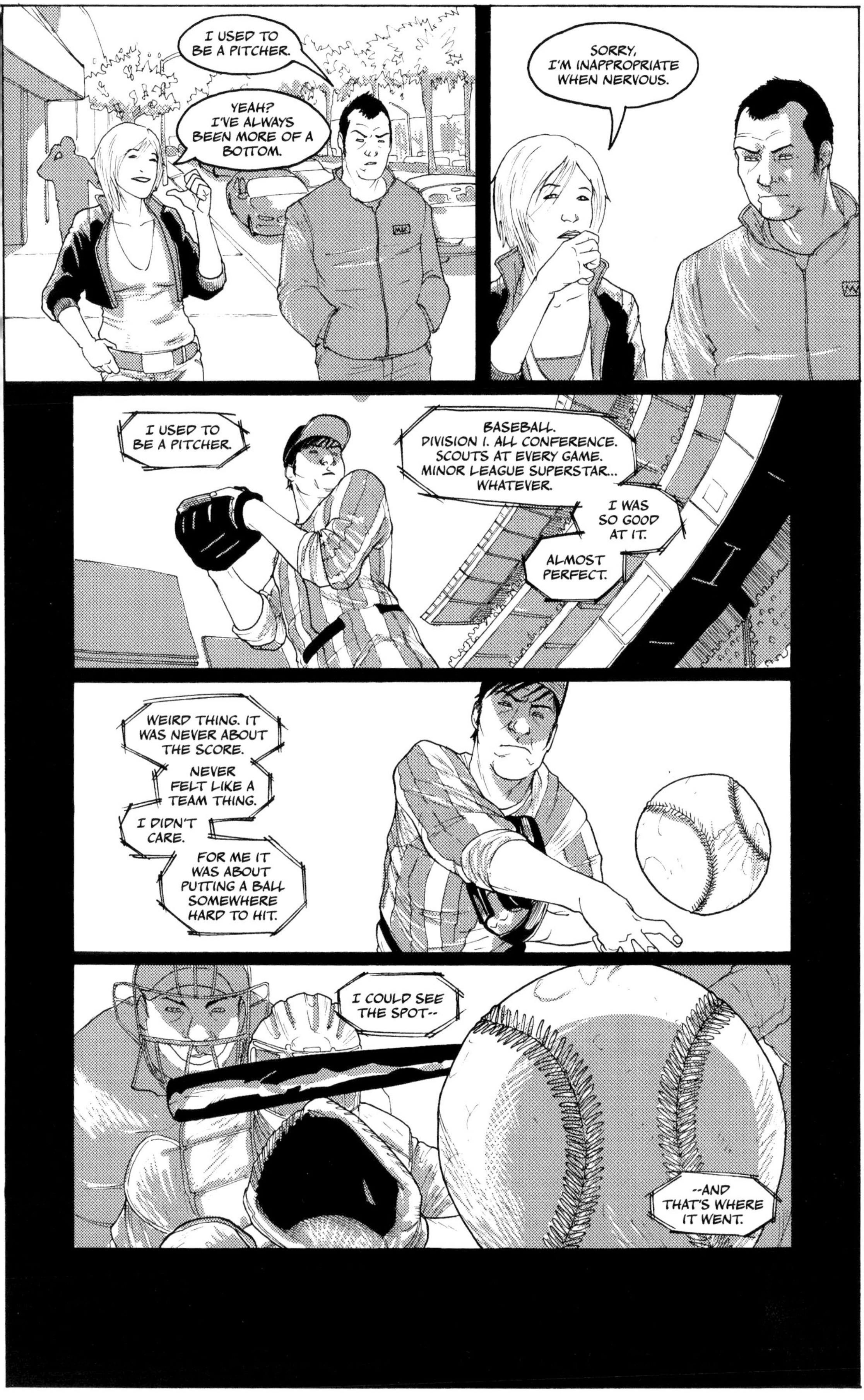
I USED TO BE A PITCHER.
YEAH? I'VE ALWAYS BEEN MORE OF A BOTTOM.
SORRY, I'M INAPPROPRIATE WHEN NERVOUS.
I USED TO BE A PITCHER.
BASEBALL. DIVISION I. ALL CONFERENCE. SCOUTS AT EVERY GAME. MINOR LEAGUE SUPERSTAR... WHATEVER.
I WAS SO GOOD AT IT.
ALMOST PERFECT.
WEIRD THING. IT WAS NEVER ABOUT THE SCORE.
NEVER FELT LIKE A TEAM THING.
I DIDN'T CARE.
FOR ME IT WAS ABOUT PUTTING A BALL SOMEWHERE HARD TO HIT.
I COULD SEE THE SPOT--
--AND THAT'S WHERE IT WENT.

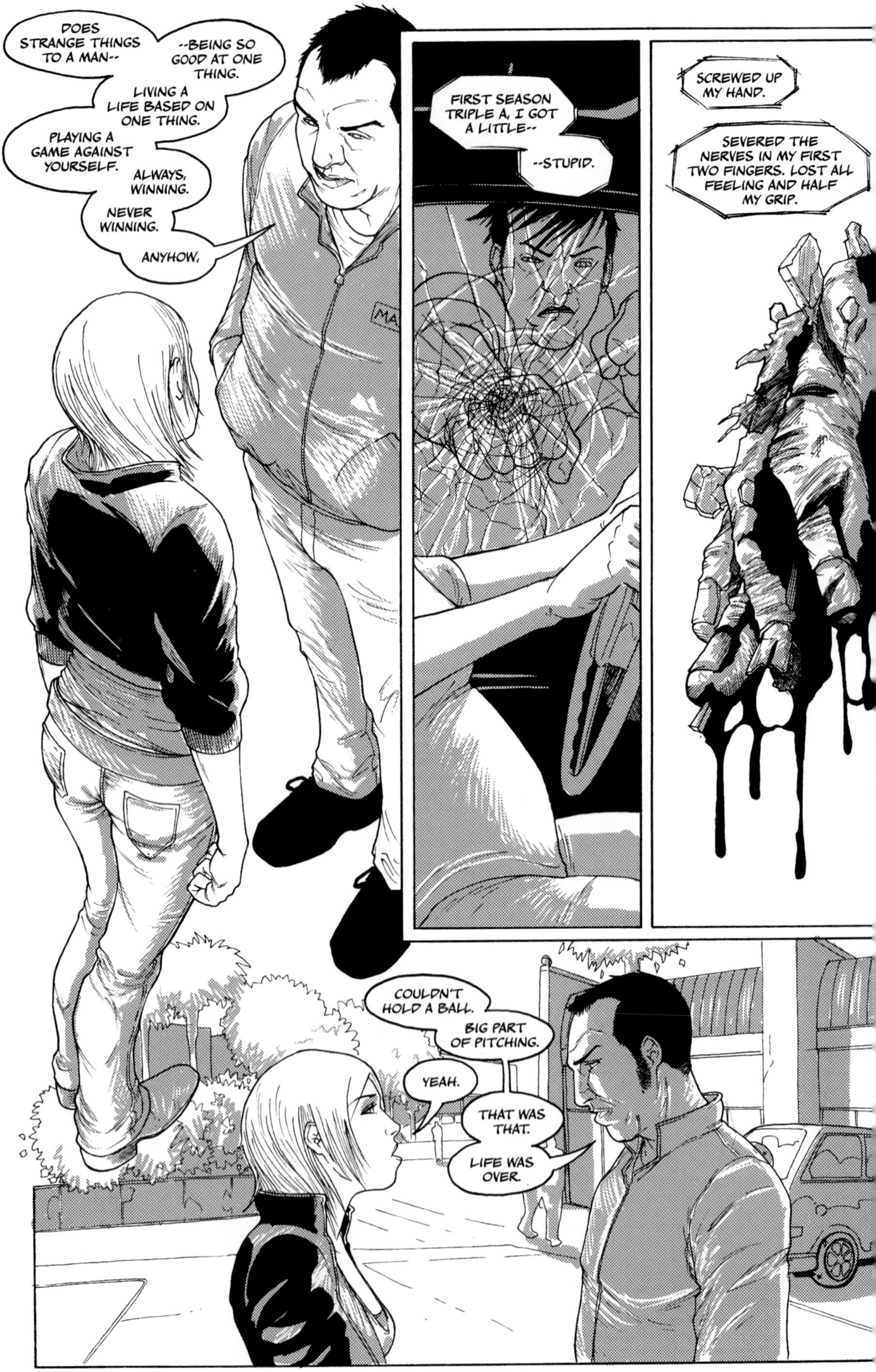

DOES STRANGE THINGS TO A MAN--
--BEING SO GOOD AT ONE THING.
LIVING A LIFE BASED ON ONE THING.
PLAYING A GAME AGAINST YOURSELF.
ALWAYS, WINNING.
NEVER WINNING.
ANYHOW,
FIRST SEASON TRIPLE A, I GOT A LITTLE--
--STUPID.
SCREWED UP MY HAND.
SEVERED THE NERVES IN MY FIRST TWO FINGERS. LOST ALL FEELING AND HALF MY GRIP.
COULDN'T HOLD A BALL.
BIG PART OF PITCHING.
YEAH.
THAT WAS THAT.
LIFE WAS OVER.

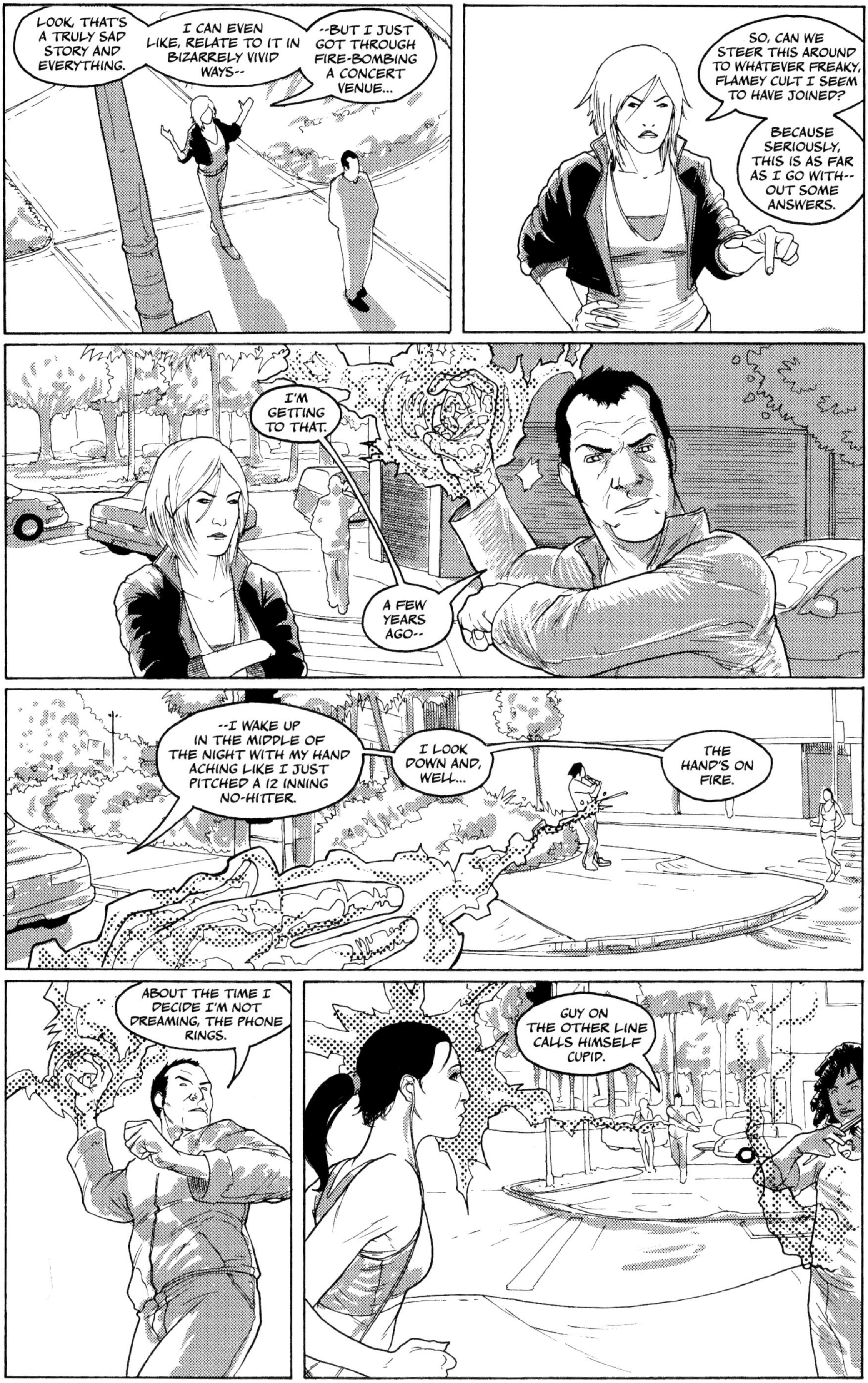
LOOK, THAT'S A TRULY SAD STORY AND EVERYTHING.
I CAN EVEN LIKE, RELATE TO IT IN BIZARRELY VIVID WAYS--
--BUT I JUST GOT THROUGH FIRE-BOMBING A CONCERT VENUE...
SO, CAN WE STEER THIS AROUND TO WHATEVER FREAKY, FLAMEY CULT I SEEM TO HAVE JOINED?
BECAUSE SERIOUSLY, THIS IS AS FAR AS I GO WITH-- OUT SOME ANSWERS.
I'M GETTING TO THAT.
A FEW YEARS AGO--
--I WAKE UP IN THE MIDDLE OF THE NIGHT WITH MY HAND ACHING LIKE I JUST PITCHED A 12 INNING NO-HITTER.
I LOOK DOWN AND, WELL...
THE HAND'S ON FIRE.
ABOUT THE TIME I DECIDE I'M NOT DREAMING, THE PHONE RINGS.
GUY ON THE OTHER LINE CALLS HIMSELF CUPID.

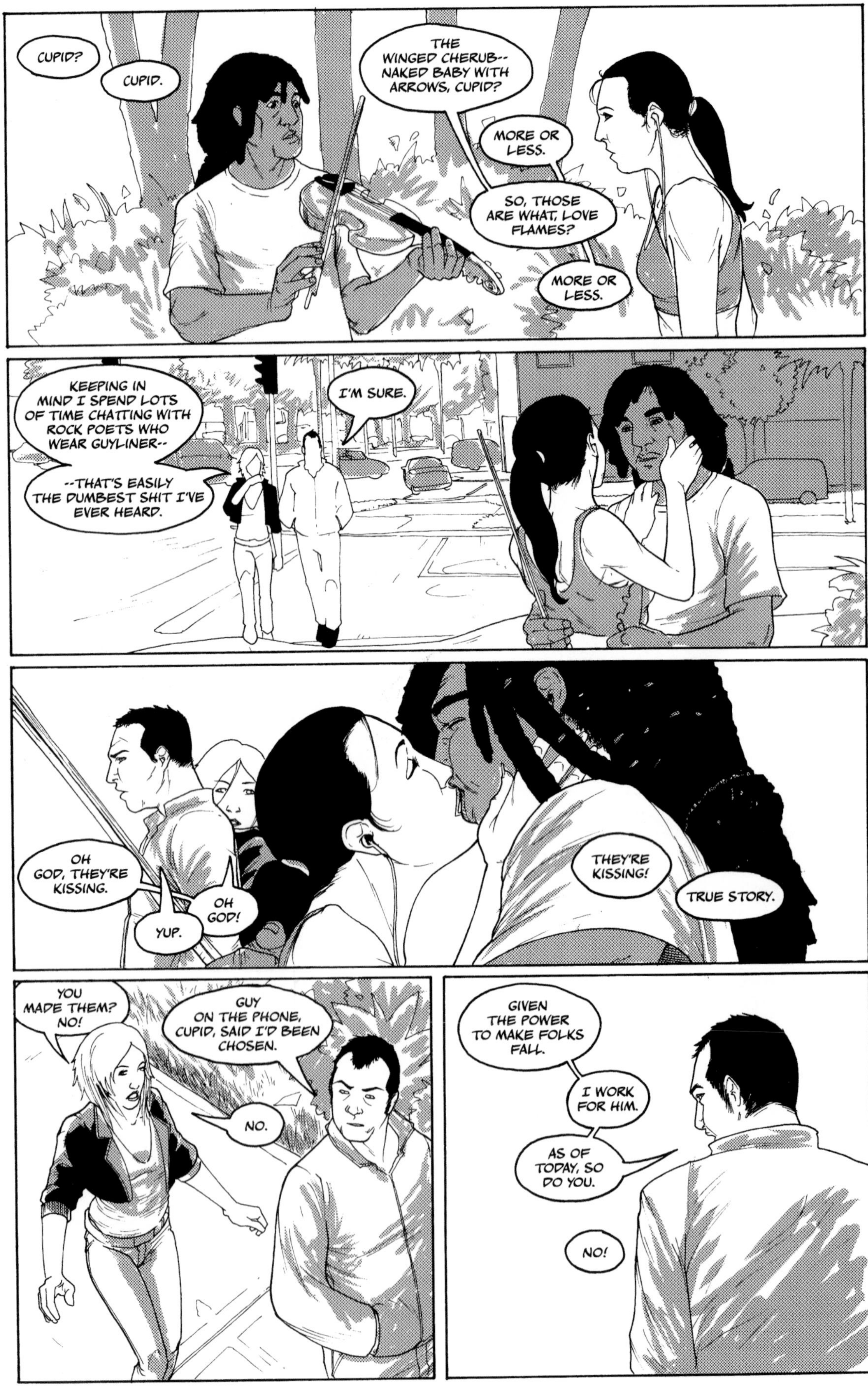
CUPID?
CUPID.
THE WINGED CHERUB--NAKED BABY WITH ARROWS, CUPID?
MORE OR LESS.
SO, THOSE ARE WHAT, LOVE FLAMES?
MORE OR LESS.
KEEPING IN MIND I SPEND LOTS OF TIME CHATTING WITH ROCK POETS WHO WEAR GUYLINER--
--THAT'S EASILY THE DUMBEST SHIT I'VE EVER HEARD.
I'M SURE.
OH GOD, THEY'RE KISSING.
YUP.
OH GOD!
THEY'RE KISSING!
TRUE STORY.
YOU MADE THEM? NO!
GUY ON THE PHONE, CUPID, SAID I'D BEEN CHOSEN.
NO.
GIVEN THE POWER TO MAKE FOLKS FALL.
I WORK FOR HIM.
AS OF TODAY, SO DO YOU.
NO!

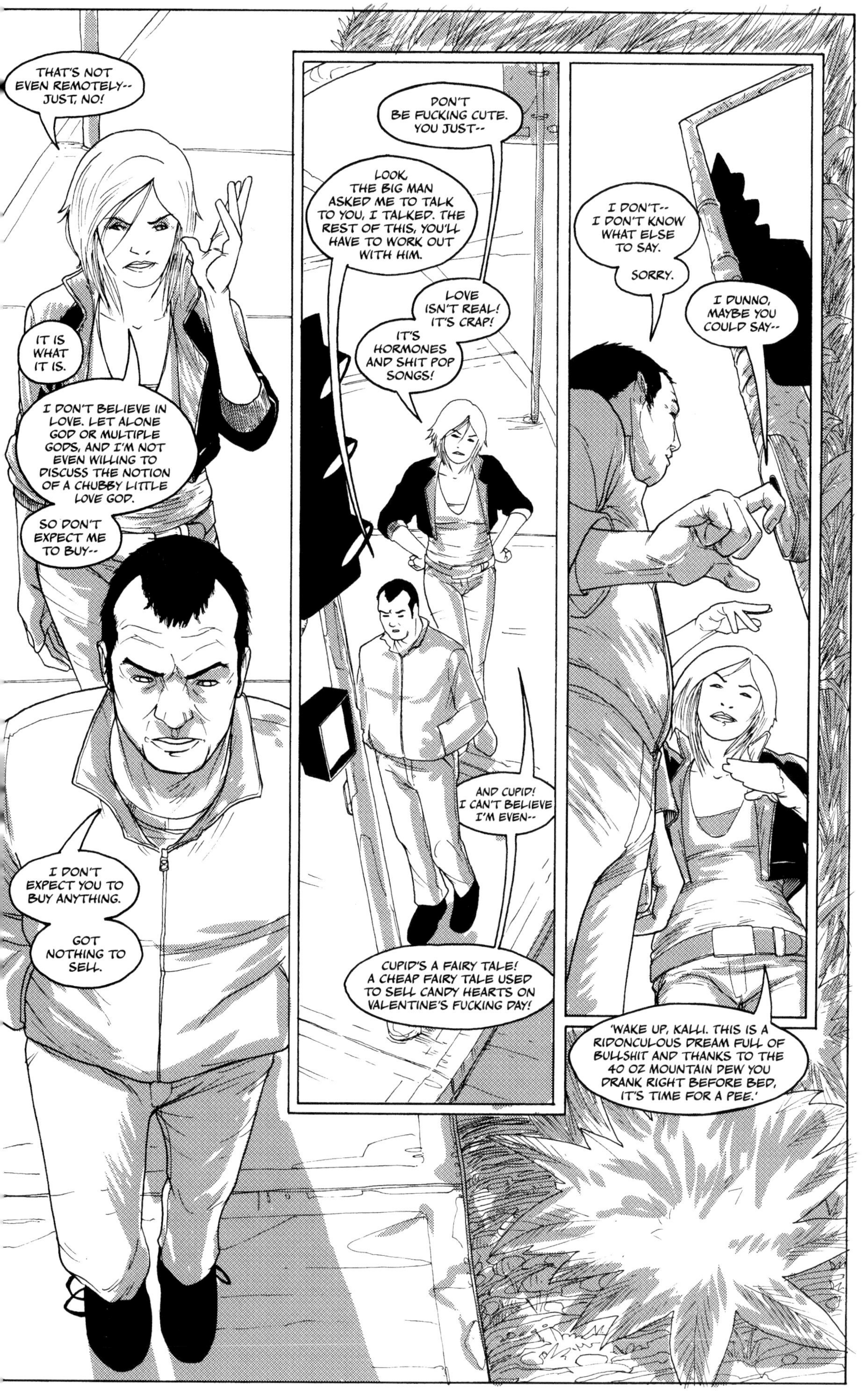
THAT'S NOT EVEN REMOTELY-- JUST, NO!
IT IS WHAT IT IS.
I DON'T BELIEVE IN LOVE. LET ALONE GOD OR MULTIPLE GODS, AND I'M NOT EVEN WILLING TO DISCUSS THE NOTION OF A CHUBBY LITTLE LOVE GOD.
SO DON'T EXPECT ME TO BUY--
I DON'T EXPECT YOU TO BUY ANYTHING.
GOT NOTHING TO SELL.
DON'T BE FUCKING CUTE. YOU JUST--
LOOK, THE BIG MAN ASKED ME TO TALK TO YOU, I TALKED. THE REST OF THIS, YOU'LL HAVE TO WORK OUT WITH HIM.
LOVE ISN'T REAL! IT'S CRAP!
IT'S HORMONES AND SHIT POP SONGS!
AND CUPID! I CAN'T BELIEVE I'M EVEN--
CUPID'S A FAIRY TALE! A CHEAP FAIRY TALE USED TO SELL CANDY HEARTS ON VALENTINE'S FUCKING DAY!
I DON'T-- I DON'T KNOW WHAT ELSE TO SAY.
SORRY.
I DUNNO, MAYBE YOU COULD SAY--
'WAKE UP, KALLI. THIS IS A RIDONCULOUS DREAM FULL OF BULLSHIT AND THANKS TO THE 40 OZ MOUNTAIN DEW YOU DRANK RIGHT BEFORE BED, IT'S TIME FOR A PEE.'

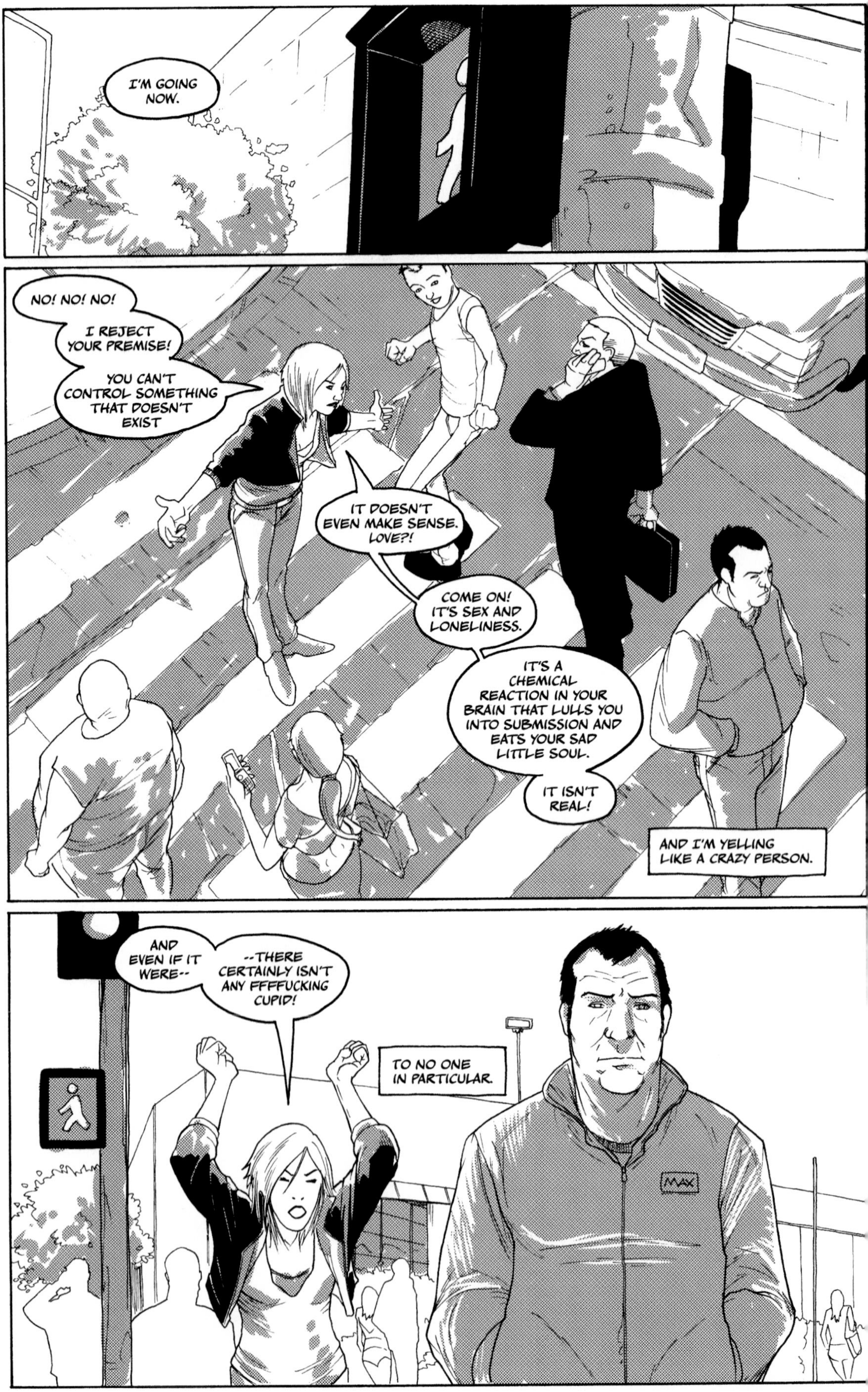
I'M GOING NOW.
NO! NO! NO!
I REJECT YOUR PREMISE!
YOU CAN'T CONTROL SOMETHING THAT DOESN'T EXIST
IT DOESN'T EVEN MAKE SENSE. LOVE?!
COME ON! IT'S SEX AND LONELINESS.
IT'S A CHEMICAL REACTION IN YOUR BRAIN THAT LULLS YOU INTO SUBMISSION AND EATS YOUR SAD LITTLE SOUL.
IT ISN'T REAL!
AND I'M YELLING LIKE A CRAZY PERSON.
AND EVEN IF IT WERE--
--THERE CERTAINLY ISN'T ANY FFFFUCKING CUPID!
TO NO ONE IN PARTICULAR.
MAX

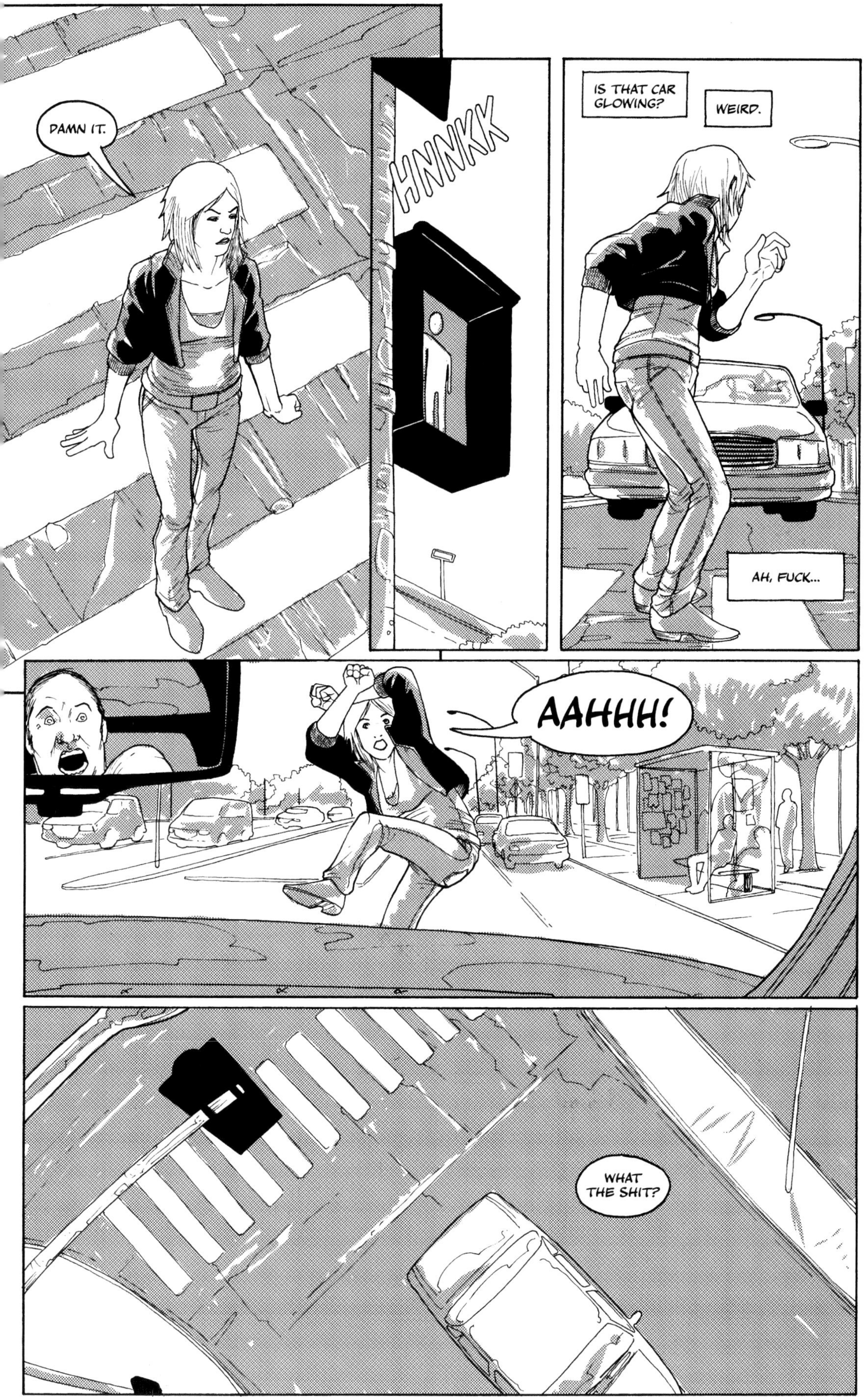
DAMN IT.
HNNKK
IS THAT CAR GLOWING?
WEIRD.
AH, FUCK...
AAHHH!
WHAT THE SHIT?

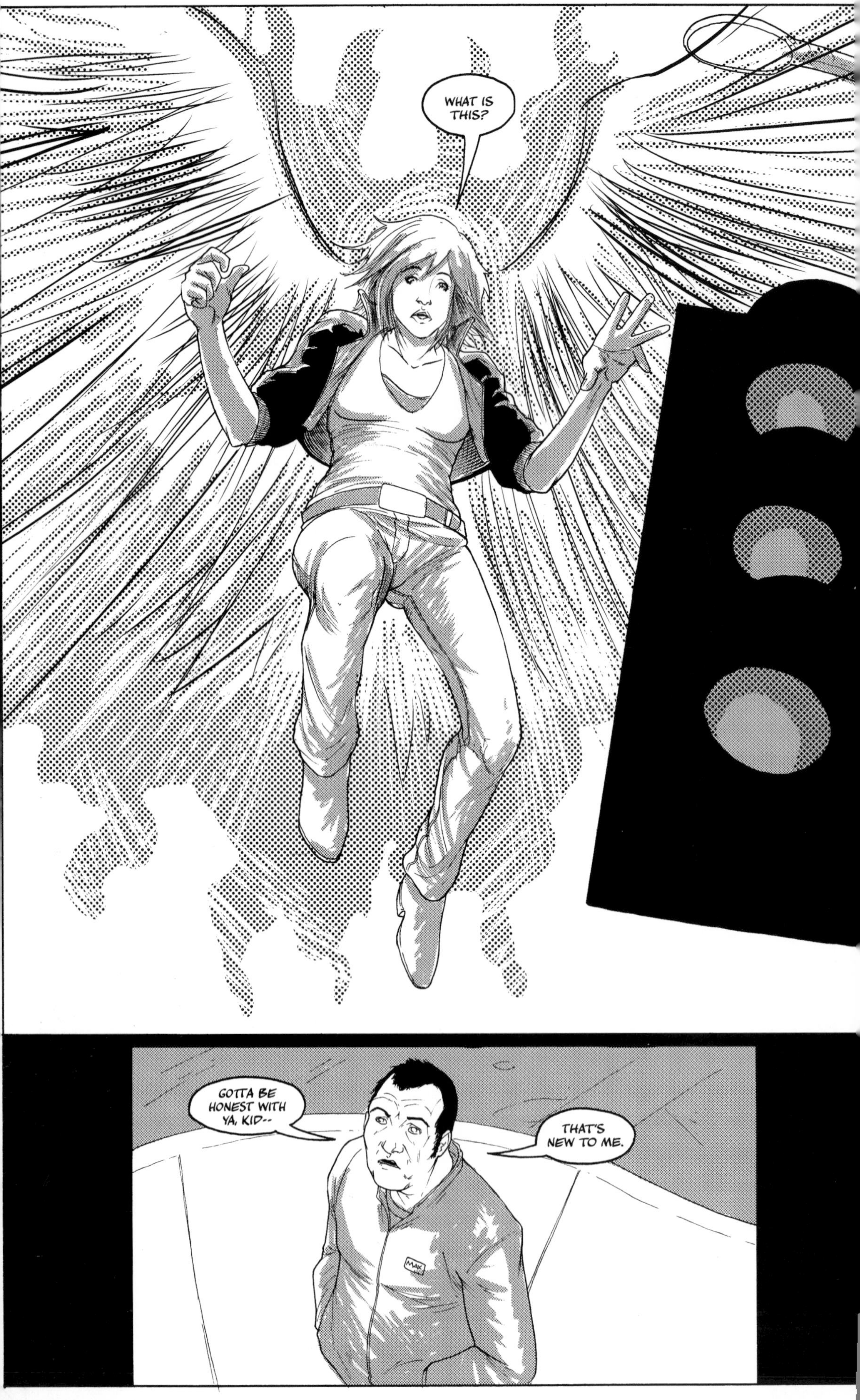
WHAT IS THIS?
GOTTA BE HONEST WITH YA, KID--
THAT'S NEW TO ME.

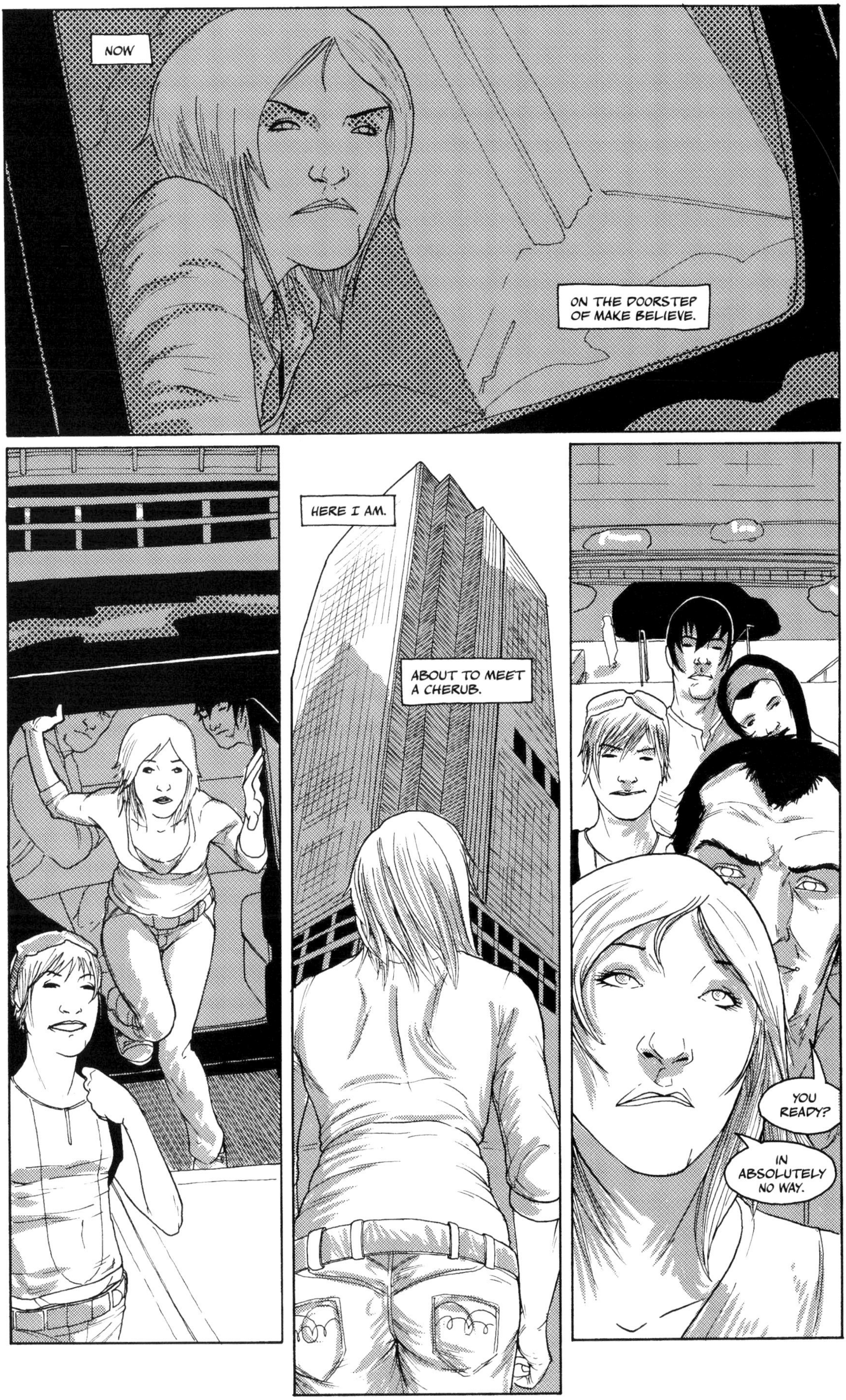
NOW
ON THE DOORSTEP OF MAKE BELIEVE.
HERE I AM.
ABOUT TO MEET A CHERUB.
YOU READY?
IN ABSOLUTELY NO WAY.

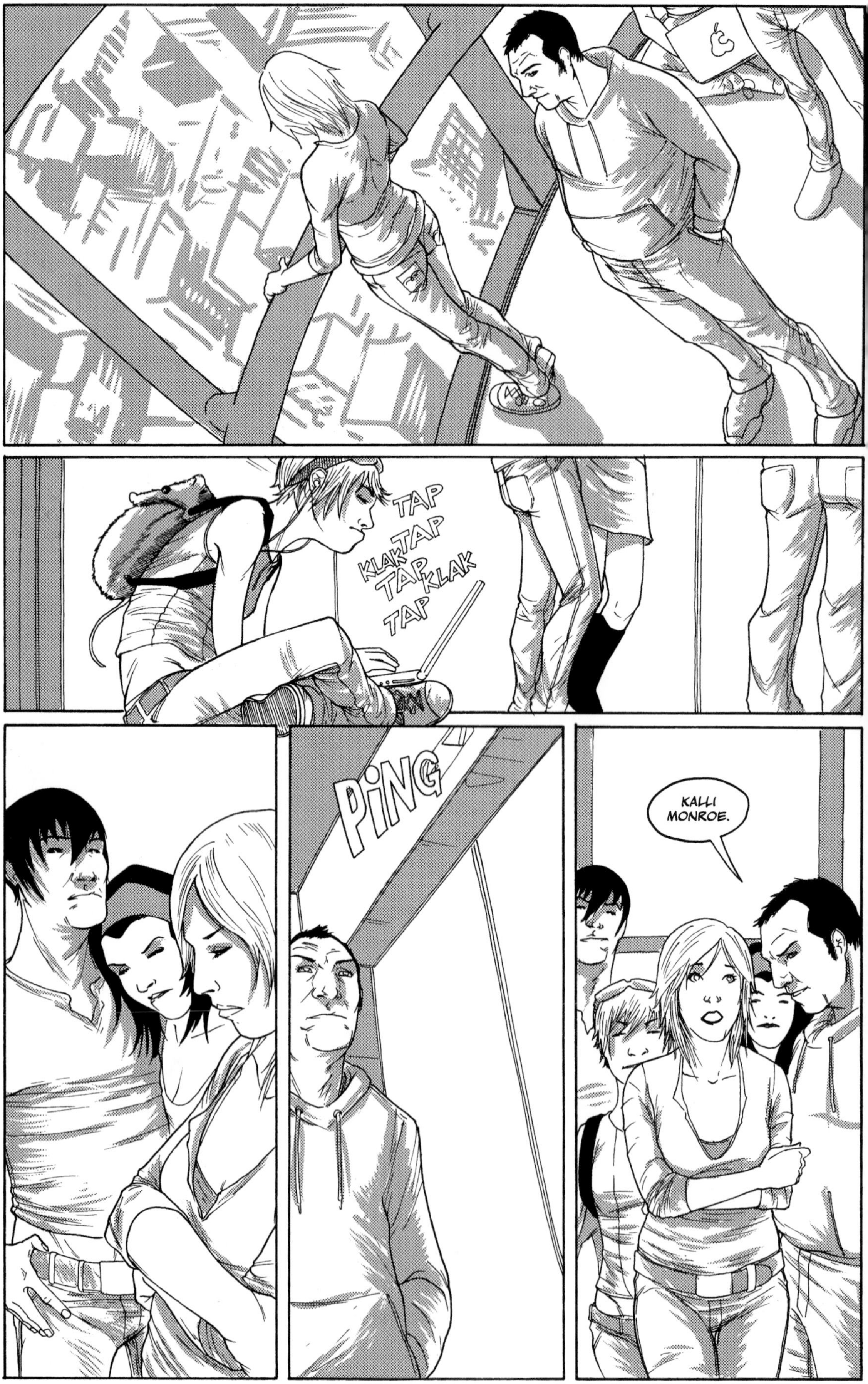
TAP
TAP
KLAK
TAP
KLAK
TAP
PING
KALLI MONROE.

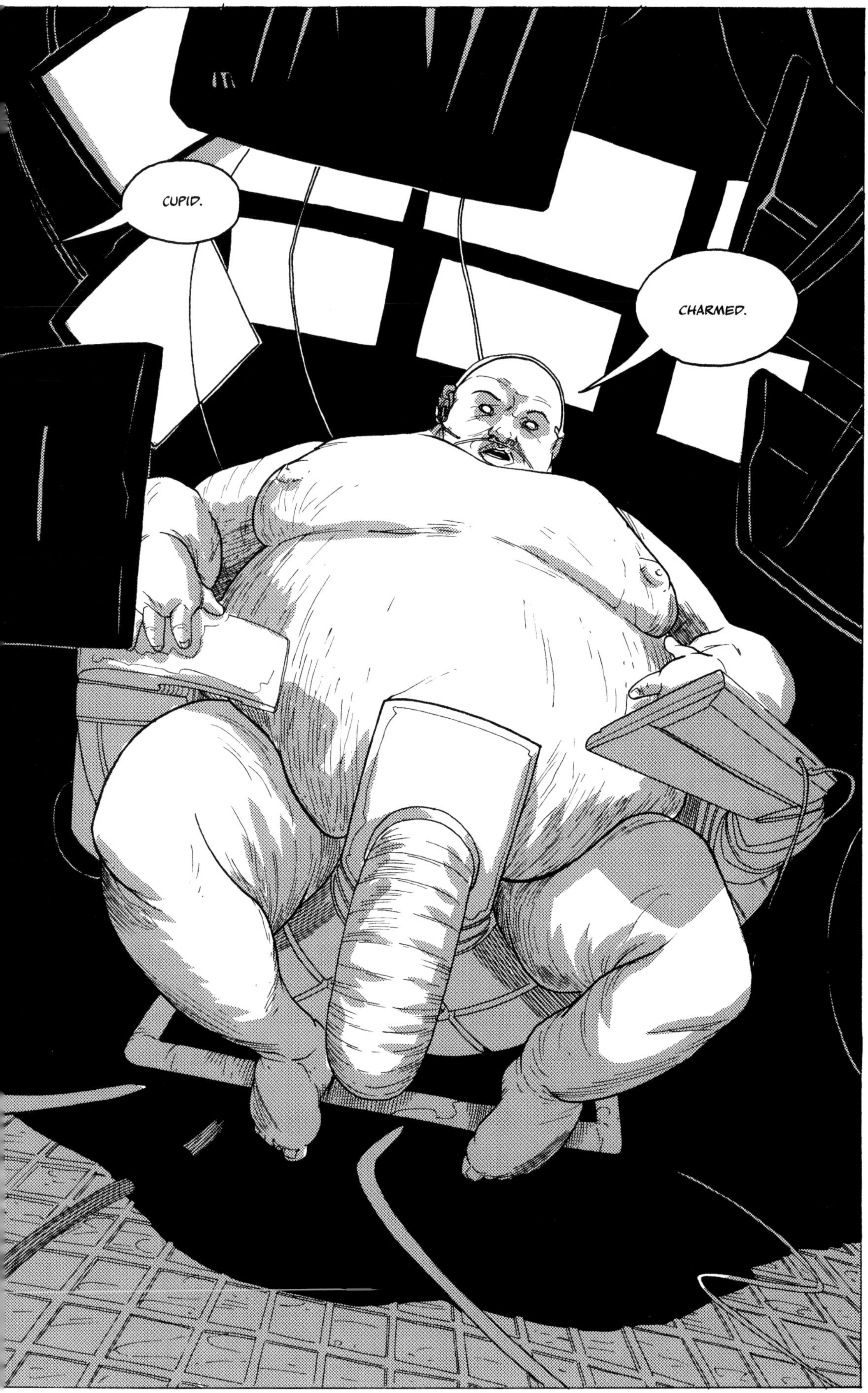
CUPID.
CHARMED.

CHAPTER 2

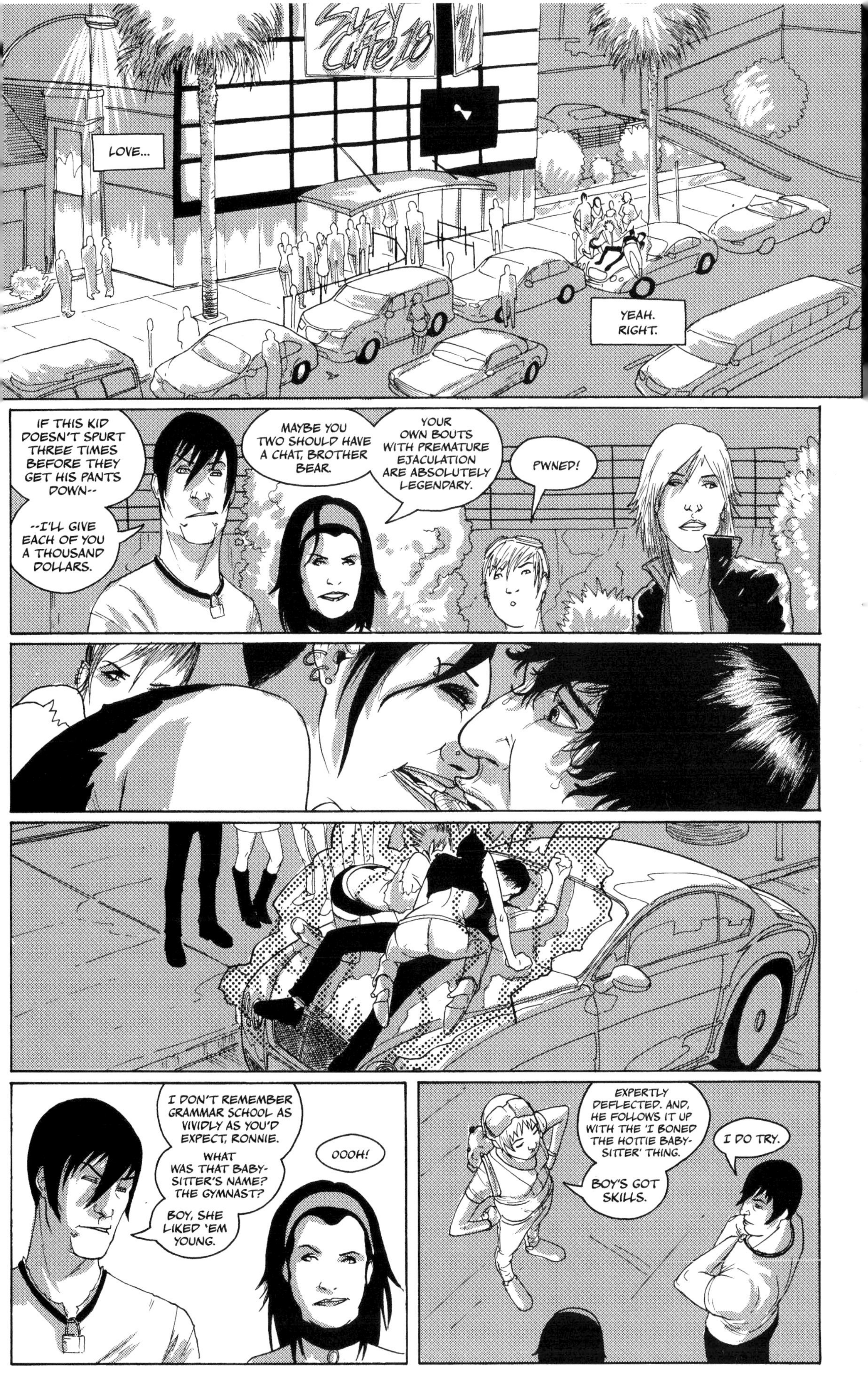
SUZY CUTE 10
LOVE...
YEAH. RIGHT.
IF THIS KID DOESN'T SPURT THREE TIMES BEFORE THEY GET HIS PANTS DOWN--
--I'LL GIVE EACH OF YOU A THOUSAND DOLLARS.
MAYBE YOU TWO SHOULD HAVE A CHAT, BROTHER BEAR.
YOUR OWN BOUTS WITH PREMATURE EJACULATION ARE ABSOLUTELY LEGENDARY.
PWNED!
I DON'T REMEMBER GRAMMAR SCHOOL AS VIVIDLY AS YOU'D EXPECT, RONNIE.
WHAT WAS THAT BABY-SITTER'S NAME? THE GYMNAST?
BOY, SHE LIKED 'EM YOUNG.
OOOH!
EXPERTLY DEFLECTED. AND, HE FOLLOWS IT UP WITH THE 'I BONED THE HOTTIE BABY-SITTER' THING.
BOY'S GOT SKILLS.
I DO TRY.

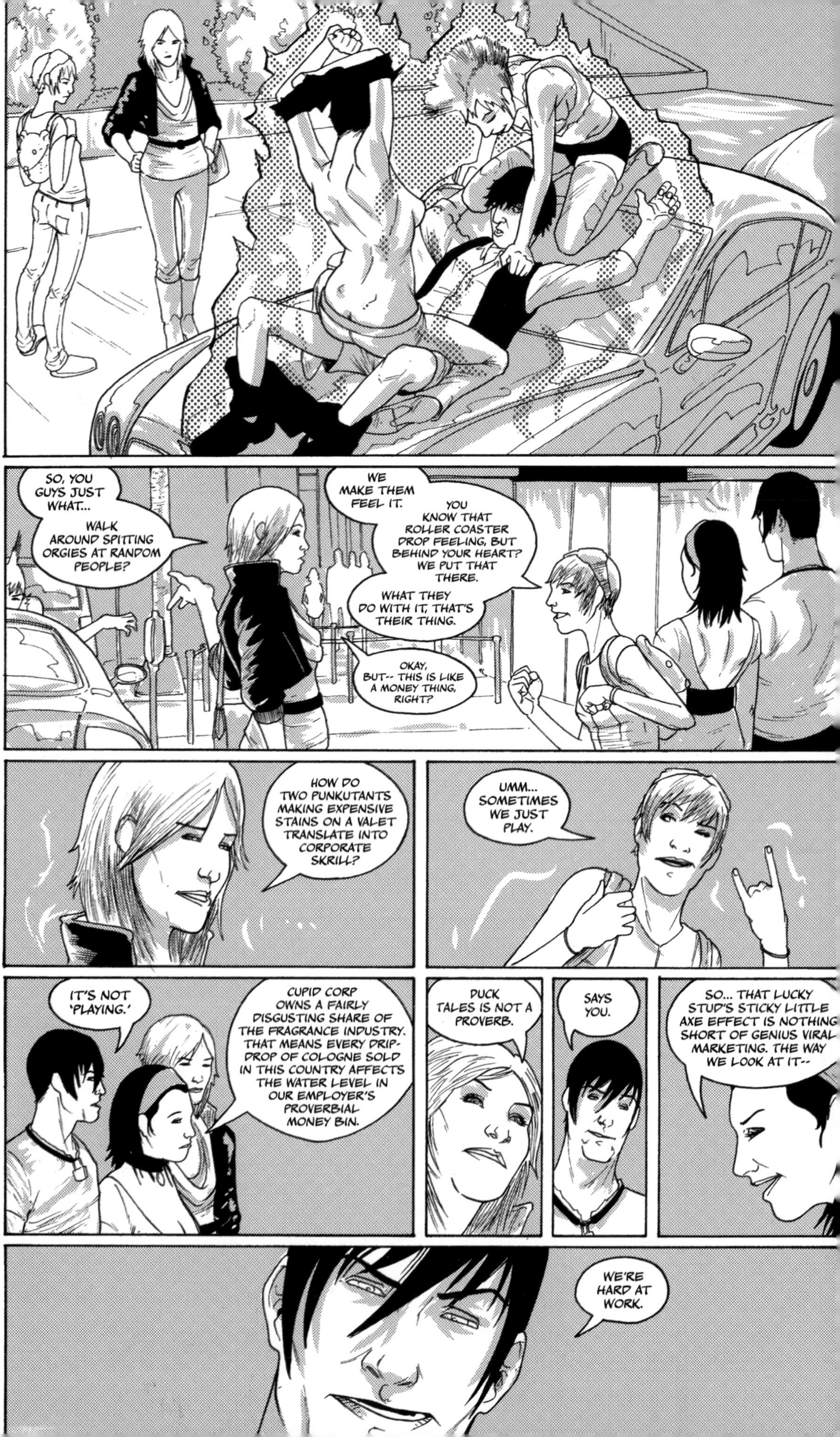

SO, YOU GUYS JUST WHAT... WALK AROUND SPITTING ORGIES AT RANDOM PEOPLE?
WE MAKE THEM FEEL IT.
YOU KNOW THAT ROLLER COASTER DROP FEELING, BUT BEHIND YOUR HEART? WE PUT THAT THERE.
WHAT THEY DO WITH IT, THAT'S THEIR THING.
OKAY, BUT-- THIS IS LIKE A MONEY THING, RIGHT?
HOW DO TWO PUNKUTANTS MAKING EXPENSIVE STAINS ON A VALET TRANSLATE INTO CORPORATE SKRILL?
UMM... SOMETIMES WE JUST PLAY.
IT'S NOT 'PLAYING.'
CUPID CORP OWNS A FAIRLY DISGUSTING SHARE OF THE FRAGRANCE INDUSTRY. THAT MEANS EVERY DRIP-DROP OF COLOGNE SOLD IN THIS COUNTRY AFFECTS THE WATER LEVEL IN OUR EMPLOYER'S PROVERBIAL MONEY BIN.
DUCK TALES IS NOT A PROVERB.
SAYS YOU.
SO... THAT LUCKY STUD'S STICKY LITTLE AXE EFFECT IS NOTHING SHORT OF GENIUS VIRAL MARKETING. THE WAY WE LOOK AT IT--
WE'RE HARD AT WORK.

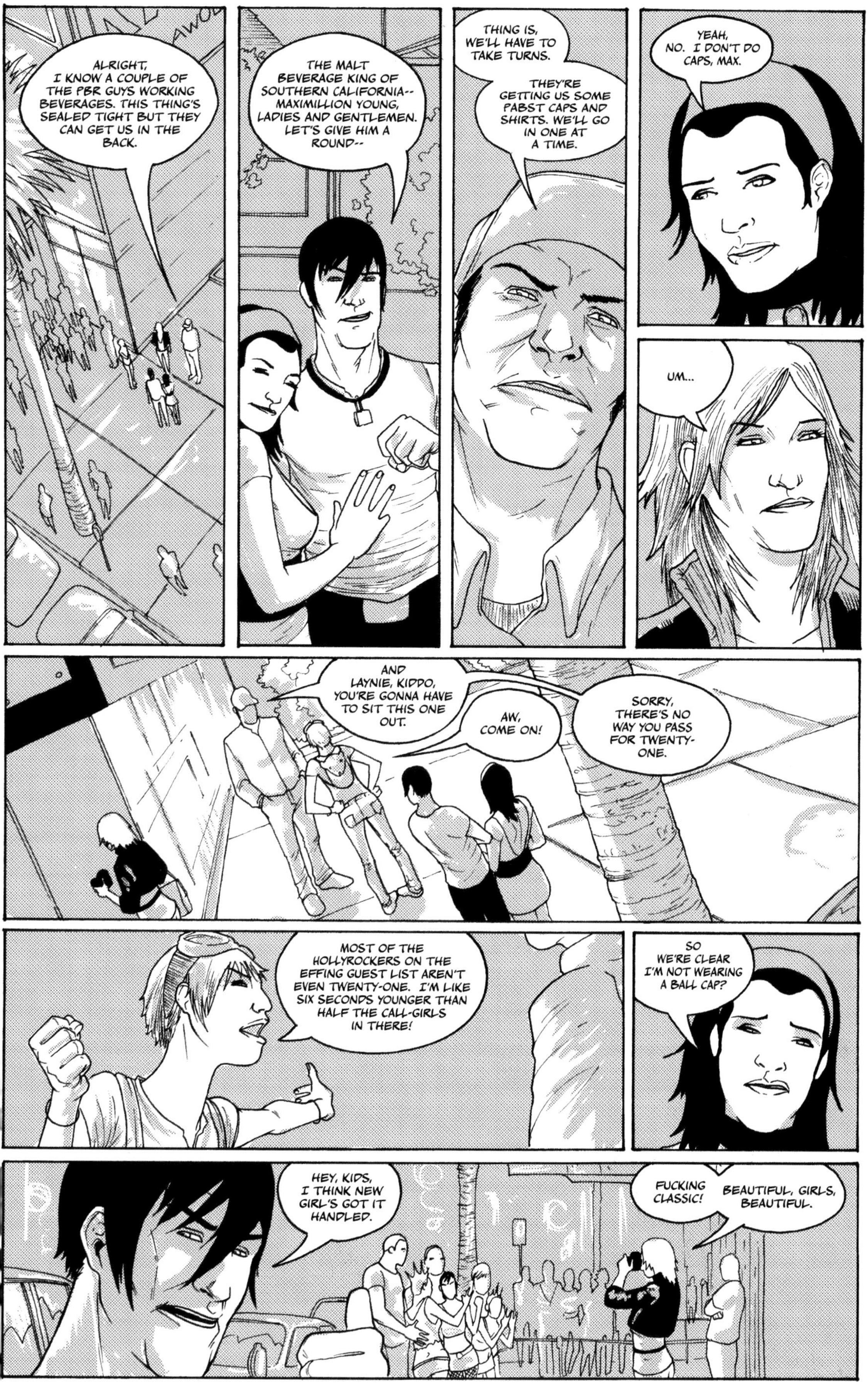
ALRIGHT, I KNOW A COUPLE OF THE PBR GUYS WORKING BEVERAGES. THIS THING'S SEALED TIGHT BUT THEY CAN GET US IN THE BACK.
THE MALT BEVERAGE KING OF SOUTHERN CALIFORNIA-- MAXIMILLION YOUNG, LADIES AND GENTLEMEN. LET'S GIVE HIM A ROUND--
THING IS, WE'LL HAVE TO TAKE TURNS.
THEY'RE GETTING US SOME PABST CAPS AND SHIRTS. WE'LL GO IN ONE AT A TIME.
YEAH, NO. I DON'T DO CAPS, MAX.
UM...
AND LAYNIE, KIDDO, YOU'RE GONNA HAVE TO SIT THIS ONE OUT.
AW, COME ON!
SORRY, THERE'S NO WAY YOU PASS FOR TWENTY-ONE.
MOST OF THE HOLLYROCKERS ON THE EFFING GUEST LIST AREN'T EVEN TWENTY-ONE. I'M LIKE SIX SECONDS YOUNGER THAN HALF THE CALL-GIRLS IN THERE!
SO WE'RE CLEAR I'M NOT WEARING A BALL CAP?
HEY, KIDS, I THINK NEW GIRL'S GOT IT HANDLED.
FUCKING CLASSIC!
BEAUTIFUL, GIRLS, BEAUTIFUL.

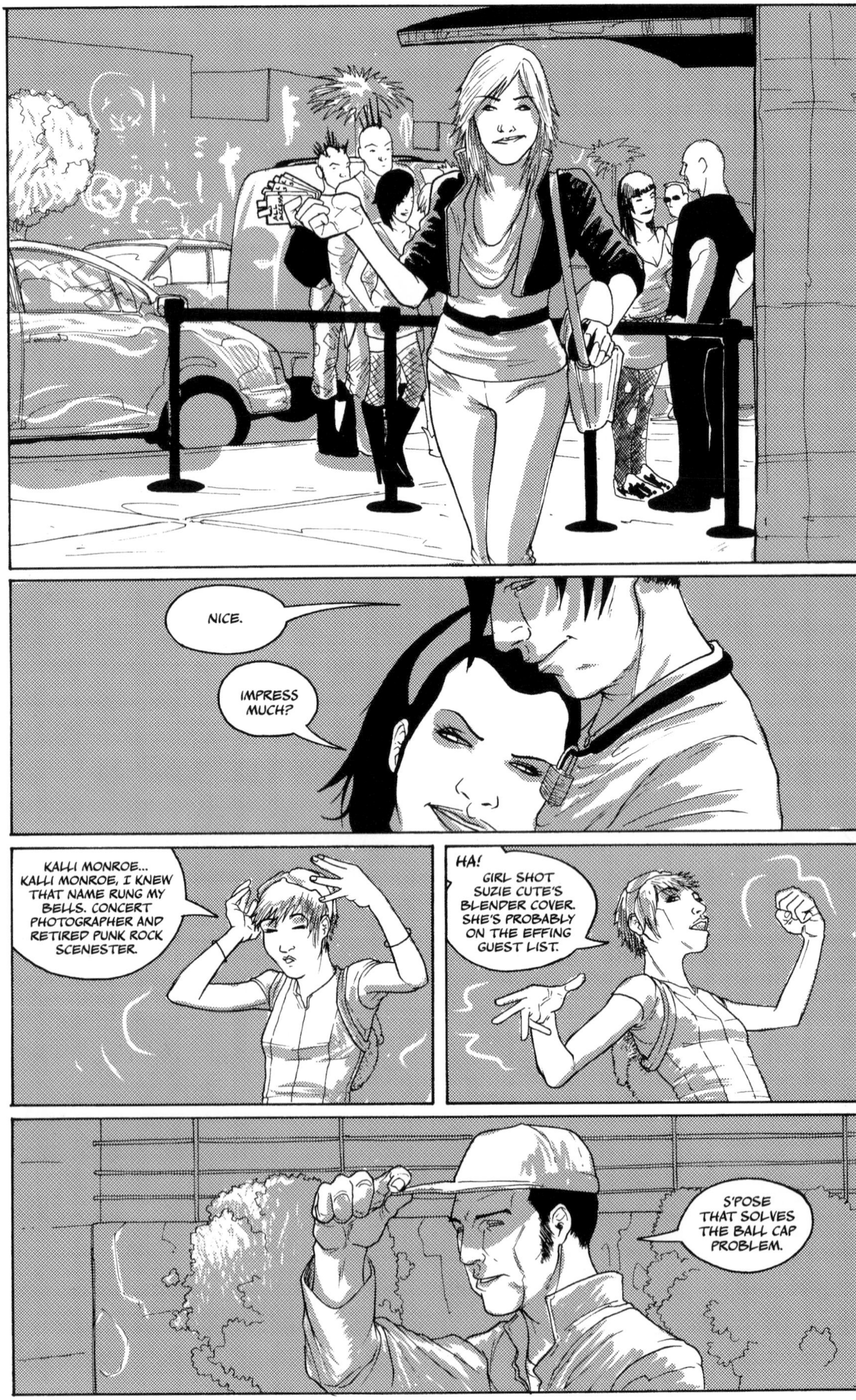
NICE.
IMPRESS MUCH?
KALLI MONROE... KALLI MONROE, I KNEW THAT NAME RUNG MY BELLS. CONCERT PHOTOGRAPHER AND RETIRED PUNK ROCK SCENESTER.
HA!
GIRL SHOT SUZIE CUTE'S BLENDER COVER. SHE'S PROBABLY ON THE EFFING GUEST LIST.
S'POSE THAT SOLVES THE BALL CAP PROBLEM.

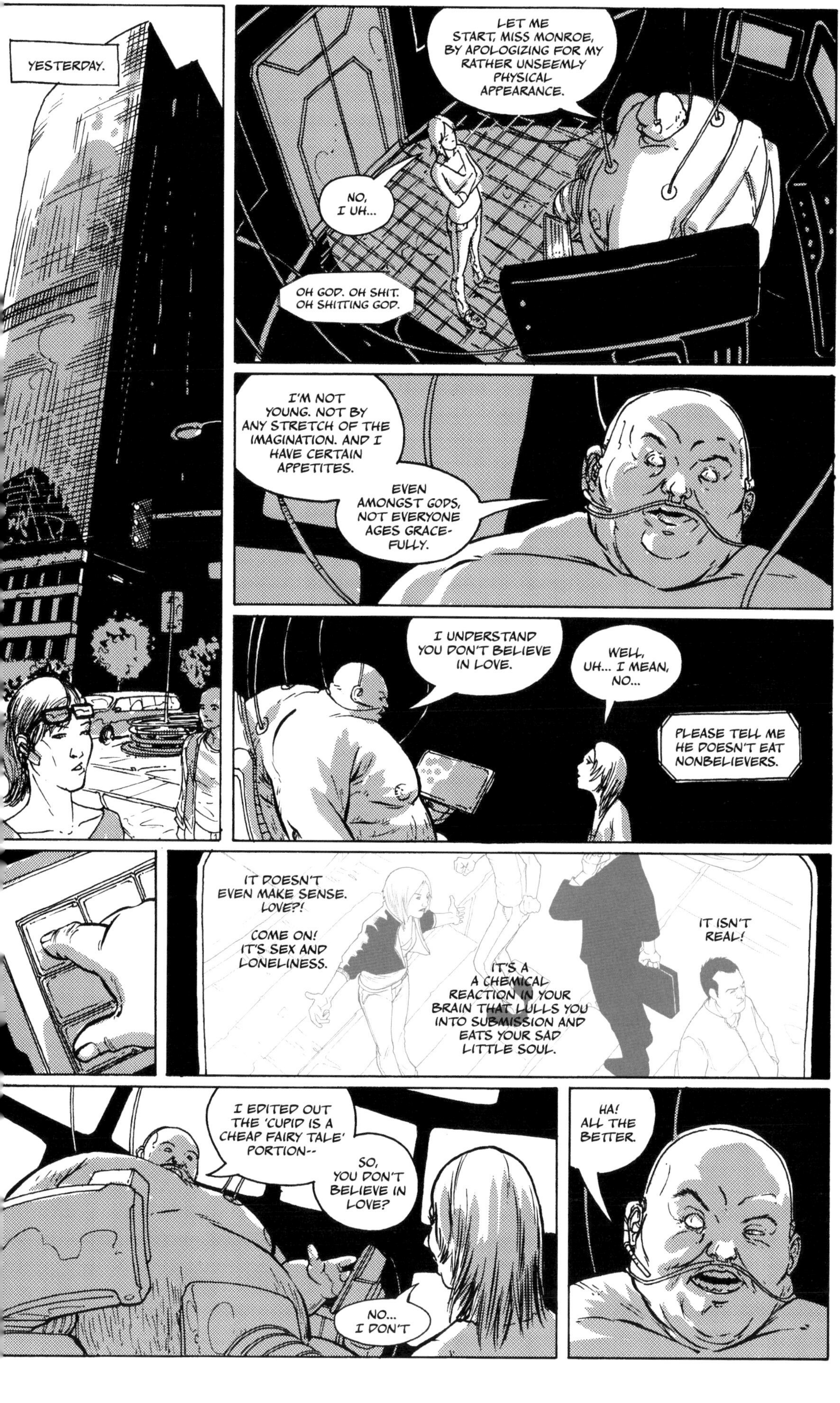
YESTERDAY.
LET ME START, MISS MONROE, BY APOLOGIZING FOR MY RATHER UNSEEMLY PHYSICAL APPEARANCE.
NO, I UH...
OH GOD. OH SHIT. OH SHITTING GOD.
I'M NOT YOUNG. NOT BY ANY STRETCH OF THE IMAGINATION. AND I HAVE CERTAIN APPETITES.
EVEN AMONGST GODS, NOT EVERYONE AGES GRACE-FULLY.
I UNDERSTAND YOU DON'T BELIEVE IN LOVE.
WELL, UH... I MEAN, NO...
PLEASE TELL ME HE DOESN'T EAT NONBELIEVERS.
IT DOESN'T EVEN MAKE SENSE. LOVE?!
COME ON! IT'S SEX AND LONELINESS.
IT'S A A CHEMICAL REACTION IN YOUR BRAIN THAT LULLS YOU INTO SUBMISSION AND EATS YOUR SAD LITTLE SOUL.
IT ISN'T REAL!
I EDITED OUT THE 'CUPID IS A CHEAP FAIRY TALE' PORTION--
SO, YOU DON'T BELIEVE IN LOVE?
NO... I DON'T
HA! ALL THE BETTER.

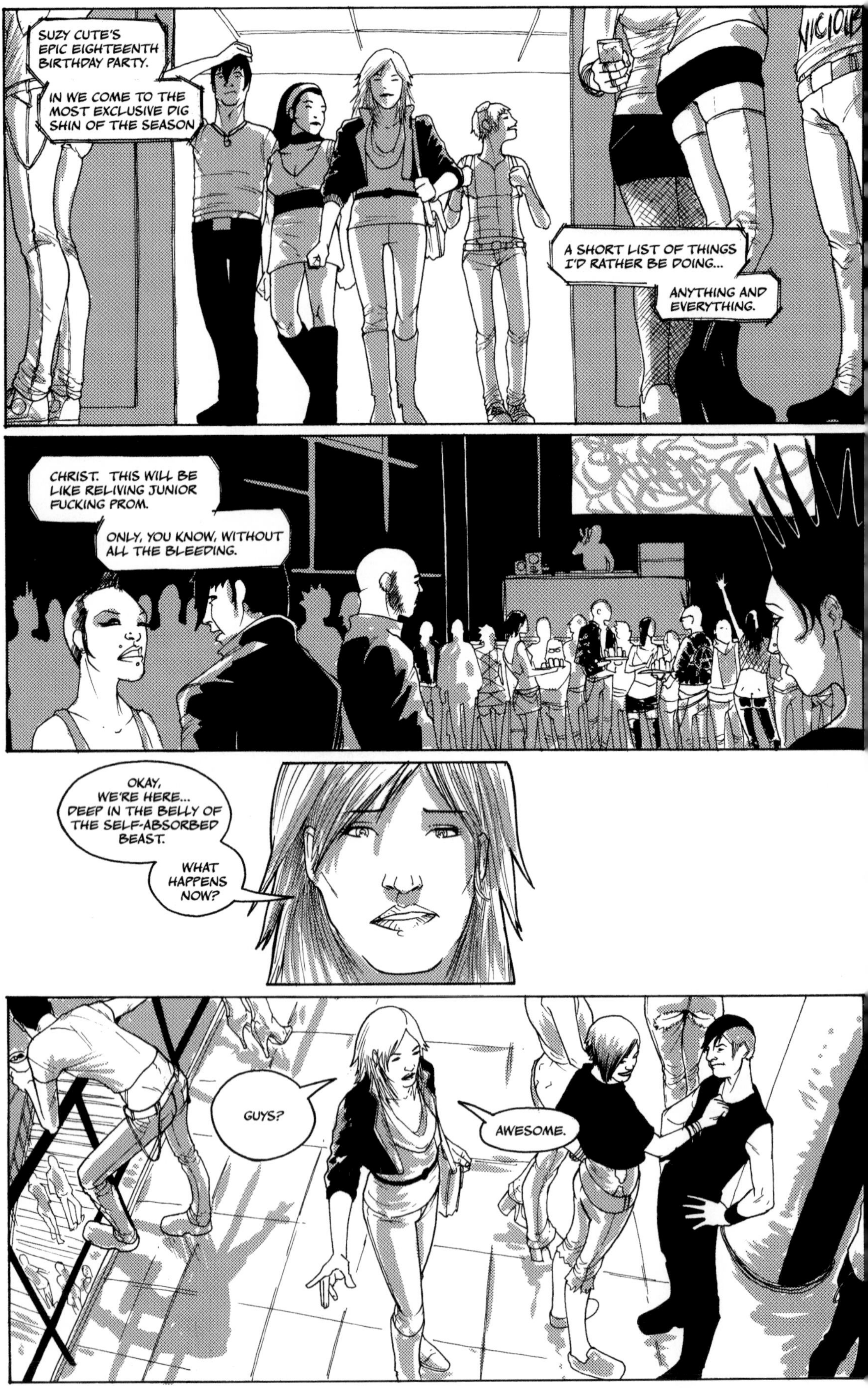
SUZY CUTE'S EPIC EIGHTEENTH BIRTHDAY PARTY.
IN WE COME TO THE MOST EXCLUSIVE DIG SHIN OF THE SEASON
A SHORT LIST OF THINGS I'D RATHER BE DOING...
ANYTHING AND EVERYTHING.
CHRIST. THIS WILL BE LIKE RELIVING JUNIOR FUCKING PROM.
ONLY, YOU KNOW, WITHOUT ALL THE BLEEDING.
OKAY, WE'RE HERE... DEEP IN THE BELLY OF THE SELF-ABSORBED BEAST.
WHAT HAPPENS NOW?
GUYS?
AWESOME.

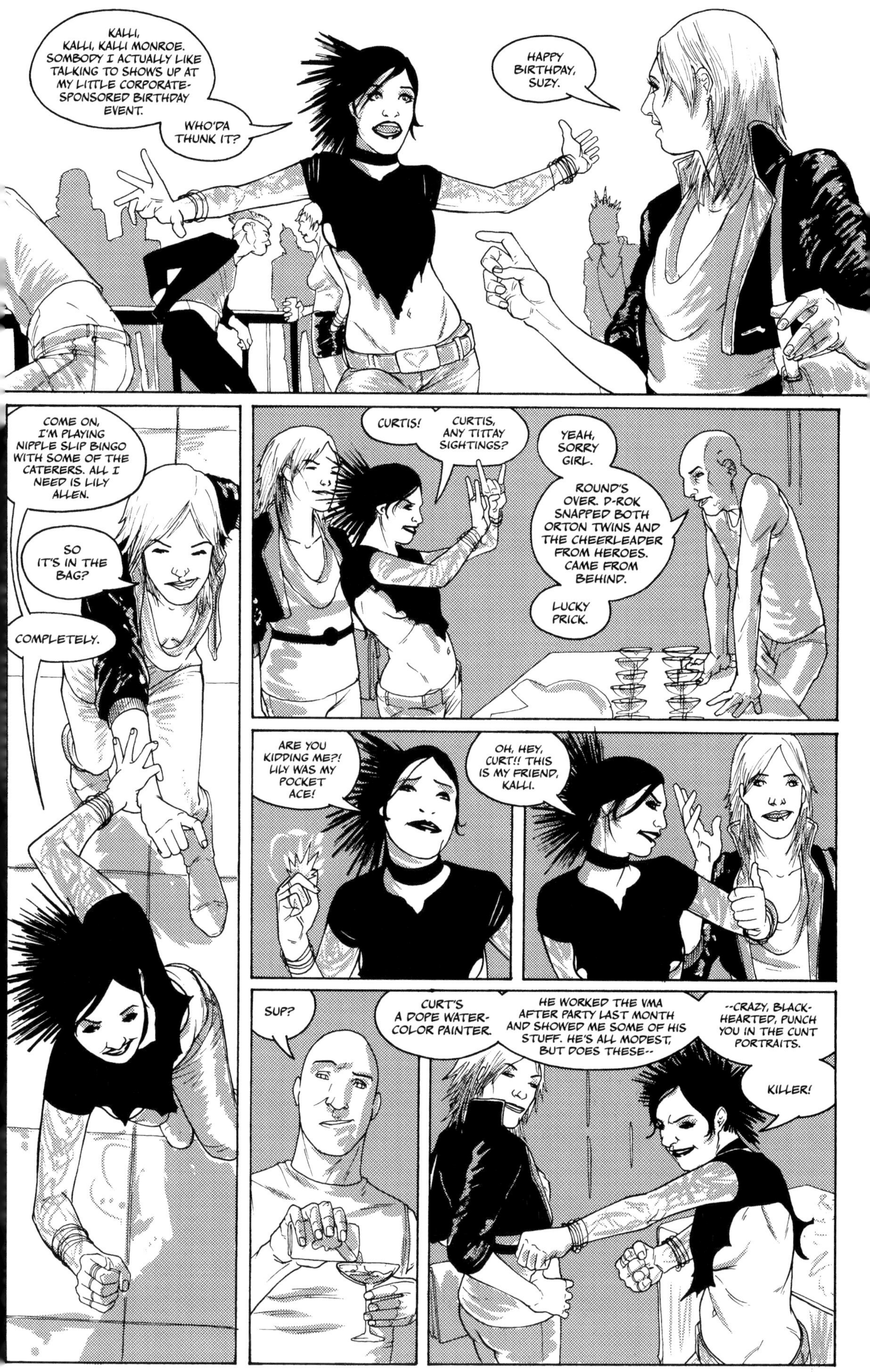
KALLI, KALLI, KALLI MONROE. SOMBODY I ACTUALLY LIKE TALKING TO SHOWS UP AT MY LITTLE CORPORATE-SPONSORED BIRTHDAY EVENT.
WHO'DA THUNK IT?
HAPPY BIRTHDAY, SUZY.
COME ON, I'M PLAYING NIPPLE SLIP BINGO WITH SOME OF THE CATERERS. ALL I NEED IS LILY ALLEN.
SO IT'S IN THE BAG?
COMPLETELY.
CURTIS!
CURTIS, ANY TITTAY SIGHTINGS?
YEAH, SORRY GIRL.
ROUND'S OVER. D-ROK SNAPPED BOTH ORTON TWINS AND THE CHEERLEADER FROM HEROES. CAME FROM BEHIND.
LUCKY PRICK.
ARE YOU KIDDING ME?! LILY WAS MY POCKET ACE!
OH, HEY, CURT!! THIS IS MY FRIEND, KALLI.
SUP?
CURT'S A DOPE WATER-COLOR PAINTER.
HE WORKED THE VMA AFTER PARTY LAST MONTH AND SHOWED ME SOME OF HIS STUFF. HE'S ALL MODEST, BUT DOES THESE--
--CRAZY, BLACK-HEARTED, PUNCH YOU IN THE CUNT PORTRAITS.
KILLER!

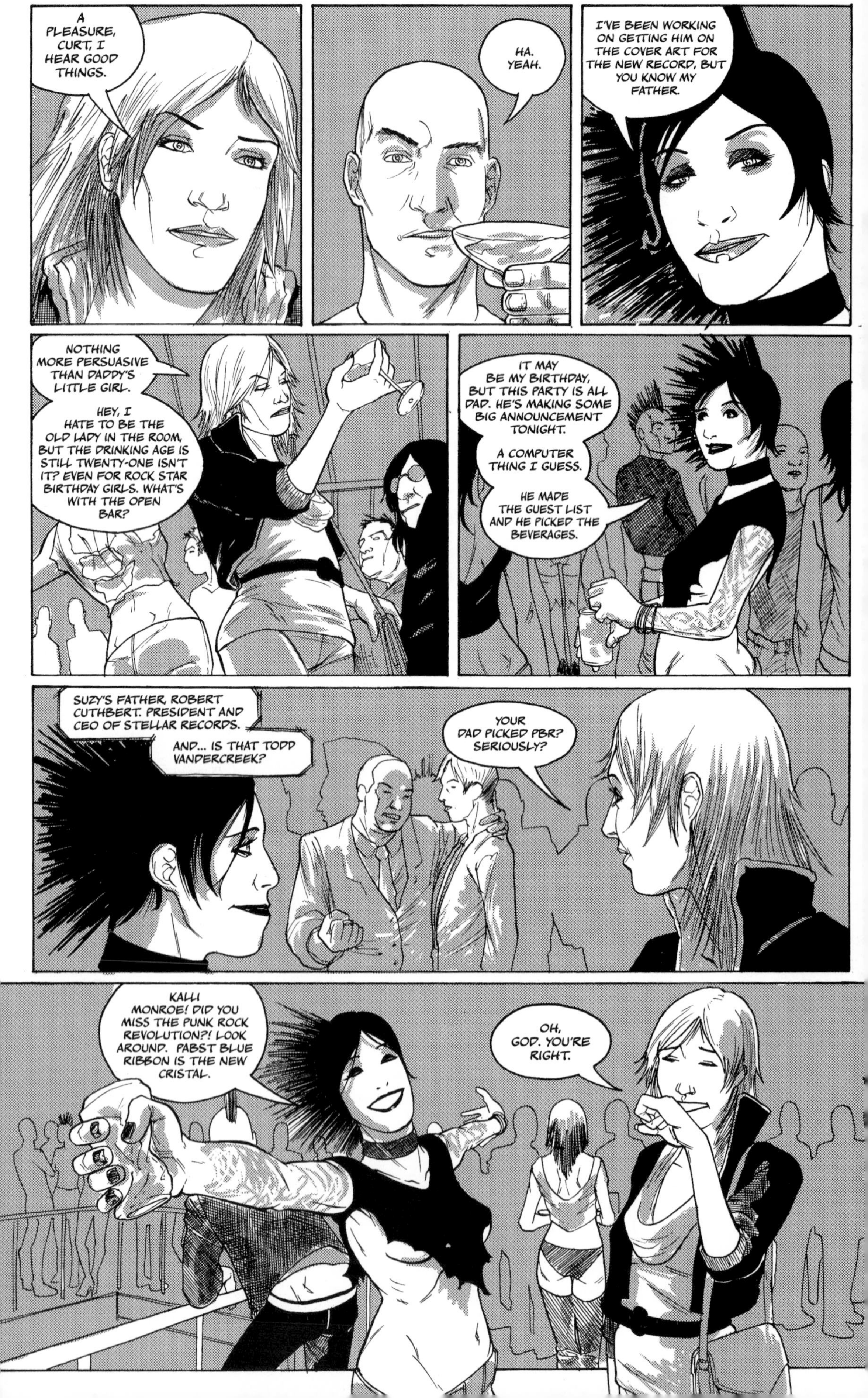
A PLEASURE, CURT, I HEAR GOOD THINGS.
HA. YEAH.
I'VE BEEN WORKING ON GETTING HIM ON THE COVER ART FOR THE NEW RECORD, BUT YOU KNOW MY FATHER.
NOTHING MORE PERSUASIVE THAN DADDY'S LITTLE GIRL.
HEY, I HATE TO BE THE OLD LADY IN THE ROOM, BUT THE DRINKING AGE IS STILL TWENTY-ONE ISN'T IT? EVEN FOR ROCK STAR BIRTHDAY GIRLS. WHAT'S WITH THE OPEN BAR?
IT MAY BE MY BIRTHDAY, BUT THIS PARTY IS ALL DAD. HE'S MAKING SOME BIG ANNOUNCEMENT TONIGHT.
A COMPUTER THING I GUESS.
HE MADE THE GUEST LIST AND HE PICKED THE BEVERAGES.
SUZY'S FATHER, ROBERT CUTHBERT. PRESIDENT AND CEO OF STELLAR RECORDS.
AND... IS THAT TODD VANDERCREEK?
YOUR DAD PICKED PBR? SERIOUSLY?
KALLI MONROE! DID YOU MISS THE PUNK ROCK REVOLUTION?! LOOK AROUND. PABST BLUE RIBBON IS THE NEW CRISTAL.
OH, GOD. YOU'RE RIGHT.

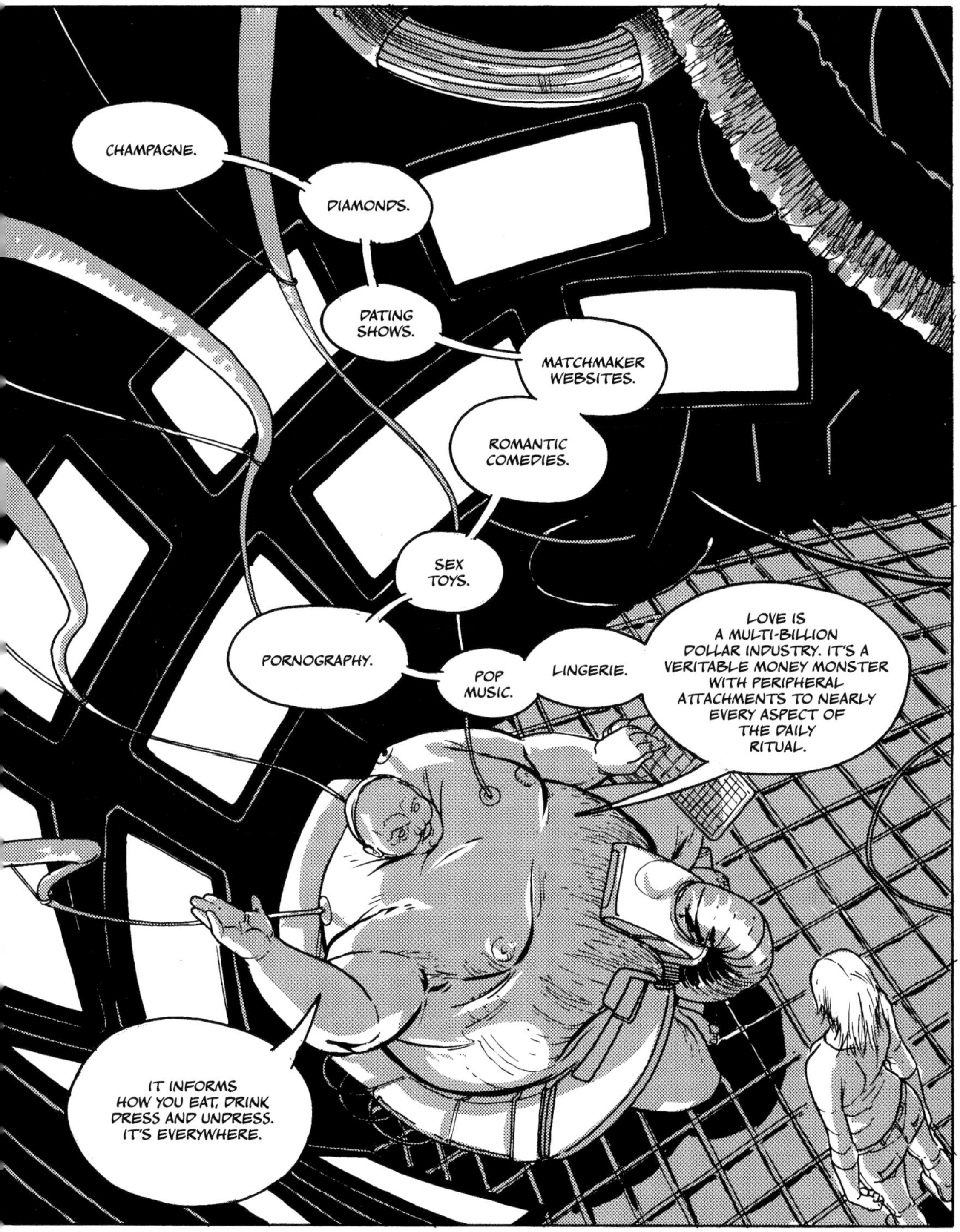
CHAMPAGNE.
DIAMONDS.
DATING SHOWS.
MATCHMAKER WEBSITES.
ROMANTIC COMEDIES.
SEX TOYS.
PORNOGRAPHY.
POP MUSIC.
LINGERIE.
LOVE IS A MULTI-BILLION DOLLAR INDUSTRY. IT'S A VERITABLE MONEY MONSTER WITH PERIPHERAL ATTACHMENTS TO NEARLY EVERY ASPECT OF THE DAILY RITUAL.
IT INFORMS HOW YOU EAT, DRINK DRESS AND UNDRESS. IT'S EVERYWHERE.

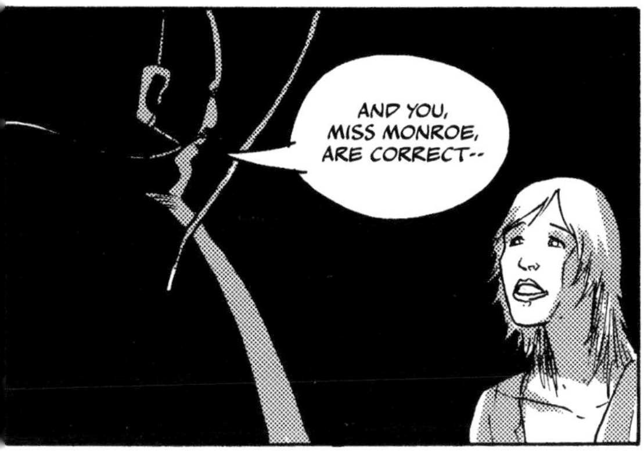
AND YOU, MISS MONROE, ARE CORRECT--

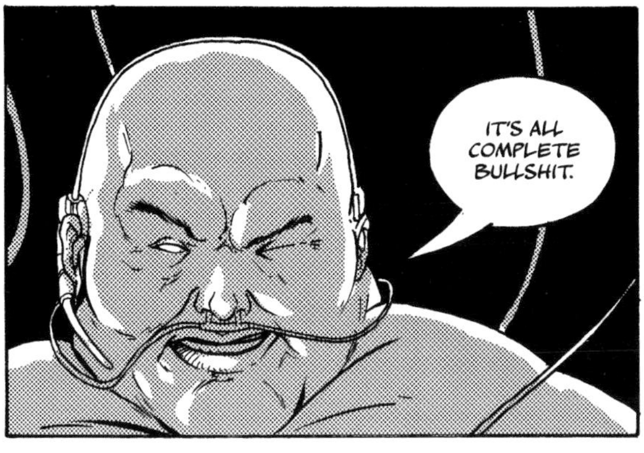
IT'S ALL COMPLETE BULLSHIT.

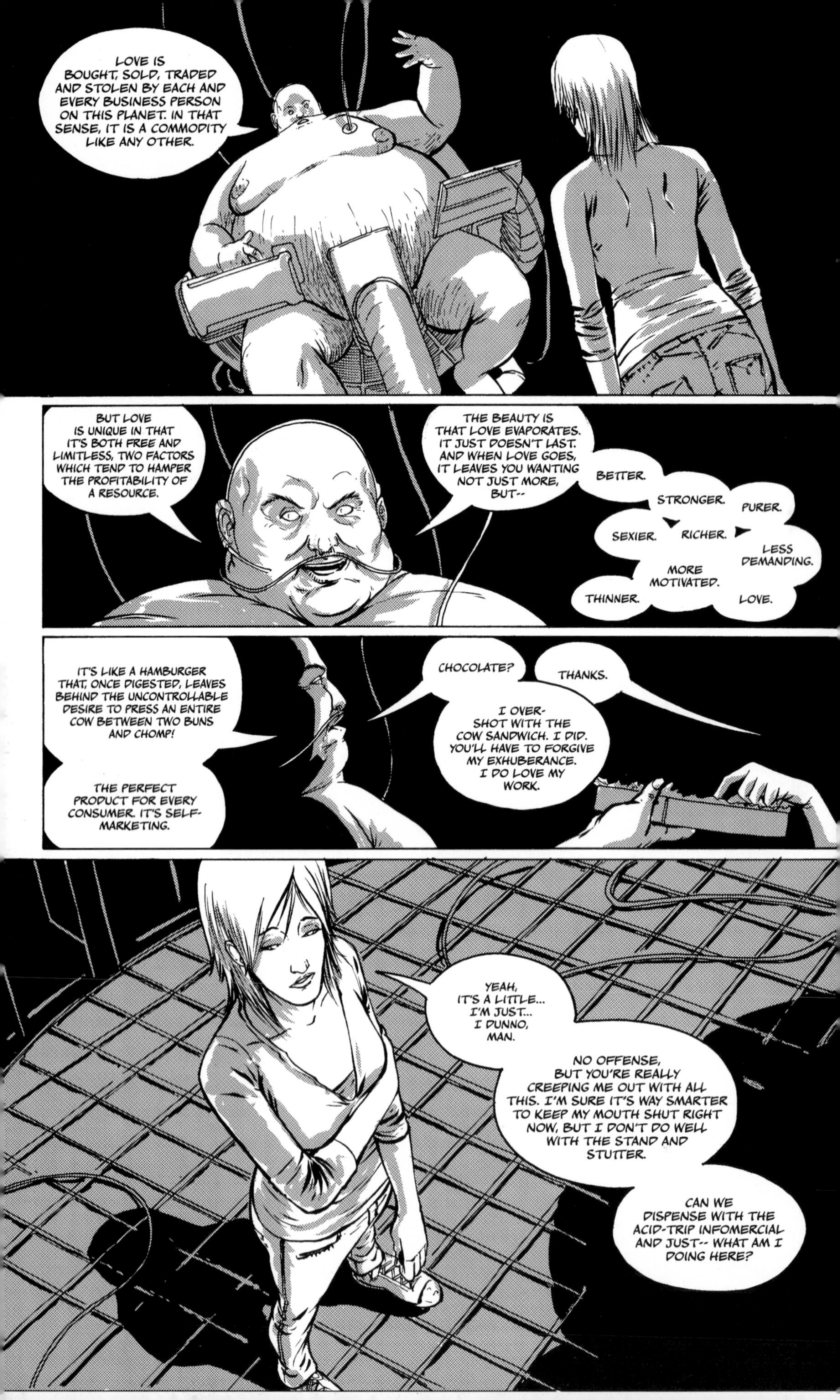
LOVE IS BOUGHT, SOLD, TRADED AND STOLEN BY EACH AND EVERY BUSINESS PERSON ON THIS PLANET. IN THAT SENSE, IT IS A COMMODITY LIKE ANY OTHER.
BUT LOVE IS UNIQUE IN THAT IT'S BOTH FREE AND LIMITLESS, TWO FACTORS WHICH TEND TO HAMPER THE PROFITABILITY OF A RESOURCE.
THE BEAUTY IS THAT LOVE EVAPORATES. IT JUST DOESN'T LAST. AND WHEN LOVE GOES, IT LEAVES YOU WANTING NOT JUST MORE, BUT--
BETTER.
STRONGER.
PURER.
SEXIER.
RICHER.
LESS DEMANDING.
MORE MOTIVATED.
THINNER.
LOVE.
IT'S LIKE A HAMBURGER THAT, ONCE DIGESTED, LEAVES BEHIND THE UNCONTROLLABLE DESIRE TO PRESS AN ENTIRE COW BETWEEN TWO BUNS AND CHOMP!
THE PERFECT PRODUCT FOR EVERY CONSUMER. IT'S SELF-MARKETING.
CHOCOLATE?
THANKS.
I OVER-SHOT WITH THE COW SANDWICH. I DID. YOU'LL HAVE TO FORGIVE MY EXHUBERANCE. I DO LOVE MY WORK.
YEAH, IT'S A LITTLE... I'M JUST... I DUNNO, MAN.
NO OFFENSE, BUT YOU'RE REALLY CREEPING ME OUT WITH ALL THIS. I'M SURE IT'S WAY SMARTER TO KEEP MY MOUTH SHUT RIGHT NOW, BUT I DON'T DO WELL WITH THE STAND AND STUTTER.
CAN WE DISPENSE WITH THE ACID-TRIP INFOMERCIAL AND JUST-- WHAT AM I DOING HERE?

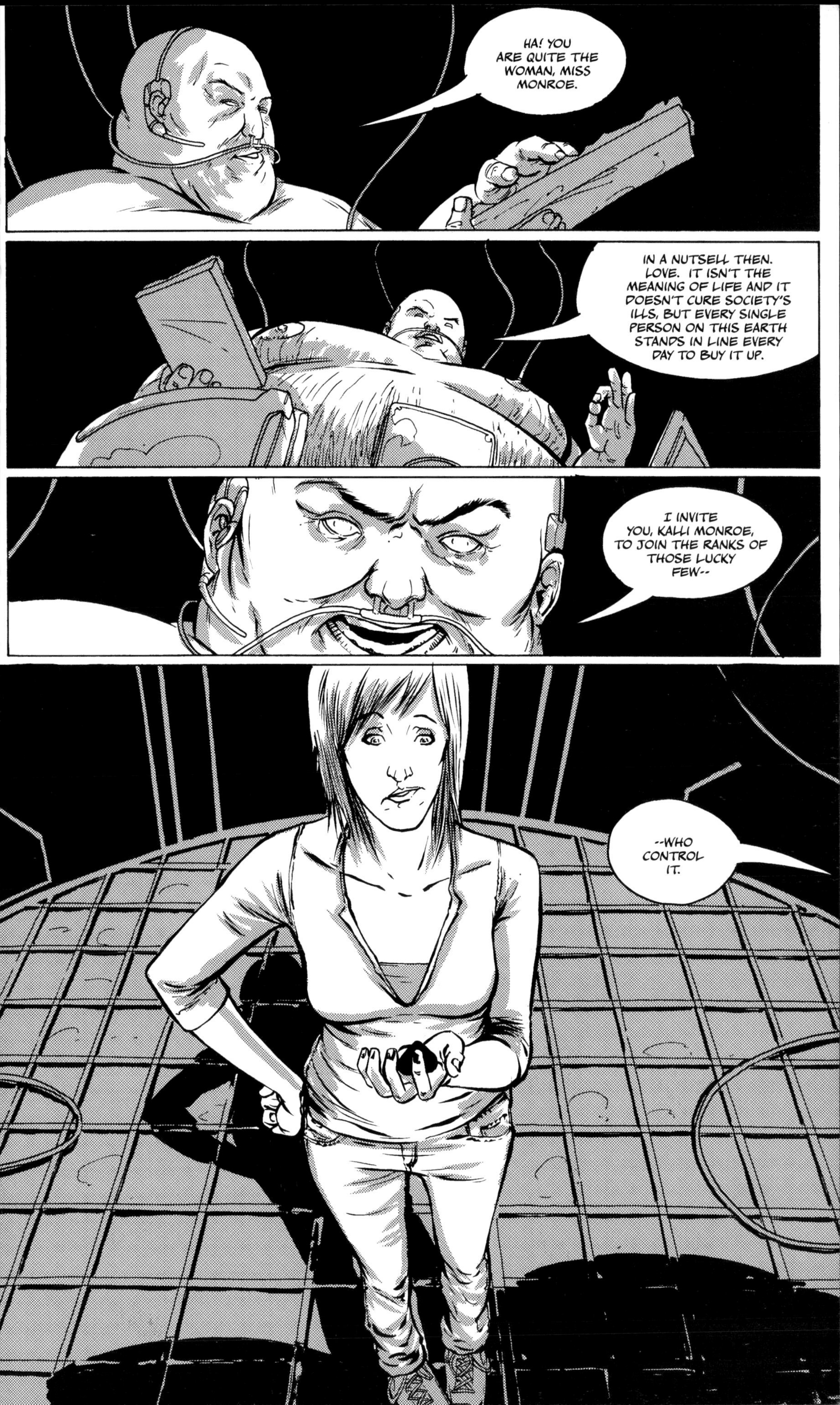
HA! YOU ARE QUITE THE WOMAN, MISS MONROE.
IN A NUTSELL THEN. LOVE. IT ISN'T THE MEANING OF LIFE AND IT DOESN'T CURE SOCIETY'S ILLS, BUT EVERY SINGLE PERSON ON THIS EARTH STANDS IN LINE EVERY DAY TO BUY IT UP.
I INVITE YOU, KALLI MONROE, TO JOIN THE RANKS OF THOSE LUCKY FEW--
--WHO CONTROL IT.

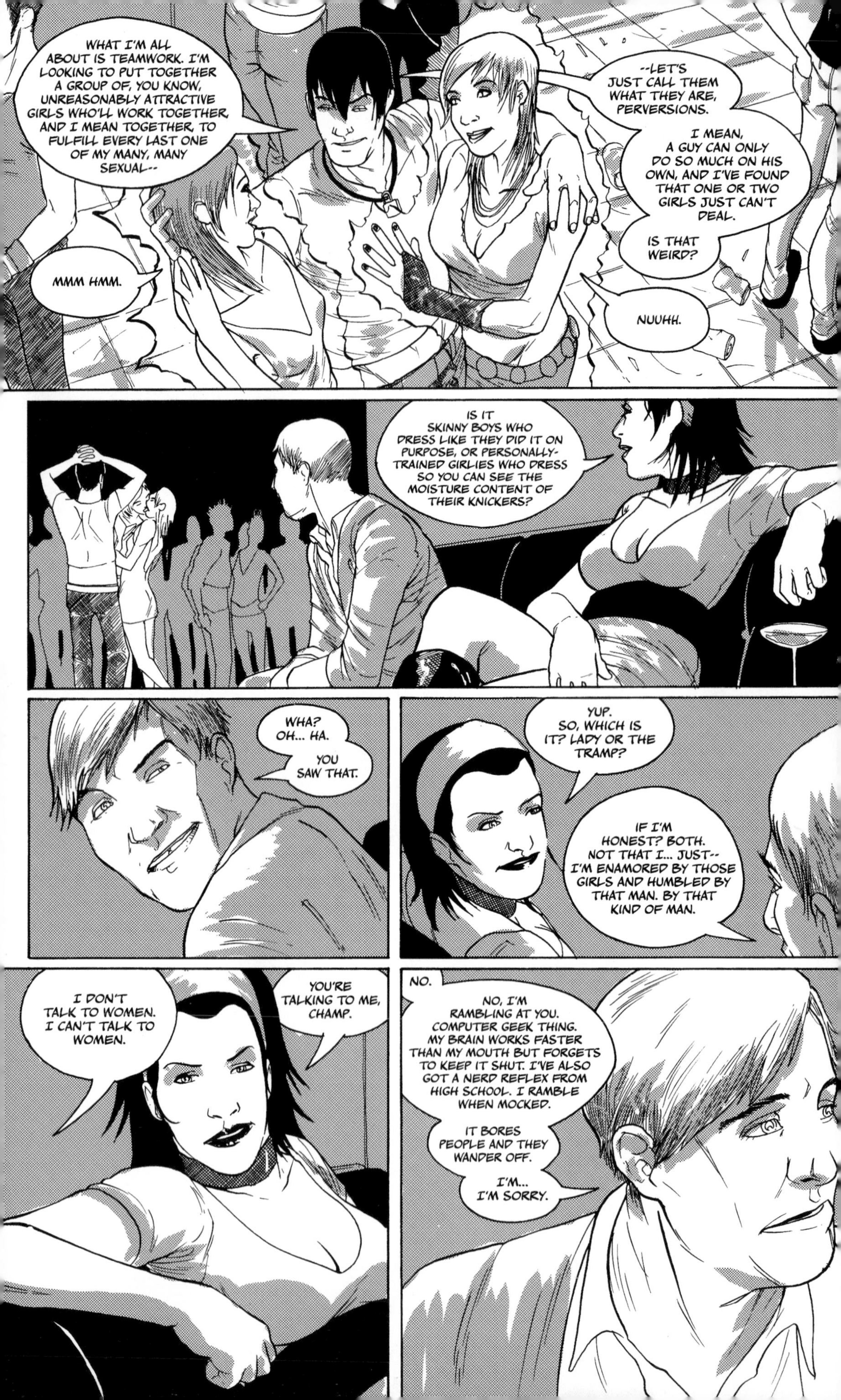
WHAT I'M ALL ABOUT IS TEAMWORK. I'M LOOKING TO PUT TOGETHER A GROUP OF, YOU KNOW, UNREASONABLY ATTRACTIVE GIRLS WHO'LL WORK TOGETHER, AND I MEAN TOGETHER, TO FULFILL EVERY LAST ONE OF MY MANY, MANY SEXUAL--
MMM HMM.
--LET'S JUST CALL THEM WHAT THEY ARE, PERVERSIONS.
I MEAN, A GUY CAN ONLY DO SO MUCH ON HIS OWN, AND I'VE FOUND THAT ONE OR TWO GIRLS JUST CAN'T DEAL.
IS THAT WEIRD?
NUUHH.
IS IT SKINNY BOYS WHO DRESS LIKE THEY DID IT ON PURPOSE, OR PERSONALLY-TRAINED GIRLIES WHO DRESS SO YOU CAN SEE THE MOISTURE CONTENT OF THEIR KNICKERS?
WHA? OH... HA.
YOU SAW THAT.
YUP. SO, WHICH IS IT? LADY OR THE TRAMP?
IF I'M HONEST? BOTH. NOT THAT I... JUST-- I'M ENAMORED BY THOSE GIRLS AND HUMBLED BY THAT MAN. BY THAT KIND OF MAN.
I DON'T TALK TO WOMEN. I CAN'T TALK TO WOMEN.
YOU'RE TALKING TO ME, CHAMP.
NO.
NO, I'M RAMBLING AT YOU. COMPUTER GEEK THING. MY BRAIN WORKS FASTER THAN MY MOUTH BUT FORGETS TO KEEP IT SHUT. I'VE ALSO GOT A NERD REFLEX FROM HIGH SCHOOL. I RAMBLE WHEN MOCKED.
IT BORES PEOPLE AND THEY WANDER OFF.
I'M... I'M SORRY.

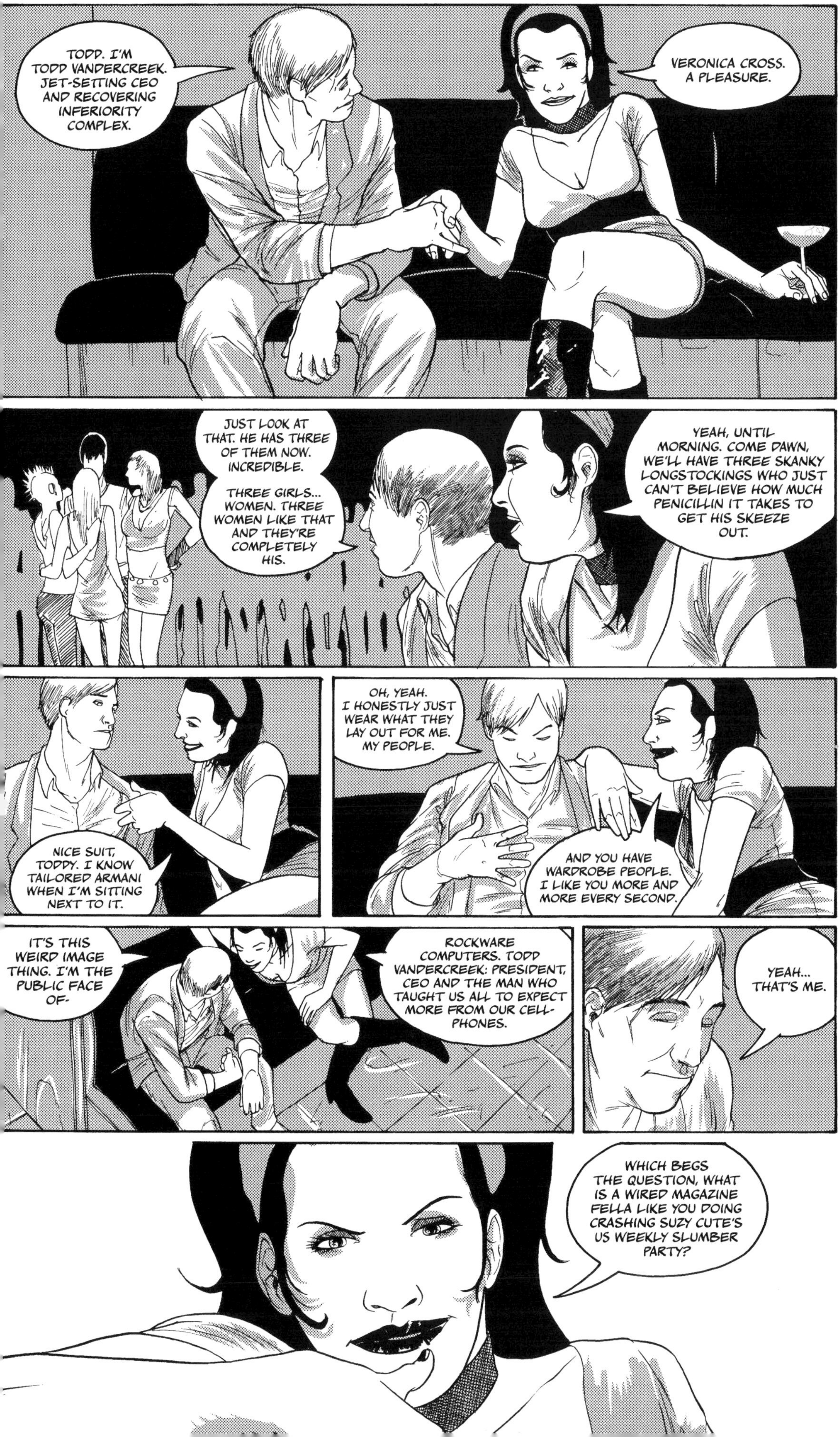
TODD. I'M TODD VANDERCREEK. JET-SETTING CEO AND RECOVERING INFERIORITY COMPLEX.
VERONICA CROSS. A PLEASURE.
JUST LOOK AT THAT. HE HAS THREE OF THEM NOW. INCREDIBLE.
THREE GIRLS... WOMEN. THREE WOMEN LIKE THAT AND THEY'RE COMPLETELY HIS.
YEAH, UNTIL MORNING. COME DAWN, WE'LL HAVE THREE SKANKY LONGSTOCKINGS WHO JUST CAN'T BELIEVE HOW MUCH PENICILLIN IT TAKES TO GET HIS SKEEZE OUT.
NICE SUIT, TODDY. I KNOW TAILORED ARMANI WHEN I'M SITTING NEXT TO IT.
OH, YEAH. I HONESTLY JUST WEAR WHAT THEY LAY OUT FOR ME. MY PEOPLE.
AND YOU HAVE WARDROBE PEOPLE. I LIKE YOU MORE AND MORE EVERY SECOND.
IT'S THIS WEIRD IMAGE THING. I'M THE PUBLIC FACE OF-
ROCKWARE COMPUTERS. TODD VANDERCREEK: PRESIDENT, CEO AND THE MAN WHO TAUGHT US ALL TO EXPECT MORE FROM OUR CELL-PHONES.
YEAH... THAT'S ME.
WHICH BEGS THE QUESTION, WHAT IS A WIRED MAGAZINE FELLA LIKE YOU DOING CRASHING SUZY CUTE'S US WEEKLY SLUMBER PARTY?

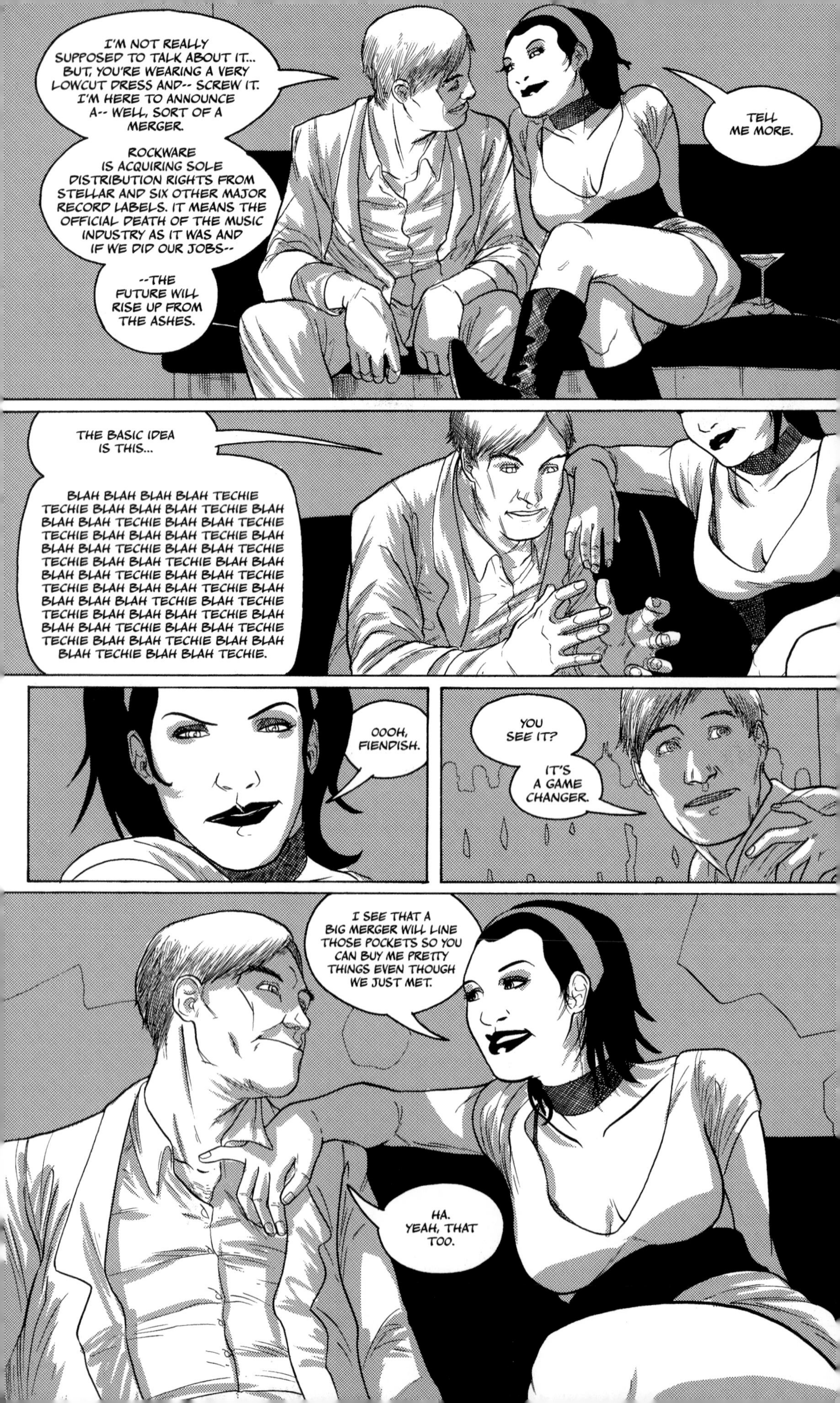
I'M NOT REALLY SUPPOSED TO TALK ABOUT IT... BUT, YOU'RE WEARING A VERY LOWCUT DRESS AND-- SCREW IT. I'M HERE TO ANNOUNCE A-- WELL, SORT OF A MERGER.
ROCKWARE IS ACQUIRING SOLE DISTRIBUTION RIGHTS FROM STELLAR AND SIX OTHER MAJOR RECORD LABELS. IT MEANS THE OFFICIAL DEATH OF THE MUSIC INDUSTRY AS IT WAS AND IF WE DID OUR JOBS--
--THE FUTURE WILL RISE UP FROM THE ASHES.
TELL ME MORE.
THE BASIC IDEA IS THIS...
BLAH BLAH BLAH BLAH TECHIE TECHIE BLAH BLAH BLAH TECHIE BLAH BLAH BLAH TECHIE BLAH BLAH TECHIE TECHIE BLAH BLAH BLAH TECHIE BLAH BLAH BLAH TECHIE BLAH BLAH TECHIE TECHIE BLAH BLAH TECHIE BLAH BLAH BLAH BLAH TECHIE BLAH BLAH TECHIE TECHIE BLAH BLAH BLAH TECHIE BLAH BLAH BLAH BLAH TECHIE BLAH TECHIE TECHIE BLAH BLAH BLAH TECHIE BLAH BLAH BLAH TECHIE BLAH BLAH TECHIE TECHIE BLAH BLAH TECHIE BLAH BLAH BLAH TECHIE BLAH BLAH TECHIE.
OOOH, FIENDISH.
YOU SEE IT?
IT'S A GAME CHANGER.
I SEE THAT A BIG MERGER WILL LINE THOSE POCKETS SO YOU CAN BUY ME PRETTY THINGS EVEN THOUGH WE JUST MET.
HA. YEAH, THAT TOO.

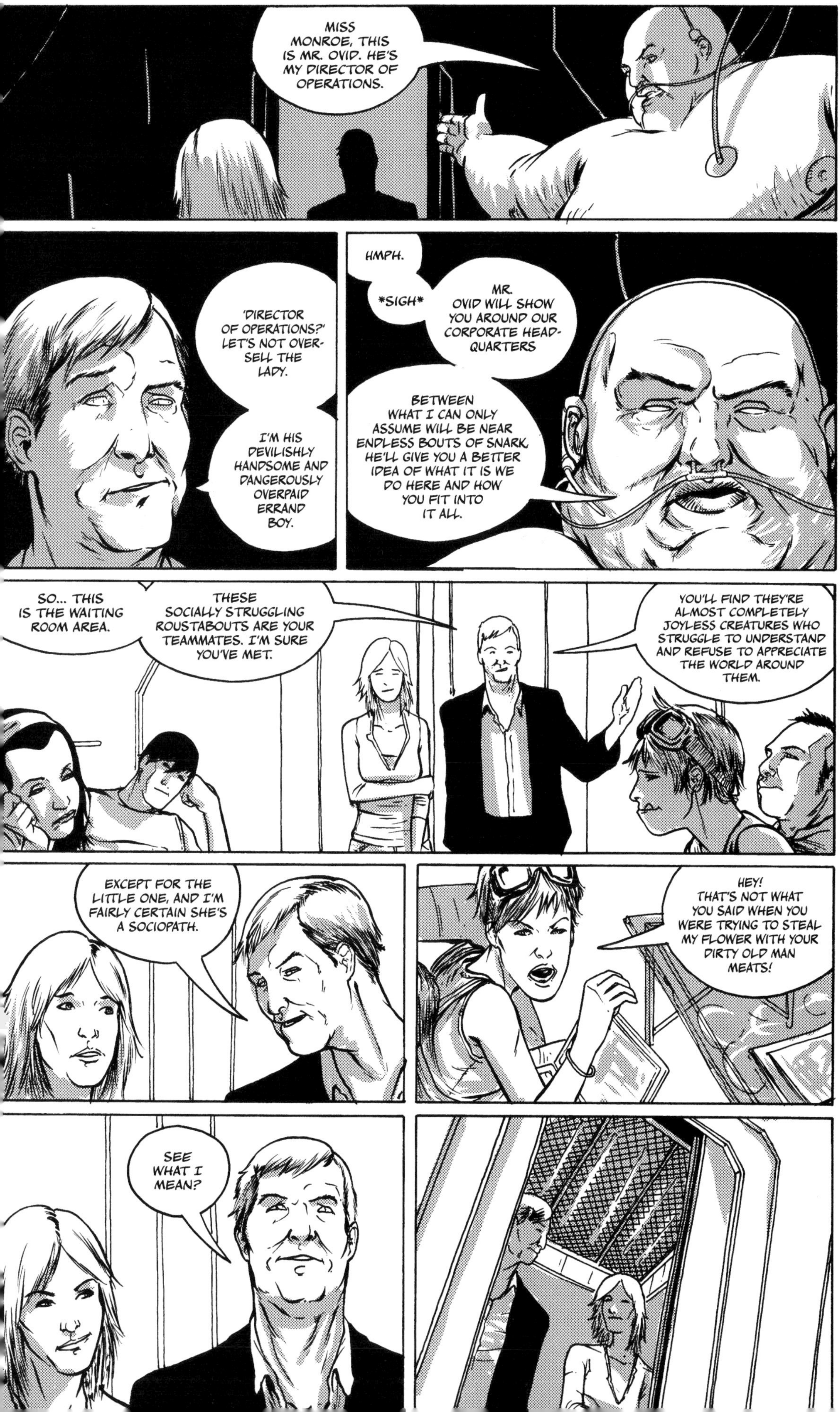
MISS MONROE, THIS IS MR. OVID. HE'S MY DIRECTOR OF OPERATIONS.
'DIRECTOR OF OPERATIONS?' LET'S NOT OVERSELL THE LADY.
I'M HIS DEVILISHLY HANDSOME AND DANGEROUSLY OVERPAID ERRAND BOY.
HMPH.
SIGH
MR. OVID WILL SHOW YOU AROUND OUR CORPORATE HEADQUARTERS
BETWEEN WHAT I CAN ONLY ASSUME WILL BE NEAR ENDLESS BOUTS OF SNARK, HE'LL GIVE YOU A BETTER IDEA OF WHAT IT IS WE DO HERE AND HOW YOU FIT INTO IT ALL.
SO... THIS IS THE WAITING ROOM AREA.
THESE SOCIALLY STRUGGLING ROUSTABOUTS ARE YOUR TEAMMATES. I'M SURE YOU'VE MET.
YOU'LL FIND THEY'RE ALMOST COMPLETELY JOYLESS CREATURES WHO STRUGGLE TO UNDERSTAND AND REFUSE TO APPRECIATE THE WORLD AROUND THEM.
EXCEPT FOR THE LITTLE ONE, AND I'M FAIRLY CERTAIN SHE'S A SOCIOPATH.
HEY! THAT'S NOT WHAT YOU SAID WHEN YOU WERE TRYING TO STEAL MY FLOWER WITH YOUR DIRTY OLD MAN MEATS!
SEE WHAT I MEAN?

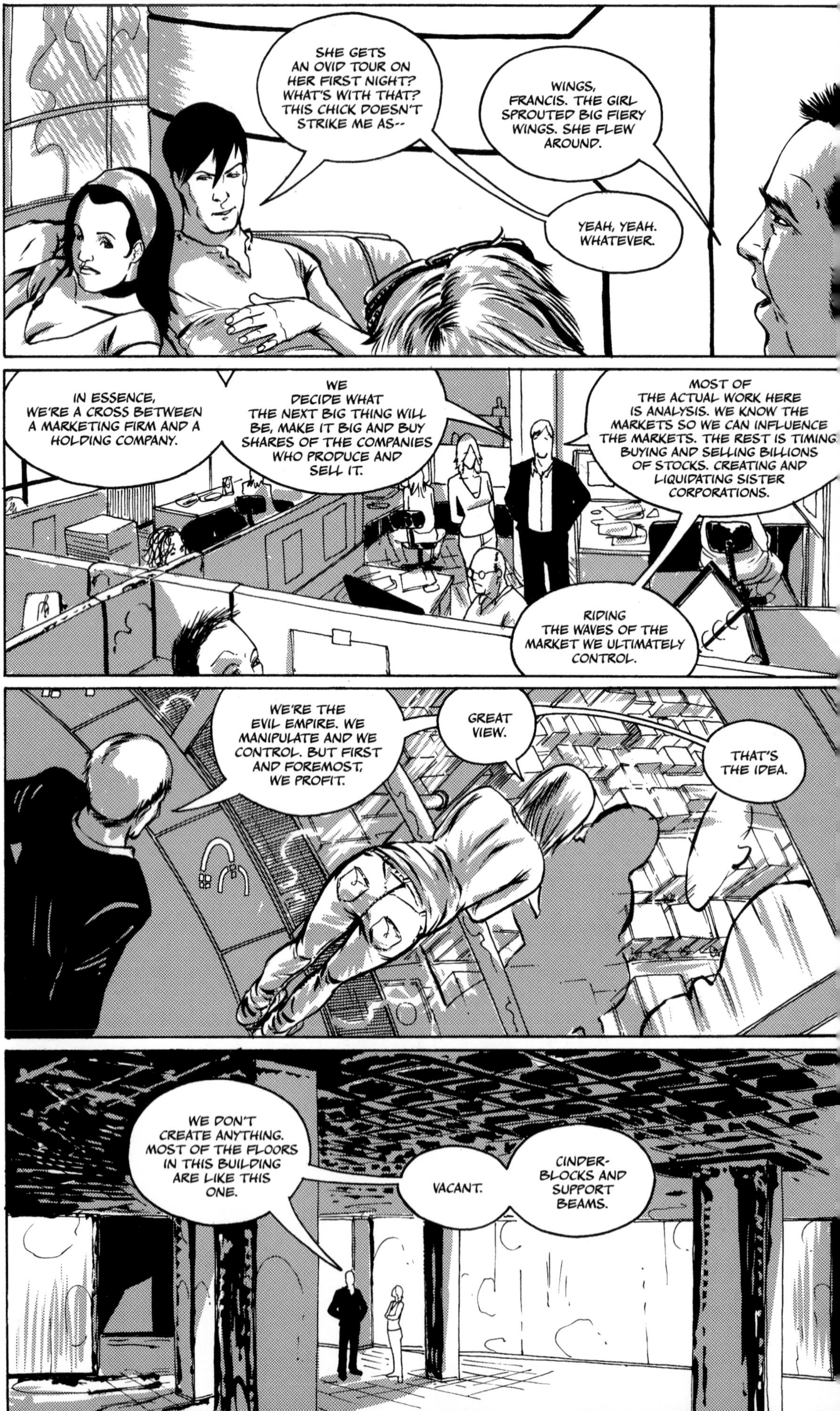
SHE GETS AN OVID TOUR ON HER FIRST NIGHT? WHAT'S WITH THAT? THIS CHICK DOESN'T STRIKE ME AS--
WINGS, FRANCIS. THE GIRL SPROUTED BIG FIERY WINGS. SHE FLEW AROUND.
YEAH, YEAH. WHATEVER.
IN ESSENCE, WE'RE A CROSS BETWEEN A MARKETING FIRM AND A HOLDING COMPANY.
WE DECIDE WHAT THE NEXT BIG THING WILL BE, MAKE IT BIG AND BUY SHARES OF THE COMPANIES WHO PRODUCE AND SELL IT.
MOST OF THE ACTUAL WORK HERE IS ANALYSIS. WE KNOW THE MARKETS SO WE CAN INFLUENCE THE MARKETS. THE REST IS TIMING. BUYING AND SELLING BILLIONS OF STOCKS. CREATING AND LIQUIDATING SISTER CORPORATIONS.
RIDING THE WAVES OF THE MARKET WE ULTIMATELY CONTROL.
WE'RE THE EVIL EMPIRE. WE MANIPULATE AND WE CONTROL. BUT FIRST AND FOREMOST, WE PROFIT.
GREAT VIEW.
THAT'S THE IDEA.
WE DON'T CREATE ANYTHING. MOST OF THE FLOORS IN THIS BUILDING ARE LIKE THIS ONE.
VACANT.
CINDER-BLOCKS AND SUPPORT BEAMS.

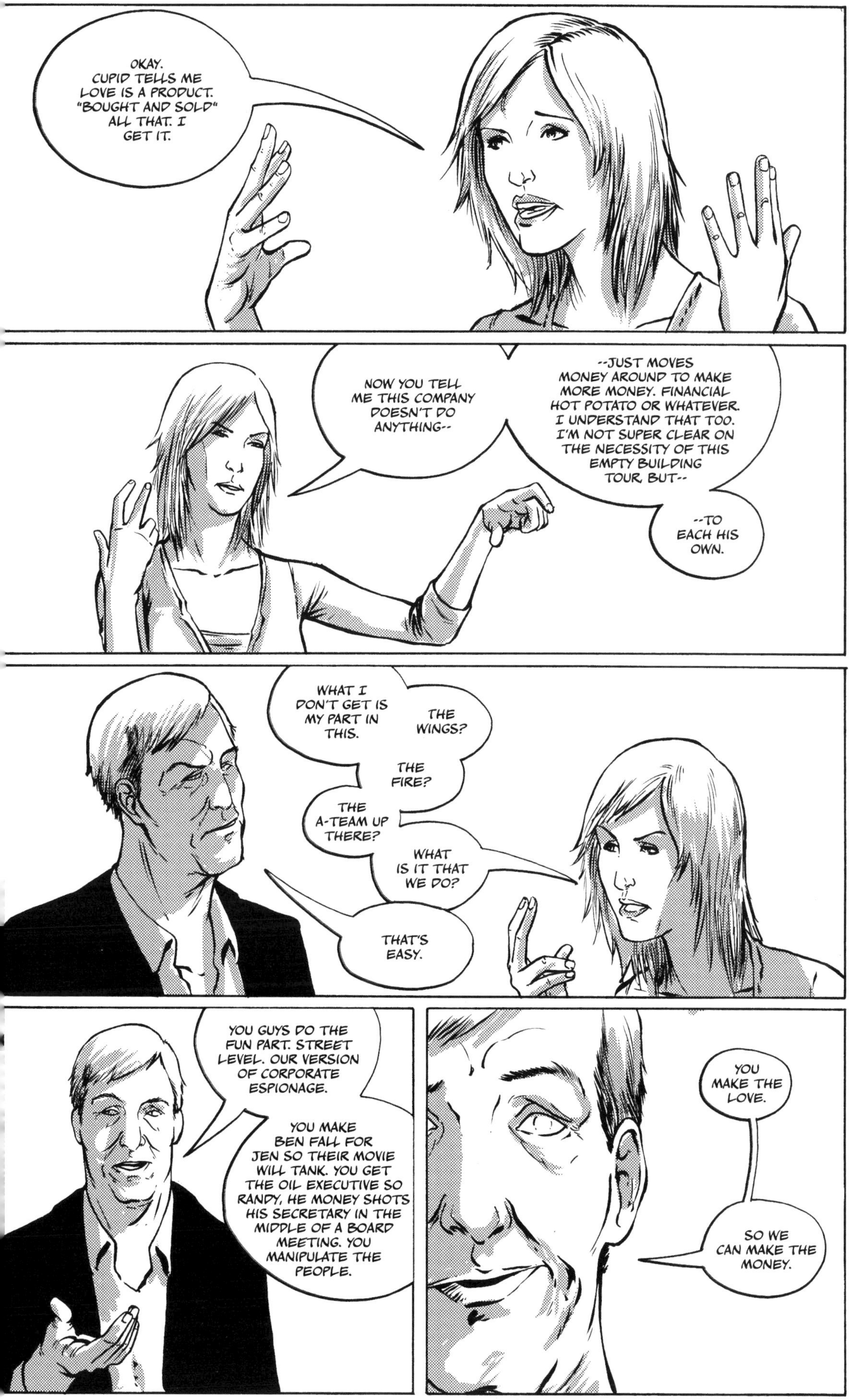
OKAY. CUPID TELLS ME LOVE IS A PRODUCT. "BOUGHT AND SOLD" ALL THAT. I GET IT.
NOW YOU TELL ME THIS COMPANY DOESN'T DO ANYTHING--
--JUST MOVES MONEY AROUND TO MAKE MORE MONEY. FINANCIAL HOT POTATO OR WHATEVER. I UNDERSTAND THAT TOO. I'M NOT SUPER CLEAR ON THE NECESSITY OF THIS EMPTY BUILDING TOUR, BUT--
--TO EACH HIS OWN.
WHAT I DON'T GET IS MY PART IN THIS.
THE WINGS?
THE FIRE?
THE A-TEAM UP THERE?
WHAT IS IT THAT WE DO?
THAT'S EASY.
YOU GUYS DO THE FUN PART. STREET LEVEL. OUR VERSION OF CORPORATE ESPIONAGE.
YOU MAKE BEN FALL FOR JEN SO THEIR MOVIE WILL TANK. YOU GET THE OIL EXECUTIVE SO RANDY, HE MONEY SHOTS HIS SECRETARY IN THE MIDDLE OF A BOARD MEETING. YOU MANIPULATE THE PEOPLE.
YOU MAKE THE LOVE.
SO WE CAN MAKE THE MONEY.

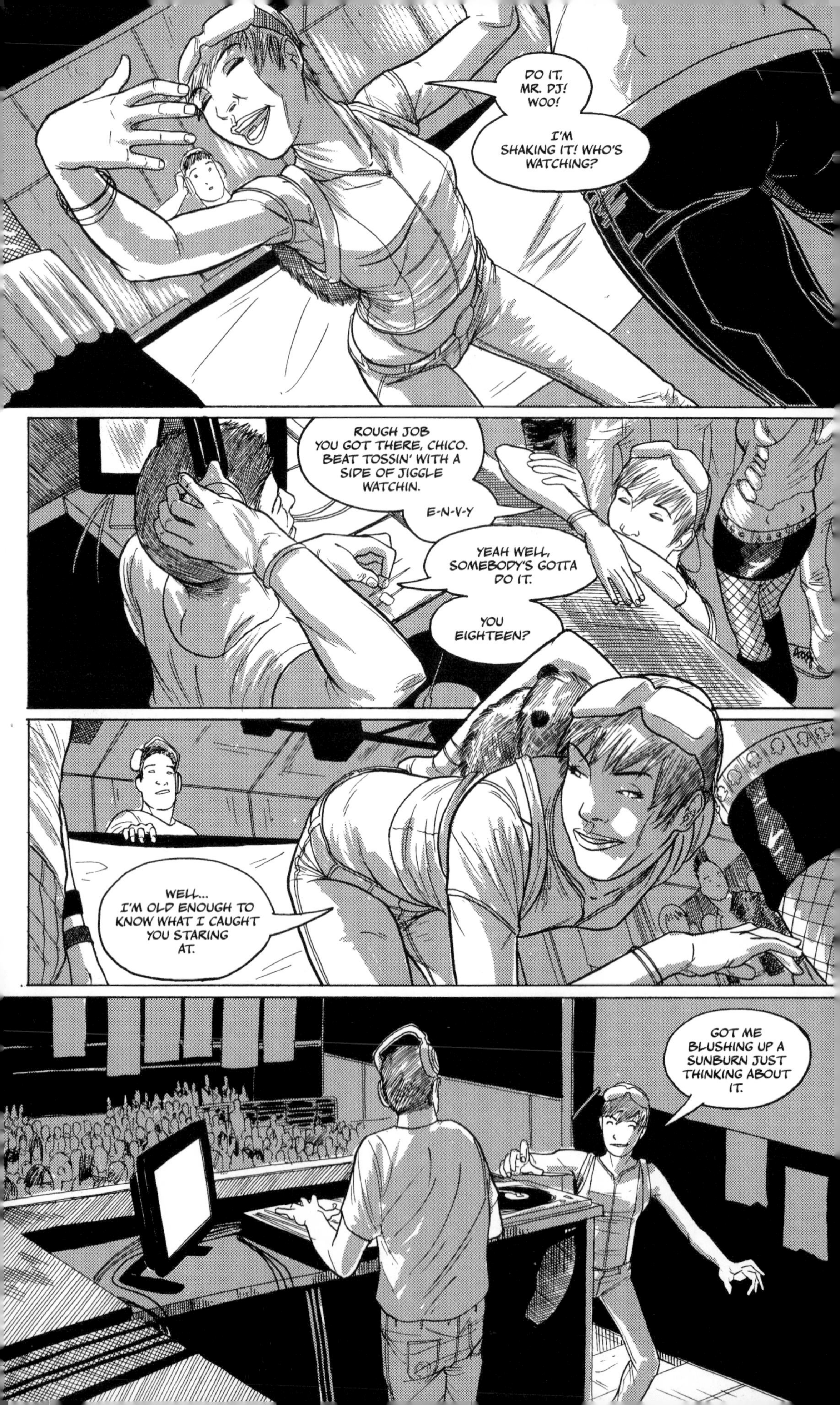
DO IT, MR. DJ! WOO!
I'M SHAKING IT! WHO'S WATCHING?
ROUGH JOB YOU GOT THERE, CHICO. BEAT TOSSIN' WITH A SIDE OF JIGGLE WATCHIN.
E-N-V-Y
YEAH WELL, SOMEBODY'S GOTTA DO IT.
YOU EIGHTEEN?
WELL... I'M OLD ENOUGH TO KNOW WHAT I CAUGHT YOU STARING AT.
GOT ME BLUSHING UP A SUNBURN JUST THINKING ABOUT IT.

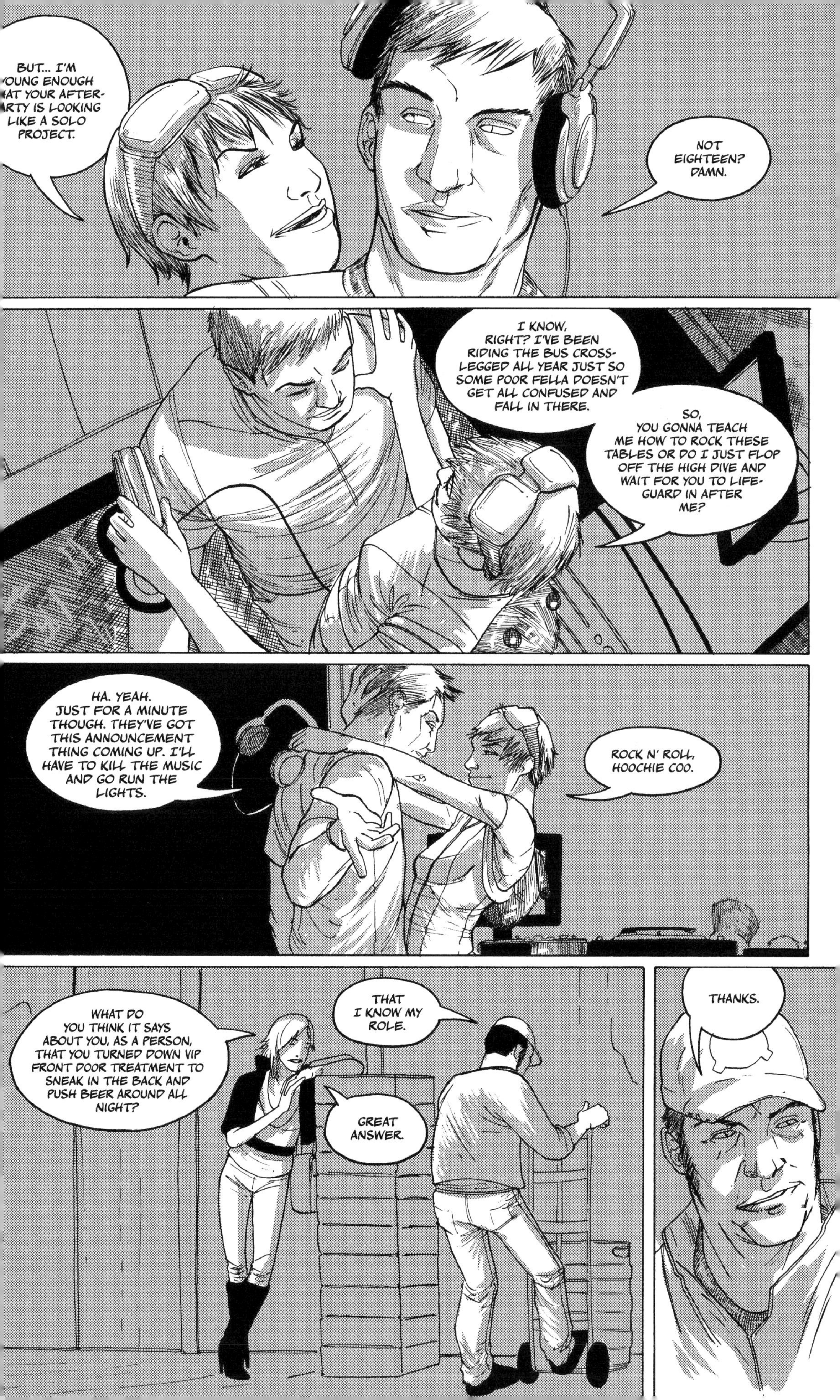
BUT... I'M
OUNG ENOUGH
AT YOUR AFTER-
ARTY IS LOOKING
LIKE A SOLO
PROJECT.
NOT EIGHTEEN? DAMN.
I KNOW, RIGHT? I'VE BEEN RIDING THE BUS CROSS-LEGGED ALL YEAR JUST SO SOME POOR FELLA DOESN'T GET ALL CONFUSED AND FALL IN THERE.
SO, YOU GONNA TEACH ME HOW TO ROCK THESE TABLES OR DO I JUST FLOP OFF THE HIGH DIVE AND WAIT FOR YOU TO LIFE-GUARD IN AFTER ME?
HA. YEAH. JUST FOR A MINUTE THOUGH. THEY'VE GOT THIS ANNOUNCEMENT THING COMING UP. I'LL HAVE TO KILL THE MUSIC AND GO RUN THE LIGHTS.
ROCK N' ROLL, HOOCHIE COO.
WHAT DO YOU THINK IT SAYS ABOUT YOU, AS A PERSON, THAT YOU TURNED DOWN VIP FRONT DOOR TREATMENT TO SNEAK IN THE BACK AND PUSH BEER AROUND ALL NIGHT?
THAT I KNOW MY ROLE.
GREAT ANSWER.
THANKS.

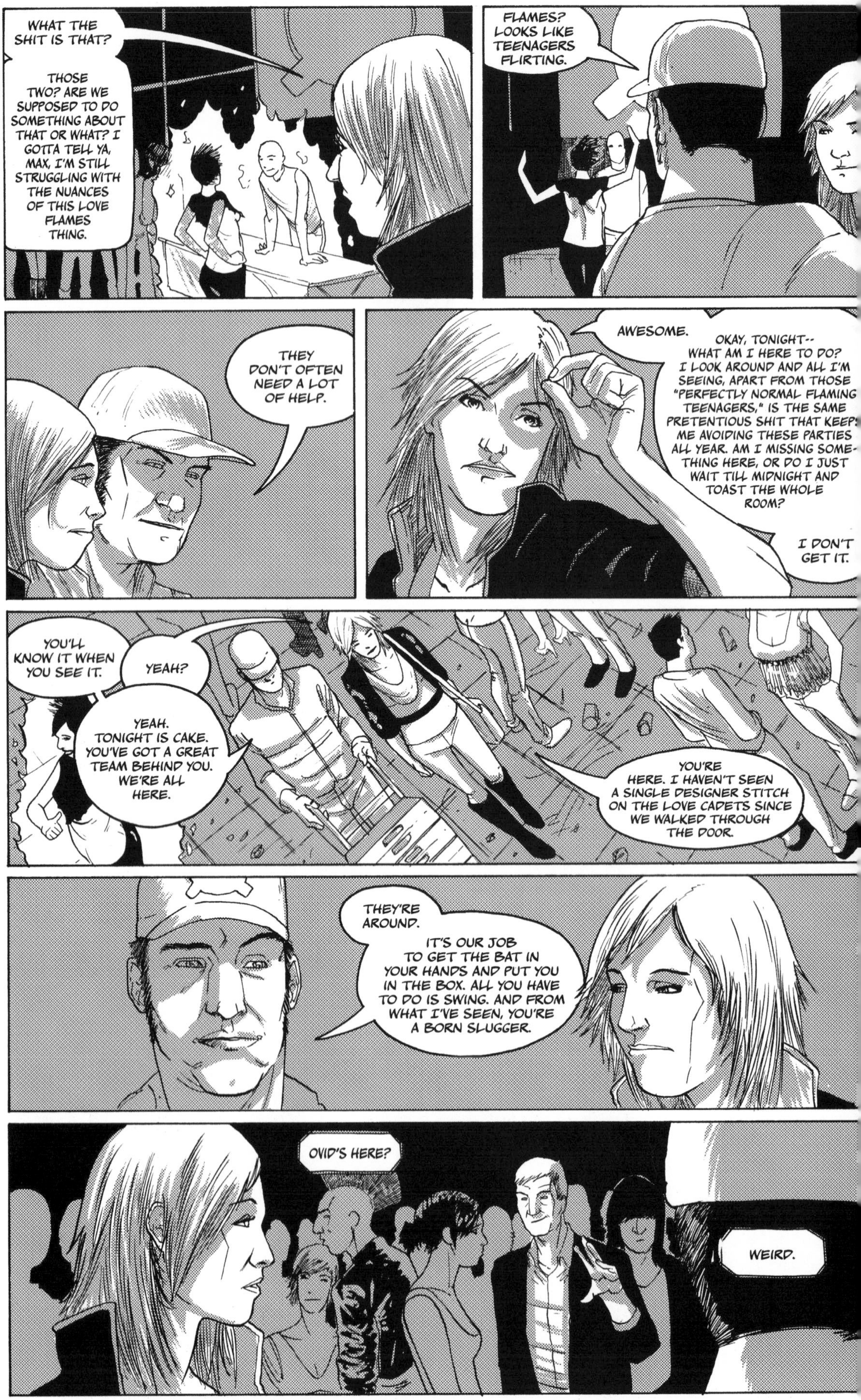
WHAT THE SHIT IS THAT?
THOSE TWO? ARE WE SUPPOSED TO DO SOMETHING ABOUT THAT OR WHAT? I GOTTA TELL YA, MAX, I'M STILL STRUGGLING WITH THE NUANCES OF THIS LOVE FLAMES THING.
FLAMES? LOOKS LIKE TEENAGERS FLIRTING.
THEY DON'T OFTEN NEED A LOT OF HELP.
AWESOME.
OKAY, TONIGHT-- WHAT AM I HERE TO DO? I LOOK AROUND AND ALL I'M SEEING, APART FROM THOSE "PERFECTLY NORMAL FLAMING TEENAGERS," IS THE SAME PRETENTIOUS SHIT THAT KEEPS ME AVOIDING THESE PARTIES ALL YEAR. AM I MISSING SOMETHING HERE, OR DO I JUST WAIT TILL MIDNIGHT AND TOAST THE WHOLE ROOM?
I DON'T GET IT.
YOU'LL KNOW IT WHEN YOU SEE IT.
YEAH?
YEAH. TONIGHT IS CAKE. YOU'VE GOT A GREAT TEAM BEHIND YOU. WE'RE ALL HERE.
YOU'RE HERE. I HAVEN'T SEEN A SINGLE DESIGNER STITCH ON THE LOVE CADETS SINCE WE WALKED THROUGH THE DOOR.
THEY'RE AROUND.
IT'S OUR JOB TO GET THE BAT IN YOUR HANDS AND PUT YOU IN THE BOX. ALL YOU HAVE TO DO IS SWING. AND FROM WHAT I'VE SEEN, YOU'RE A BORN SLUGGER.
OVID'S HERE?
WEIRD.

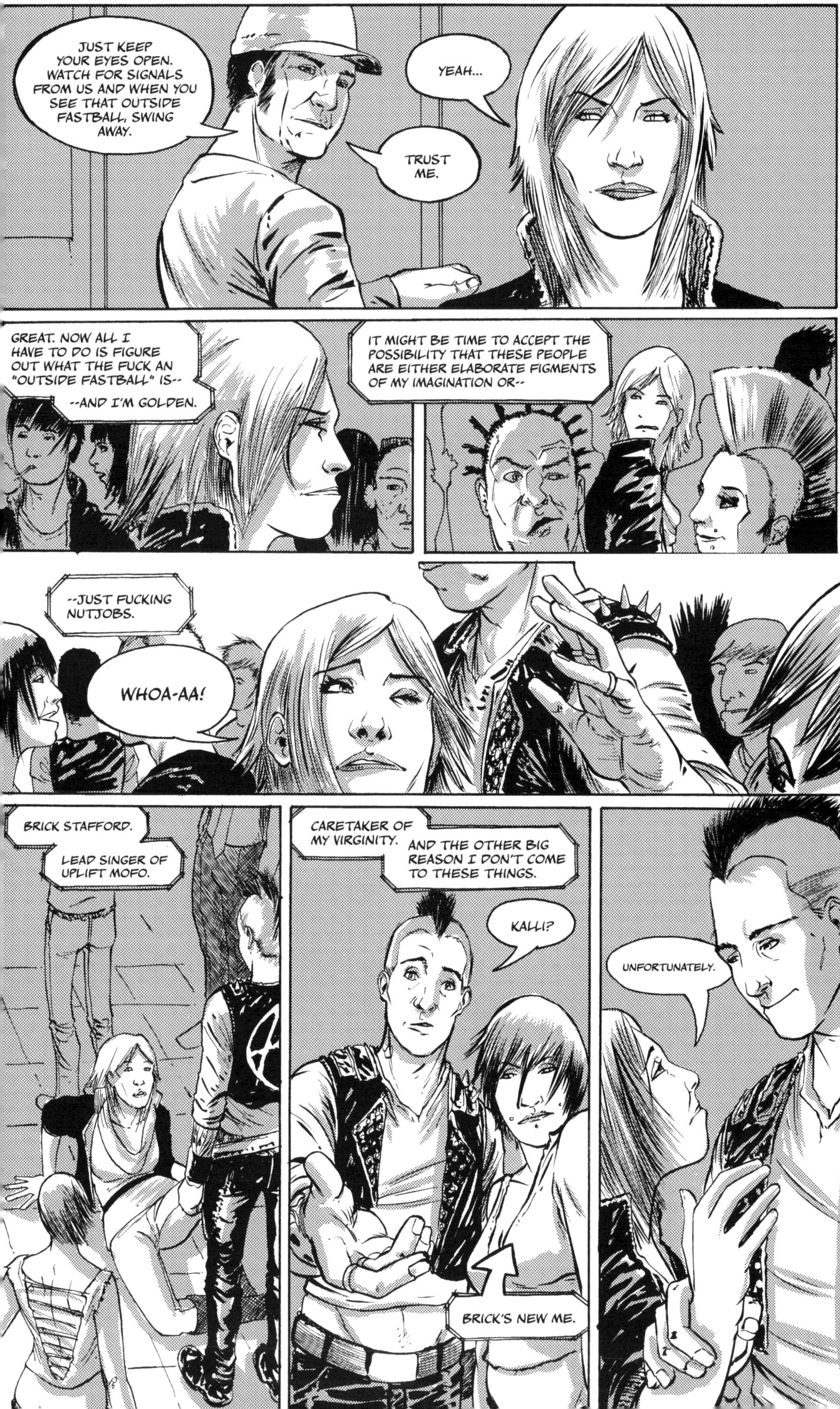
JUST KEEP YOUR EYES OPEN. WATCH FOR SIGNALS FROM US AND WHEN YOU SEE THAT OUTSIDE FASTBALL, SWING AWAY.
TRUST ME.
YEAH...
GREAT. NOW ALL I HAVE TO DO IS FIGURE OUT WHAT THE FUCK AN "OUTSIDE FASTBALL" IS--
--AND I'M GOLDEN.
IT MIGHT BE TIME TO ACCEPT THE POSSIBILITY THAT THESE PEOPLE ARE EITHER ELABORATE FIGMENTS OF MY IMAGINATION OR--
--JUST FUCKING NUTJOBS.
WHOA-AA!
BRICK STAFFORD.
LEAD SINGER OF UPLIFT MOFO.
CARETAKER OF MY VIRGINITY.
AND THE OTHER BIG REASON I DON'T COME TO THESE THINGS.
KALLI?
BRICK'S NEW ME.
UNFORTUNATELY.

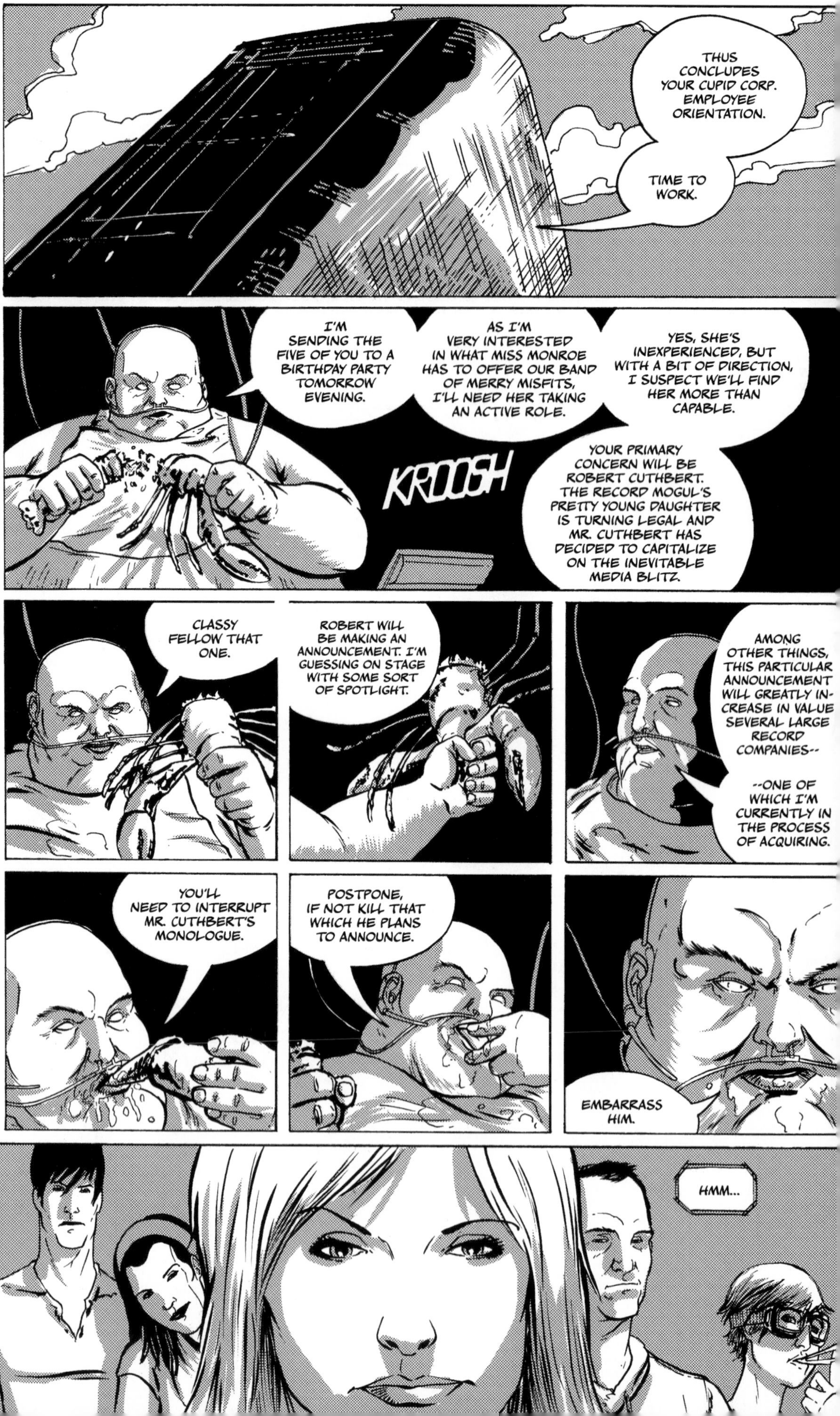
THUS CONCLUDES YOUR CUPID CORP. EMPLOYEE ORIENTATION.
TIME TO WORK.
I'M SENDING THE FIVE OF YOU TO A BIRTHDAY PARTY TOMORROW EVENING.
AS I'M VERY INTERESTED IN WHAT MISS MONROE HAS TO OFFER OUR BAND OF MERRY MISFITS, I'LL NEED HER TAKING AN ACTIVE ROLE.
YES, SHE'S INEXPERIENCED, BUT WITH A BIT OF DIRECTION, I SUSPECT WE'LL FIND HER MORE THAN CAPABLE.
KROOSH
YOUR PRIMARY CONCERN WILL BE ROBERT CUTHBERT. THE RECORD MOGUL'S PRETTY YOUNG DAUGHTER IS TURNING LEGAL AND MR. CUTHBERT HAS DECIDED TO CAPITALIZE ON THE INEVITABLE MEDIA BLITZ.
CLASSY FELLOW THAT ONE.
ROBERT WILL BE MAKING AN ANNOUNCEMENT. I'M GUESSING ON STAGE WITH SOME SORT OF SPOTLIGHT.
AMONG OTHER THINGS, THIS PARTICULAR ANNOUNCEMENT WILL GREATLY INCREASE IN VALUE SEVERAL LARGE RECORD COMPANIES--
--ONE OF WHICH I'M CURRENTLY IN THE PROCESS OF ACQUIRING.
YOU'LL NEED TO INTERRUPT MR. CUTHBERT'S MONOLOGUE.
POSTPONE, IF NOT KILL THAT WHICH HE PLANS TO ANNOUNCE.
EMBARRASS HIM.
HMM...

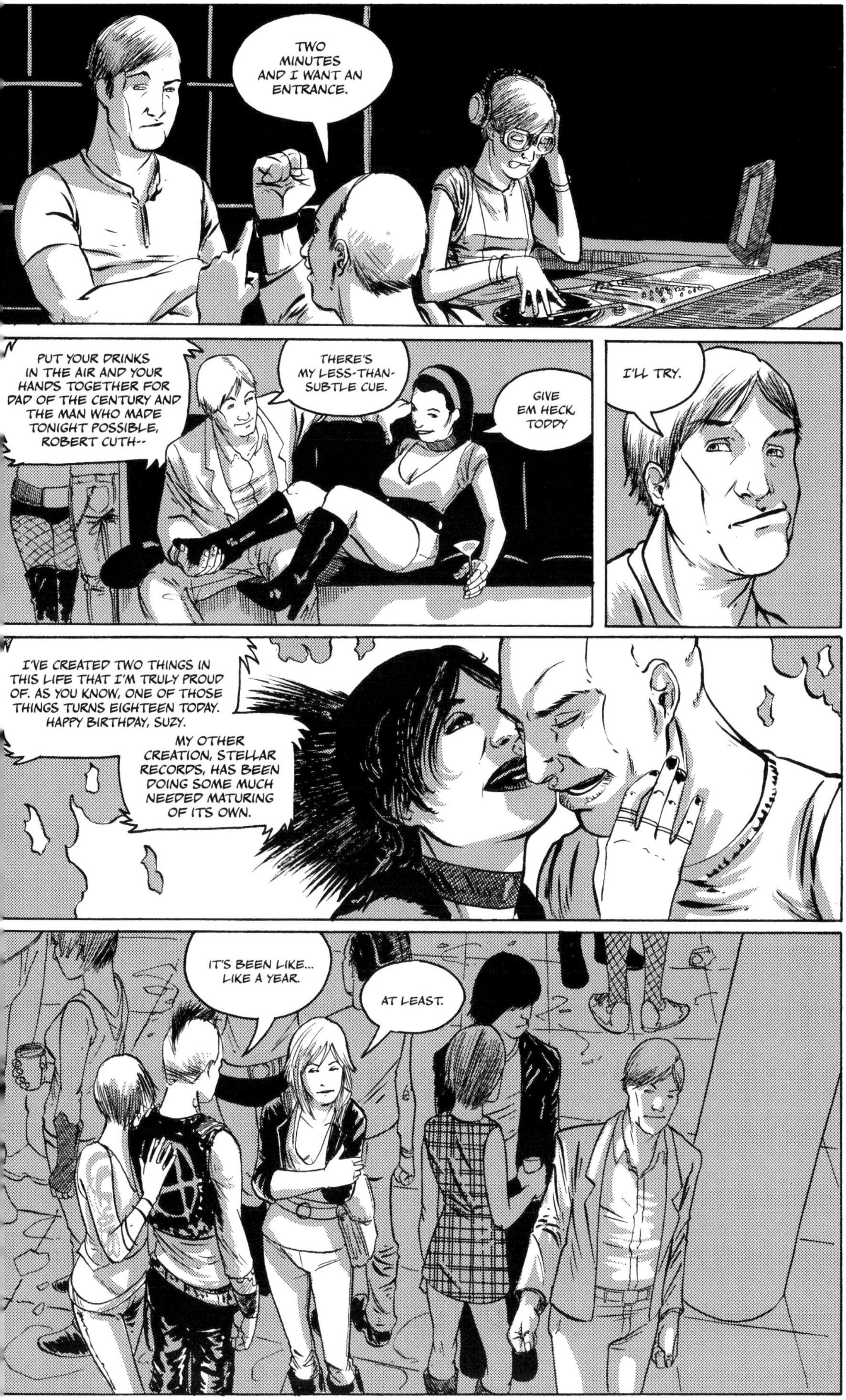
TWO MINUTES AND I WANT AN ENTRANCE.
PUT YOUR DRINKS IN THE AIR AND YOUR HANDS TOGETHER FOR DAD OF THE CENTURY AND THE MAN WHO MADE TONIGHT POSSIBLE, ROBERT CUTH--
THERE'S MY LESS-THAN-SUBTLE CUE.
GIVE EM HECK, TODDY
I'LL TRY.
I'VE CREATED TWO THINGS IN THIS LIFE THAT I'M TRULY PROUD OF. AS YOU KNOW, ONE OF THOSE THINGS TURNS EIGHTEEN TODAY. HAPPY BIRTHDAY, SUZY.
MY OTHER CREATION, STELLAR RECORDS, HAS BEEN DOING SOME MUCH NEEDED MATURING OF ITS OWN.
IT'S BEEN LIKE... LIKE A YEAR.
AT LEAST.

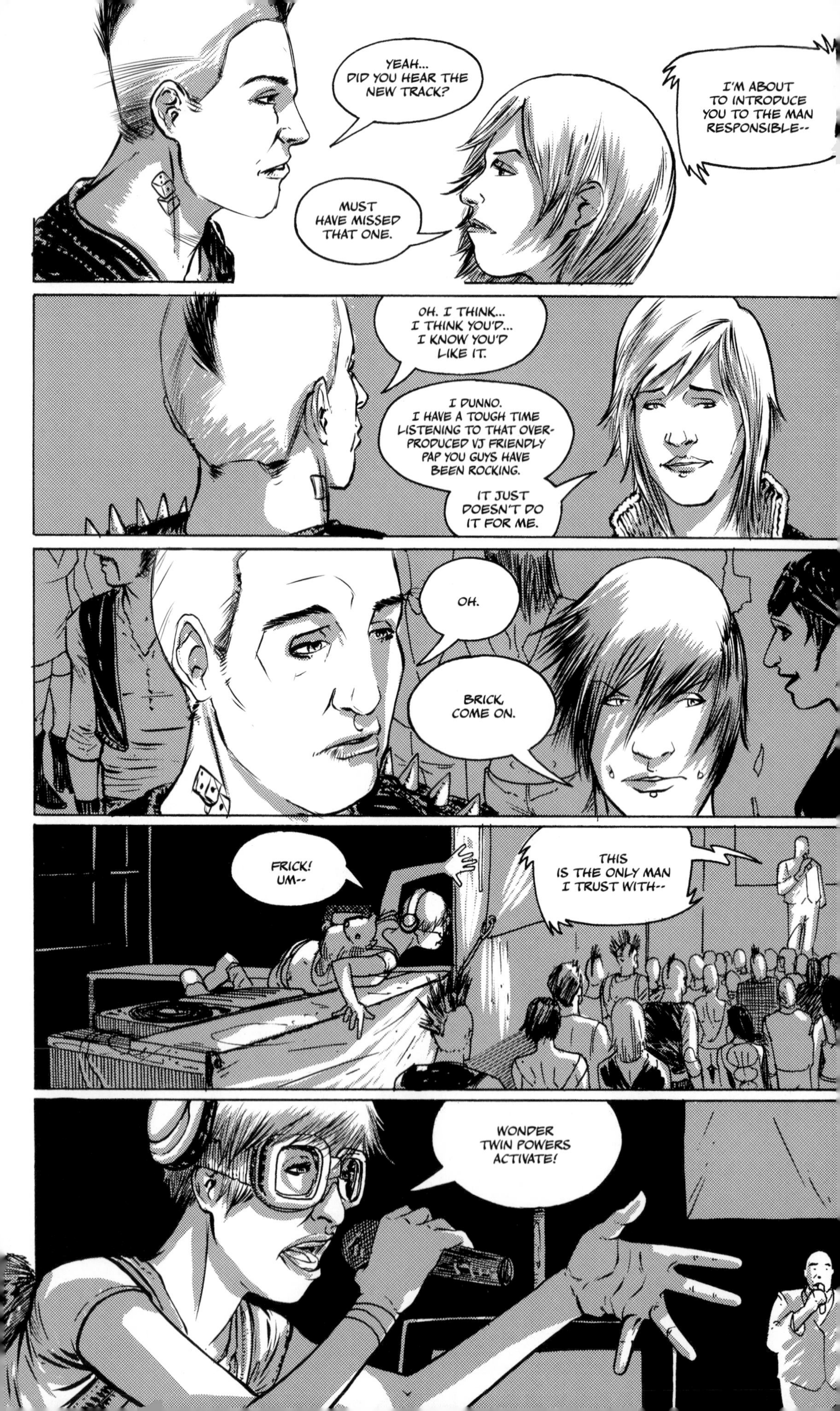
YEAH... DID YOU HEAR THE NEW TRACK?
I'M ABOUT TO INTRODUCE YOU TO THE MAN RESPONSIBLE--
MUST HAVE MISSED THAT ONE.
OH. I THINK... I THINK YOU'D... I KNOW YOU'D LIKE IT.
I DUNNO. I HAVE A TOUGH TIME LISTENING TO THAT OVER-PRODUCED VJ FRIENDLY PAP YOU GUYS HAVE BEEN ROCKING.
IT JUST DOESN'T DO IT FOR ME.
OH.
BRICK, COME ON.
FRICK! UM--
THIS IS THE ONLY MAN I TRUST WITH--
WONDER TWIN POWERS ACTIVATE!

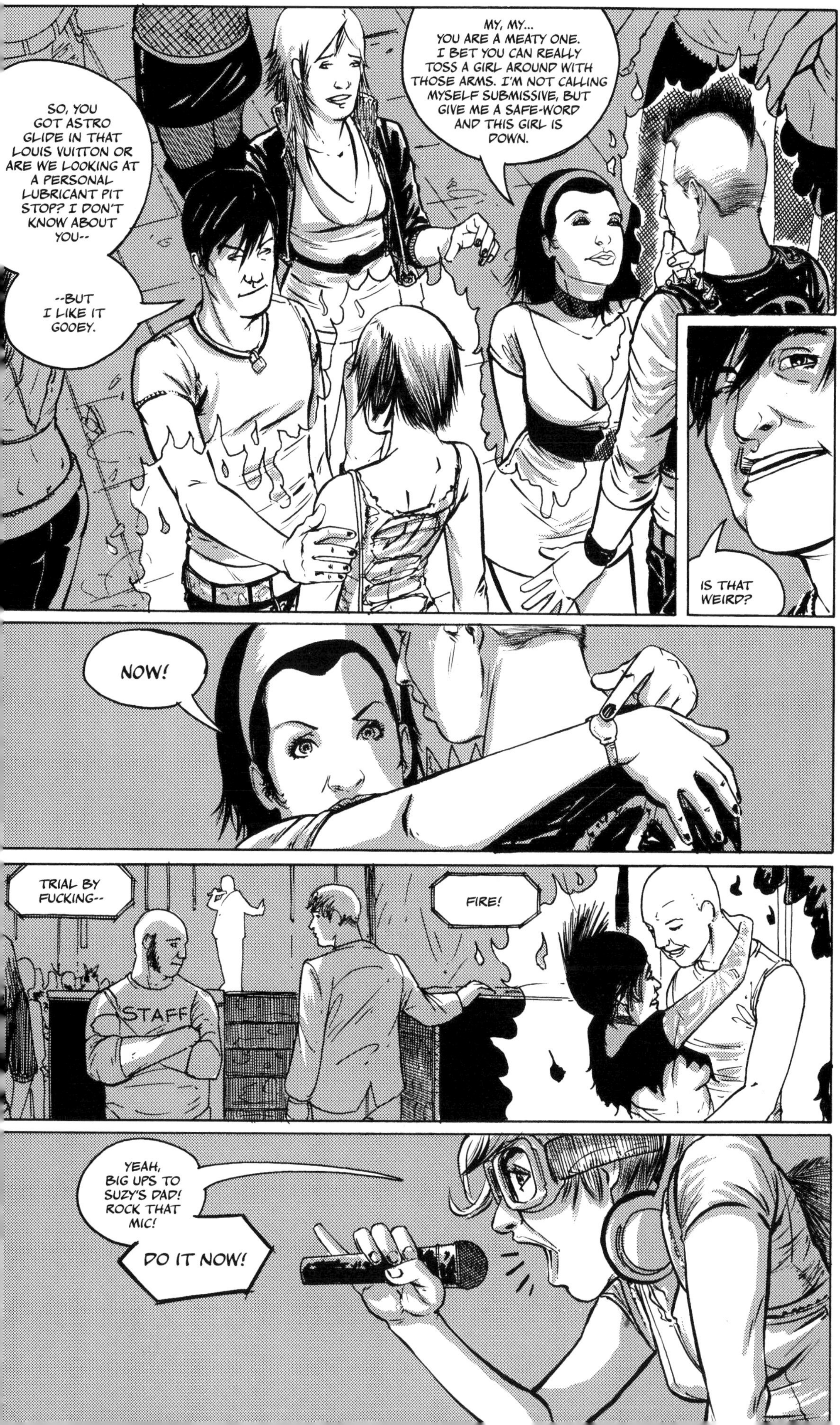

SO, YOU GOT ASTRO GLIDE IN THAT LOUIS VUITTON OR ARE WE LOOKING AT A PERSONAL LUBRICANT PIT STOP? I DON'T KNOW ABOUT YOU--
--BUT I LIKE IT GOOEY.
MY, MY... YOU ARE A MEATY ONE. I BET YOU CAN REALLY TOSS A GIRL AROUND WITH THOSE ARMS. I'M NOT CALLING MYSELF SUBMISSIVE, BUT GIVE ME A SAFE-WORD AND THIS GIRL IS DOWN.
IS THAT WEIRD?
NOW!
TRIAL BY FUCKING--
STAFF
FIRE!
YEAH, BIG UPS TO SUZY'S DAD! ROCK THAT MIC!
DO IT NOW!

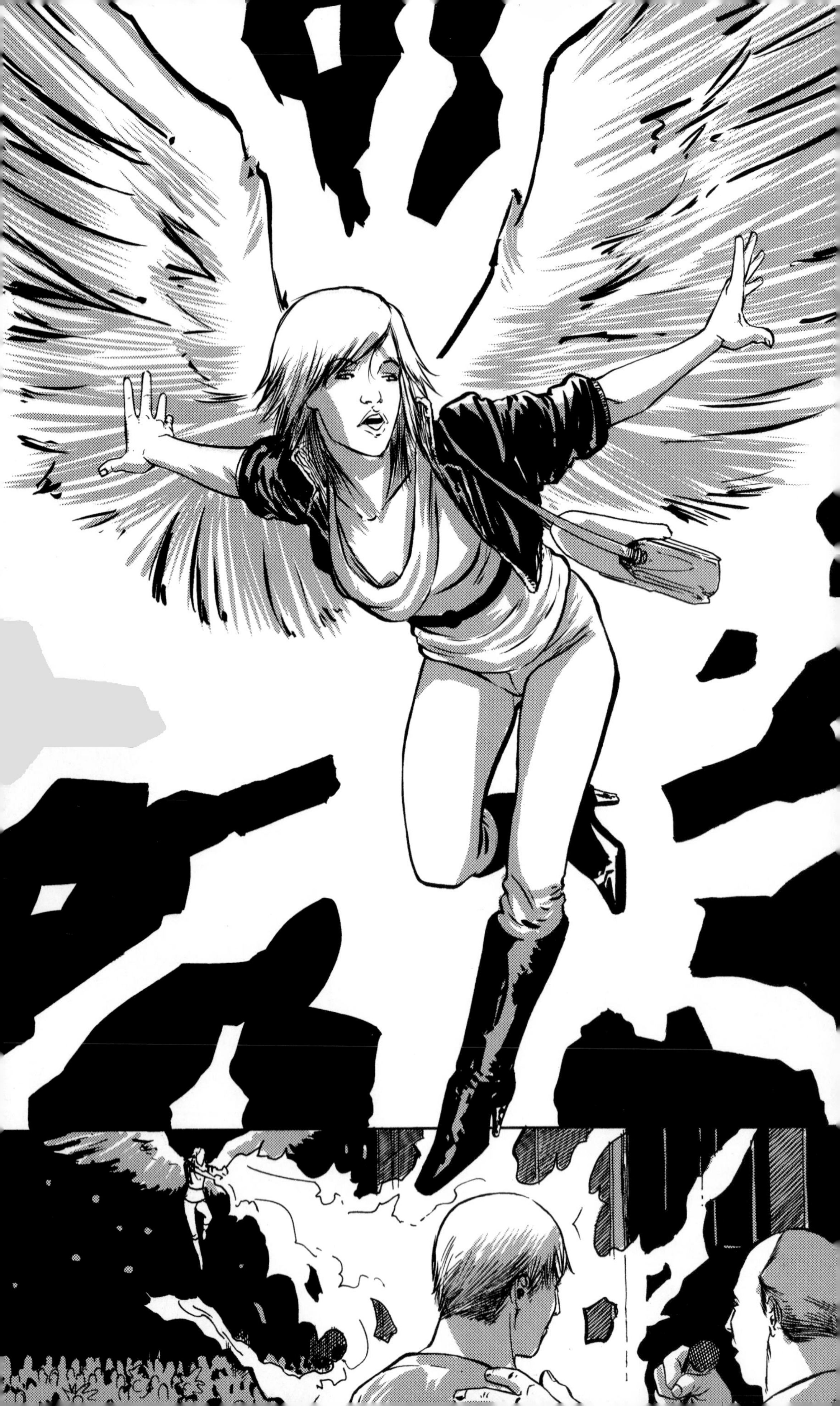

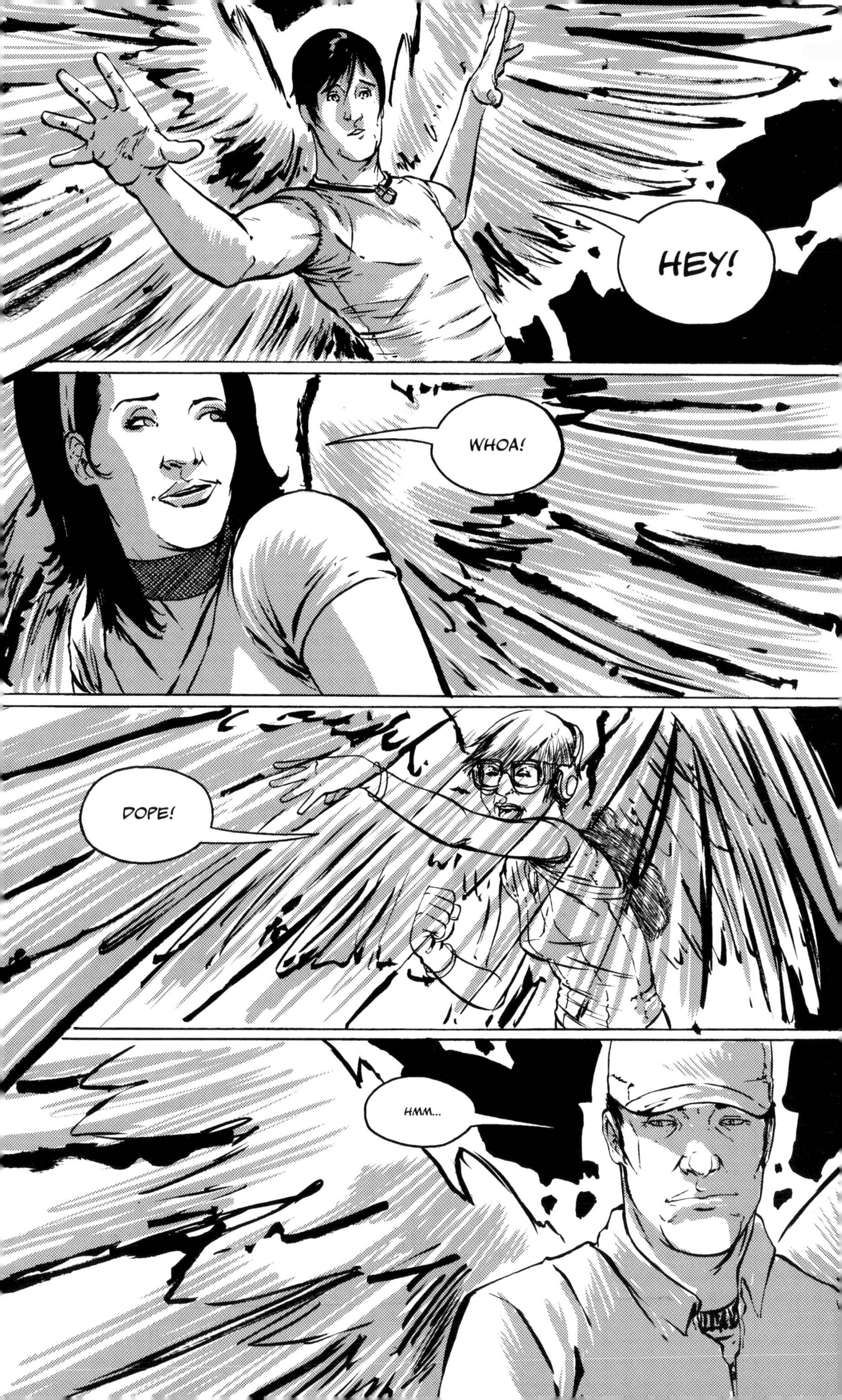
HEY!
WHOA!
DOPE!
HMM...

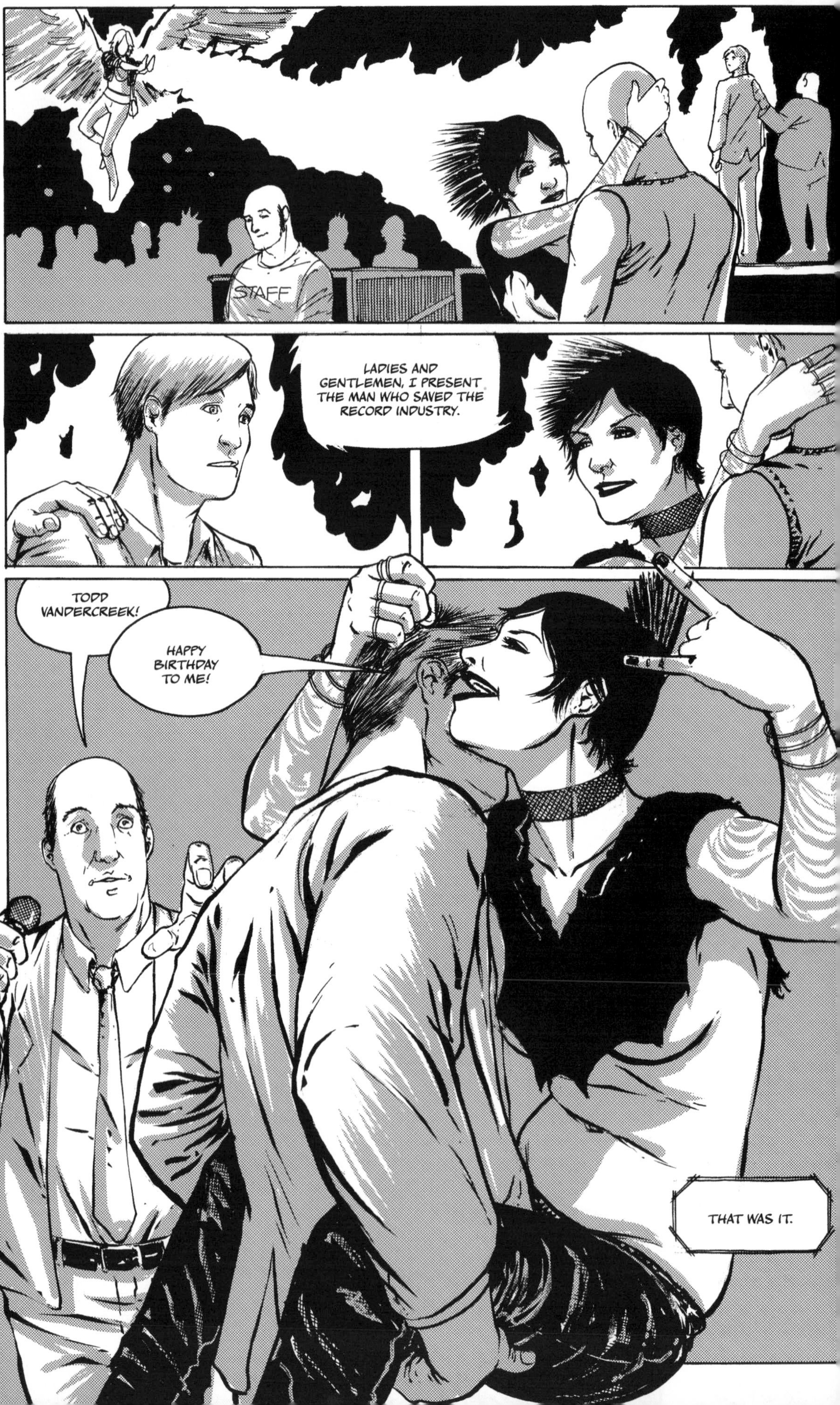
STAFF
LADIES AND GENTLEMEN, I PRESENT THE MAN WHO SAVED THE RECORD INDUSTRY.
TODD VANDERCREEK!
HAPPY BIRTHDAY TO ME!
THAT WAS IT.

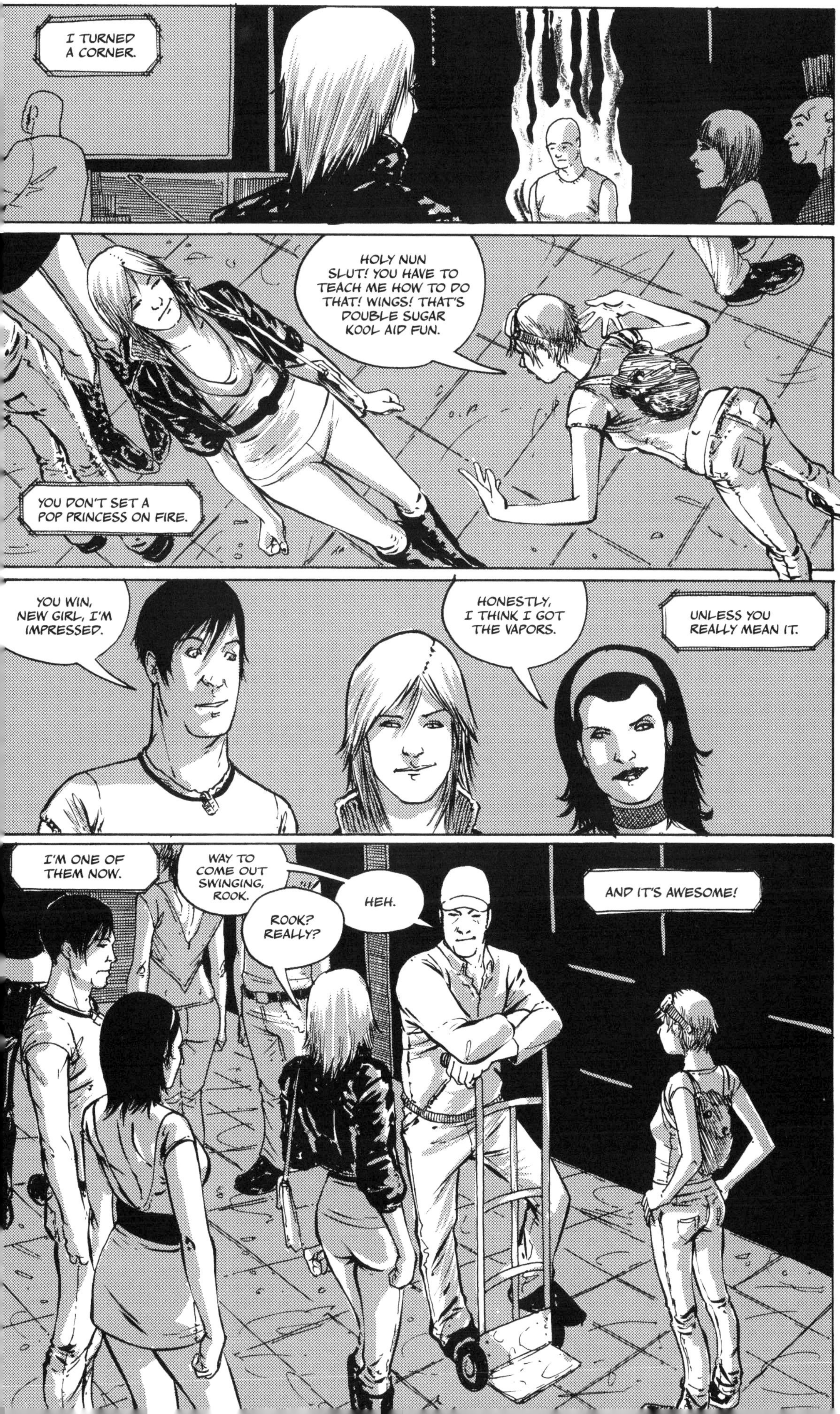
I TURNED A CORNER.
HOLY NUN SLUT! YOU HAVE TO TEACH ME HOW TO DO THAT! WINGS! THAT'S DOUBLE SUGAR KOOL AID FUN.
YOU DON'T SET A POP PRINCESS ON FIRE.
YOU WIN, NEW GIRL, I'M IMPRESSED.
HONESTLY, I THINK I GOT THE VAPORS.
UNLESS YOU REALLY MEAN IT.
I'M ONE OF THEM NOW.
WAY TO COME OUT SWINGING, ROOK.
ROOK? REALLY?
HEH.
AND IT'S AWESOME!

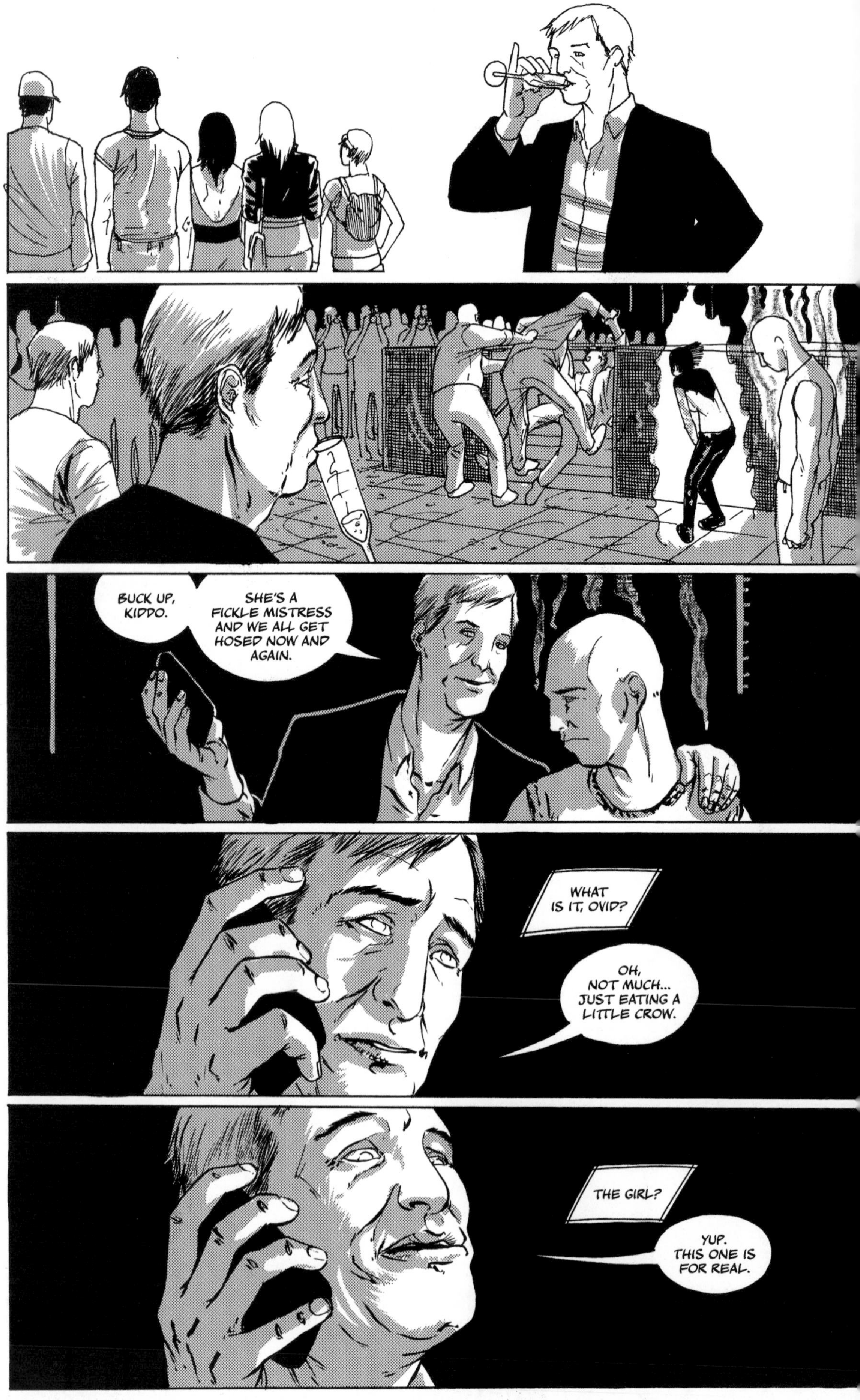
BUCK UP, KIDDO.
SHE'S A FICKLE MISTRESS AND WE ALL GET HOSED NOW AND AGAIN.
WHAT IS IT, OVID?
OH, NOT MUCH... JUST EATING A LITTLE CROW.
THE GIRL?
YUP. THIS ONE IS FOR REAL.

CHAPTER 3

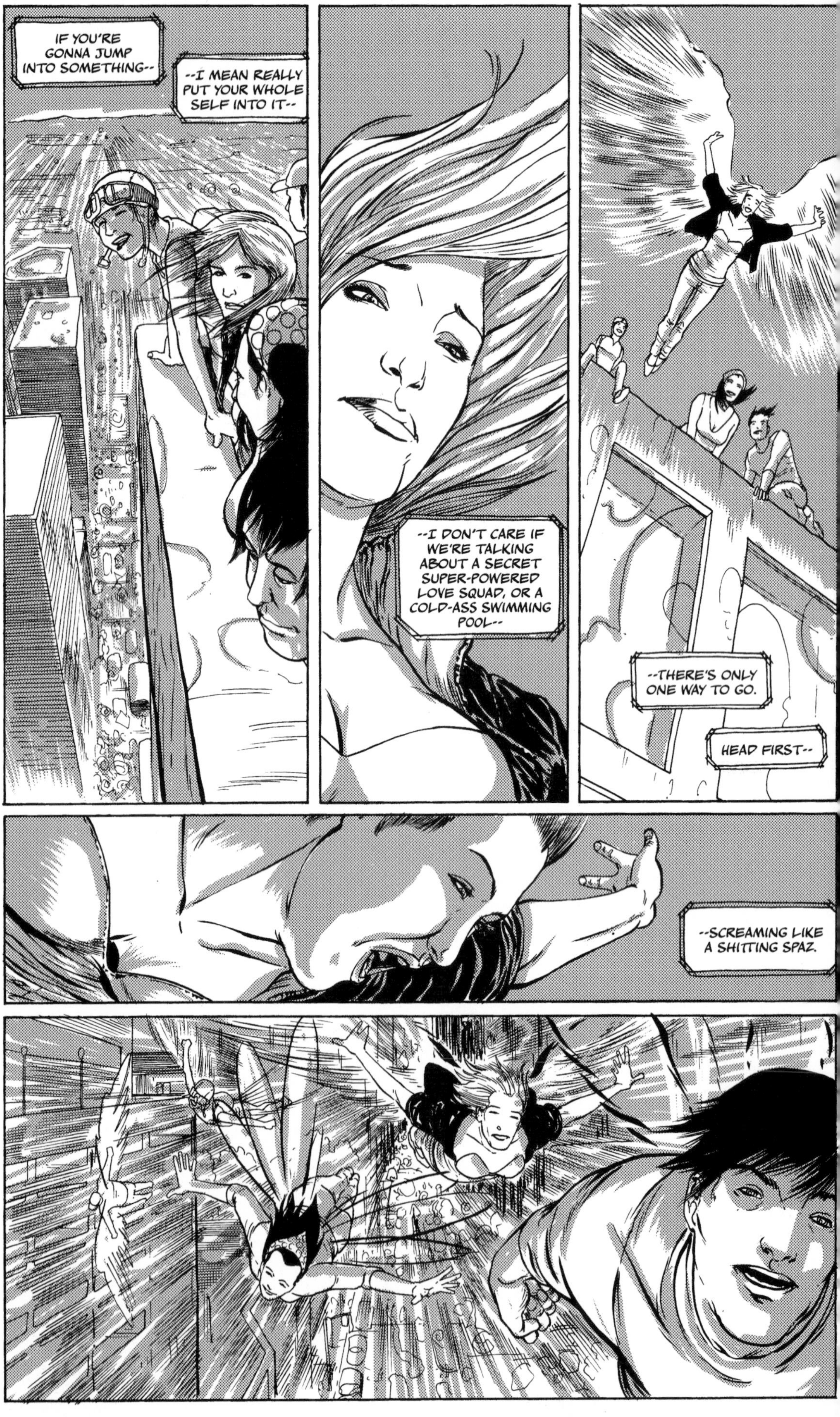
IF YOU'RE GONNA JUMP INTO SOMETHING--
--I MEAN REALLY PUT YOUR WHOLE SELF INTO IT--
--I DON'T CARE IF WE'RE TALKING ABOUT A SECRET SUPER-POWERED LOVE SQUAD, OR A COLD-ASS SWIMMING POOL--
--THERE'S ONLY ONE WAY TO GO.
HEAD FIRST--
--SCREAMING LIKE A SHITTING SPAZ.

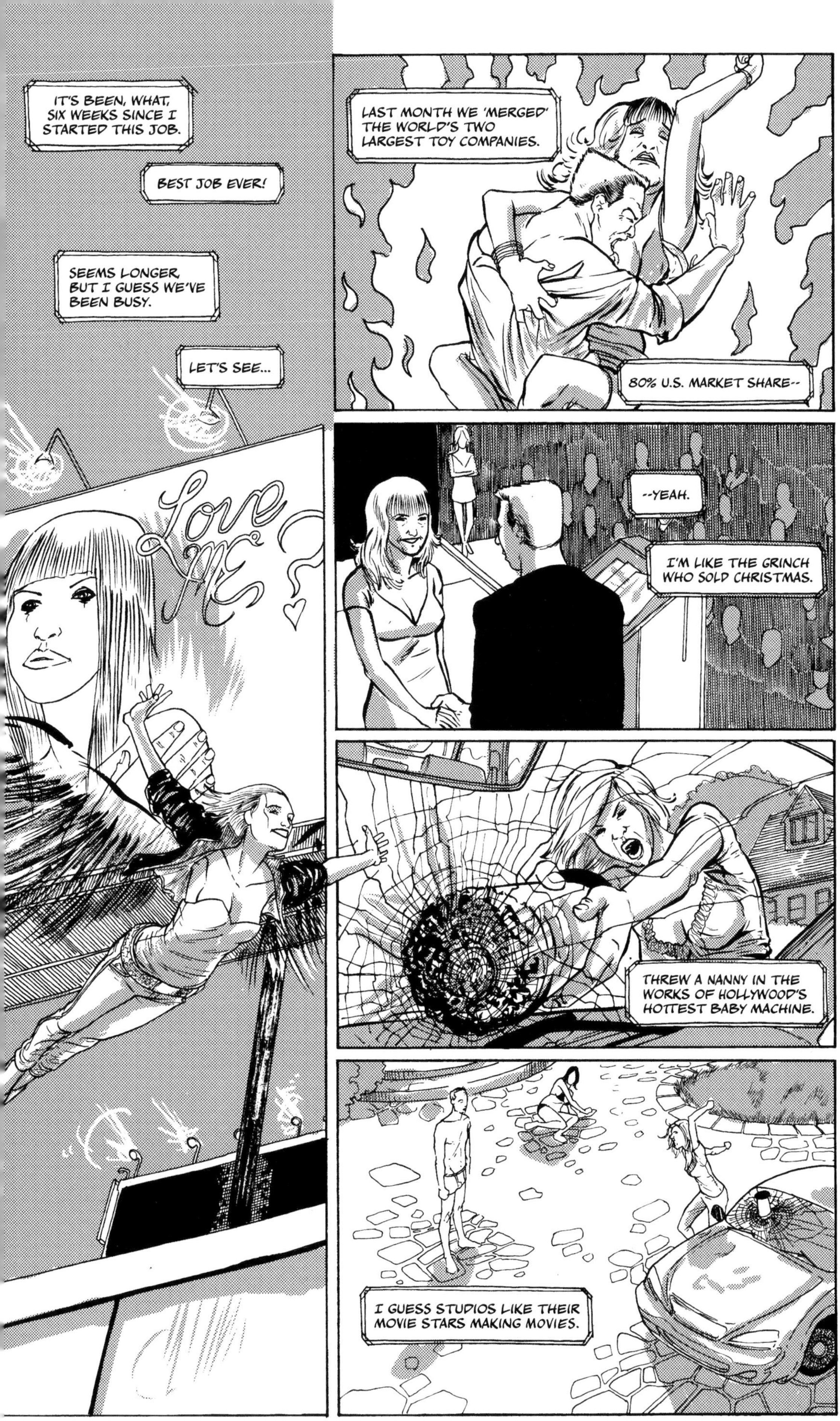
IT'S BEEN, WHAT, SIX WEEKS SINCE I STARTED THIS JOB.
BEST JOB EVER!
SEEMS LONGER, BUT I GUESS WE'VE BEEN BUSY.
LET'S SEE...
Love Me
LAST MONTH WE 'MERGED' THE WORLD'S TWO LARGEST TOY COMPANIES.
80% U.S. MARKET SHARE--
--YEAH.
I'M LIKE THE GRINCH WHO SOLD CHRISTMAS.
THREW A NANNY IN THE WORKS OF HOLLYWOOD'S HOTTEST BABY MACHINE.
I GUESS STUDIOS LIKE THEIR MOVIE STARS MAKING MOVIES.

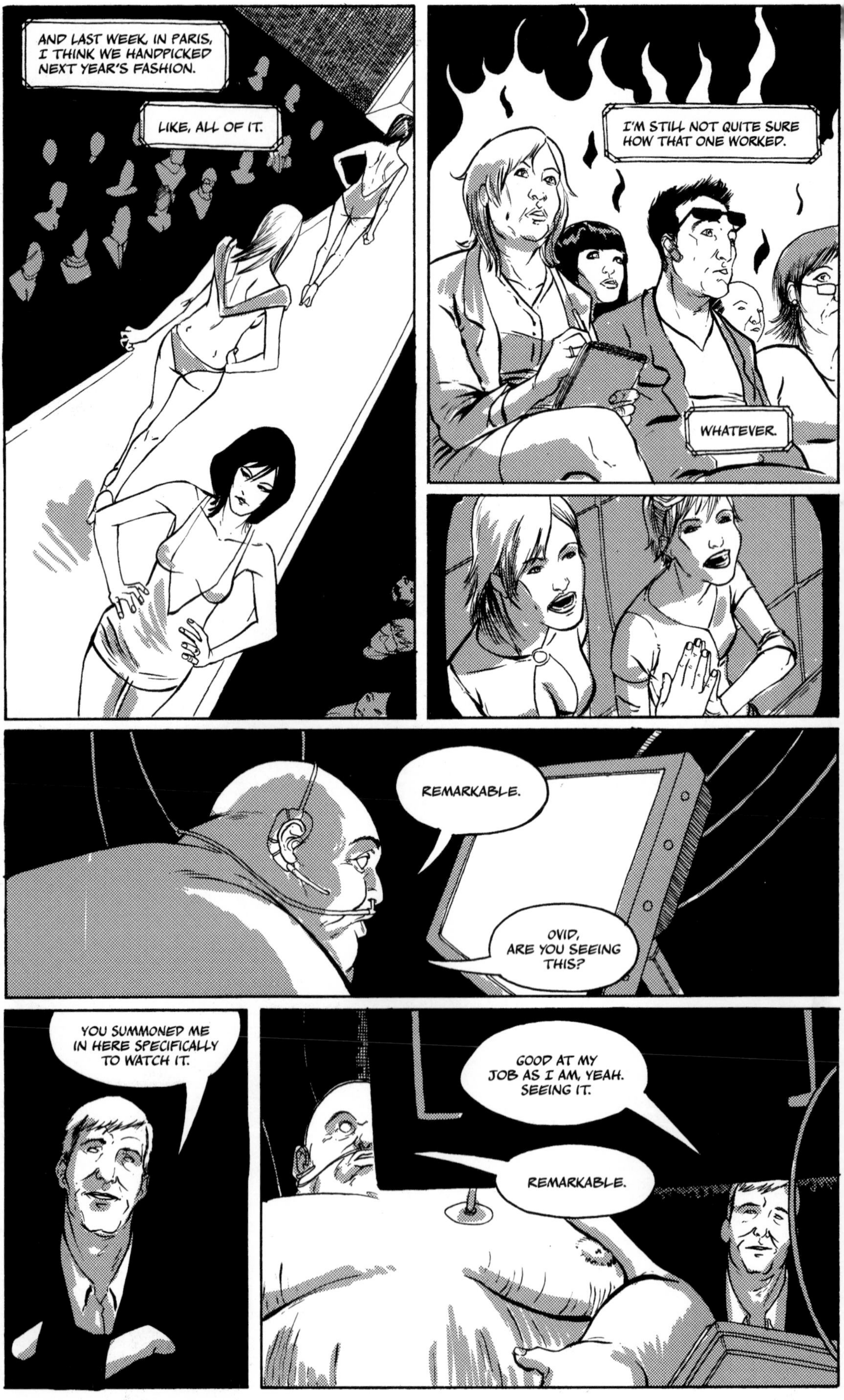
AND LAST WEEK, IN PARIS, I THINK WE HANDPICKED NEXT YEAR'S FASHION.
LIKE, ALL OF IT.
I'M STILL NOT QUITE SURE HOW THAT ONE WORKED.
WHATEVER.
REMARKABLE.
OVID, ARE YOU SEEING THIS?
YOU SUMMONED ME IN HERE SPECIFICALLY TO WATCH IT.
GOOD AT MY JOB AS I AM, YEAH. SEEING IT.
REMARKABLE.

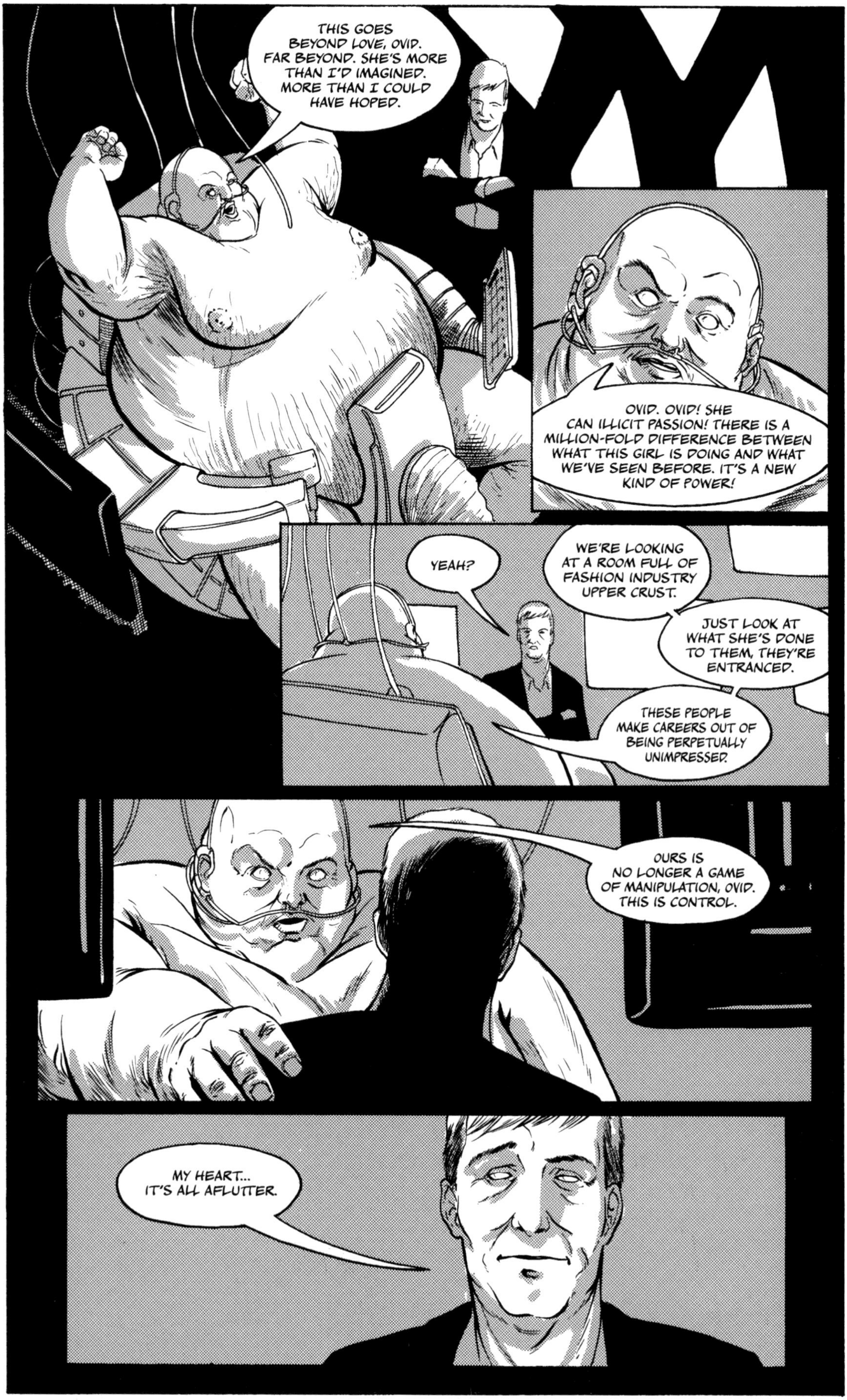
THIS GOES BEYOND LOVE, OVID. FAR BEYOND. SHE'S MORE THAN I'D IMAGINED. MORE THAN I COULD HAVE HOPED.
OVID. OVID! SHE CAN ILLICIT PASSION! THERE IS A MILLION-FOLD DIFFERENCE BETWEEN WHAT THIS GIRL IS DOING AND WHAT WE'VE SEEN BEFORE. IT'S A NEW KIND OF POWER!
YEAH?
WE'RE LOOKING AT A ROOM FULL OF FASHION INDUSTRY UPPER CRUST.
JUST LOOK AT WHAT SHE'S DONE TO THEM, THEY'RE ENTRANCED.
THESE PEOPLE MAKE CAREERS OUT OF BEING PERPETUALLY UNIMPRESSED.
OURS IS NO LONGER A GAME OF MANIPULATION, OVID. THIS IS CONTROL.
MY HEART... IT'S ALL AFLUTTER.

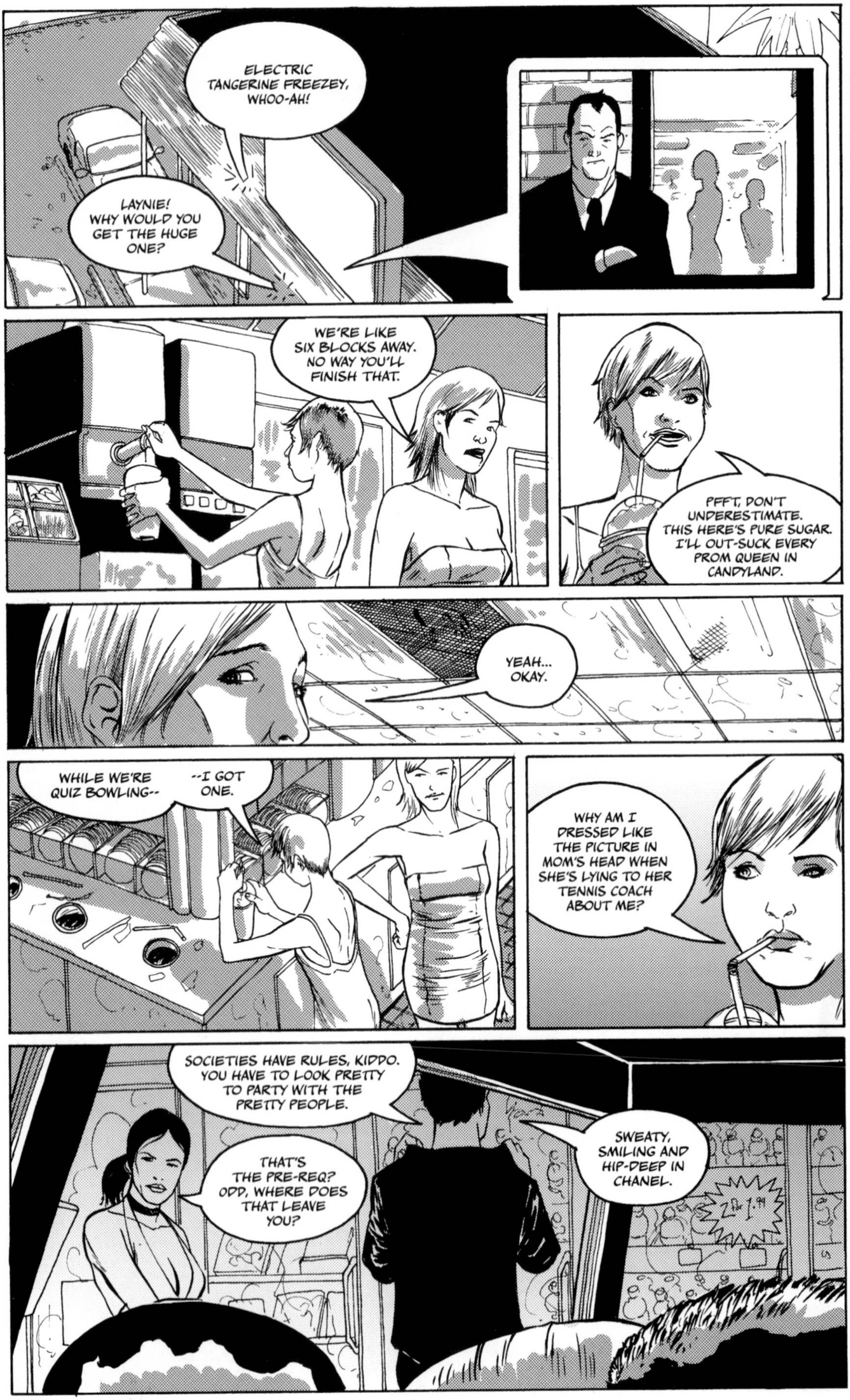
ELECTRIC TANGERINE FREEZEY, WHOO-AH!
LAYNIE! WHY WOULD YOU GET THE HUGE ONE?
WE'RE LIKE SIX BLOCKS AWAY. NO WAY YOU'LL FINISH THAT.
PFFT, DON'T UNDERESTIMATE. THIS HERE'S PURE SUGAR. I'LL OUT-SUCK EVERY PROM QUEEN IN CANDYLAND.
YEAH... OKAY.
WHILE WE'RE QUIZ BOWLING--
--I GOT ONE.
WHY AM I DRESSED LIKE THE PICTURE IN MOM'S HEAD WHEN SHE'S LYING TO HER TENNIS COACH ABOUT ME?
SOCIETIES HAVE RULES, KIDDO. YOU HAVE TO LOOK PRETTY TO PARTY WITH THE PRETTY PEOPLE.
THAT'S THE PRE-REQ? ODD, WHERE DOES THAT LEAVE YOU?
SWEATY, SMILING AND HIP-DEEP IN CHANEL.

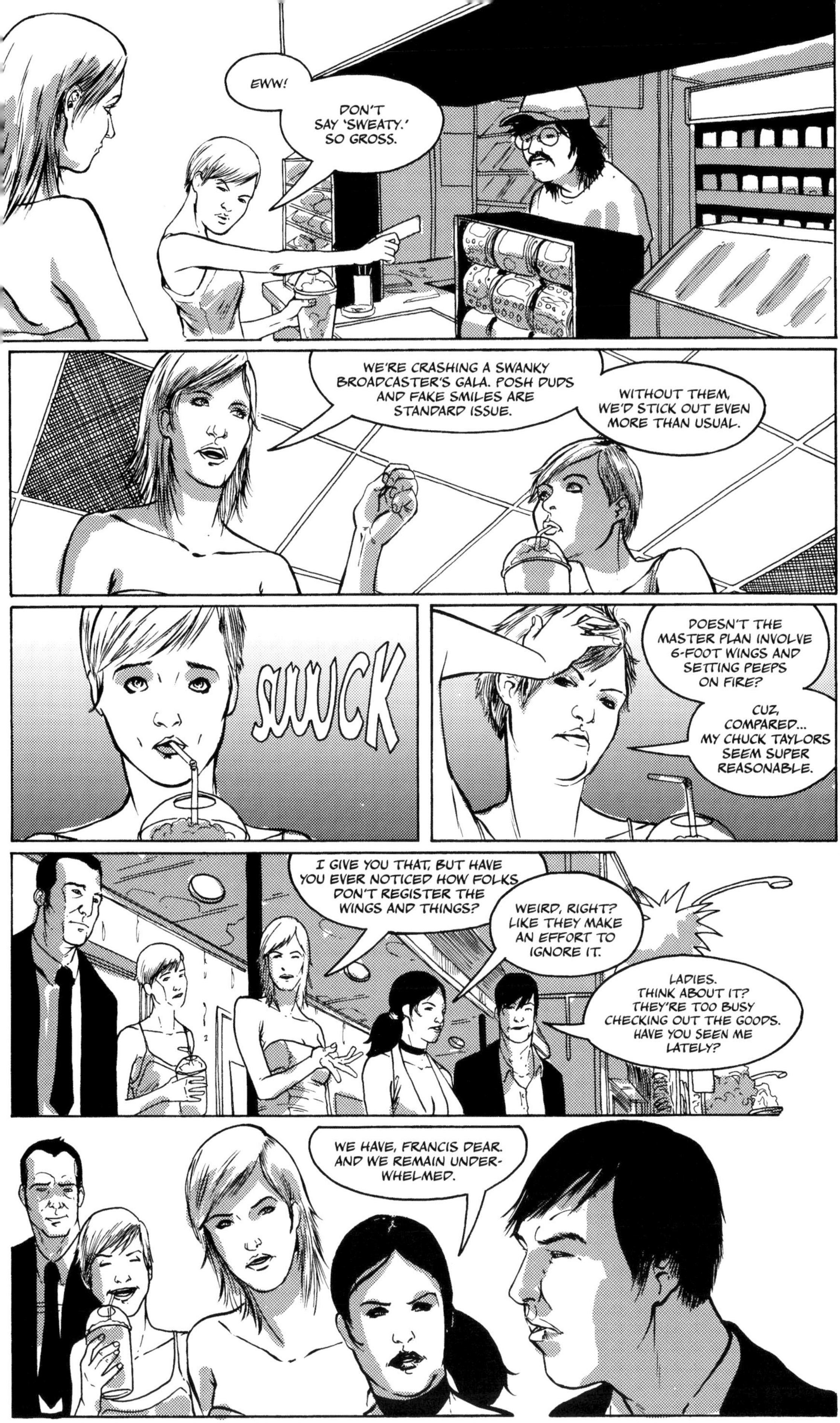
EWW!
DON'T SAY 'SWEATY.' SO GROSS.
WE'RE CRASHING A SWANKY BROADCASTER'S GALA. POSH DUDS AND FAKE SMILES ARE STANDARD ISSUE.
WITHOUT THEM, WE'D STICK OUT EVEN MORE THAN USUAL.
SUUUCK
DOESN'T THE MASTER PLAN INVOLVE 6-FOOT WINGS AND SETTING PEEPS ON FIRE?
CUZ, COMPARED... MY CHUCK TAYLORS SEEM SUPER REASONABLE.
I GIVE YOU THAT, BUT HAVE YOU EVER NOTICED HOW FOLKS DON'T REGISTER THE WINGS AND THINGS?
WEIRD, RIGHT? LIKE THEY MAKE AN EFFORT TO IGNORE IT.
LADIES. THINK ABOUT IT? THEY'RE TOO BUSY CHECKING OUT THE GOODS. HAVE YOU SEEN ME LATELY?
WE HAVE, FRANCIS DEAR. AND WE REMAIN UNDER-WHELMED.

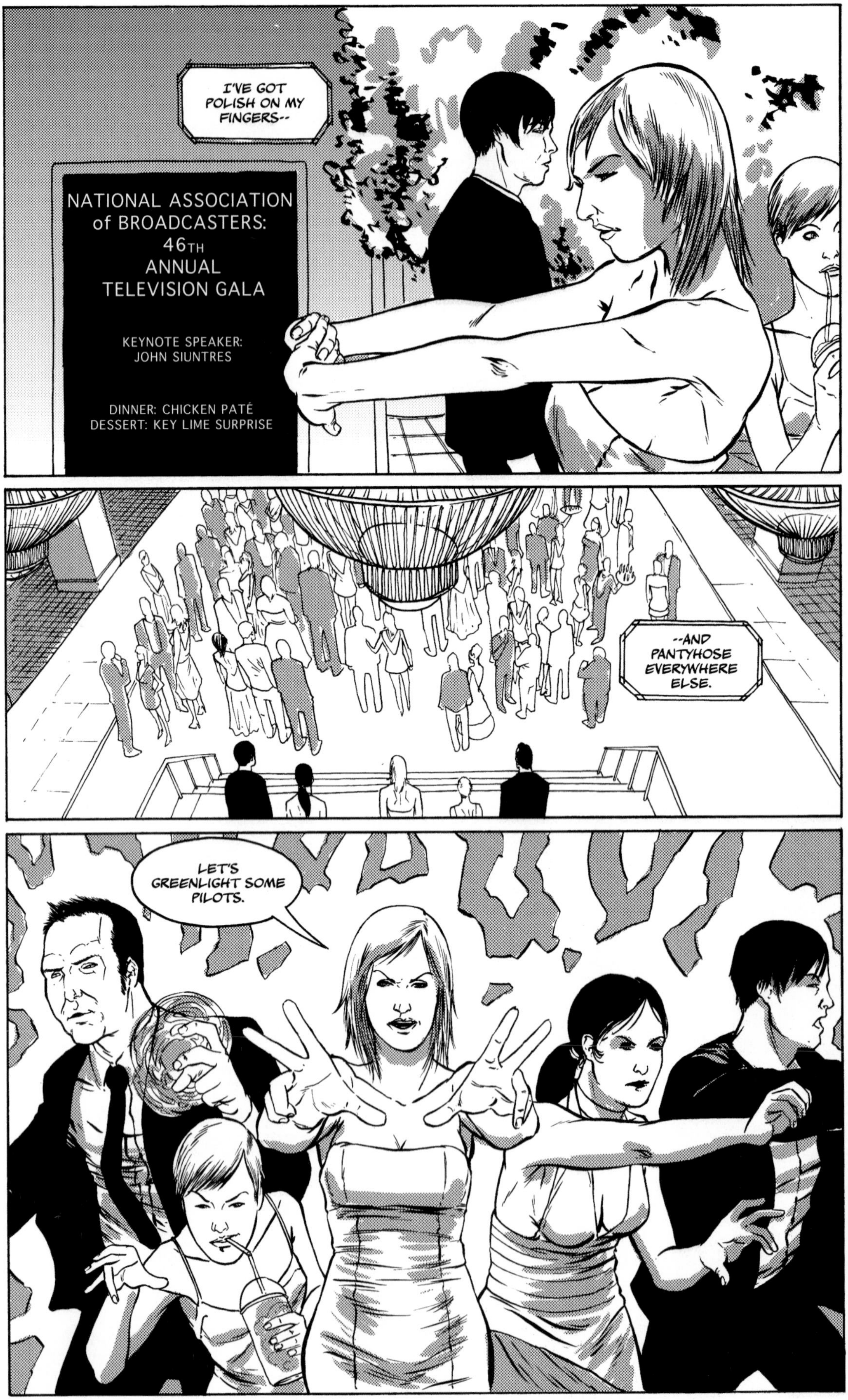

I'VE GOT POLISH ON MY FINGERS--
NATIONAL ASSOCIATION of BROADCASTERS: 46TH ANNUAL TELEVISION GALA
KEYNOTE SPEAKER: JOHN SIUNTRES
DINNER: CHICKEN PATÉ
DESSERT: KEY LIME SURPRISE
--AND PANTYHOSE EVERYWHERE ELSE.
LET'S GREENLIGHT SOME PILOTS.

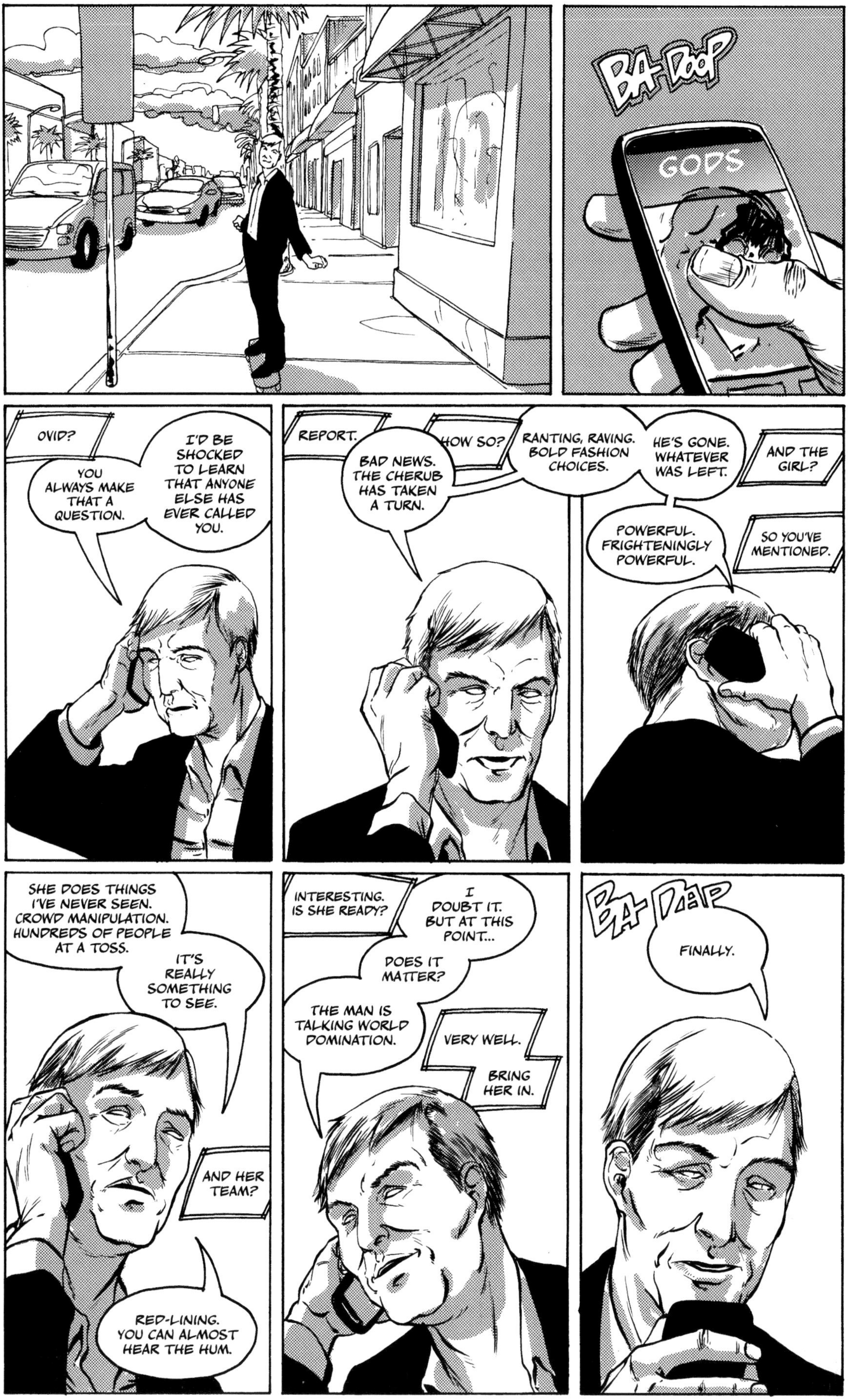
BA-DOOP
GODS
OVID?
YOU ALWAYS MAKE THAT A QUESTION.
I'D BE SHOCKED TO LEARN THAT ANYONE ELSE HAS EVER CALLED YOU.
REPORT.
BAD NEWS. THE CHERUB HAS TAKEN A TURN.
HOW SO?
RANTING, RAVING. BOLD FASHION CHOICES.
HE'S GONE. WHATEVER WAS LEFT.
AND THE GIRL?
POWERFUL. FRIGHTENINGLY POWERFUL.
SO YOU'VE MENTIONED.
SHE DOES THINGS I'VE NEVER SEEN. CROWD MANIPULATION. HUNDREDS OF PEOPLE AT A TOSS.
IT'S REALLY SOMETHING TO SEE.
AND HER TEAM?
RED-LINING. YOU CAN ALMOST HEAR THE HUM.
INTERESTING. IS SHE READY?
I DOUBT IT. BUT AT THIS POINT...
DOES IT MATTER?
THE MAN IS TALKING WORLD DOMINATION.
VERY WELL.
BRING HER IN.
BA-DAP
FINALLY.

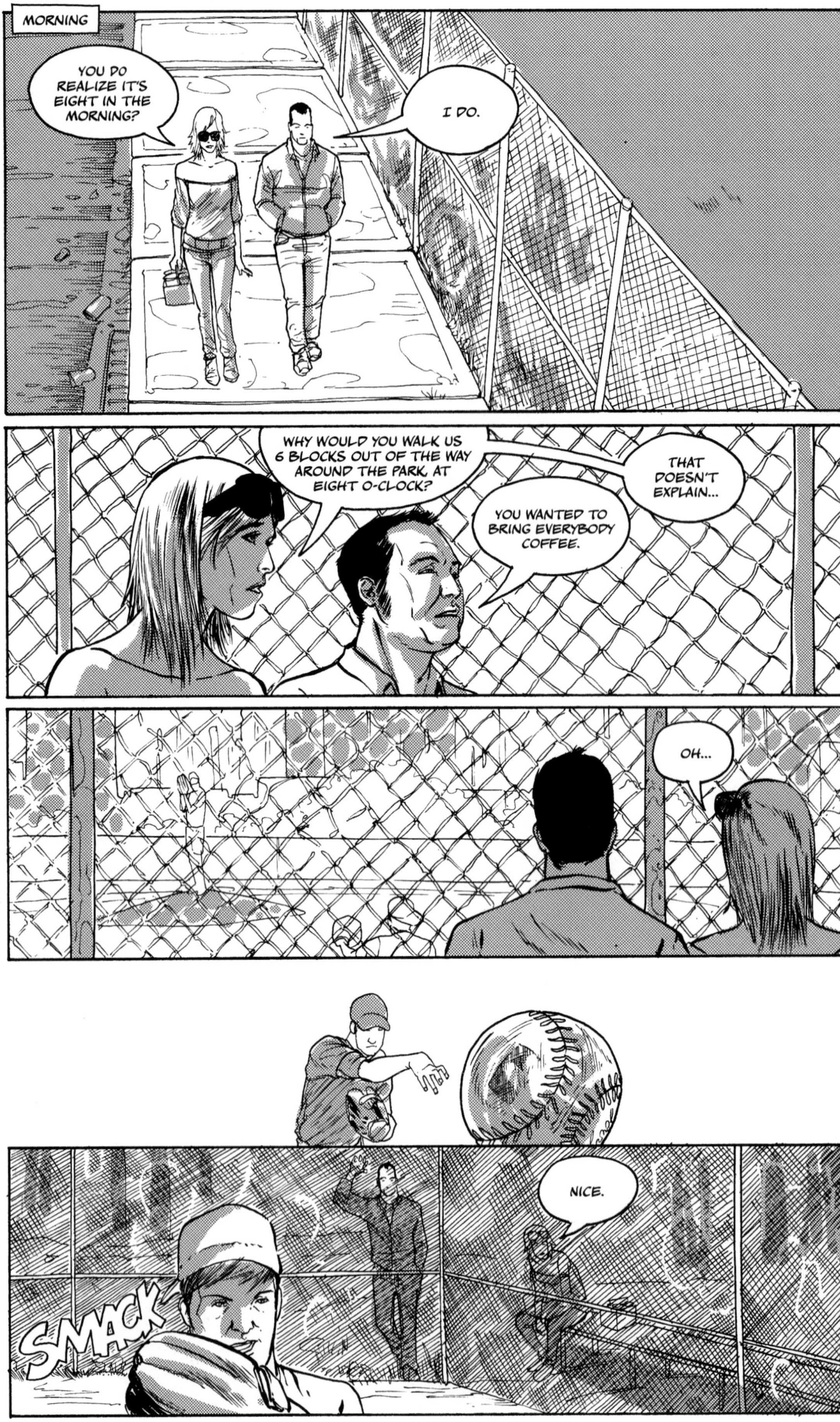
MORNING
YOU DO REALIZE IT'S EIGHT IN THE MORNING?
I DO.
WHY WOULD YOU WALK US 6 BLOCKS OUT OF THE WAY AROUND THE PARK, AT EIGHT O-CLOCK?
YOU WANTED TO BRING EVERYBODY COFFEE.
THAT DOESN'T EXPLAIN...
OH...
SMACK
NICE.

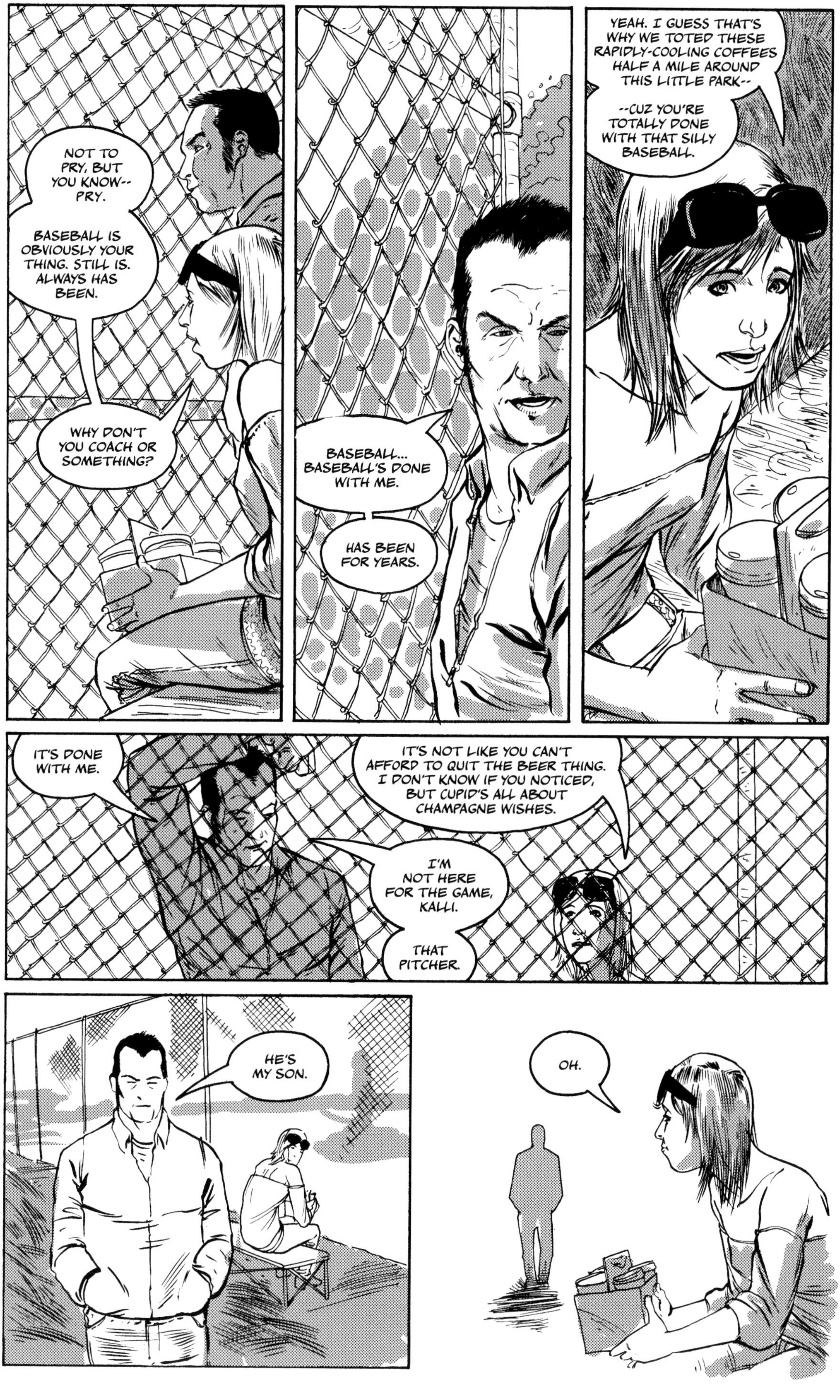
NOT TO PRY, BUT YOU KNOW-- PRY.
BASEBALL IS OBVIOUSLY YOUR THING. STILL IS. ALWAYS HAS BEEN.
WHY DON'T YOU COACH OR SOMETHING?
BASEBALL... BASEBALL'S DONE WITH ME.
HAS BEEN FOR YEARS.
YEAH. I GUESS THAT'S WHY WE TOTED THESE RAPIDLY-COOLING COFFEES HALF A MILE AROUND THIS LITTLE PARK--
--CUZ YOU'RE TOTALLY DONE WITH THAT SILLY BASEBALL.
IT'S DONE WITH ME.
IT'S NOT LIKE YOU CAN'T AFFORD TO QUIT THE BEER THING. I DON'T KNOW IF YOU NOTICED, BUT CUPID'S ALL ABOUT CHAMPAGNE WISHES.
I'M NOT HERE FOR THE GAME, KALLI.
THAT PITCHER.
HE'S MY SON.
OH.

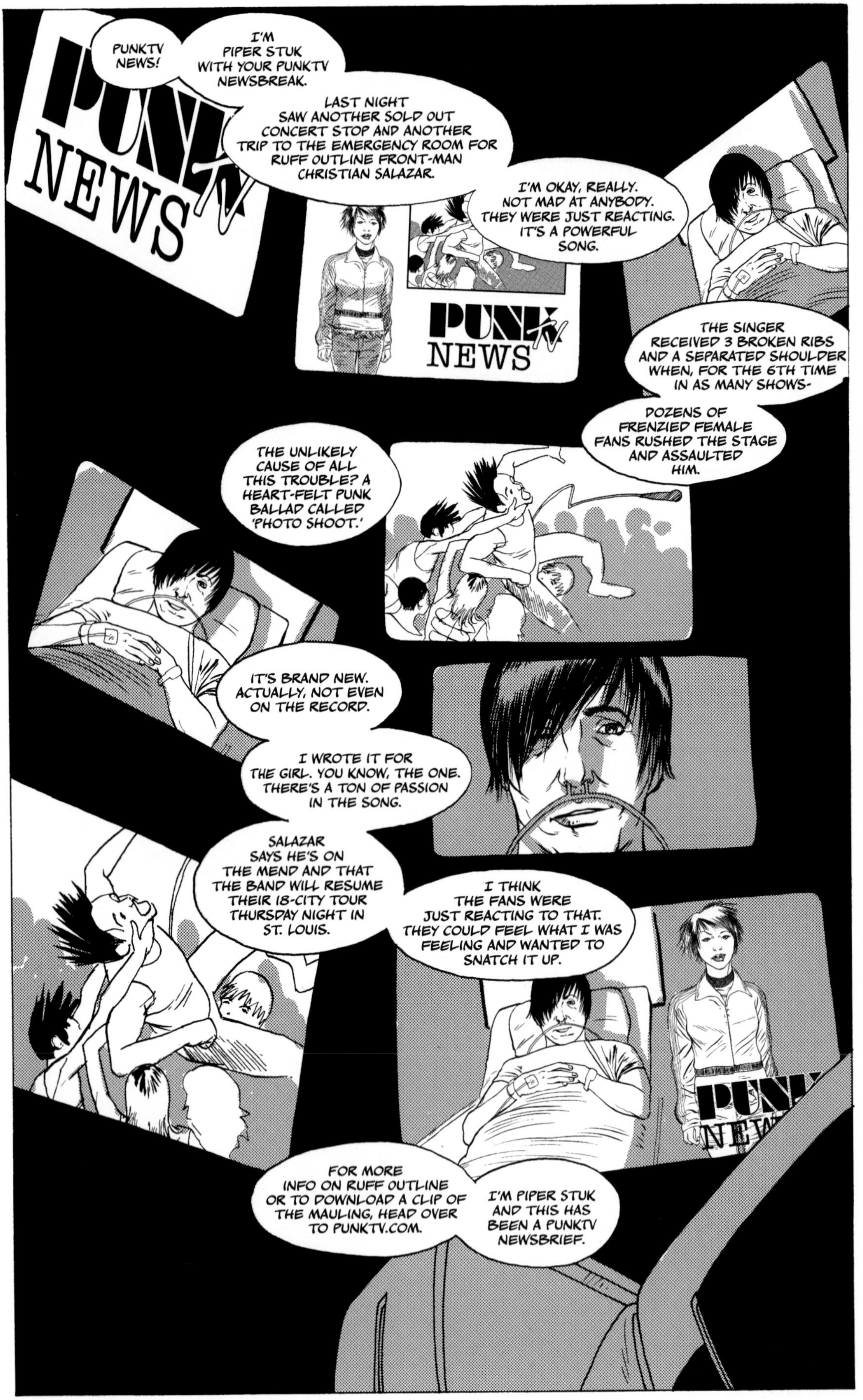
PUNKTV NEWS!
I'M PIPER STUK WITH YOUR PUNKTV NEWSBREAK.
LAST NIGHT SAW ANOTHER SOLD OUT CONCERT STOP AND ANOTHER TRIP TO THE EMERGENCY ROOM FOR RUFF OUTLINE FRONT-MAN CHRISTIAN SALAZAR.
PUNK TV NEWS
I'M OKAY, REALLY. NOT MAD AT ANYBODY. THEY WERE JUST REACTING. IT'S A POWERFUL SONG.
PUNK TV NEWS
THE SINGER RECEIVED 3 BROKEN RIBS AND A SEPARATED SHOULDER WHEN, FOR THE 6TH TIME IN AS MANY SHOWS-
DOZENS OF FRENZIED FEMALE FANS RUSHED THE STAGE AND ASSAULTED HIM.
THE UNLIKELY CAUSE OF ALL THIS TROUBLE? A HEART-FELT PUNK BALLAD CALLED 'PHOTO SHOOT.'
IT'S BRAND NEW. ACTUALLY, NOT EVEN ON THE RECORD.
I WROTE IT FOR THE GIRL. YOU KNOW, THE ONE. THERE'S A TON OF PASSION IN THE SONG.
SALAZAR SAYS HE'S ON THE MEND AND THAT THE BAND WILL RESUME THEIR 18-CITY TOUR THURSDAY NIGHT IN ST. LOUIS.
I THINK THE FANS WERE JUST REACTING TO THAT. THEY COULD FEEL WHAT I WAS FEELING AND WANTED TO SNATCH IT UP.
FOR MORE INFO ON RUFF OUTLINE OR TO DOWNLOAD A CLIP OF THE MAULING, HEAD OVER TO PUNKTV.COM.
I'M PIPER STUK AND THIS HAS BEEN A PUNKTV NEWSBRIEF.

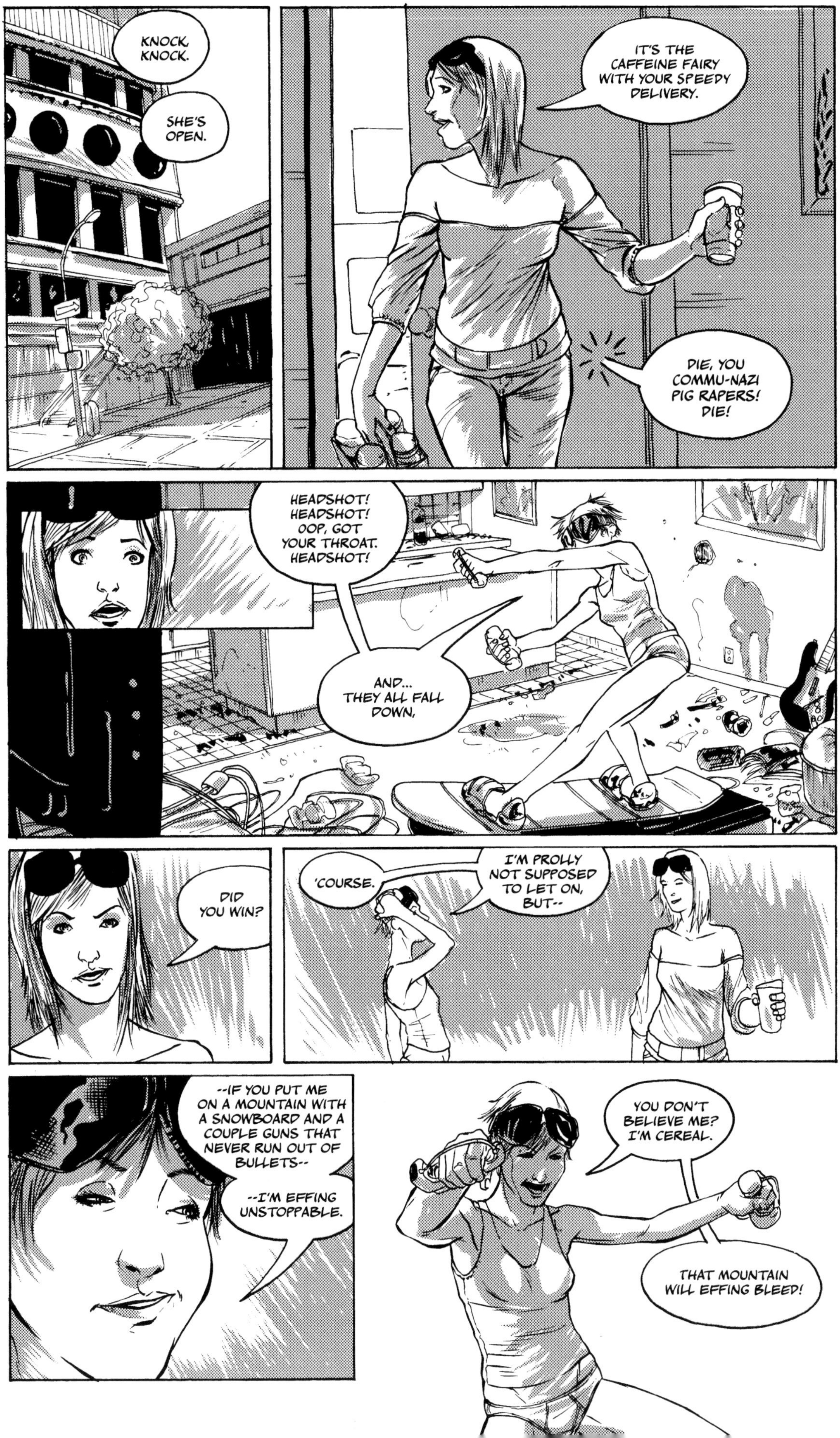
KNOCK, KNOCK.
SHE'S OPEN.
IT'S THE CAFFEINE FAIRY WITH YOUR SPEEDY DELIVERY.
DIE, YOU COMMU-NAZI PIG RAPERS! DIE!
HEADSHOT! HEADSHOT! OOP, GOT YOUR THROAT. HEADSHOT!
AND... THEY ALL FALL DOWN.
DID YOU WIN?
'COURSE.
I'M PROLLY NOT SUPPOSED TO LET ON, BUT--
--IF YOU PUT ME ON A MOUNTAIN WITH A SNOWBOARD AND A COUPLE GUNS THAT NEVER RUN OUT OF BULLETS--
--I'M EFFING UNSTOPPABLE.
YOU DON'T BELIEVE ME? I'M CEREAL.
THAT MOUNTAIN WILL EFFING BLEED!

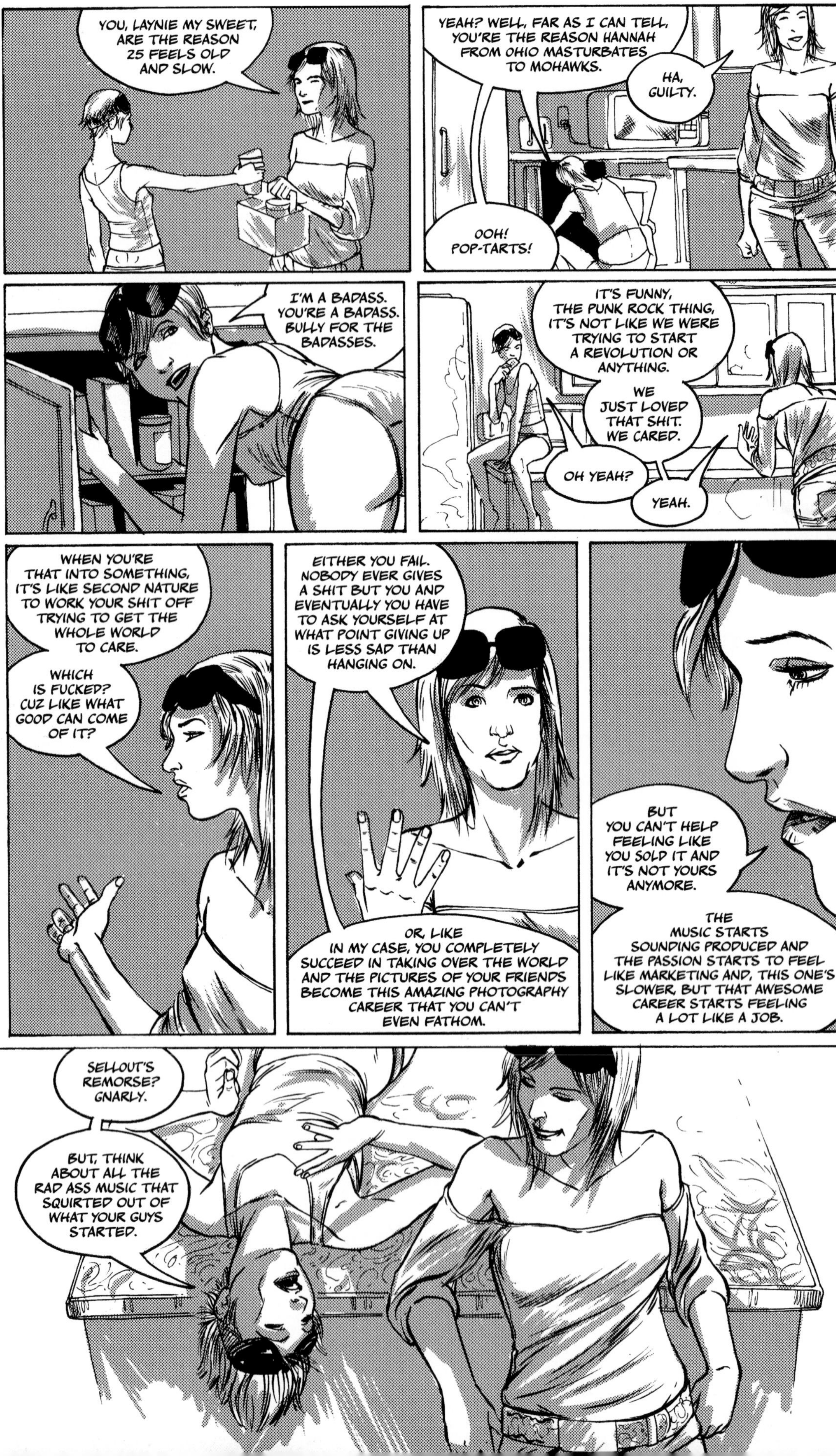

YOU, LAYNIE MY SWEET, ARE THE REASON 25 FEELS OLD AND SLOW.
YEAH? WELL, FAR AS I CAN TELL, YOU'RE THE REASON HANNAH FROM OHIO MASTURBATES TO MOHAWKS.
HA, GUILTY.
OOH! POP-TARTS!
I'M A BADASS. YOU'RE A BADASS. BULLY FOR THE BADASSES.
IT'S FUNNY, THE PUNK ROCK THING, IT'S NOT LIKE WE WERE TRYING TO START A REVOLUTION OR ANYTHING.
WE JUST LOVED THAT SHIT. WE CARED.
OH YEAH?
YEAH.
WHEN YOU'RE THAT INTO SOMETHING, IT'S LIKE SECOND NATURE TO WORK YOUR SHIT OFF TRYING TO GET THE WHOLE WORLD TO CARE.
WHICH IS FUCKED? CUZ LIKE WHAT GOOD CAN COME OF IT?
EITHER YOU FAIL. NOBODY EVER GIVES A SHIT BUT YOU AND EVENTUALLY YOU HAVE TO ASK YOURSELF AT WHAT POINT GIVING UP IS LESS SAD THAN HANGING ON.
OR, LIKE IN MY CASE, YOU COMPLETELY SUCCEED IN TAKING OVER THE WORLD AND THE PICTURES OF YOUR FRIENDS BECOME THIS AMAZING PHOTOGRAPHY CAREER THAT YOU CAN'T EVEN FATHOM.
BUT YOU CAN'T HELP FEELING LIKE YOU SOLD IT AND IT'S NOT YOURS ANYMORE.
THE MUSIC STARTS SOUNDING PRODUCED AND THE PASSION STARTS TO FEEL LIKE MARKETING AND, THIS ONE'S SLOWER, BUT THAT AWESOME CAREER STARTS FEELING A LOT LIKE A JOB.
SELLOUT'S REMORSE? GNARLY.
BUT, THINK ABOUT ALL THE RAD ASS MUSIC THAT SQUIRTED OUT OF WHAT YOUR GUYS STARTED.

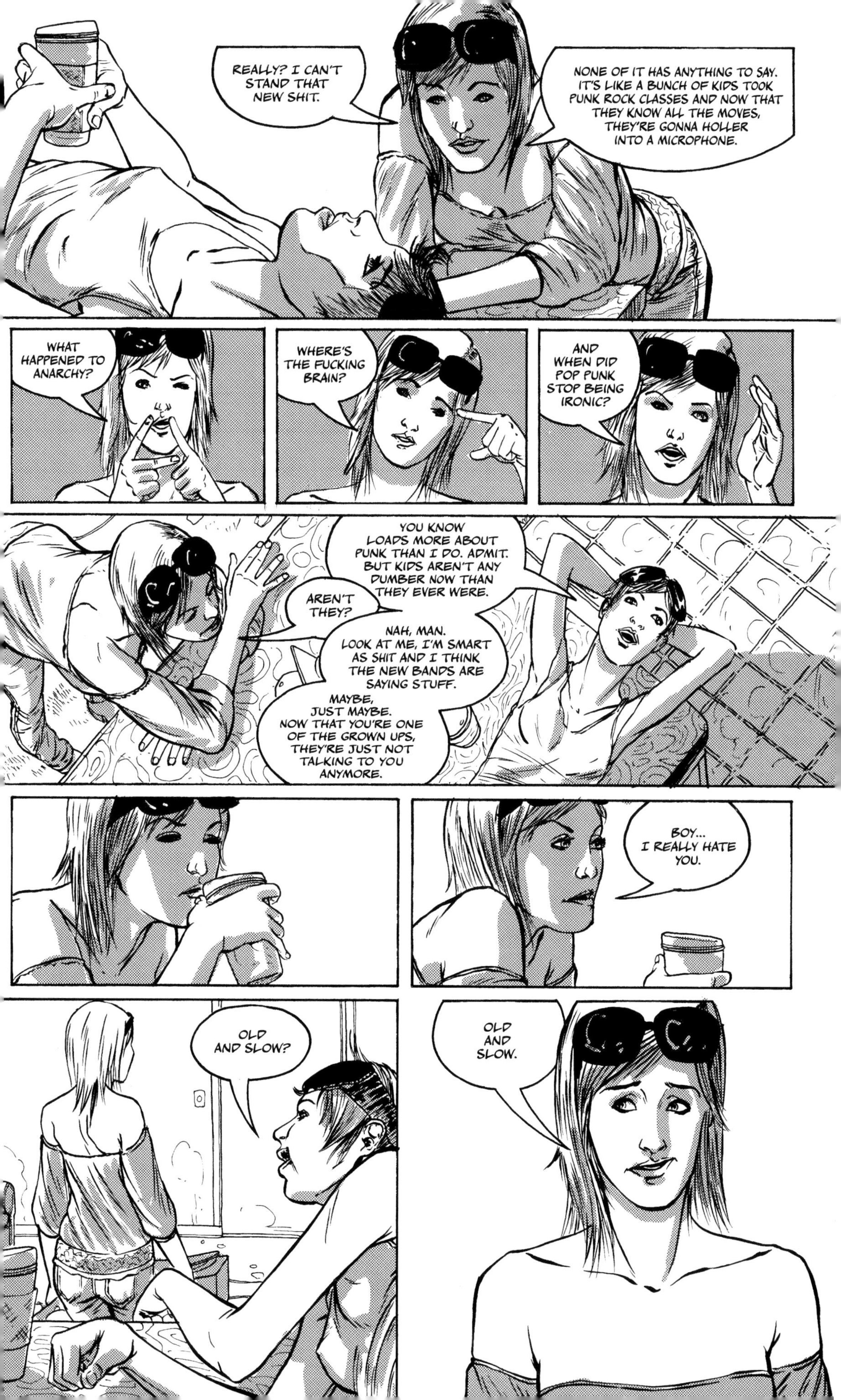
REALLY? I CAN'T STAND THAT NEW SHIT.
NONE OF IT HAS ANYTHING TO SAY. IT'S LIKE A BUNCH OF KIDS TOOK PUNK ROCK CLASSES AND NOW THAT THEY KNOW ALL THE MOVES, THEY'RE GONNA HOLLER INTO A MICROPHONE.
WHAT HAPPENED TO ANARCHY?
WHERE'S THE FUCKING BRAIN?
AND WHEN DID POP PUNK STOP BEING IRONIC?
YOU KNOW LOADS MORE ABOUT PUNK THAN I DO. ADMIT. BUT KIDS AREN'T ANY DUMBER NOW THAN THEY EVER WERE.
AREN'T THEY?
NAH, MAN. LOOK AT ME, I'M SMART AS SHIT AND I THINK THE NEW BANDS ARE SAYING STUFF.
MAYBE, JUST MAYBE. NOW THAT YOU'RE ONE OF THE GROWN UPS, THEY'RE JUST NOT TALKING TO YOU ANYMORE.
BOY... I REALLY HATE YOU.
OLD AND SLOW?
OLD AND SLOW.

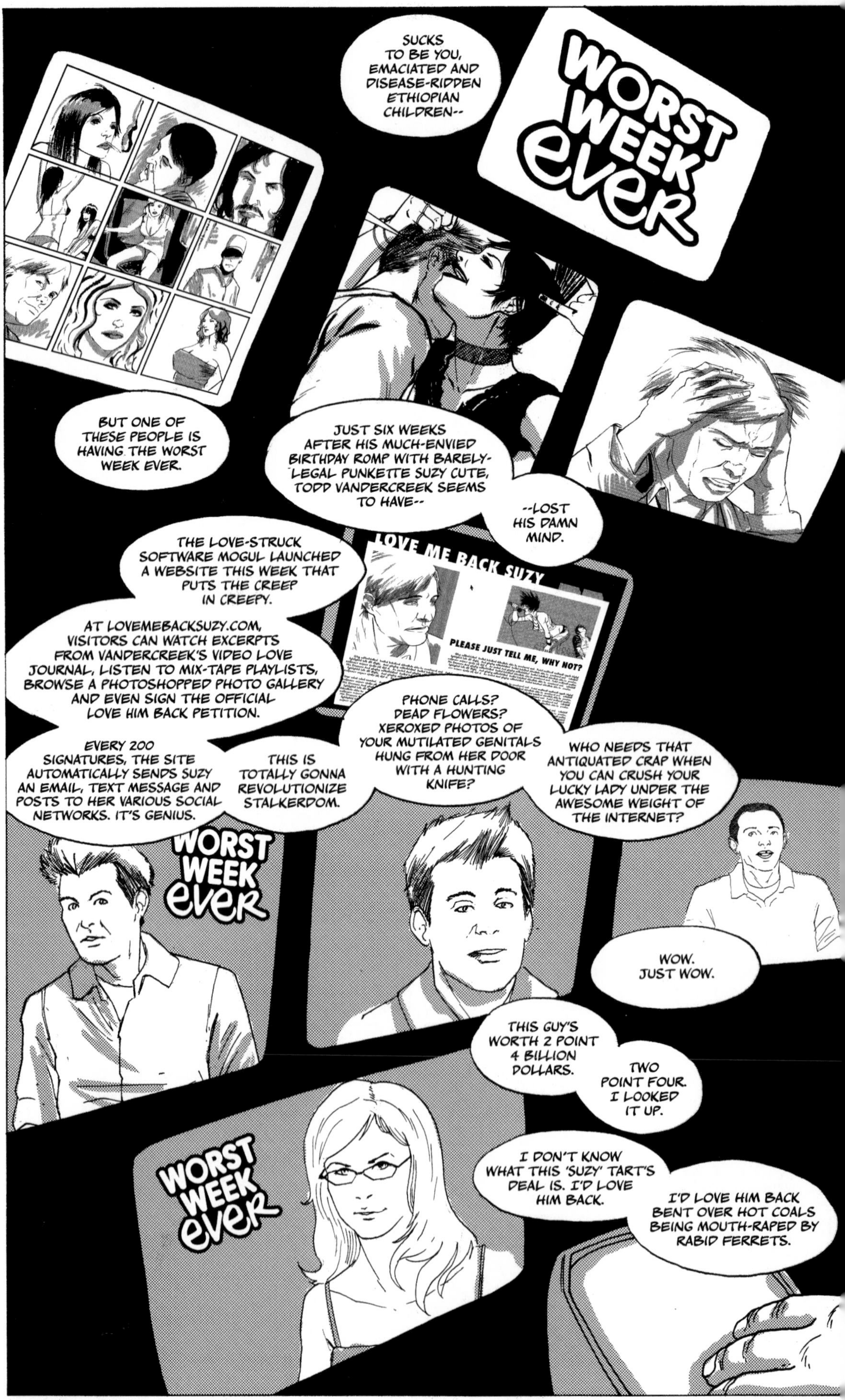

SUCKS TO BE YOU, EMACIATED AND DISEASE-RIDDEN ETHIOPIAN CHILDREN--
WORST WEEK ever
BUT ONE OF THESE PEOPLE IS HAVING THE WORST WEEK EVER.
JUST SIX WEEKS AFTER HIS MUCH-ENVIED BIRTHDAY ROMP WITH BARELY-LEGAL PUNKETTE SUZY CUTE, TODD VANDERCREEK SEEMS TO HAVE--
--LOST HIS DAMN MIND.
THE LOVE-STRUCK SOFTWARE MOGUL LAUNCHED A WEBSITE THIS WEEK THAT PUTS THE CREEP IN CREEPY.
LOVE ME BACK SUZY
PLEASE JUST TELL ME, WHY NOT?
AT LOVEMEBACKSUZY.COM, VISITORS CAN WATCH EXCERPTS FROM VANDERCREEK'S VIDEO LOVE JOURNAL, LISTEN TO MIX-TAPE PLAYLISTS, BROWSE A PHOTOSHOPPED PHOTO GALLERY AND EVEN SIGN THE OFFICIAL LOVE HIM BACK PETITION.
EVERY 200 SIGNATURES, THE SITE AUTOMATICALLY SENDS SUZY AN EMAIL, TEXT MESSAGE AND POSTS TO HER VARIOUS SOCIAL NETWORKS. IT'S GENIUS.
THIS IS TOTALLY GONNA REVOLUTIONIZE STALKERDOM.
PHONE CALLS? DEAD FLOWERS? XEROXED PHOTOS OF YOUR MUTILATED GENITALS HUNG FROM HER DOOR WITH A HUNTING KNIFE?
WHO NEEDS THAT ANTIQUATED CRAP WHEN YOU CAN CRUSH YOUR LUCKY LADY UNDER THE AWESOME WEIGHT OF THE INTERNET?
WORST WEEK ever
WOW. JUST WOW.
THIS GUY'S WORTH 2 POINT 4 BILLION DOLLARS.
TWO POINT FOUR. I LOOKED IT UP.
WORST WEEK ever
I DON'T KNOW WHAT THIS 'SUZY' TART'S DEAL IS. I'D LOVE HIM BACK.
I'D LOVE HIM BACK BENT OVER HOT COALS BEING MOUTH-RAPED BY RABID FERRETS.

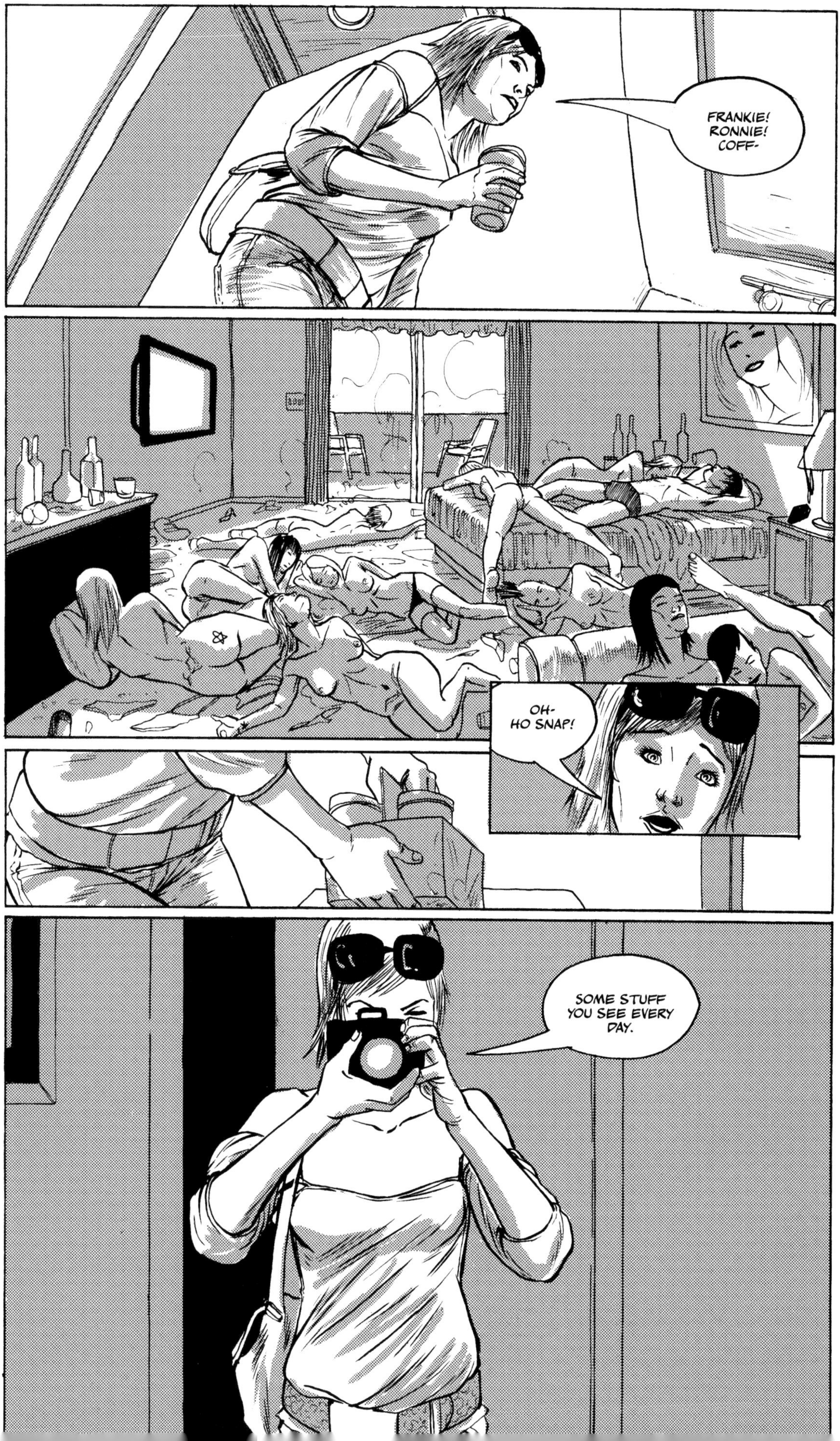
FRANKIE! RONNIE! COFF-
OH- HO SNAP!
SOME STUFF YOU SEE EVERY DAY.

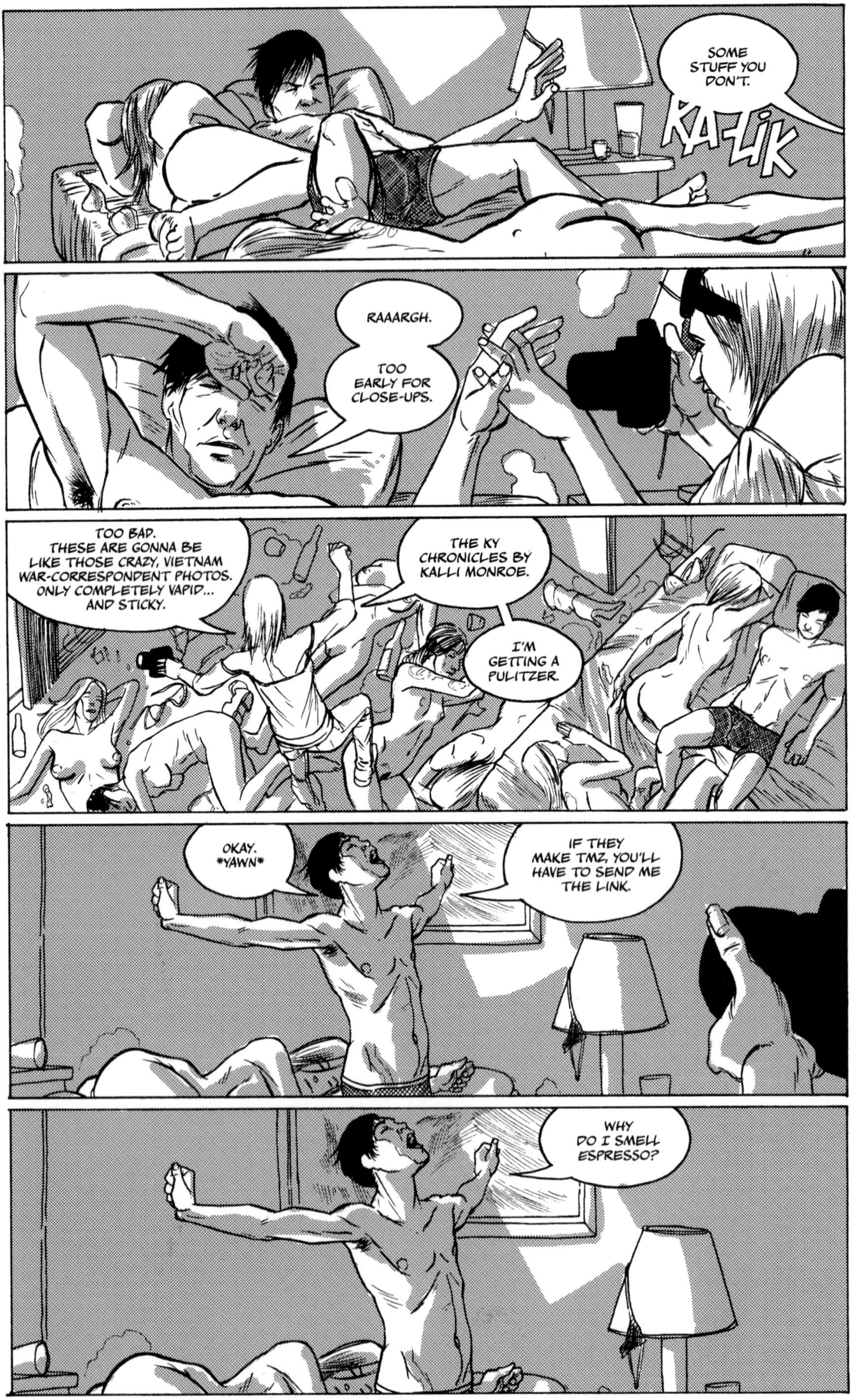

SOME STUFF YOU DON'T.
KA-LIK
RAAARGH.
TOO EARLY FOR CLOSE-UPS.
TOO BAD. THESE ARE GONNA BE LIKE THOSE CRAZY, VIETNAM WAR-CORRESPONDENT PHOTOS. ONLY COMPLETELY VAPID... AND STICKY.
THE KY CHRONICLES BY KALLI MONROE.
I'M GETTING A PULITZER.
OKAY. *YAWN*
IF THEY MAKE TMZ, YOU'LL HAVE TO SEND ME THE LINK.
WHY DO I SMELL ESPRESSO?

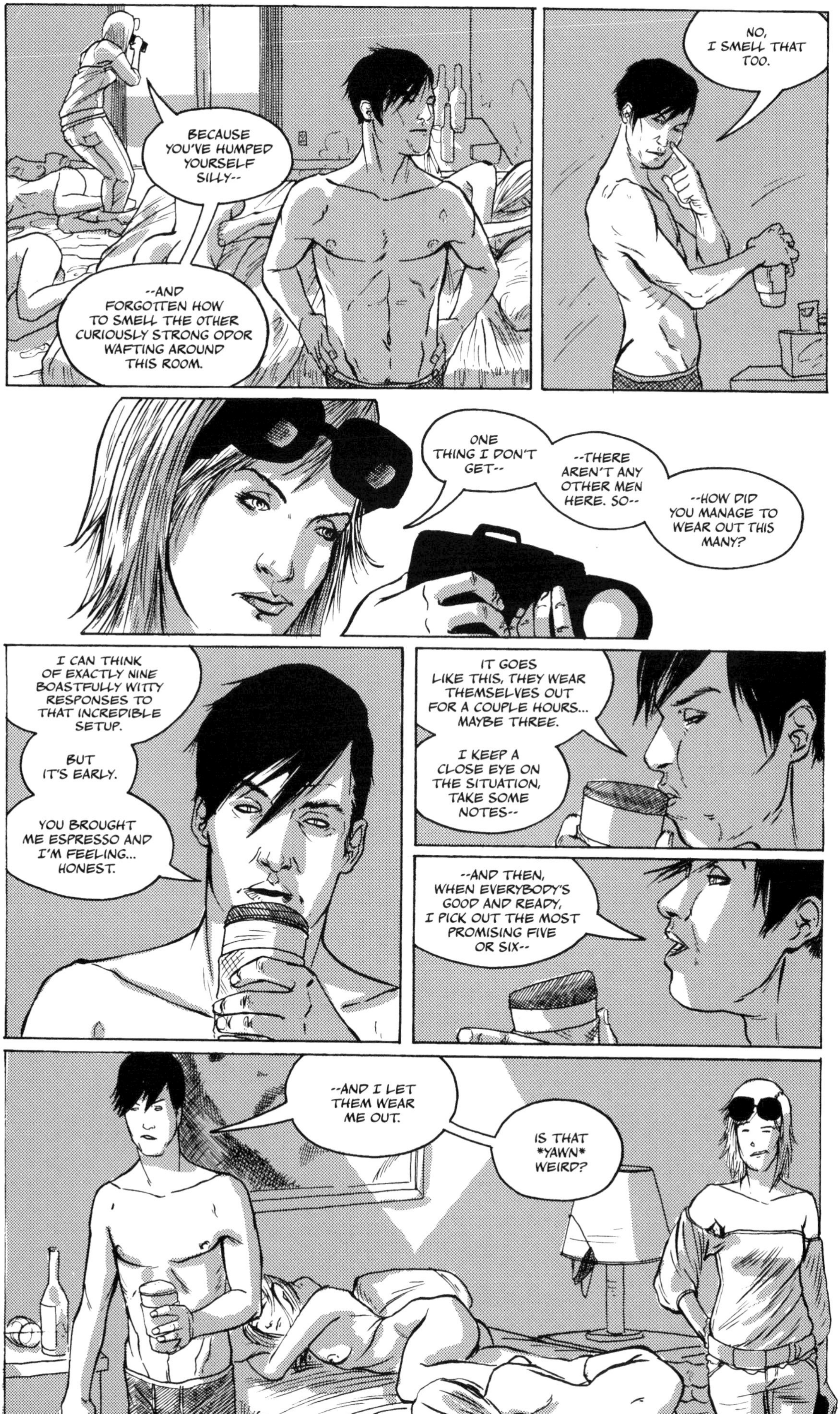
BECAUSE YOU'VE HUMPED YOURSELF SILLY--
--AND FORGOTTEN HOW TO SMELL THE OTHER CURIOUSLY STRONG ODOR WAFTING AROUND THIS ROOM.
NO, I SMELL THAT TOO.
ONE THING I DON'T GET--
--THERE AREN'T ANY OTHER MEN HERE. SO--
--HOW DID YOU MANAGE TO WEAR OUT THIS MANY?
I CAN THINK OF EXACTLY NINE BOASTFULLY WITTY RESPONSES TO THAT INCREDIBLE SETUP.
BUT IT'S EARLY.
YOU BROUGHT ME ESPRESSO AND I'M FEELING... HONEST.
IT GOES LIKE THIS, THEY WEAR THEMSELVES OUT FOR A COUPLE HOURS... MAYBE THREE.
I KEEP A CLOSE EYE ON THE SITUATION, TAKE SOME NOTES--
--AND THEN, WHEN EVERYBODY'S GOOD AND READY, I PICK OUT THE MOST PROMISING FIVE OR SIX--
--AND I LET THEM WEAR ME OUT.
IS THAT *YAWN* WEIRD?

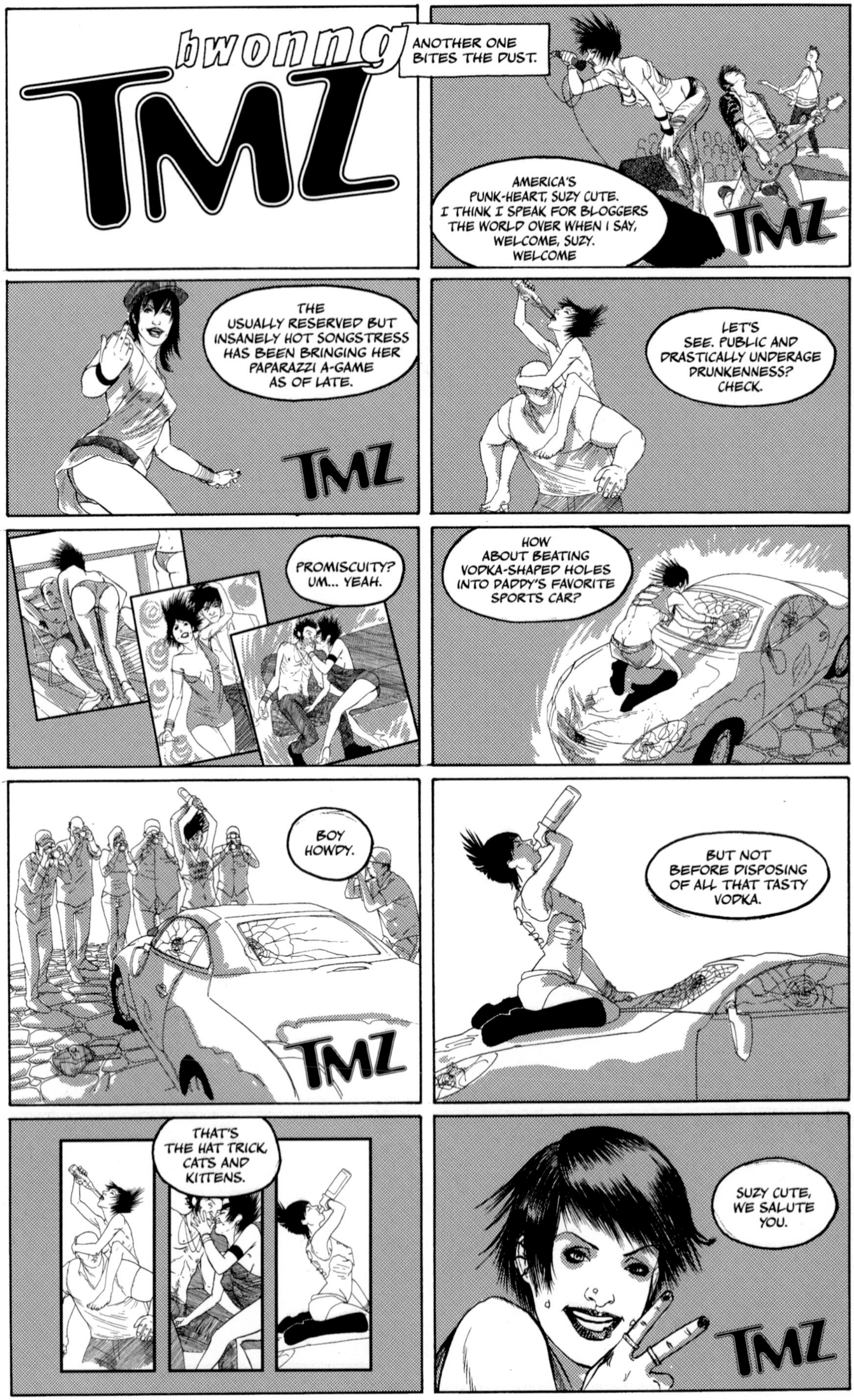
bwonng
TMZ
ANOTHER ONE BITES THE DUST.
AMERICA'S PUNK-HEART, SUZY CUTE. I THINK I SPEAK FOR BLOGGERS THE WORLD OVER WHEN I SAY, WELCOME, SUZY. WELCOME
TMZ
THE USUALLY RESERVED BUT INSANELY HOT SONGSTRESS HAS BEEN BRINGING HER PAPARAZZI A-GAME AS OF LATE.
TMZ
LET'S SEE. PUBLIC AND DRASTICALLY UNDERAGE DRUNKENNESS? CHECK.
PROMISCUITY? UM... YEAH.
HOW ABOUT BEATING VODKA-SHAPED HOLES INTO DADDY'S FAVORITE SPORTS CAR?
BOY HOWDY.
TMZ
BUT NOT BEFORE DISPOSING OF ALL THAT TASTY VODKA.
THAT'S THE HAT TRICK, CATS AND KITTENS.
SUZY CUTE, WE SALUTE YOU.
TMZ

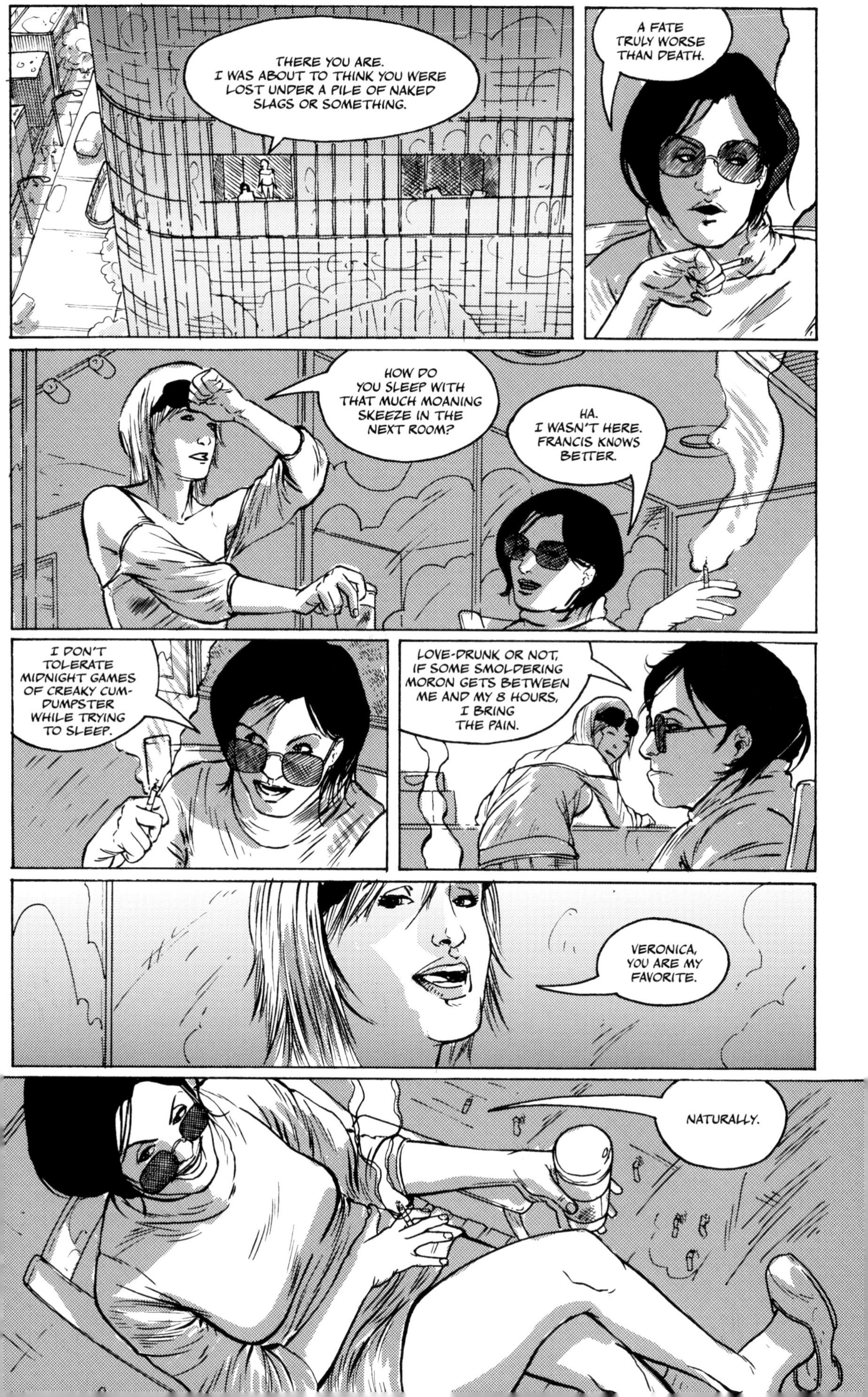
THERE YOU ARE. I WAS ABOUT TO THINK YOU WERE LOST UNDER A PILE OF NAKED SLAGS OR SOMETHING.
A FATE TRULY WORSE THAN DEATH.
HOW DO YOU SLEEP WITH THAT MUCH MOANING SKEEZE IN THE NEXT ROOM?
HA. I WASN'T HERE. FRANCIS KNOWS BETTER.
I DON'T TOLERATE MIDNIGHT GAMES OF CREAKY CUM-DUMPSTER WHILE TRYING TO SLEEP.
LOVE-DRUNK OR NOT, IF SOME SMOLDERING MORON GETS BETWEEN ME AND MY 8 HOURS, I BRING THE PAIN.
VERONICA, YOU ARE MY FAVORITE.
NATURALLY.

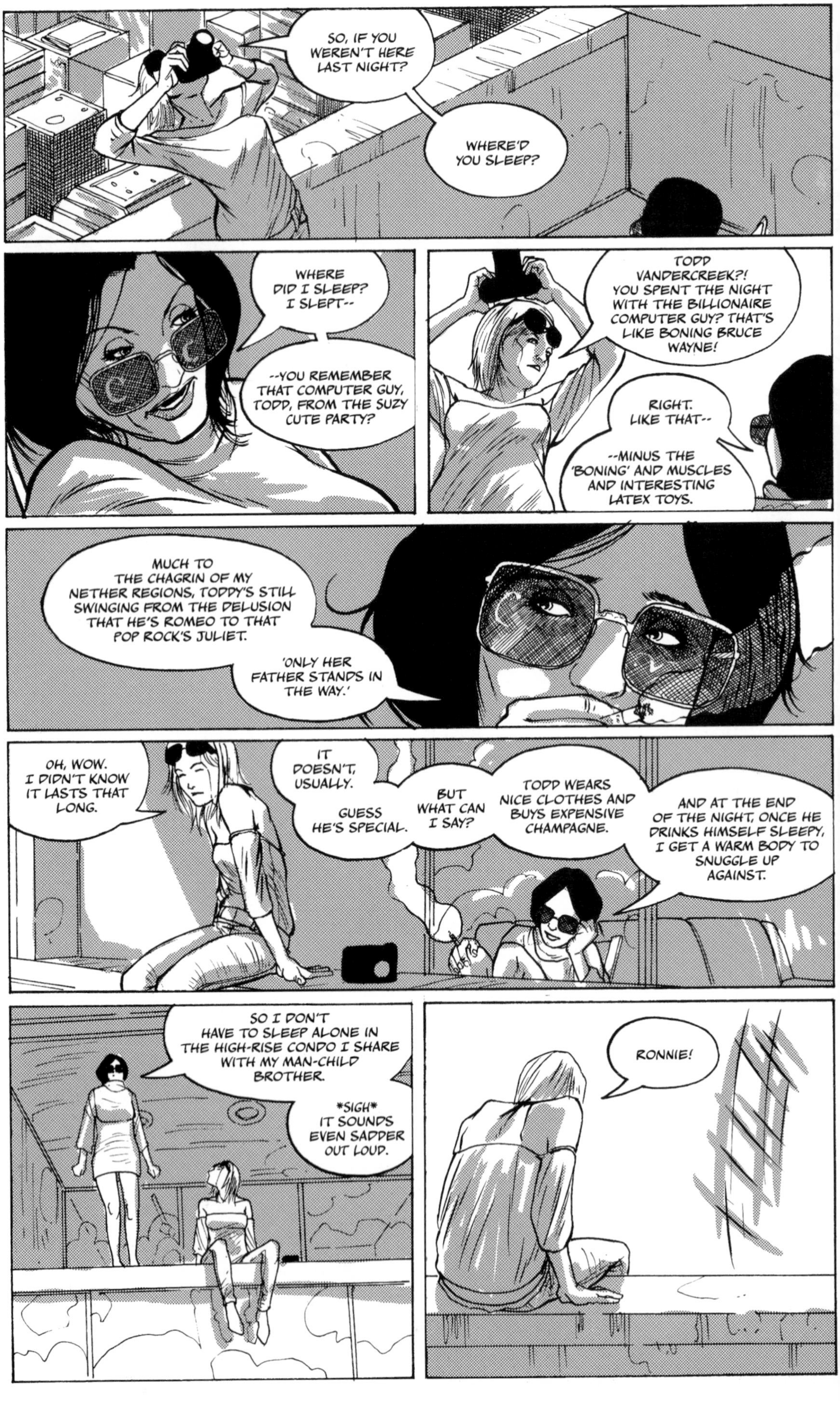
SO, IF YOU WEREN'T HERE LAST NIGHT?
WHERE'D YOU SLEEP?
WHERE DID I SLEEP? I SLEPT--
--YOU REMEMBER THAT COMPUTER GUY, TODD, FROM THE SUZY CUTE PARTY?
TODD VANDERCREEK?! YOU SPENT THE NIGHT WITH THE BILLIONAIRE COMPUTER GUY? THAT'S LIKE BONING BRUCE WAYNE!
RIGHT. LIKE THAT--
--MINUS THE 'BONING' AND MUSCLES AND INTERESTING LATEX TOYS.
MUCH TO THE CHAGRIN OF MY NETHER REGIONS, TODDY'S STILL SWINGING FROM THE DELUSION THAT HE'S ROMEO TO THAT POP ROCK'S JULIET.
'ONLY HER FATHER STANDS IN THE WAY.'
OH, WOW. I DIDN'T KNOW IT LASTS THAT LONG.
IT DOESN'T, USUALLY.
GUESS HE'S SPECIAL.
BUT WHAT CAN I SAY?
TODD WEARS NICE CLOTHES AND BUYS EXPENSIVE CHAMPAGNE.
AND AT THE END OF THE NIGHT, ONCE HE DRINKS HIMSELF SLEEPY, I GET A WARM BODY TO SNUGGLE UP AGAINST.
SO I DON'T HAVE TO SLEEP ALONE IN THE HIGH-RISE CONDO I SHARE WITH MY MAN-CHILD BROTHER.
SIGH IT SOUNDS EVEN SADDER OUT LOUD.
RONNIE!

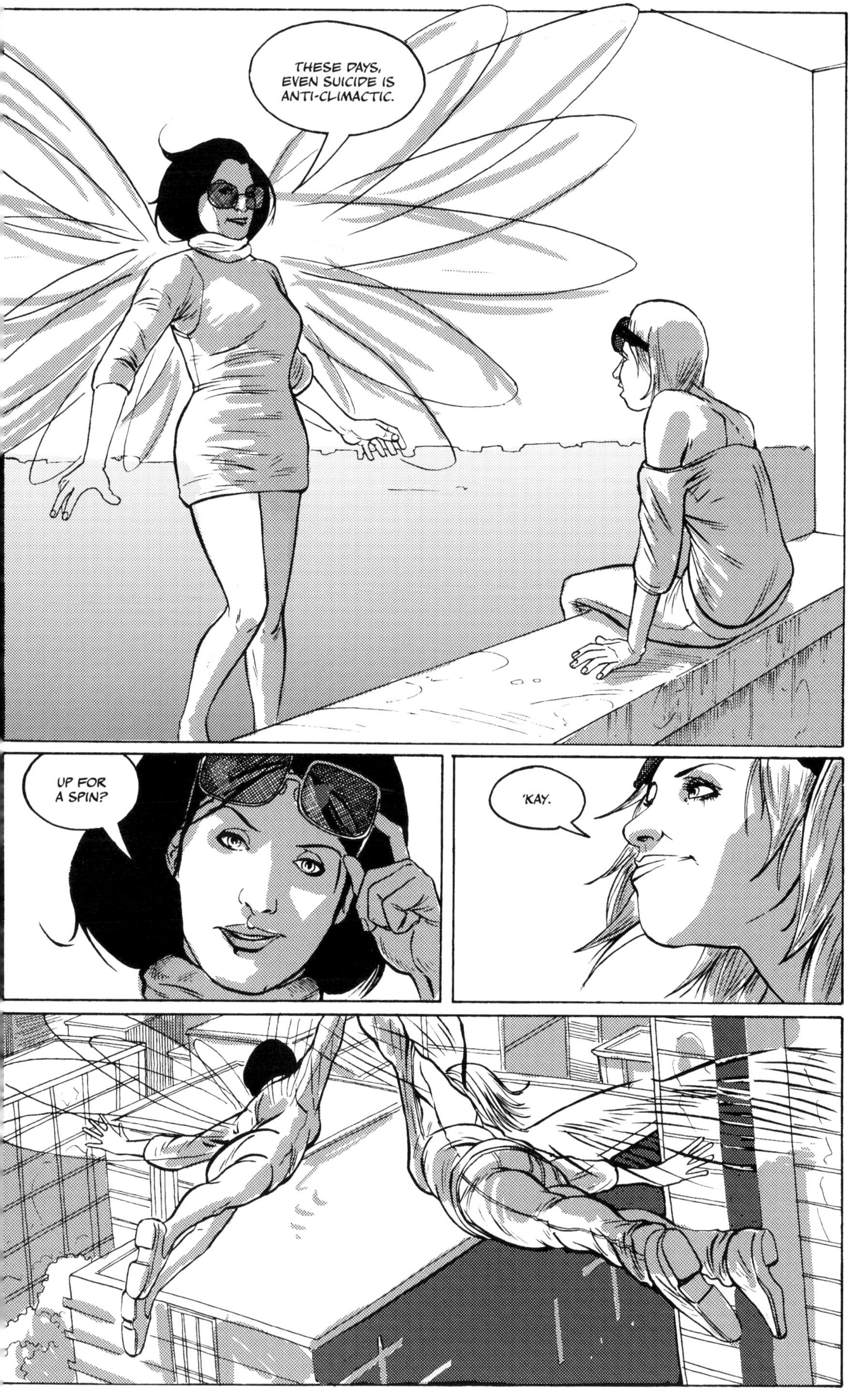
THESE DAYS, EVEN SUICIDE IS ANTI-CLIMACTIC.
UP FOR A SPIN?
'KAY.

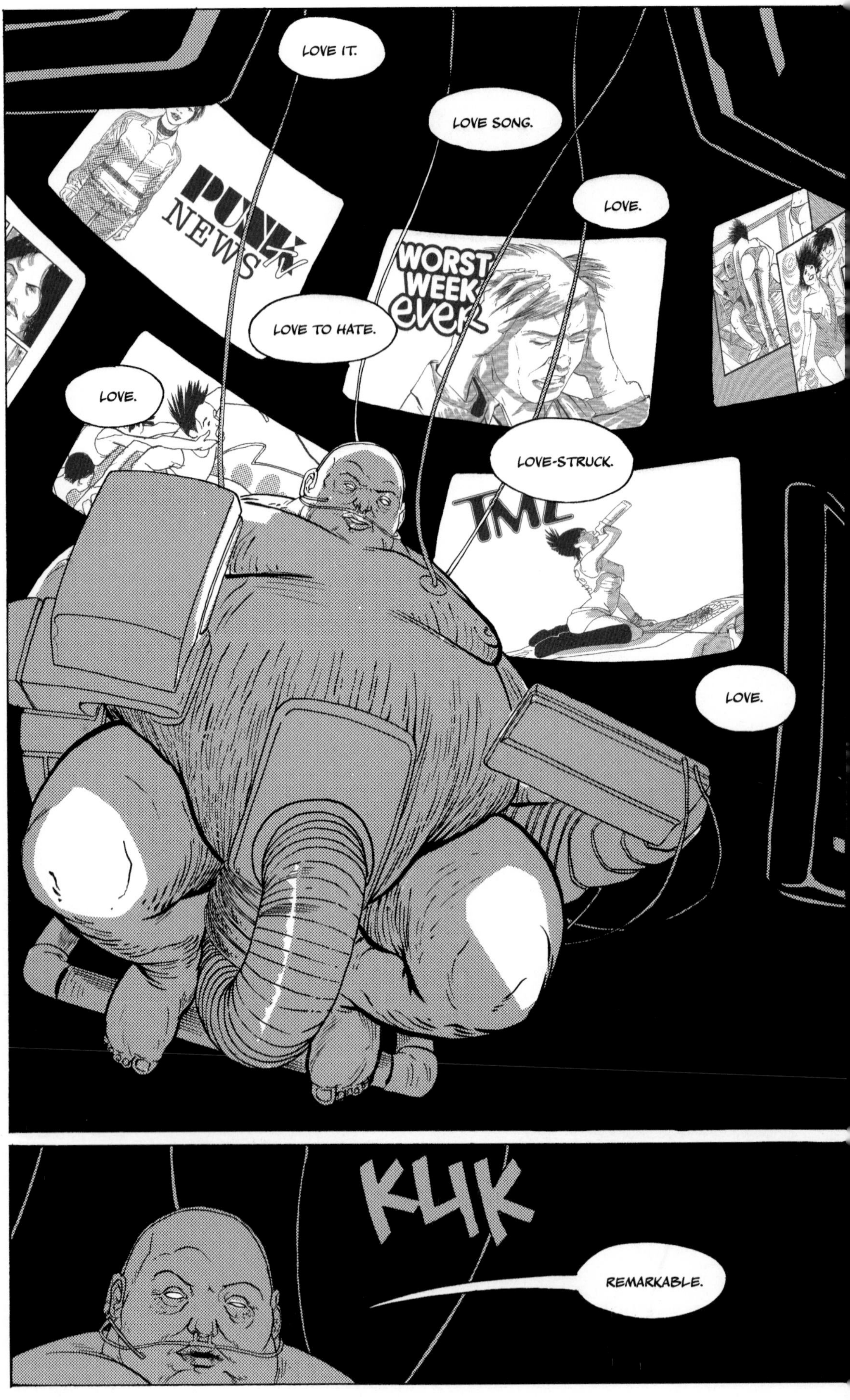

LOVE IT.
LOVE SONG.
PUNK
NEWS
LOVE.
WORST
WEEK
ever
LOVE TO HATE.
LOVE.
LOVE-STRUCK.
LOVE.
KUK
REMARKABLE.

CHAPTER 4

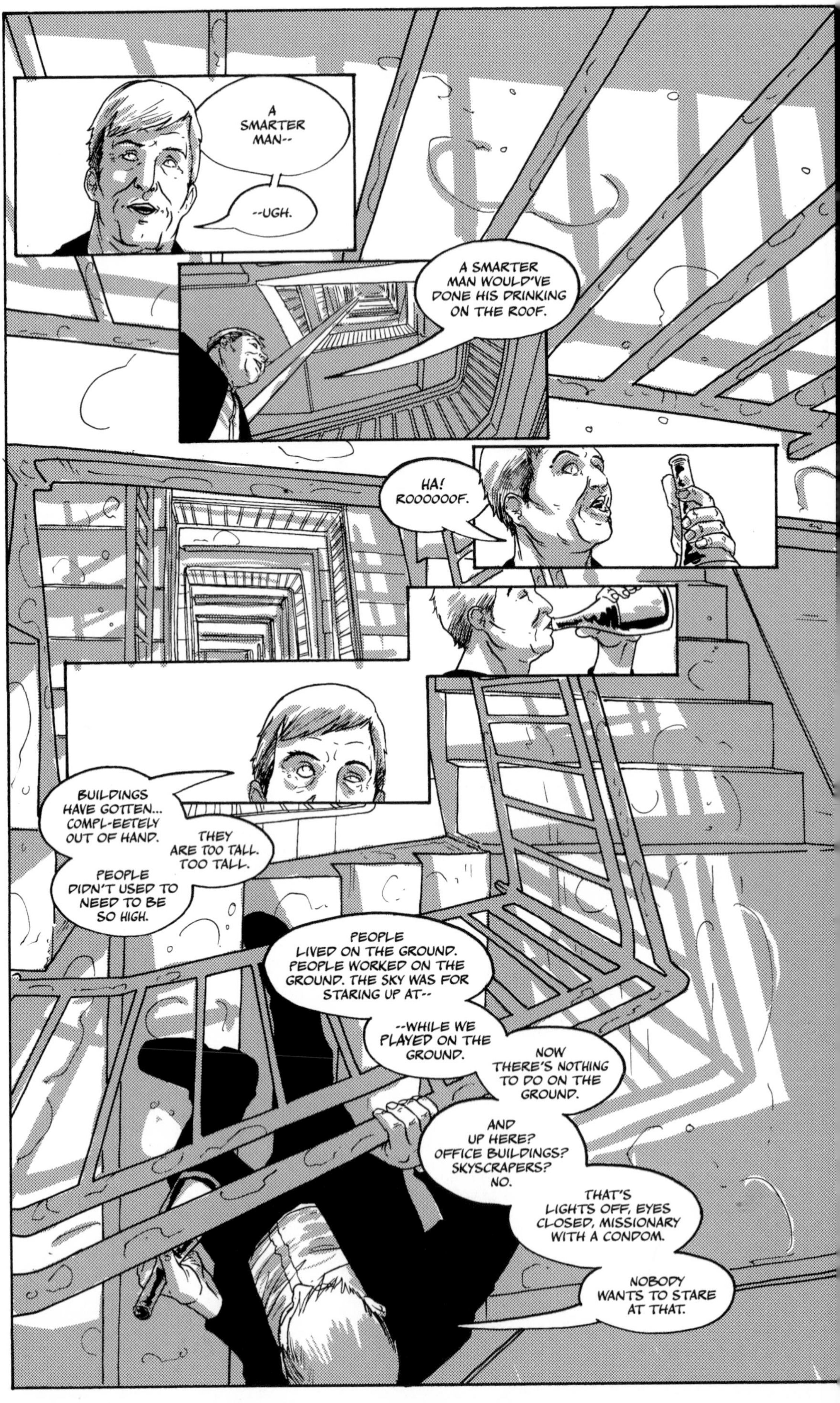
A SMARTER MAN--
--UGH.
A SMARTER MAN WOULD'VE DONE HIS DRINKING ON THE ROOF.
HA! ROOOOOOF.
BUILDINGS HAVE GOTTEN... COMPL-EETELY OUT OF HAND.
THEY ARE TOO TALL. TOO TALL.
PEOPLE DIDN'T USED TO NEED TO BE SO HIGH.
PEOPLE LIVED ON THE GROUND. PEOPLE WORKED ON THE GROUND. THE SKY WAS FOR STARING UP AT--
--WHILE WE PLAYED ON THE GROUND.
NOW THERE'S NOTHING TO DO ON THE GROUND.
AND UP HERE? OFFICE BUILDINGS? SKYSCRAPERS? NO.
THAT'S LIGHTS OFF, EYES CLOSED, MISSIONARY WITH A CONDOM.
NOBODY WANTS TO STARE AT THAT.

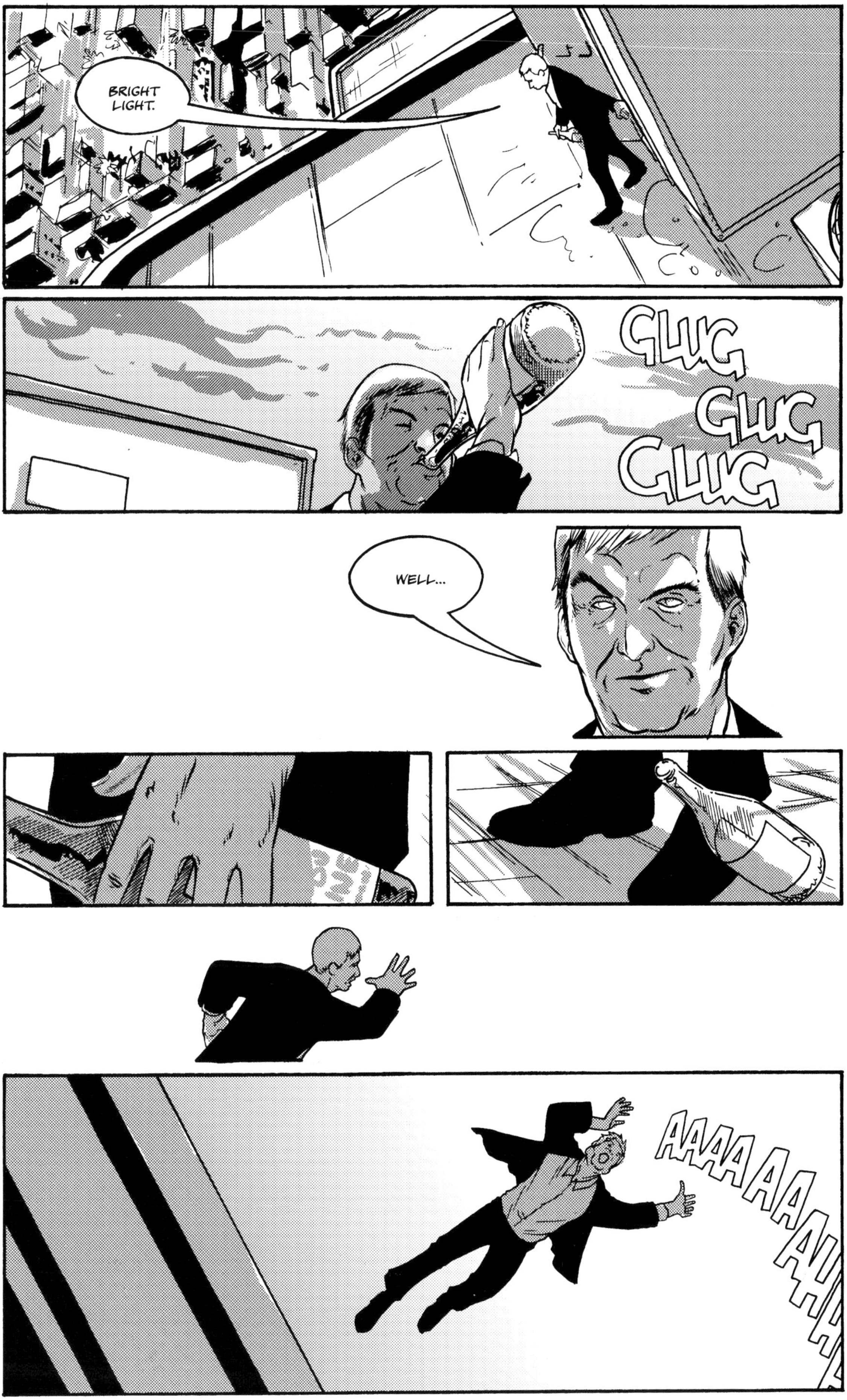
BRIGHT LIGHT.
GLUG
GLUG
GLUG
WELL...
AAAAAAAAHHH

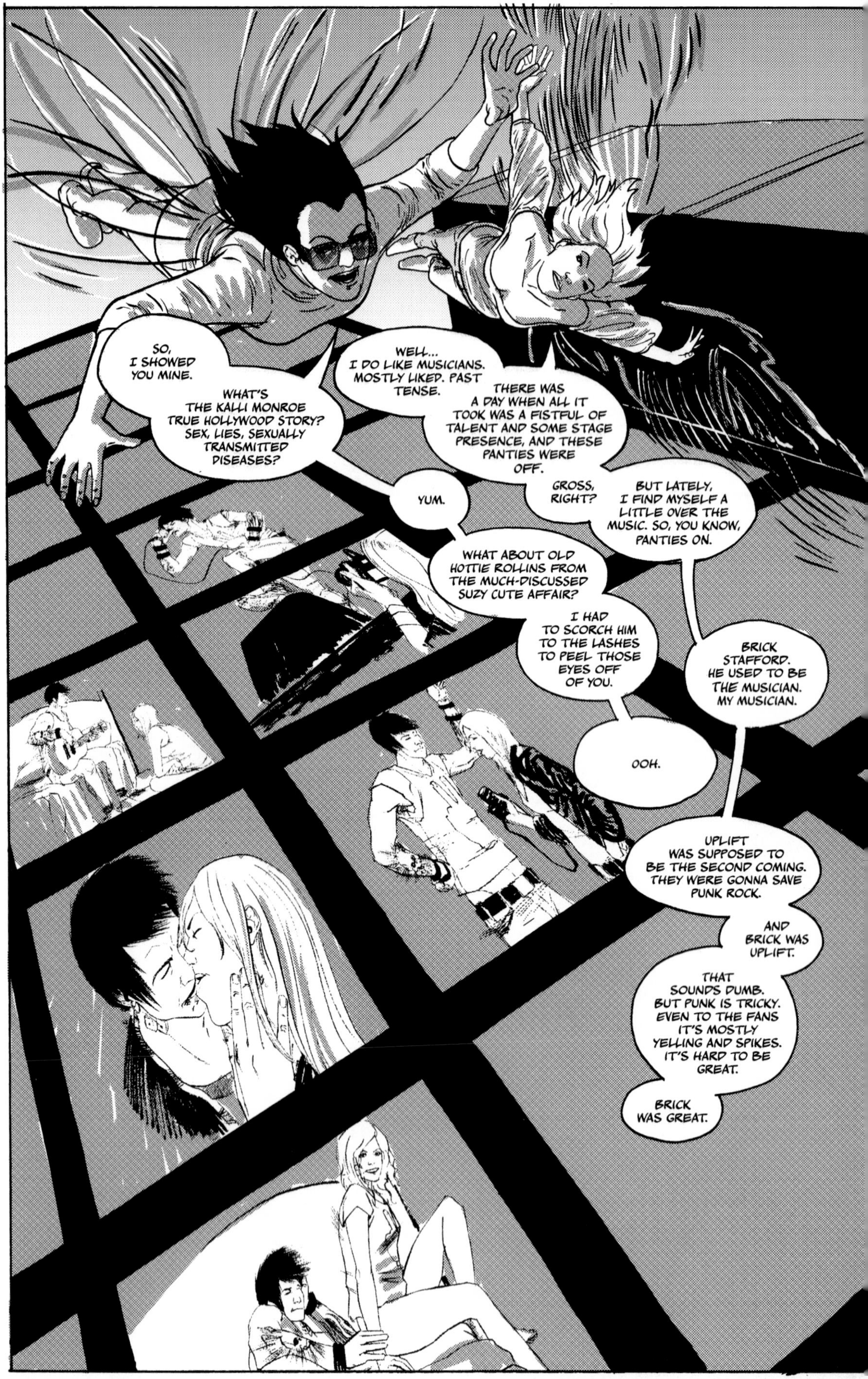
SO, I SHOWED YOU MINE.
WHAT'S THE KALLI MONROE TRUE HOLLYWOOD STORY? SEX, LIES, SEXUALLY TRANSMITTED DISEASES?
WELL... I DO LIKE MUSICIANS. MOSTLY LIKED. PAST TENSE.
THERE WAS A DAY WHEN ALL IT TOOK WAS A FISTFUL OF TALENT AND SOME STAGE PRESENCE, AND THESE PANTIES WERE OFF.
YUM.
GROSS, RIGHT?
BUT LATELY, I FIND MYSELF A LITTLE OVER THE MUSIC. SO, YOU KNOW, PANTIES ON.
WHAT ABOUT OLD HOTTIE ROLLINS FROM THE MUCH-DISCUSSED SUZY CUTE AFFAIR?
I HAD TO SCORCH HIM TO THE LASHES TO PEEL THOSE EYES OFF OF YOU.
BRICK STAFFORD. HE USED TO BE THE MUSICIAN. MY MUSICIAN.
OOH.
UPLIFT WAS SUPPOSED TO BE THE SECOND COMING. THEY WERE GONNA SAVE PUNK ROCK.
AND BRICK WAS UPLIFT.
THAT SOUNDS DUMB. BUT PUNK IS TRICKY. EVEN TO THE FANS IT'S MOSTLY YELLING AND SPIKES. IT'S HARD TO BE GREAT.
BRICK WAS GREAT.

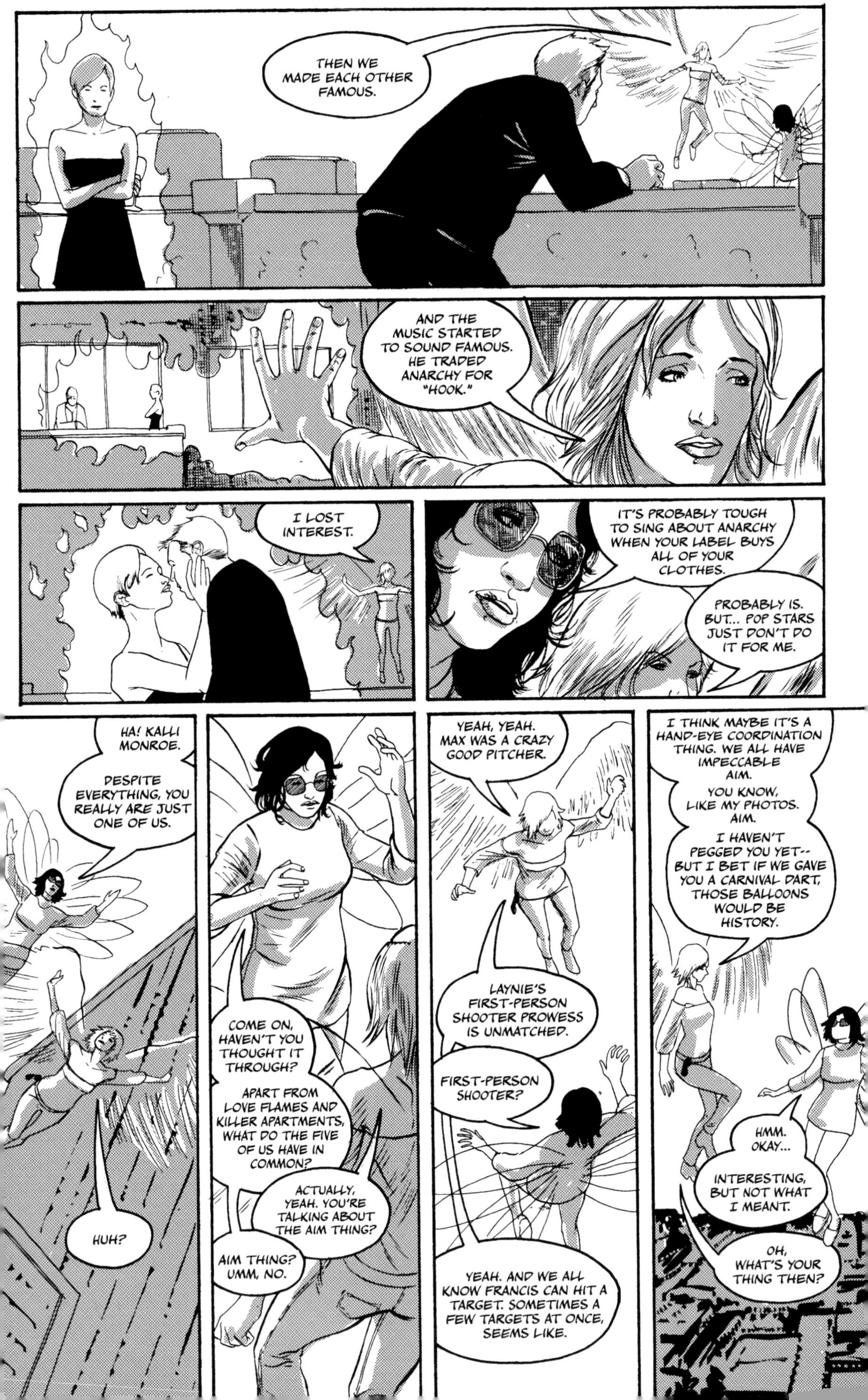
THEN WE MADE EACH OTHER FAMOUS.
AND THE MUSIC STARTED TO SOUND FAMOUS. HE TRADED ANARCHY FOR "HOOK."
I LOST INTEREST.
IT'S PROBABLY TOUGH TO SING ABOUT ANARCHY WHEN YOUR LABEL BUYS ALL OF YOUR CLOTHES.
PROBABLY IS. BUT... POP STARS JUST DON'T DO IT FOR ME.
HA! KALLI MONROE.
DESPITE EVERYTHING, YOU REALLY ARE JUST ONE OF US.
HUH?
COME ON, HAVEN'T YOU THOUGHT IT THROUGH?
APART FROM LOVE FLAMES AND KILLER APARTMENTS, WHAT DO THE FIVE OF US HAVE IN COMMON?
ACTUALLY, YEAH. YOU'RE TALKING ABOUT THE AIM THING?
AIM THING? UMM, NO.
YEAH, YEAH. MAX WAS A CRAZY GOOD PITCHER.
LAYNIE'S FIRST-PERSON SHOOTER PROWESS IS UNMATCHED.
FIRST-PERSON SHOOTER?
YEAH. AND WE ALL KNOW FRANCIS CAN HIT A TARGET. SOMETIMES A FEW TARGETS AT ONCE, SEEMS LIKE.
I THINK MAYBE IT'S A HAND-EYE COORDINATION THING. WE ALL HAVE IMPECCABLE AIM.
YOU KNOW, LIKE MY PHOTOS. AIM.
I HAVEN'T PEGGED YOU YET-- BUT I BET IF WE GAVE YOU A CARNIVAL DART, THOSE BALLOONS WOULD BE HISTORY.
HMM. OKAY...
INTERESTING, BUT NOT WHAT I MEANT.
OH, WHAT'S YOUR THING THEN?

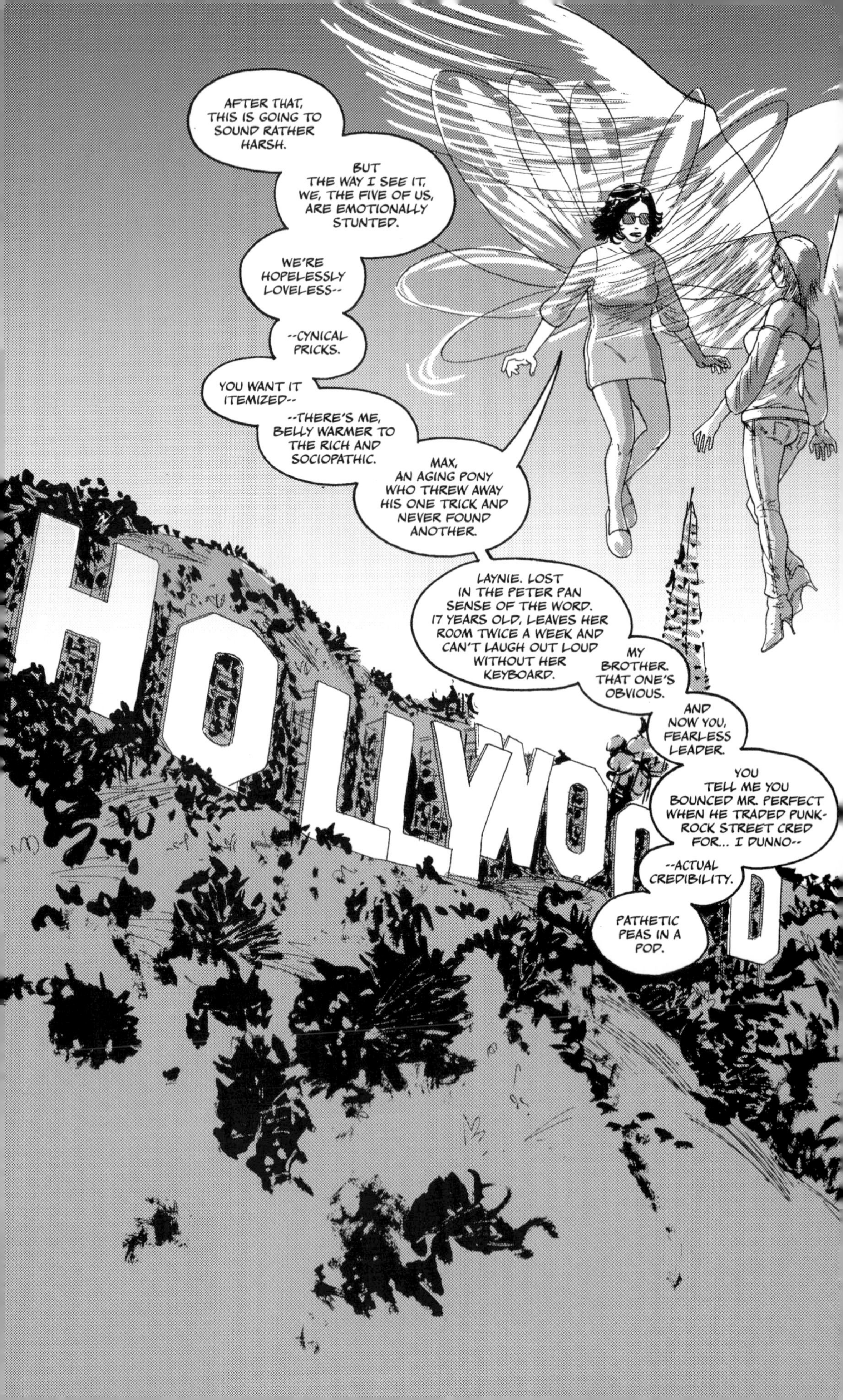

AFTER THAT, THIS IS GOING TO SOUND RATHER HARSH.
BUT THE WAY I SEE IT, WE, THE FIVE OF US, ARE EMOTIONALLY STUNTED.
WE'RE HOPELESSLY LOVELESS--
--CYNICAL PRICKS.
YOU WANT IT ITEMIZED--
--THERE'S ME, BELLY WARMER TO THE RICH AND SOCIOPATHIC.
MAX, AN AGING PONY WHO THREW AWAY HIS ONE TRICK AND NEVER FOUND ANOTHER.
LAYNIE. LOST IN THE PETER PAN SENSE OF THE WORD. 17 YEARS OLD, LEAVES HER ROOM TWICE A WEEK AND CAN'T LAUGH OUT LOUD WITHOUT HER KEYBOARD.
MY BROTHER. THAT ONE'S OBVIOUS.
AND NOW YOU, FEARLESS LEADER.
YOU TELL ME YOU BOUNCED MR. PERFECT WHEN HE TRADED PUNK-ROCK STREET CRED FOR... I DUNNO--
--ACTUAL CREDIBILITY.
PATHETIC PEAS IN A POD.
HOLLYWOOD

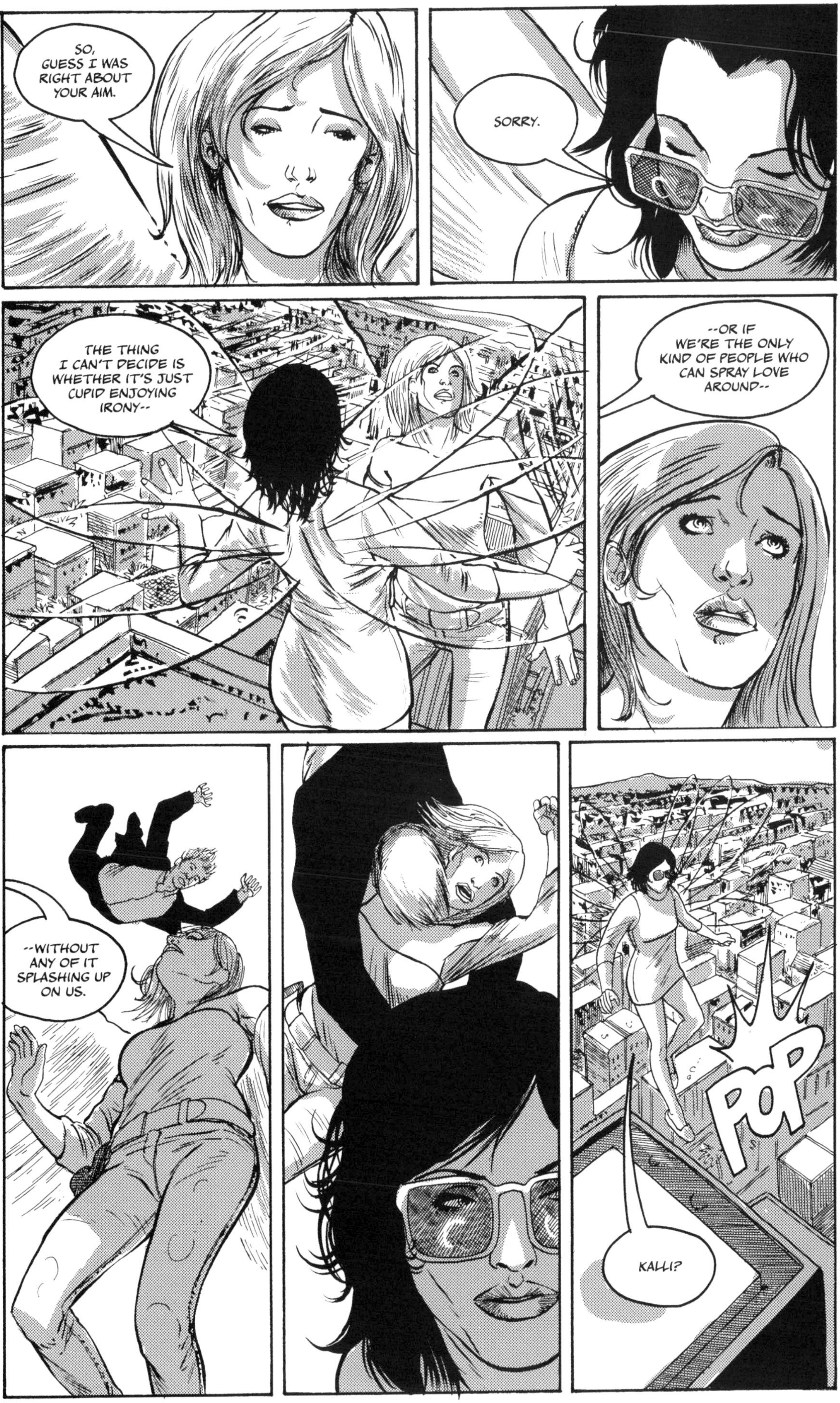
SO, GUESS I WAS RIGHT ABOUT YOUR AIM.
SORRY.
THE THING I CAN'T DECIDE IS WHETHER IT'S JUST CUPID ENJOYING IRONY--
--OR IF WE'RE THE ONLY KIND OF PEOPLE WHO CAN SPRAY LOVE AROUND--
--WITHOUT ANY OF IT SPLASHING UP ON US.
POP
KALLI?

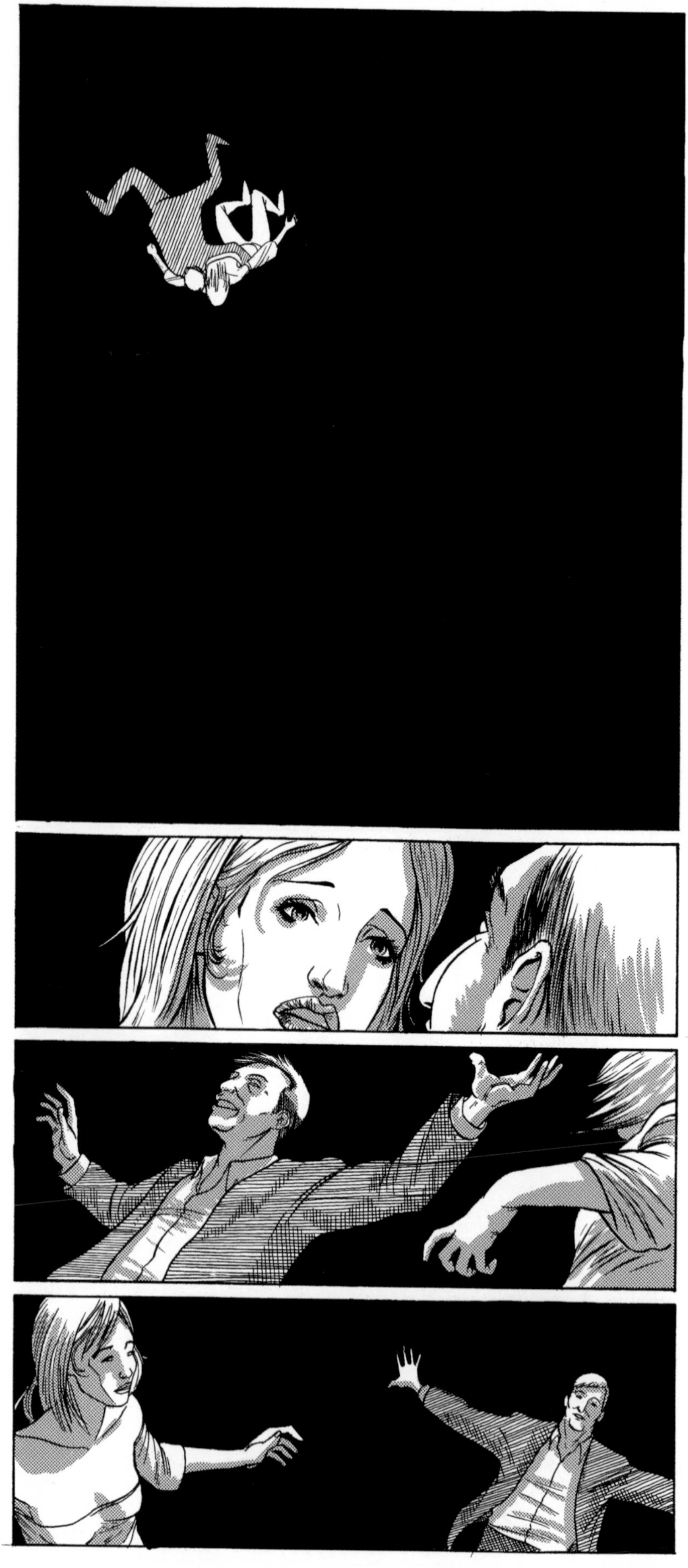

Ovid?!

Kalli.

Ovid, what the shit?!
Where are we?

***I honestly…
I can't say. I have an idea,
but as to where exactly.
I am awfully sorry.***

It's black. Just black.
We're in black, Ovid!

Yeah?

Yeah!

***See, that doesn't sound good.
Never is good.
The thing is, right now,
my eyes are closed.
I seem to handle the trip
better this way.***

What trip? Where are-
Are you DRUNK?

***Ha.
I just love when
people ask that.
"Why, Ovid...
Your words are all slurry.
And… and yes,
you seem to be sweating
a great deal.
Do I smell very cheap wine?***

***You're not…
Are you drunk?"
Ha Ha Ha.
Of course I'm drunk, Kalli.
You said it yourself,
we're in black.
When I intend to be in black,
I come prepared.***

Ovid! Where is this?

***Well, It's nowhere at all.
And everywhere at once.
And, well...
everywhere else in between.***

Great. Thanks for that,
Willy fucking Wonka.

***Just close your eyes
till we get there, love.***

***Next time
I'll bring wine for two.
It was inconsiderate
and I'm sorry.***

Get where?
Where are we going?

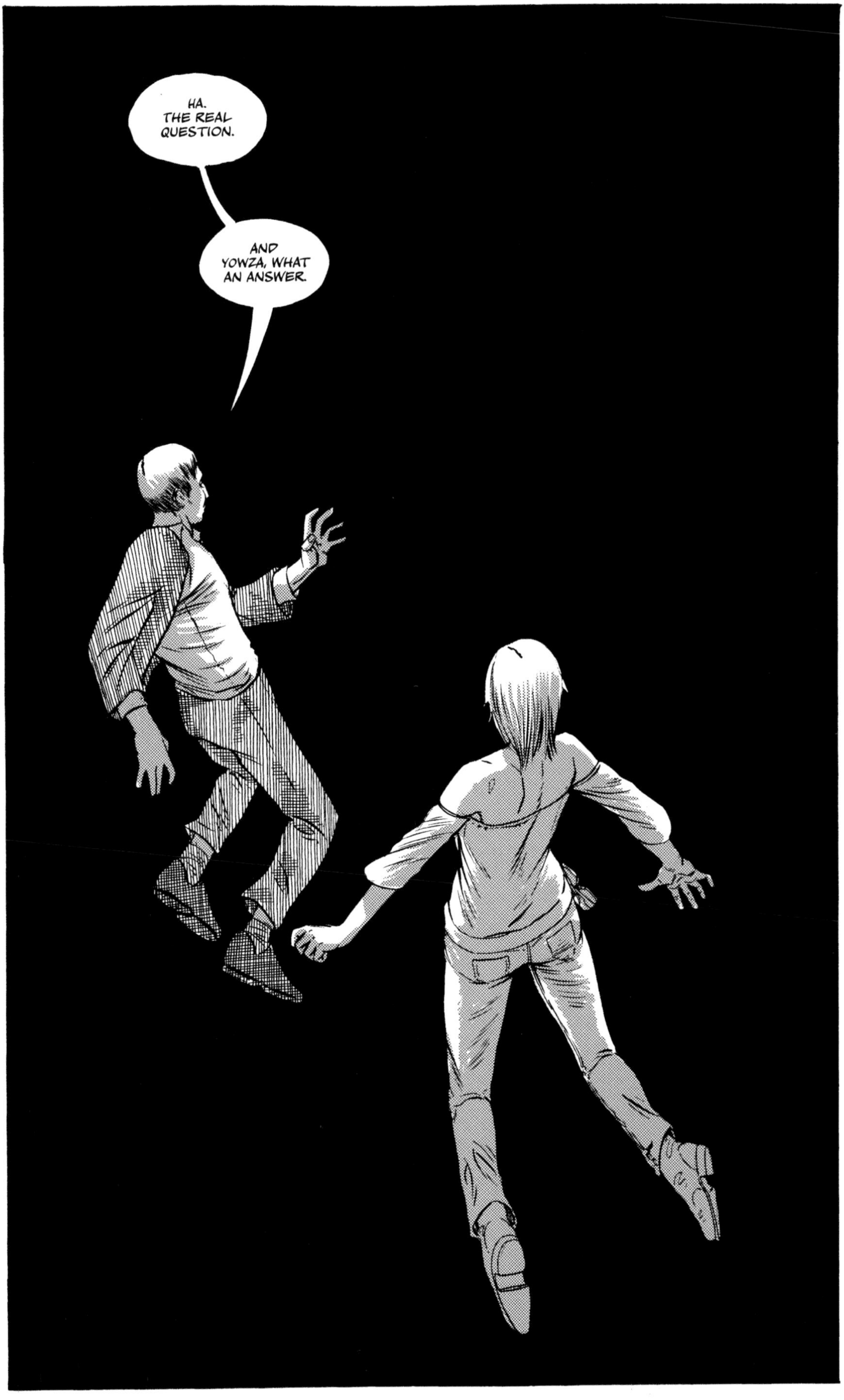
HA.
THE REAL
QUESTION.
AND
YOWZA, WHAT
AN ANSWER.

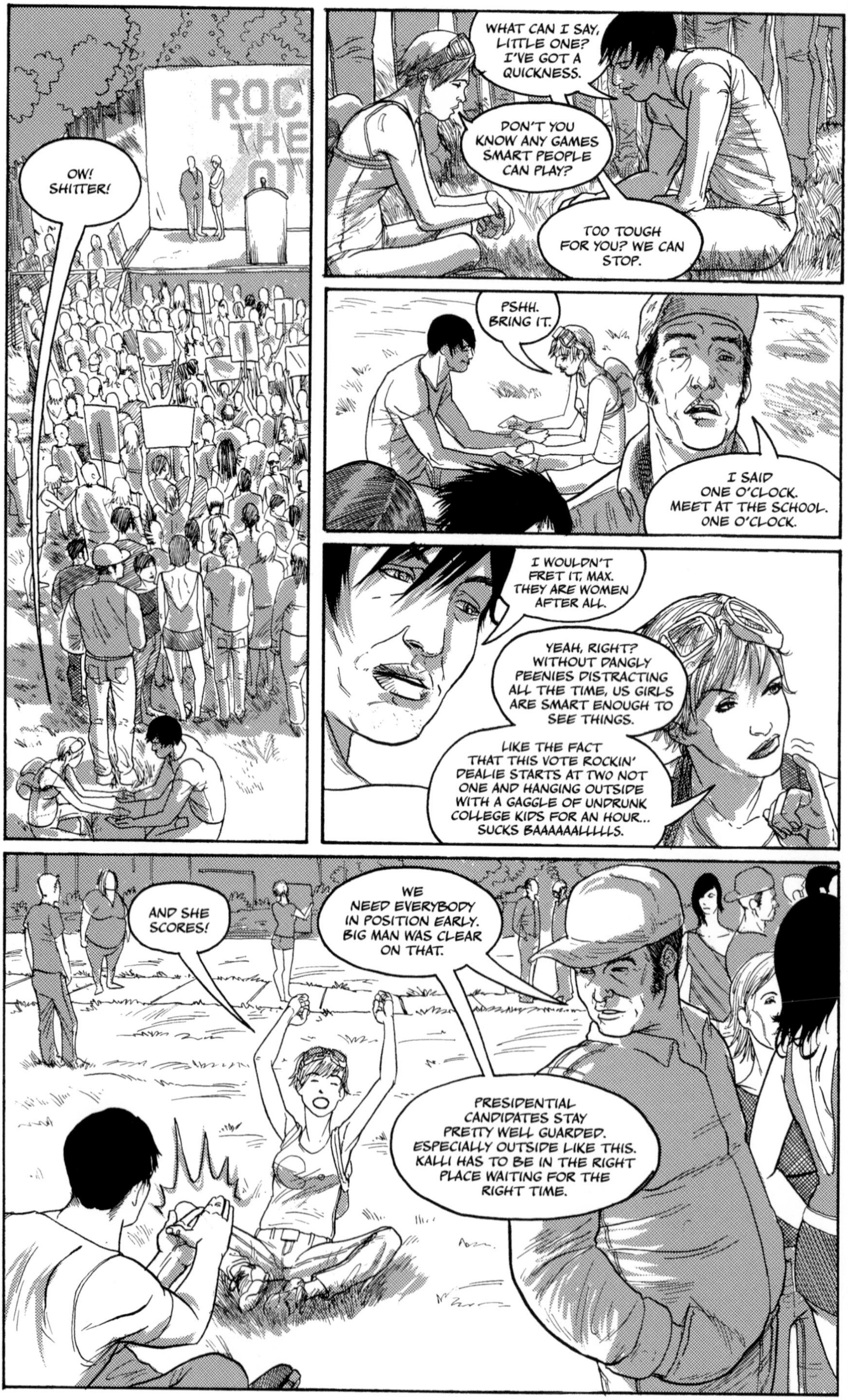
OW!
SHITTER!
WHAT CAN I SAY, LITTLE ONE? I'VE GOT A QUICKNESS.
DON'T YOU KNOW ANY GAMES SMART PEOPLE CAN PLAY?
TOO TOUGH FOR YOU? WE CAN STOP.
PSHH. BRING IT.
I SAID ONE O'CLOCK. MEET AT THE SCHOOL. ONE O'CLOCK.
I WOULDN'T FRET IT, MAX. THEY ARE WOMEN AFTER ALL.
YEAH, RIGHT? WITHOUT DANGLY PEENIES DISTRACTING ALL THE TIME, US GIRLS ARE SMART ENOUGH TO SEE THINGS.
LIKE THE FACT THAT THIS VOTE ROCKIN' DEALIE STARTS AT TWO NOT ONE AND HANGING OUTSIDE WITH A GAGGLE OF UNDRUNK COLLEGE KIDS FOR AN HOUR... SUCKS BAAAAAALLLLLS.
AND SHE SCORES!
WE NEED EVERYBODY IN POSITION EARLY. BIG MAN WAS CLEAR ON THAT.
PRESIDENTIAL CANDIDATES STAY PRETTY WELL GUARDED. ESPECIALLY OUTSIDE LIKE THIS. KALLI HAS TO BE IN THE RIGHT PLACE WAITING FOR THE RIGHT TIME.

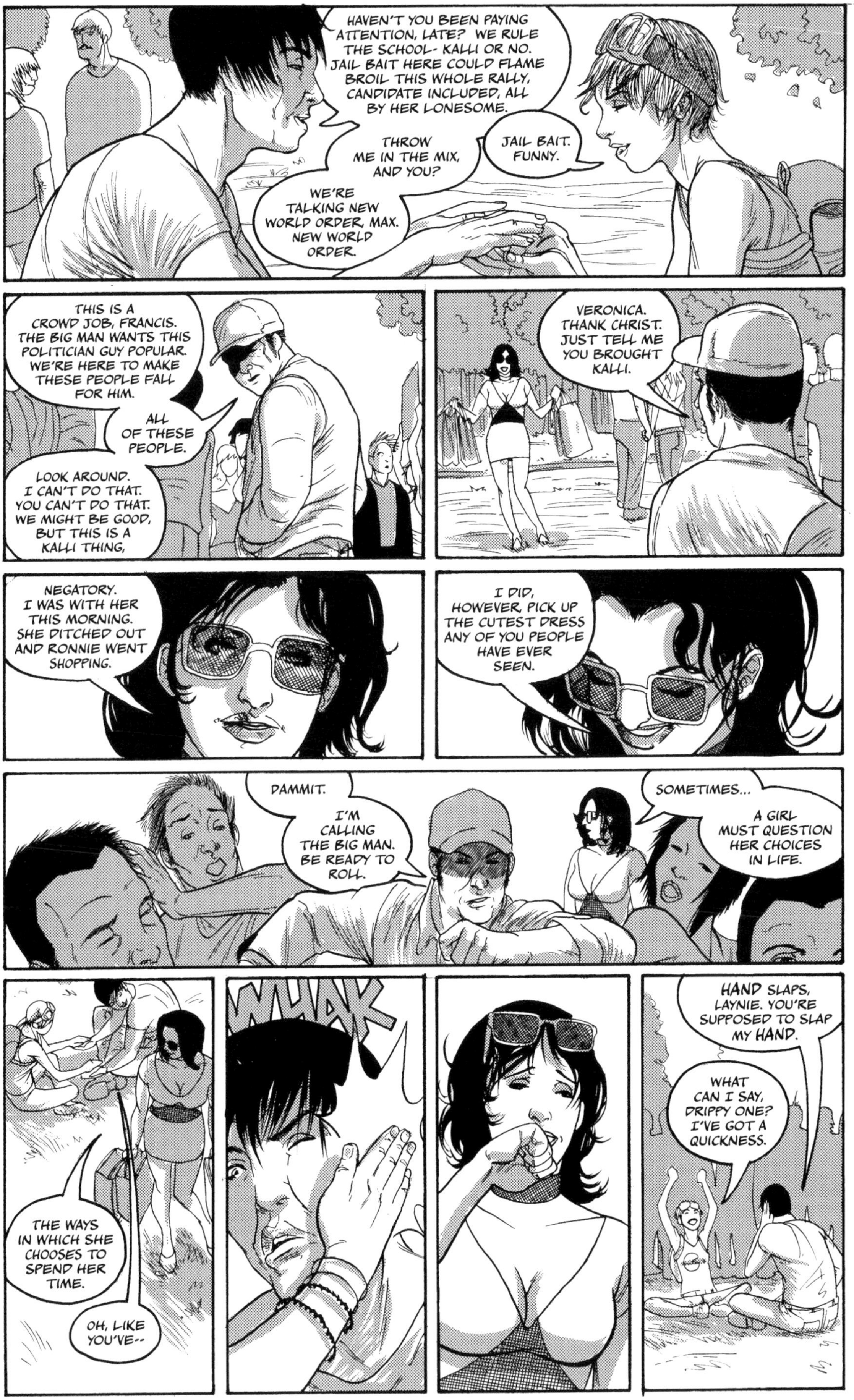
HAVEN'T YOU BEEN PAYING ATTENTION, LATE? WE RULE THE SCHOOL- KALLI OR NO. JAIL BAIT HERE COULD FLAME BROIL THIS WHOLE RALLY, CANDIDATE INCLUDED, ALL BY HER LONESOME.
JAIL BAIT. FUNNY.
THROW ME IN THE MIX, AND YOU?
WE'RE TALKING NEW WORLD ORDER, MAX. NEW WORLD ORDER.
THIS IS A CROWD JOB, FRANCIS. THE BIG MAN WANTS THIS POLITICIAN GUY POPULAR. WE'RE HERE TO MAKE THESE PEOPLE FALL FOR HIM.
ALL OF THESE PEOPLE.
LOOK AROUND. I CAN'T DO THAT. YOU CAN'T DO THAT. WE MIGHT BE GOOD, BUT THIS IS A KALLI THING,
VERONICA. THANK CHRIST. JUST TELL ME YOU BROUGHT KALLI.
NEGATORY. I WAS WITH HER THIS MORNING. SHE DITCHED OUT AND RONNIE WENT SHOPPING.
I DID, HOWEVER, PICK UP THE CUTEST DRESS ANY OF YOU PEOPLE HAVE EVER SEEN.
DAMMIT.
I'M CALLING THE BIG MAN. BE READY TO ROLL.
SOMETIMES...
A GIRL MUST QUESTION HER CHOICES IN LIFE.
THE WAYS IN WHICH SHE CHOOSES TO SPEND HER TIME.
OH, LIKE YOU'VE--
WHAK
HAND SLAPS, LAYNIE. YOU'RE SUPPOSED TO SLAP MY HAND.
WHAT CAN I SAY, DRIPPY ONE? I'VE GOT A QUICKNESS.

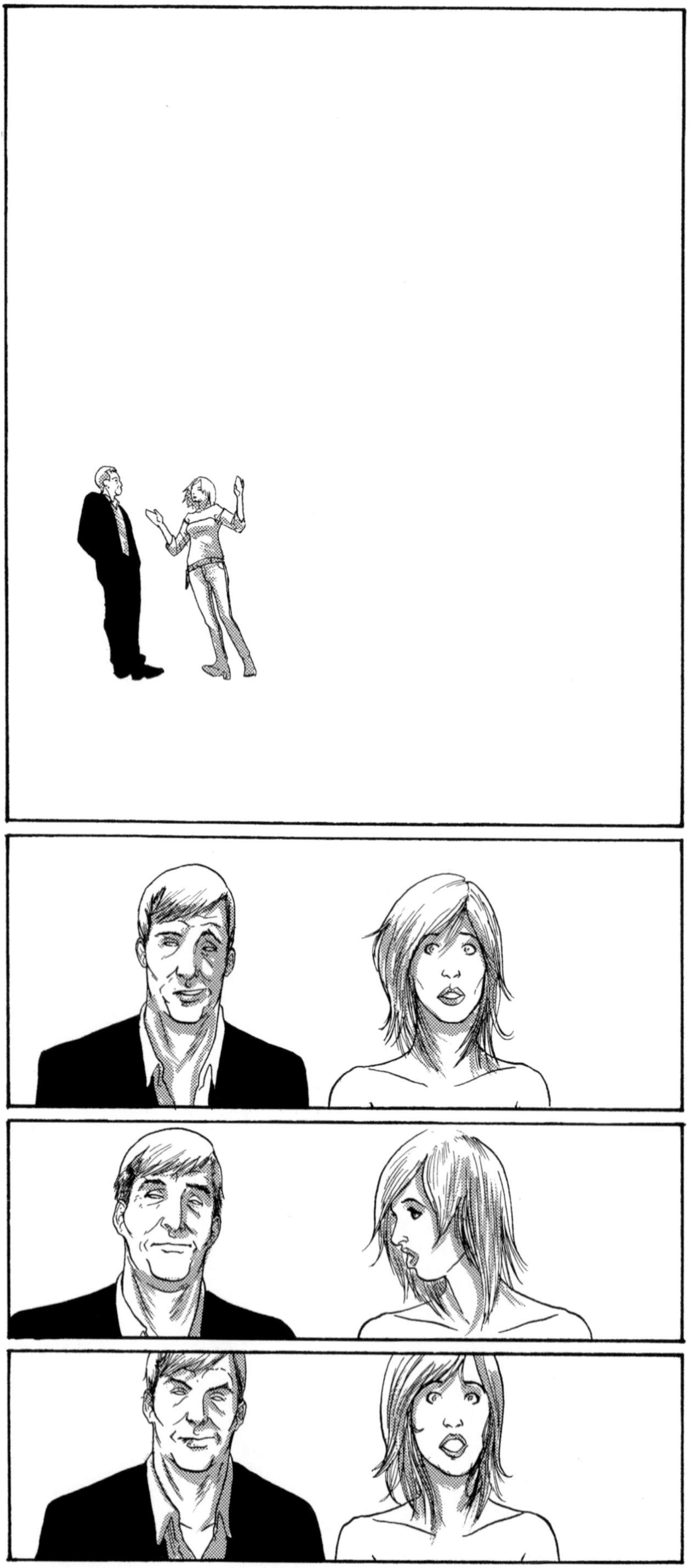

From BLACK to creepy nothingness void.

This is a real whiz-bang trip you brought me on.

Lucky for you, I specialize in whiz-bang.

No worries, though… We have arrived.

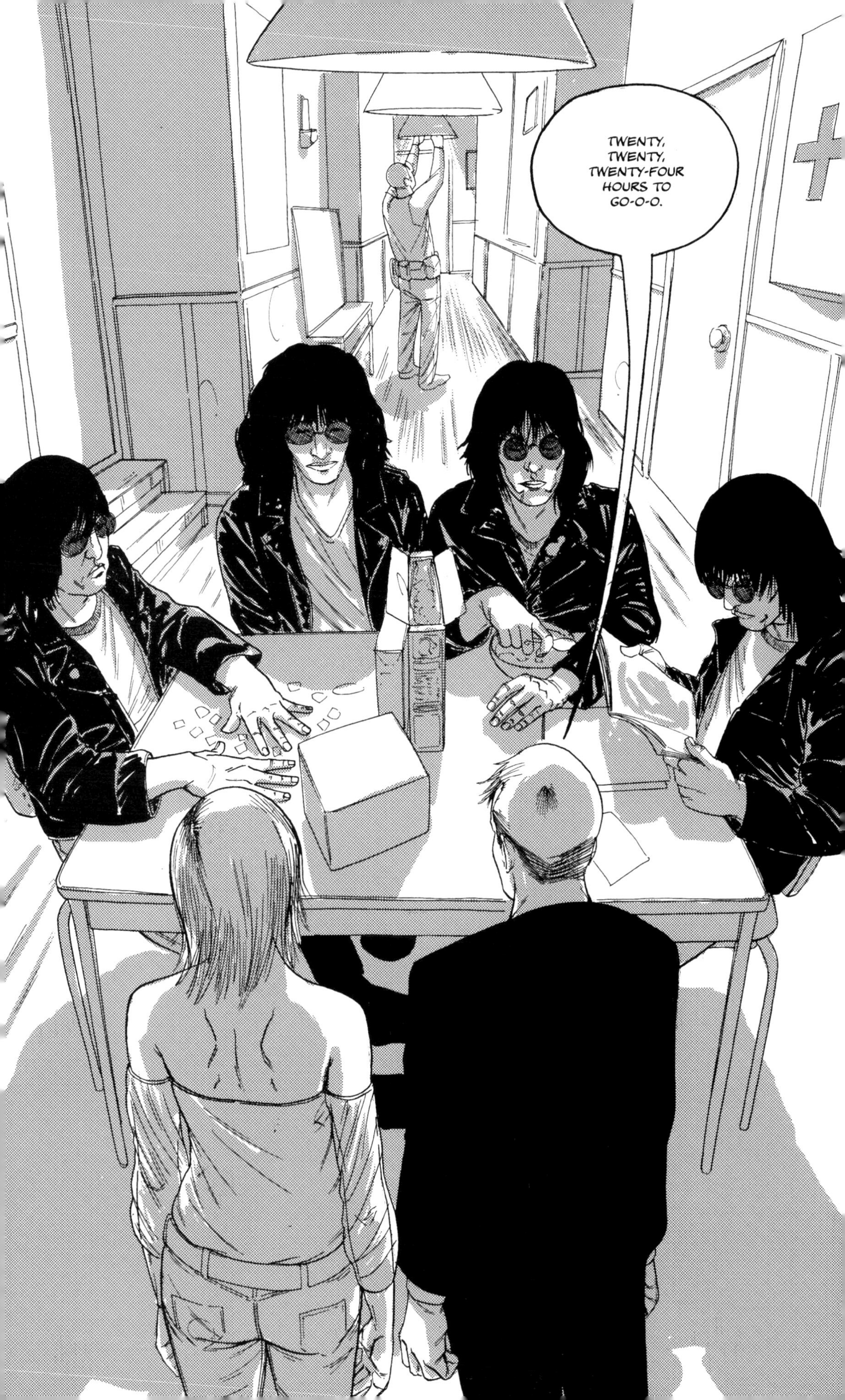
TWENTY, TWENTY, TWENTY-FOUR HOURS TO GO-O-O.

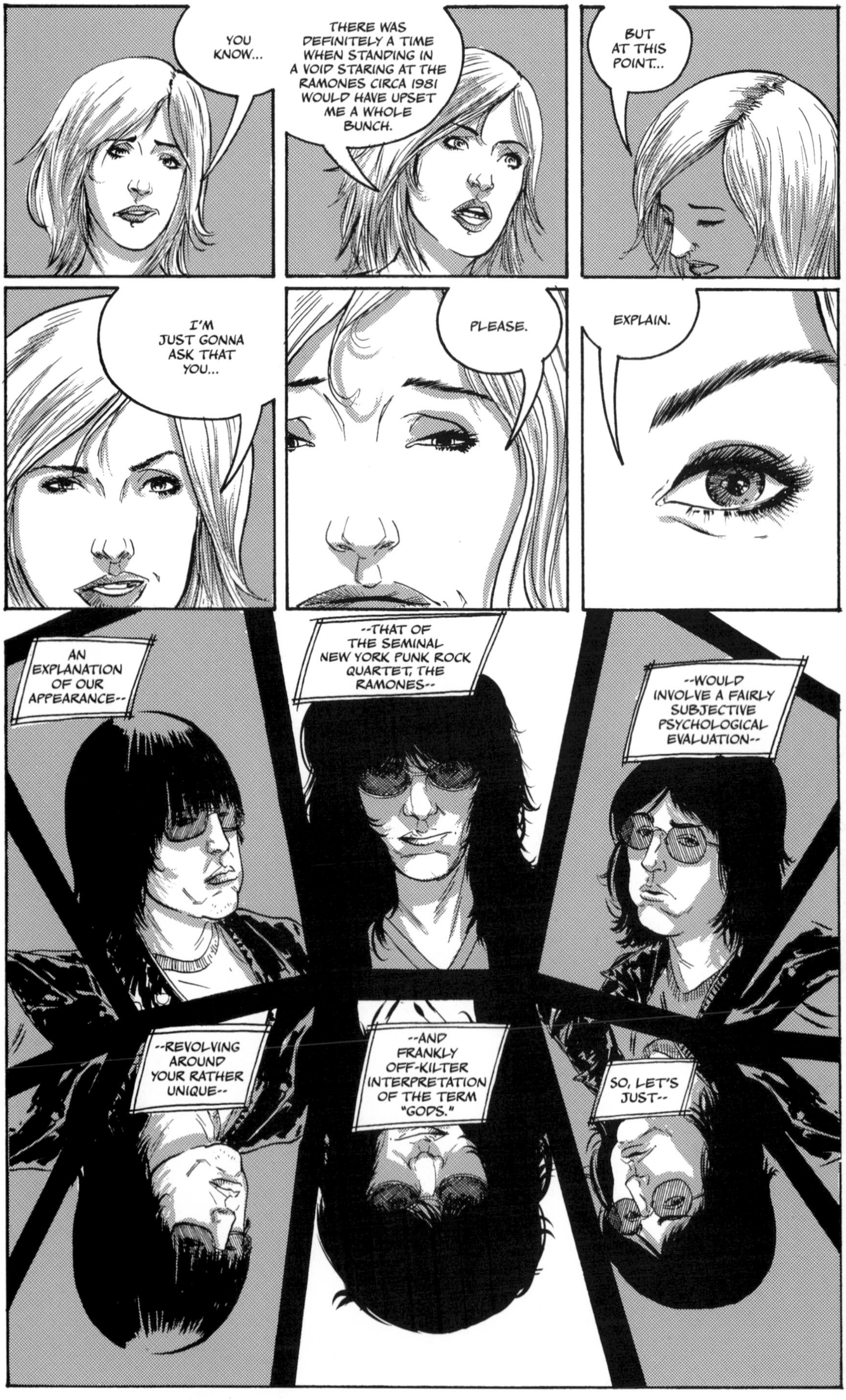
YOU KNOW...
THERE WAS DEFINITELY A TIME WHEN STANDING IN A VOID STARING AT THE RAMONES CIRCA 1981 WOULD HAVE UPSET ME A WHOLE BUNCH.
BUT AT THIS POINT...
I'M JUST GONNA ASK THAT YOU...
PLEASE.
EXPLAIN.
AN EXPLANATION OF OUR APPEARANCE--
--THAT OF THE SEMINAL NEW YORK PUNK ROCK QUARTET, THE RAMONES--
--WOULD INVOLVE A FAIRLY SUBJECTIVE PSYCHOLOGICAL EVALUATION--
--REVOLVING AROUND YOUR RATHER UNIQUE--
--AND FRANKLY OFF-KILTER INTERPRETATION OF THE TERM "GODS."
SO, LET'S JUST--

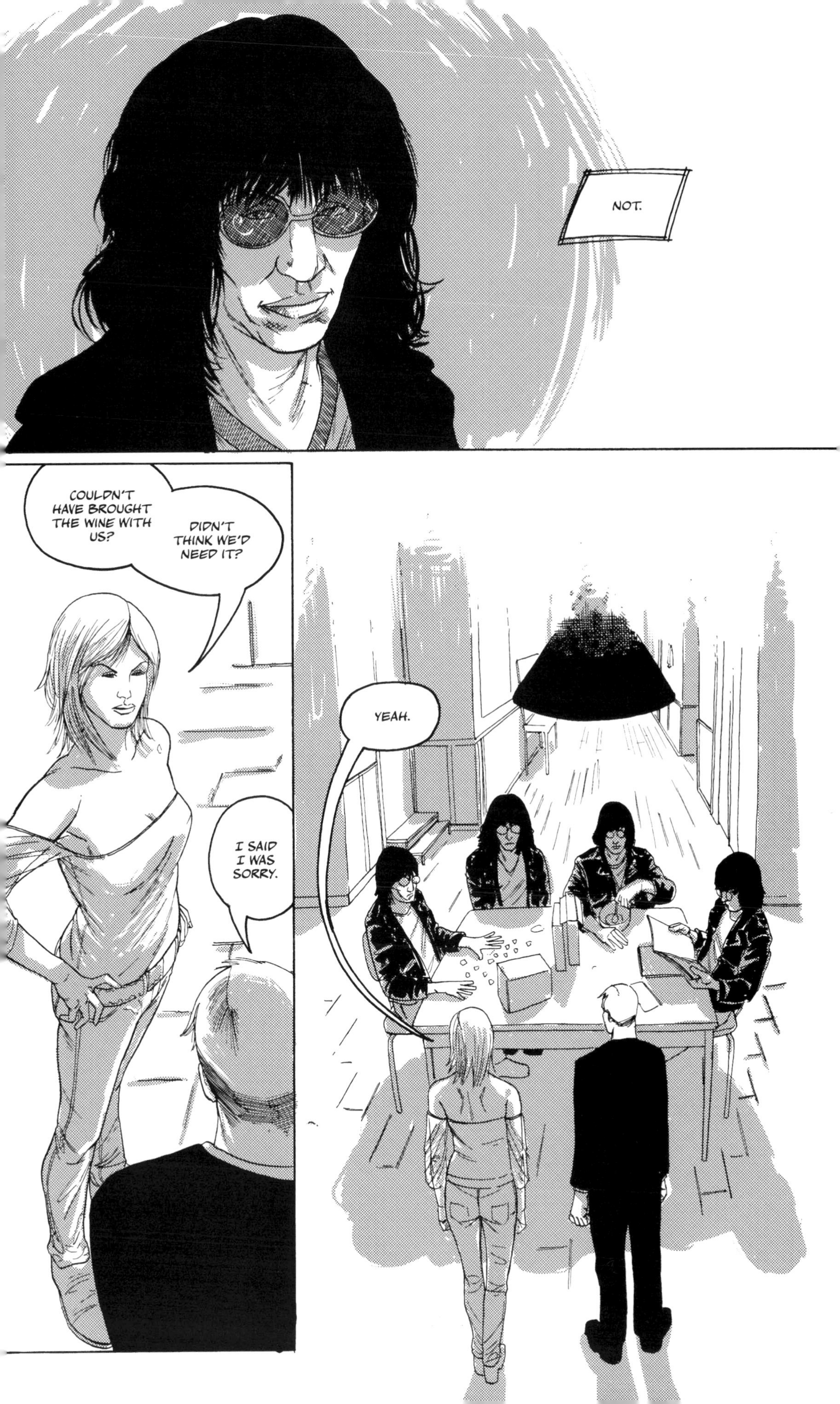
NOT.
COULDN'T HAVE BROUGHT THE WINE WITH US?
DIDN'T THINK WE'D NEED IT?
I SAID I WAS SORRY.
YEAH.

I'M SAYING I DON'T KNOW HOW TO MAKE A GIRL APPEAR OUT OF THE THIN AIR.

ANY SUGGESTIONS AS TO--

RIGHT.

FINE.

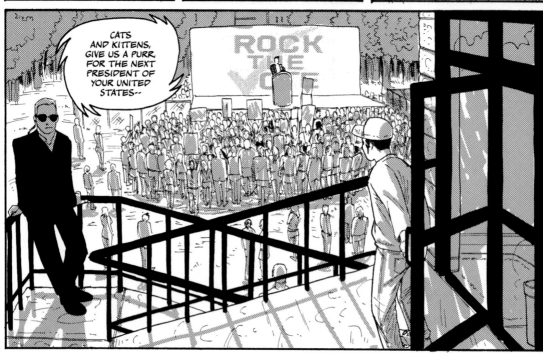

CATS AND KITTENS, GIVE US A PURR, FOR THE NEXT PRESIDENT OF YOUR UNITED STATES--

ROCK THE VOTE

--SENATOR DEREK GREY!

SHIT.

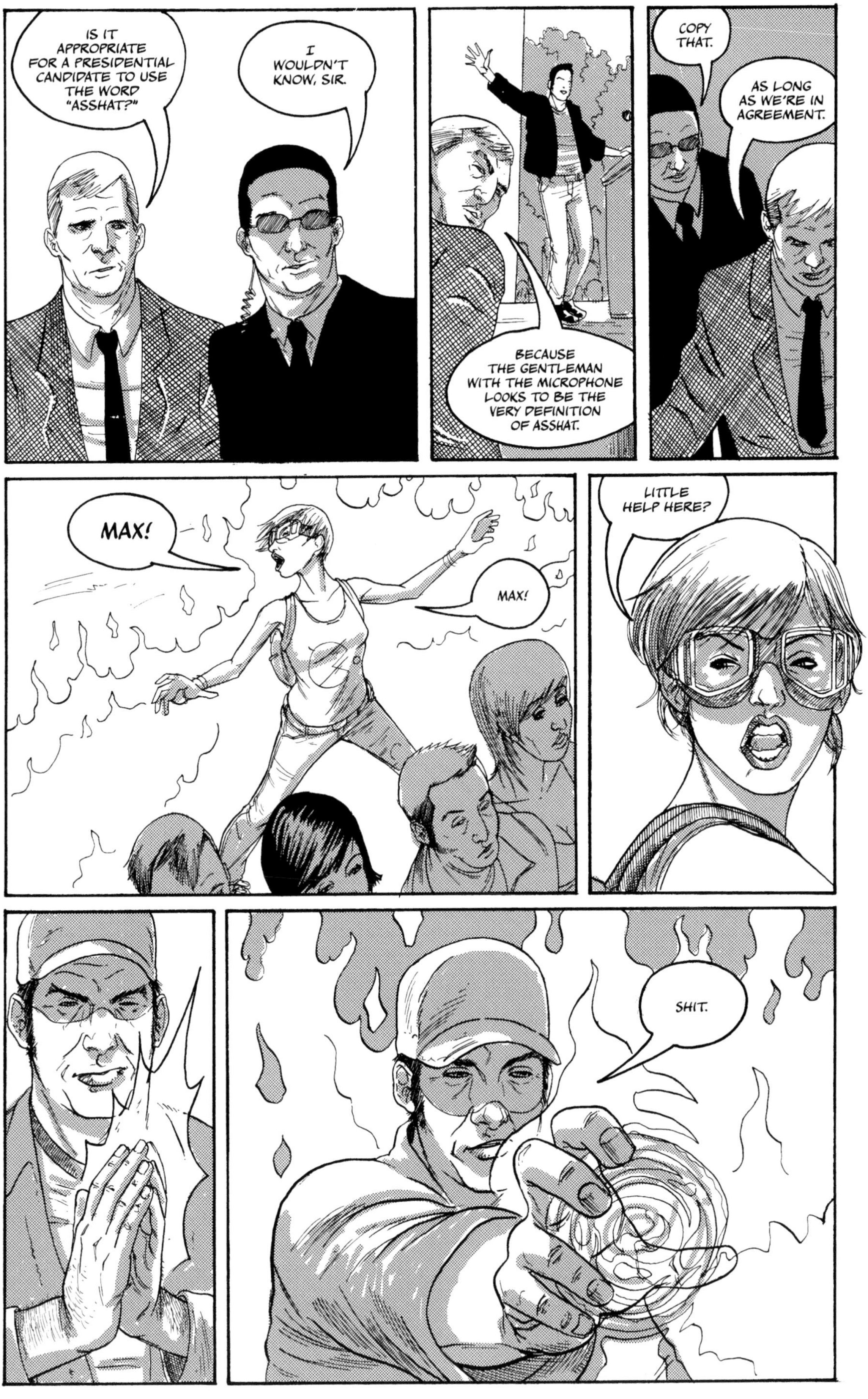
IS IT APPROPRIATE FOR A PRESIDENTIAL CANDIDATE TO USE THE WORD "ASSHAT?"
I WOULDN'T KNOW, SIR.
BECAUSE THE GENTLEMAN WITH THE MICROPHONE LOOKS TO BE THE VERY DEFINITION OF ASSHAT.
COPY THAT.
AS LONG AS WE'RE IN AGREEMENT.
MAX!
MAX!
LITTLE HELP HERE?
SHIT.

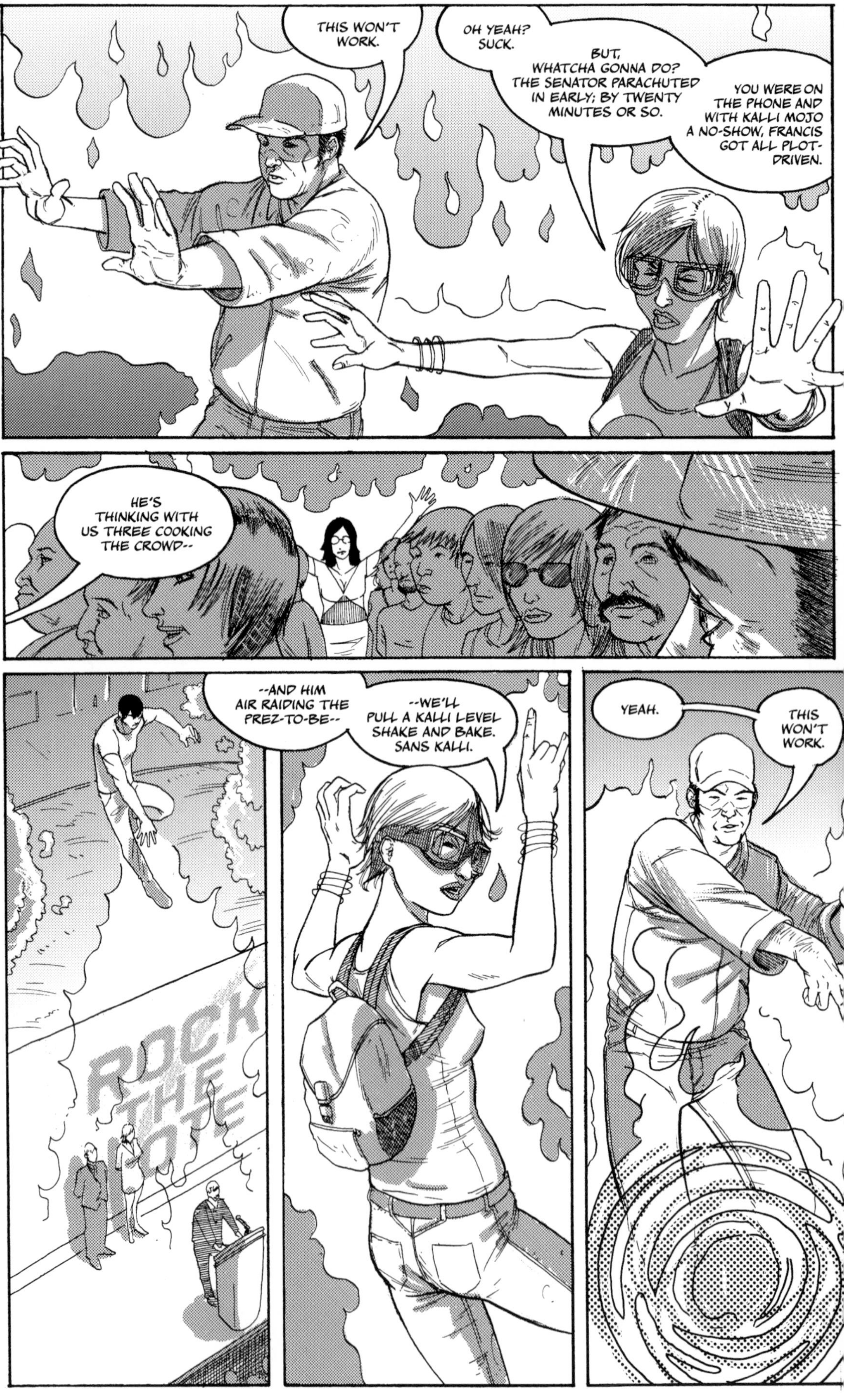
THIS WON'T WORK.
OH YEAH? SUCK.
BUT, WHATCHA GONNA DO? THE SENATOR PARACHUTED IN EARLY; BY TWENTY MINUTES OR SO.
YOU WERE ON THE PHONE AND WITH KALLI MOJO A NO-SHOW, FRANCIS GOT ALL PLOT-DRIVEN.
HE'S THINKING WITH US THREE COOKING THE CROWD--
--AND HIM AIR RAIDING THE PREZ-TO-BE--
--WE'LL PULL A KALLI LEVEL SHAKE AND BAKE. SANS KALLI.
ROCK THE VOTE
YEAH.
THIS WON'T WORK.

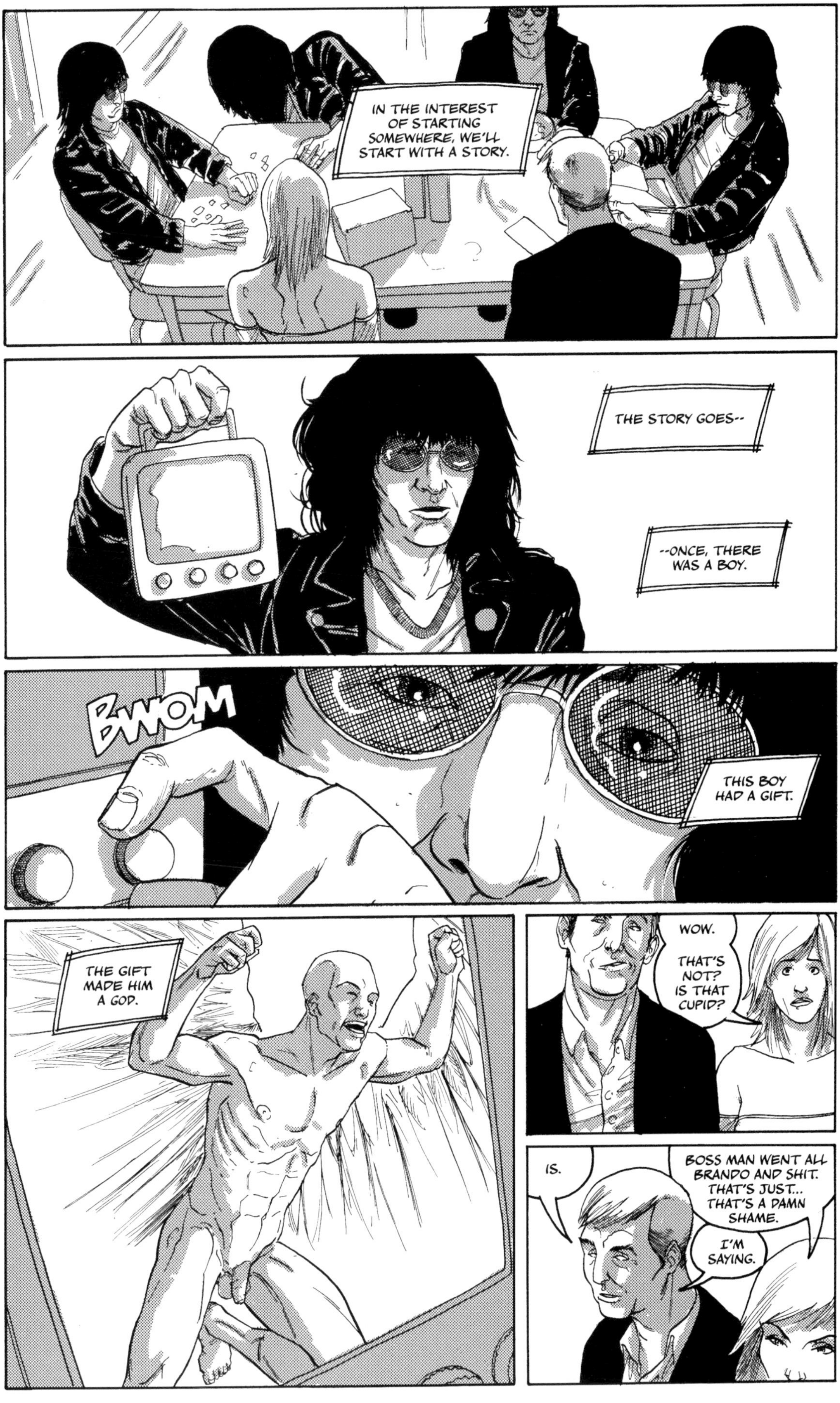
IN THE INTEREST OF STARTING SOMEWHERE, WE'LL START WITH A STORY.
THE STORY GOES--
--ONCE, THERE WAS A BOY.
BWOM
THIS BOY HAD A GIFT.
THE GIFT MADE HIM A GOD.
WOW.
THAT'S NOT? IS THAT CUPID?
IS.
BOSS MAN WENT ALL BRANDO AND SHIT. THAT'S JUST... THAT'S A DAMN SHAME.
I'M SAYING.

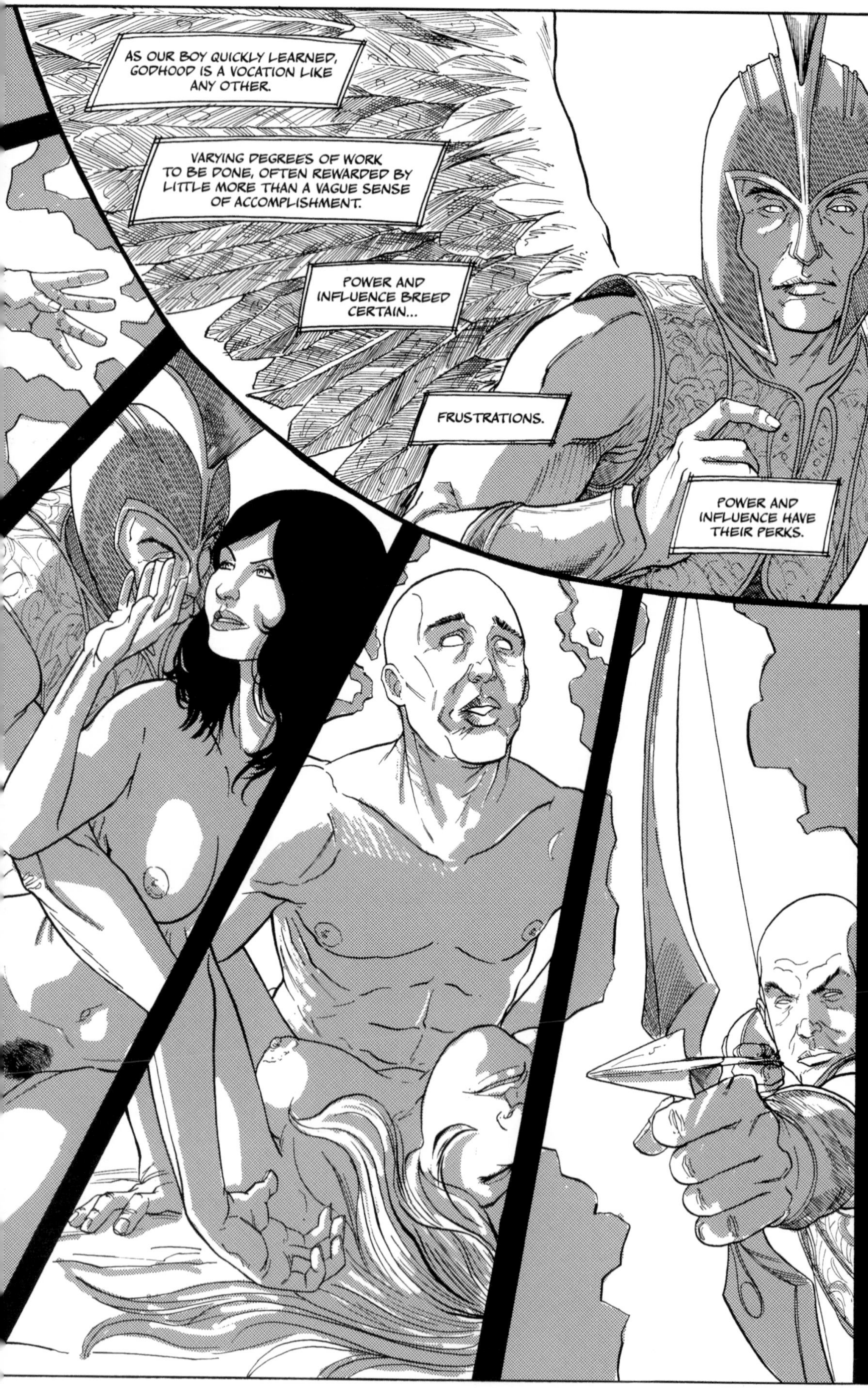
AS OUR BOY QUICKLY LEARNED, GODHOOD IS A VOCATION LIKE ANY OTHER.
VARYING DEGREES OF WORK TO BE DONE, OFTEN REWARDED BY LITTLE MORE THAN A VAGUE SENSE OF ACCOMPLISHMENT.
POWER AND INFLUENCE BREED CERTAIN...
FRUSTRATIONS.
POWER AND INFLUENCE HAVE THEIR PERKS.

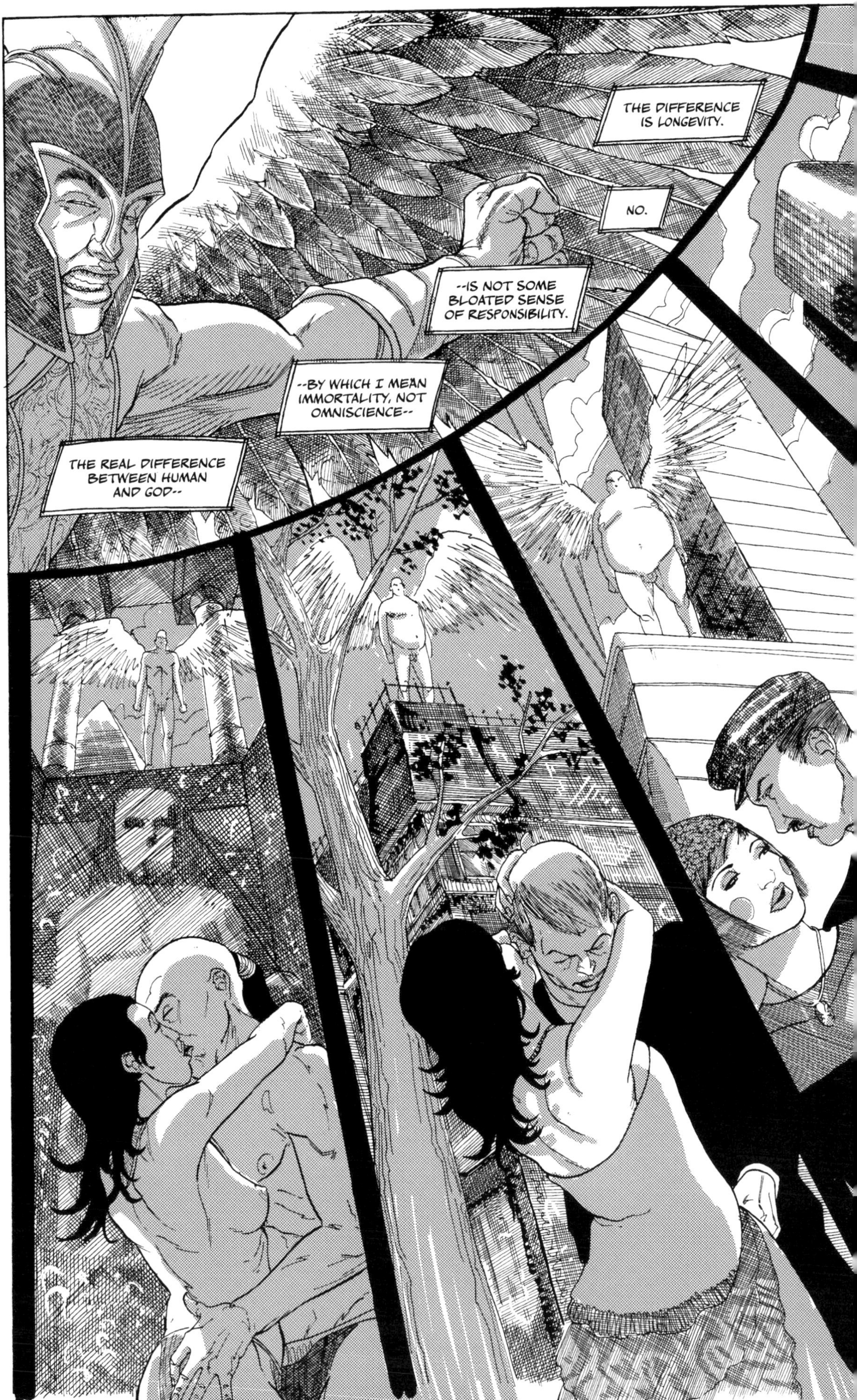
THE REAL DIFFERENCE BETWEEN HUMAN AND GOD--
--BY WHICH I MEAN IMMORTALITY, NOT OMNISCIENCE--
--IS NOT SOME BLOATED SENSE OF RESPONSIBILITY.
NO.
THE DIFFERENCE IS LONGEVITY.

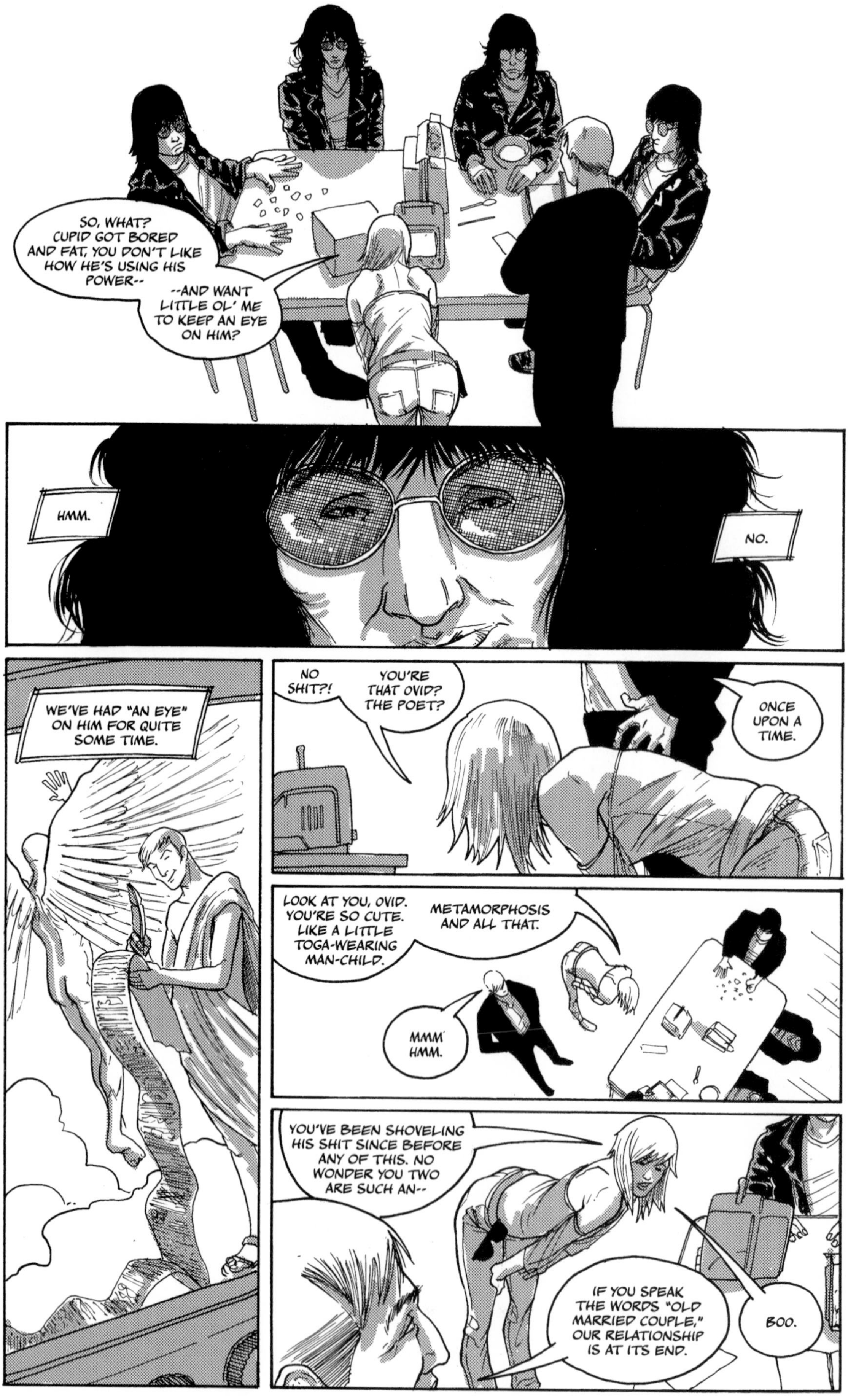
SO, WHAT? CUPID GOT BORED AND FAT, YOU DON'T LIKE HOW HE'S USING HIS POWER--
--AND WANT LITTLE OL' ME TO KEEP AN EYE ON HIM?
HMM.
NO.
WE'VE HAD "AN EYE" ON HIM FOR QUITE SOME TIME.
NO SHIT?!
YOU'RE THAT OVID? THE POET?
ONCE UPON A TIME.
LOOK AT YOU, OVID. YOU'RE SO CUTE. LIKE A LITTLE TOGA-WEARING MAN-CHILD.
METAMORPHOSIS AND ALL THAT.
MMM HMM.
YOU'VE BEEN SHOVELING HIS SHIT SINCE BEFORE ANY OF THIS. NO WONDER YOU TWO ARE SUCH AN--
IF YOU SPEAK THE WORDS "OLD MARRIED COUPLE," OUR RELATIONSHIP IS AT ITS END.
BOO.

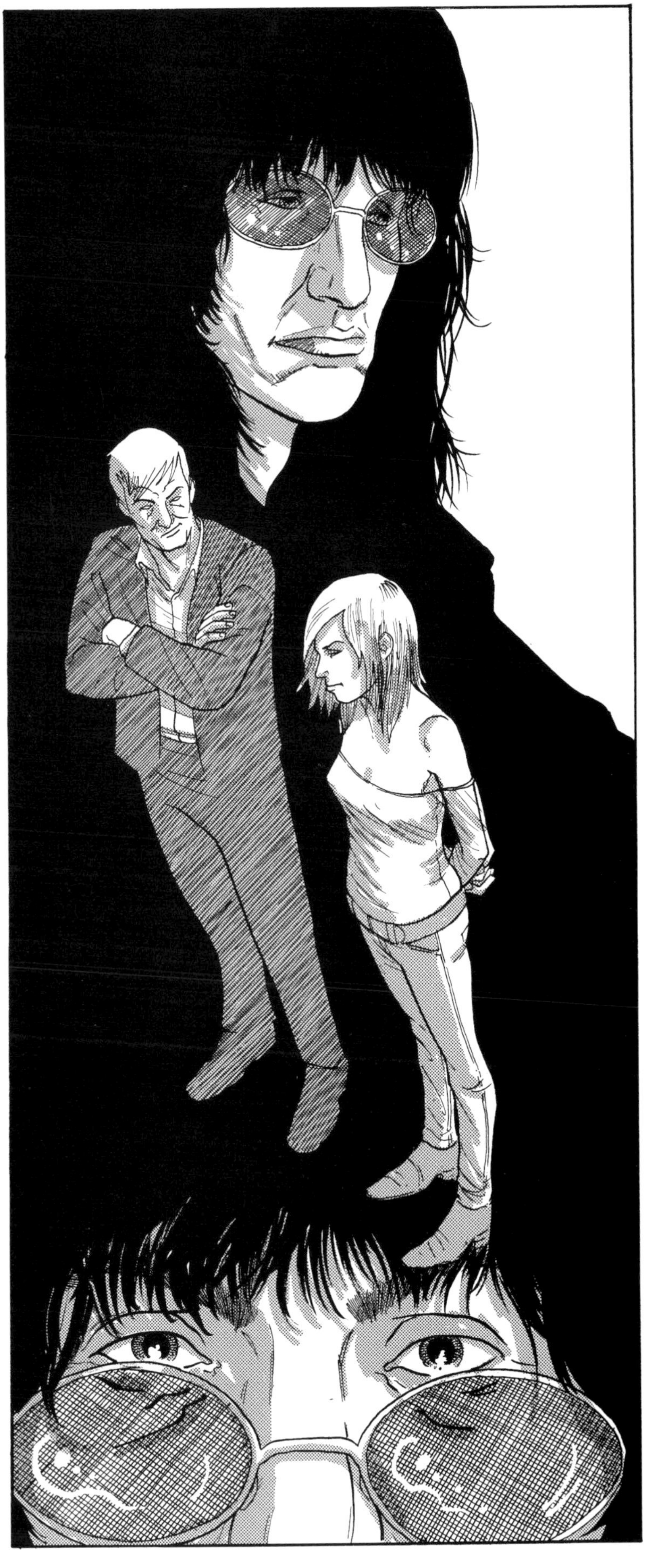

Ahem.

Sorry

As I was saying, Ovid has been our eyes and ears. YOUR role, however--

IS TO BE SLIGHTLY MORE INVOLVED.

AHHH!

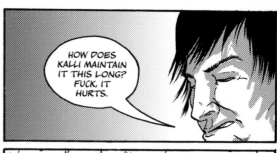

HOW DOES KALLI MAINTAIN IT THIS LONG? FUCK, IT HURTS.

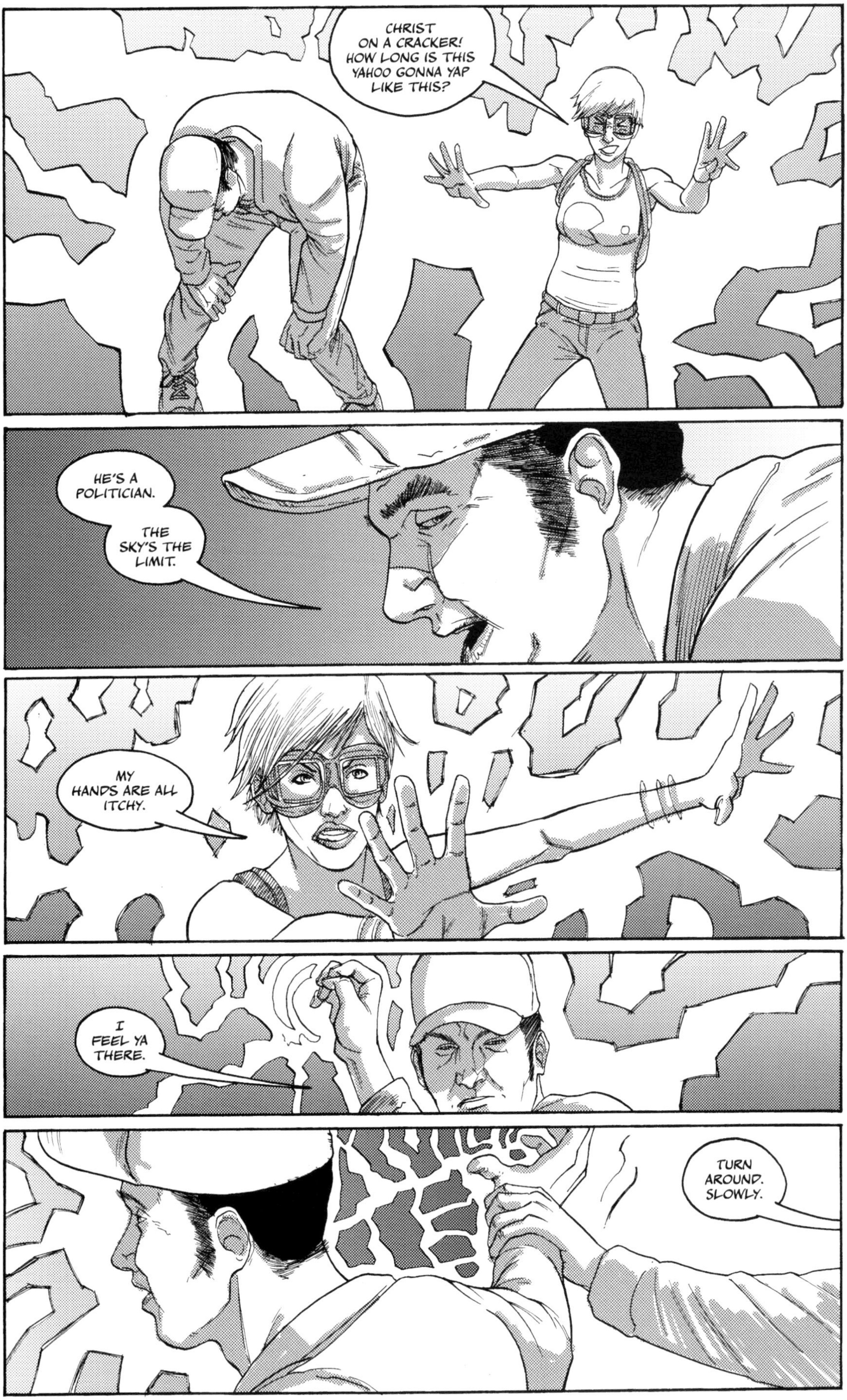
CHRIST ON A CRACKER! HOW LONG IS THIS YAHOO GONNA YAP LIKE THIS?
HE'S A POLITICIAN.
THE SKY'S THE LIMIT.
MY HANDS ARE ALL ITCHY.
I FEEL YA THERE.
TURN AROUND. SLOWLY.

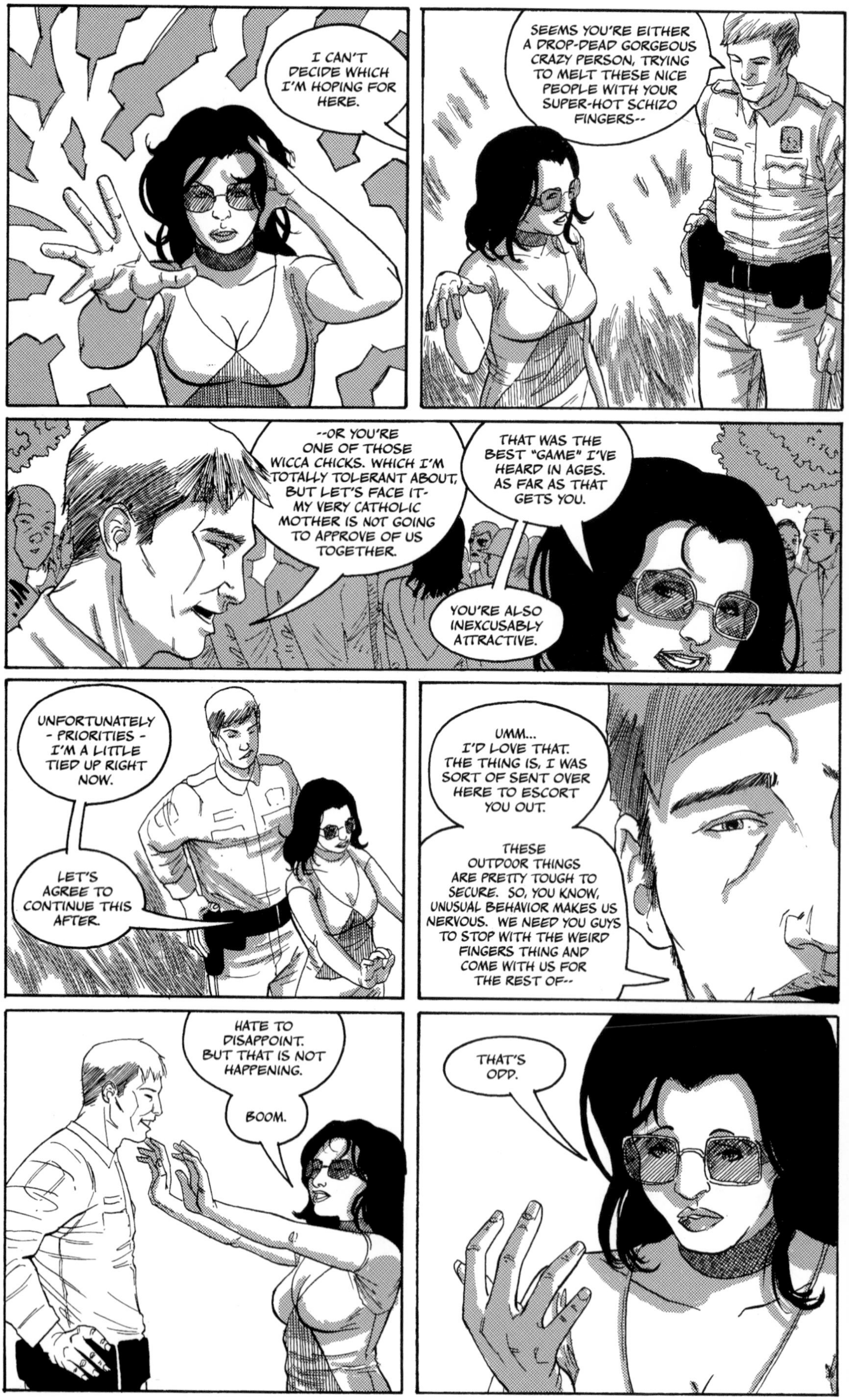
I CAN'T DECIDE WHICH I'M HOPING FOR HERE.
SEEMS YOU'RE EITHER A DROP-DEAD GORGEOUS CRAZY PERSON, TRYING TO MELT THESE NICE PEOPLE WITH YOUR SUPER-HOT SCHIZO FINGERS--
--OR YOU'RE ONE OF THOSE WICCA CHICKS. WHICH I'M TOTALLY TOLERANT ABOUT, BUT LET'S FACE IT- MY VERY CATHOLIC MOTHER IS NOT GOING TO APPROVE OF US TOGETHER.
THAT WAS THE BEST "GAME" I'VE HEARD IN AGES. AS FAR AS THAT GETS YOU.
YOU'RE ALSO INEXCUSABLY ATTRACTIVE.
UNFORTUNATELY - PRIORITIES - I'M A LITTLE TIED UP RIGHT NOW.
LET'S AGREE TO CONTINUE THIS AFTER.
UMM... I'D LOVE THAT. THE THING IS, I WAS SORT OF SENT OVER HERE TO ESCORT YOU OUT.
THESE OUTDOOR THINGS ARE PRETTY TOUGH TO SECURE. SO, YOU KNOW, UNUSUAL BEHAVIOR MAKES US NERVOUS. WE NEED YOU GUYS TO STOP WITH THE WEIRD FINGERS THING AND COME WITH US FOR THE REST OF--
HATE TO DISAPPOINT. BUT THAT IS NOT HAPPENING.
BOOM.
THAT'S ODD.

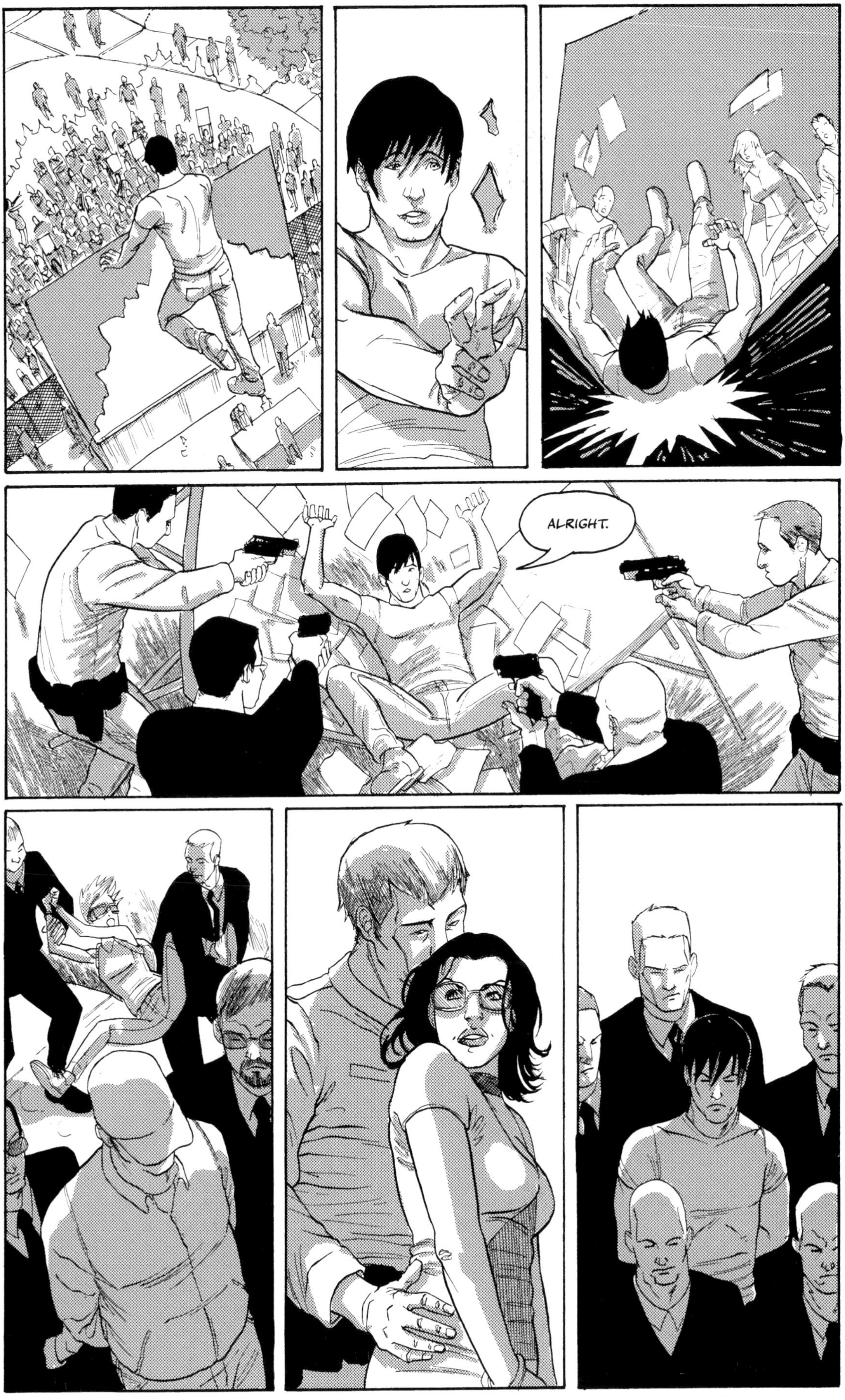
ALRIGHT.

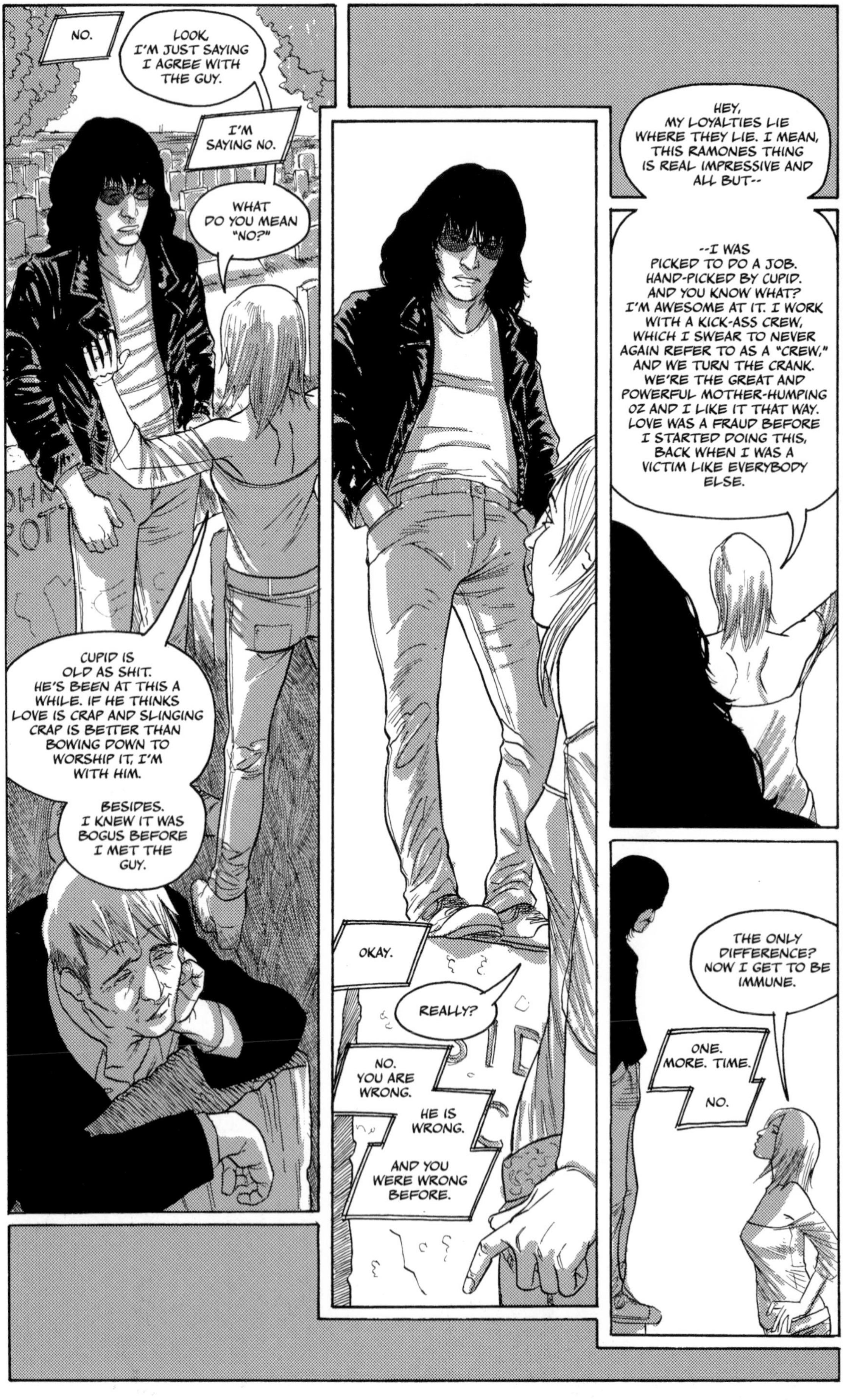
NO.
LOOK, I'M JUST SAYING I AGREE WITH THE GUY.
I'M SAYING NO.
WHAT DO YOU MEAN "NO?"
CUPID IS OLD AS SHIT. HE'S BEEN AT THIS A WHILE. IF HE THINKS LOVE IS CRAP AND SLINGING CRAP IS BETTER THAN BOWING DOWN TO WORSHIP IT, I'M WITH HIM.
BESIDES. I KNEW IT WAS BOGUS BEFORE I MET THE GUY.
OKAY.
REALLY?
NO. YOU ARE WRONG.
HE IS WRONG.
AND YOU WERE WRONG BEFORE.
HEY, MY LOYALTIES LIE WHERE THEY LIE. I MEAN, THIS RAMONES THING IS REAL IMPRESSIVE AND ALL BUT--
--I WAS PICKED TO DO A JOB. HAND-PICKED BY CUPID. AND YOU KNOW WHAT? I'M AWESOME AT IT. I WORK WITH A KICK-ASS CREW, WHICH I SWEAR TO NEVER AGAIN REFER TO AS A "CREW," AND WE TURN THE CRANK. WE'RE THE GREAT AND POWERFUL MOTHER-HUMPING OZ AND I LIKE IT THAT WAY. LOVE WAS A FRAUD BEFORE I STARTED DOING THIS, BACK WHEN I WAS A VICTIM LIKE EVERYBODY ELSE.
THE ONLY DIFFERENCE? NOW I GET TO BE IMMUNE.
ONE. MORE. TIME.
NO.

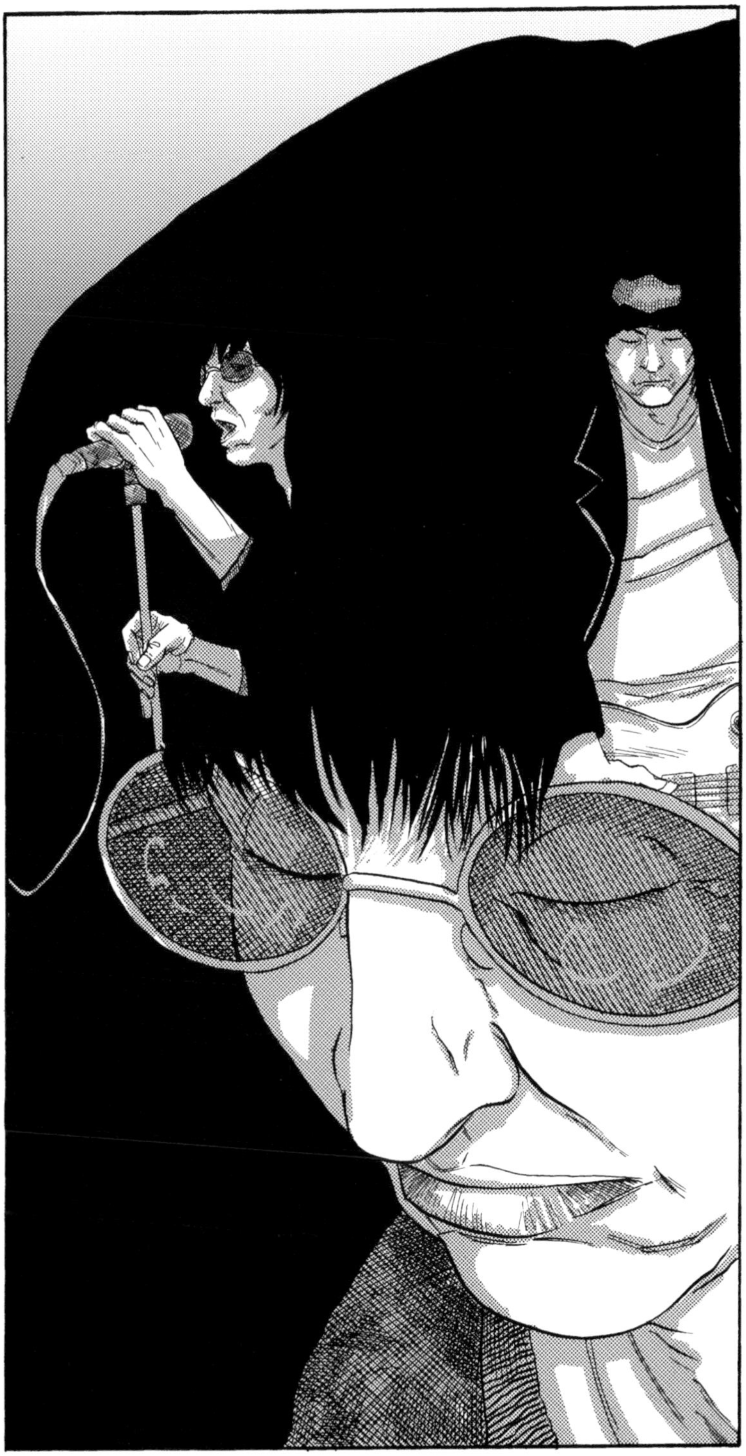

Cupid did NOT choose you.

You WERE chosen.

Not by him.

Love is a natural order. One of many. It is pure and it is vital. Love is one of the very few things without which humanity CANNOT prosper.

So, I'm sorry but you are wrong.

I grant you this, love HAS been corrupted. It has become an instrument of gluttony and obsession. It fuels a society of excess and it ruins lives.

All of which is Cupid's doing. It was his responsibility and IS his failure.

The LOVE that you know.

The world in which you live.

ALL Cupid.

Who do we blame, the gun or the gunman?

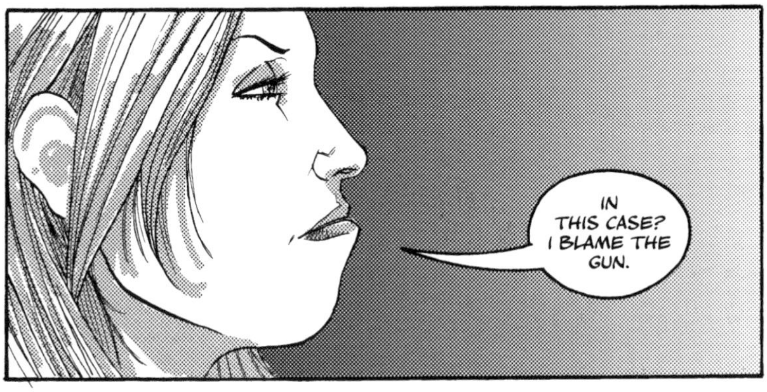
IN THIS CASE? I BLAME THE GUN.

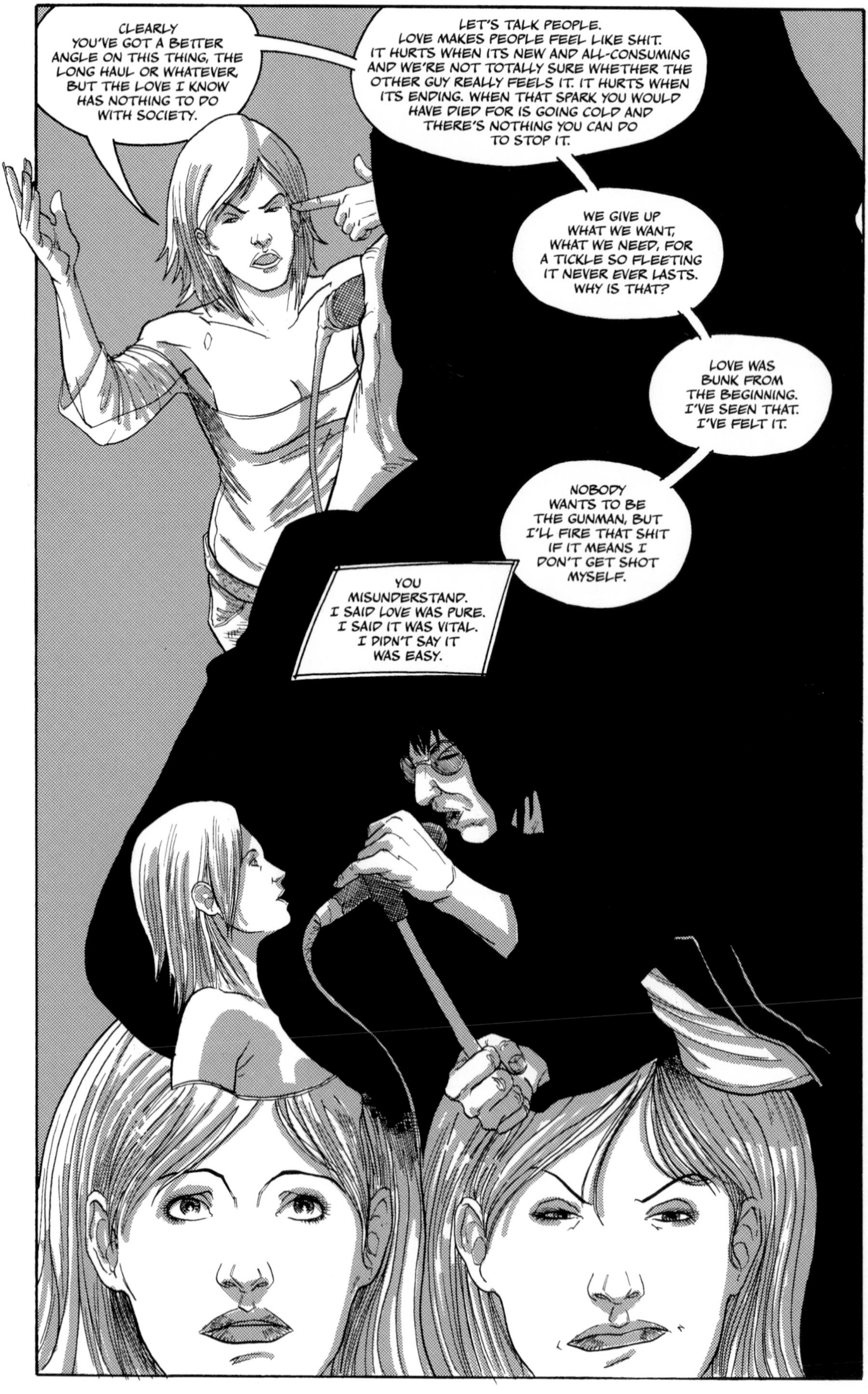
CLEARLY YOU'VE GOT A BETTER ANGLE ON THIS THING, THE LONG HAUL OR WHATEVER, BUT THE LOVE I KNOW HAS NOTHING TO DO WITH SOCIETY.
LET'S TALK PEOPLE. LOVE MAKES PEOPLE FEEL LIKE SHIT. IT HURTS WHEN ITS NEW AND ALL-CONSUMING AND WE'RE NOT TOTALLY SURE WHETHER THE OTHER GUY REALLY FEELS IT. IT HURTS WHEN ITS ENDING. WHEN THAT SPARK YOU WOULD HAVE DIED FOR IS GOING COLD AND THERE'S NOTHING YOU CAN DO TO STOP IT.
WE GIVE UP WHAT WE WANT, WHAT WE NEED, FOR A TICKLE SO FLEETING IT NEVER EVER LASTS. WHY IS THAT?
LOVE WAS BUNK FROM THE BEGINNING. I'VE SEEN THAT. I'VE FELT IT.
NOBODY WANTS TO BE THE GUNMAN, BUT I'LL FIRE THAT SHIT IF IT MEANS I DON'T GET SHOT MYSELF.
YOU MISUNDERSTAND. I SAID LOVE WAS PURE. I SAID IT WAS VITAL. I DIDN'T SAY IT WAS EASY.

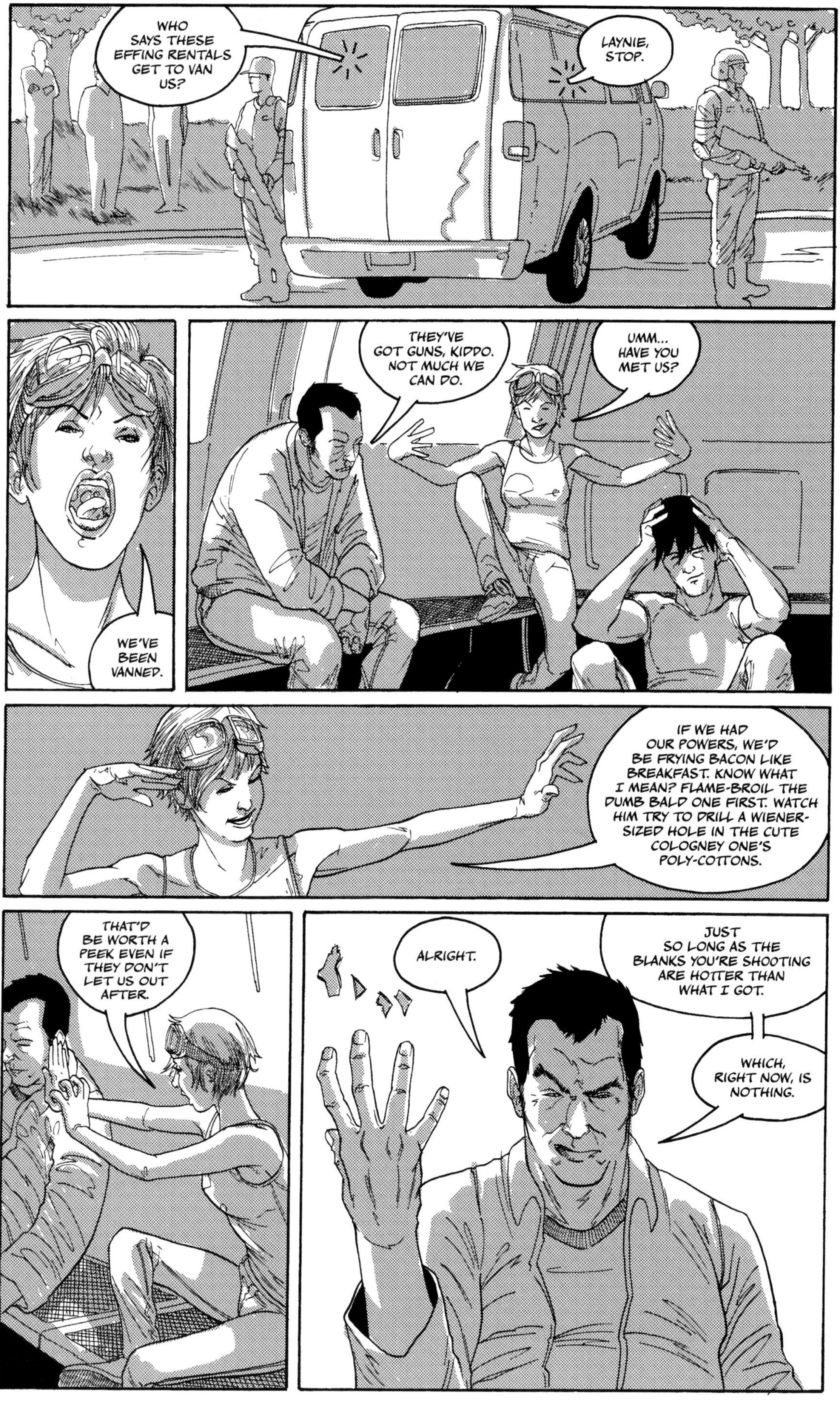
WHO SAYS THESE EFFING RENTALS GET TO VAN US?
LAYNIE, STOP.
WE'VE BEEN VANNED.
THEY'VE GOT GUNS, KIDDO. NOT MUCH WE CAN DO.
UMM... HAVE YOU MET US?
IF WE HAD OUR POWERS, WE'D BE FRYING BACON LIKE BREAKFAST. KNOW WHAT I MEAN? FLAME-BROIL THE DUMB BALD ONE FIRST. WATCH HIM TRY TO DRILL A WIENER-SIZED HOLE IN THE CUTE COLOGNEY ONE'S POLY-COTTONS.
THAT'D BE WORTH A PEEK EVEN IF THEY DON'T LET US OUT AFTER.
ALRIGHT.
JUST SO LONG AS THE BLANKS YOU'RE SHOOTING ARE HOTTER THAN WHAT I GOT.
WHICH, RIGHT NOW, IS NOTHING.

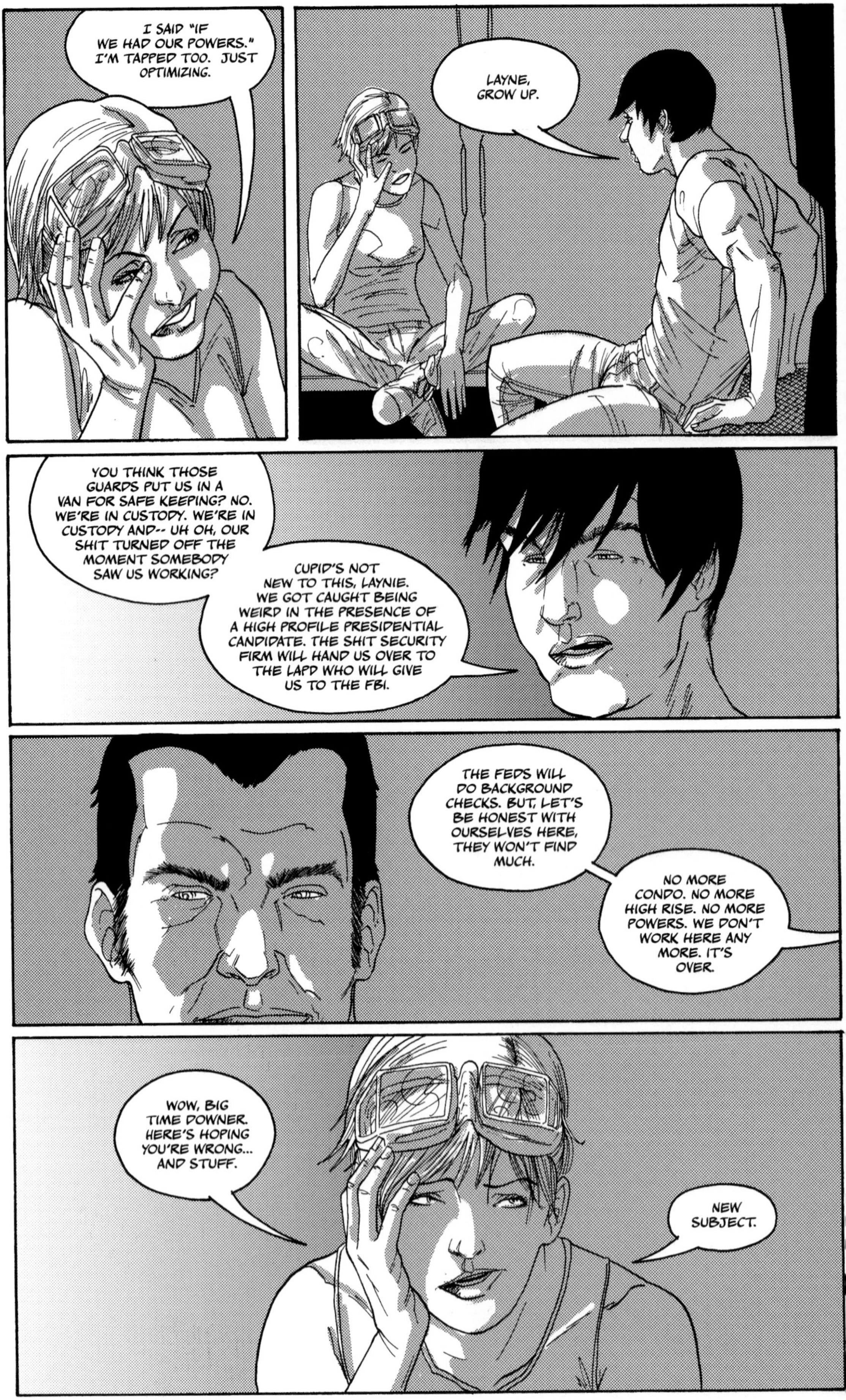
I SAID "IF WE HAD OUR POWERS." I'M TAPPED TOO. JUST OPTIMIZING.
LAYNE, GROW UP.
YOU THINK THOSE GUARDS PUT US IN A VAN FOR SAFE KEEPING? NO. WE'RE IN CUSTODY. WE'RE IN CUSTODY AND-- UH OH, OUR SHIT TURNED OFF THE MOMENT SOMEBODY SAW US WORKING?
CUPID'S NOT NEW TO THIS, LAYNIE. WE GOT CAUGHT BEING WEIRD IN THE PRESENCE OF A HIGH PROFILE PRESIDENTIAL CANDIDATE. THE SHIT SECURITY FIRM WILL HAND US OVER TO THE LAPD WHO WILL GIVE US TO THE FBI.
THE FEDS WILL DO BACKGROUND CHECKS. BUT, LET'S BE HONEST WITH OURSELVES HERE, THEY WON'T FIND MUCH.
NO MORE CONDO. NO MORE HIGH RISE. NO MORE POWERS. WE DON'T WORK HERE ANY MORE. IT'S OVER.
WOW, BIG TIME DOWNER. HERE'S HOPING YOU'RE WRONG... AND STUFF.
NEW SUBJECT.

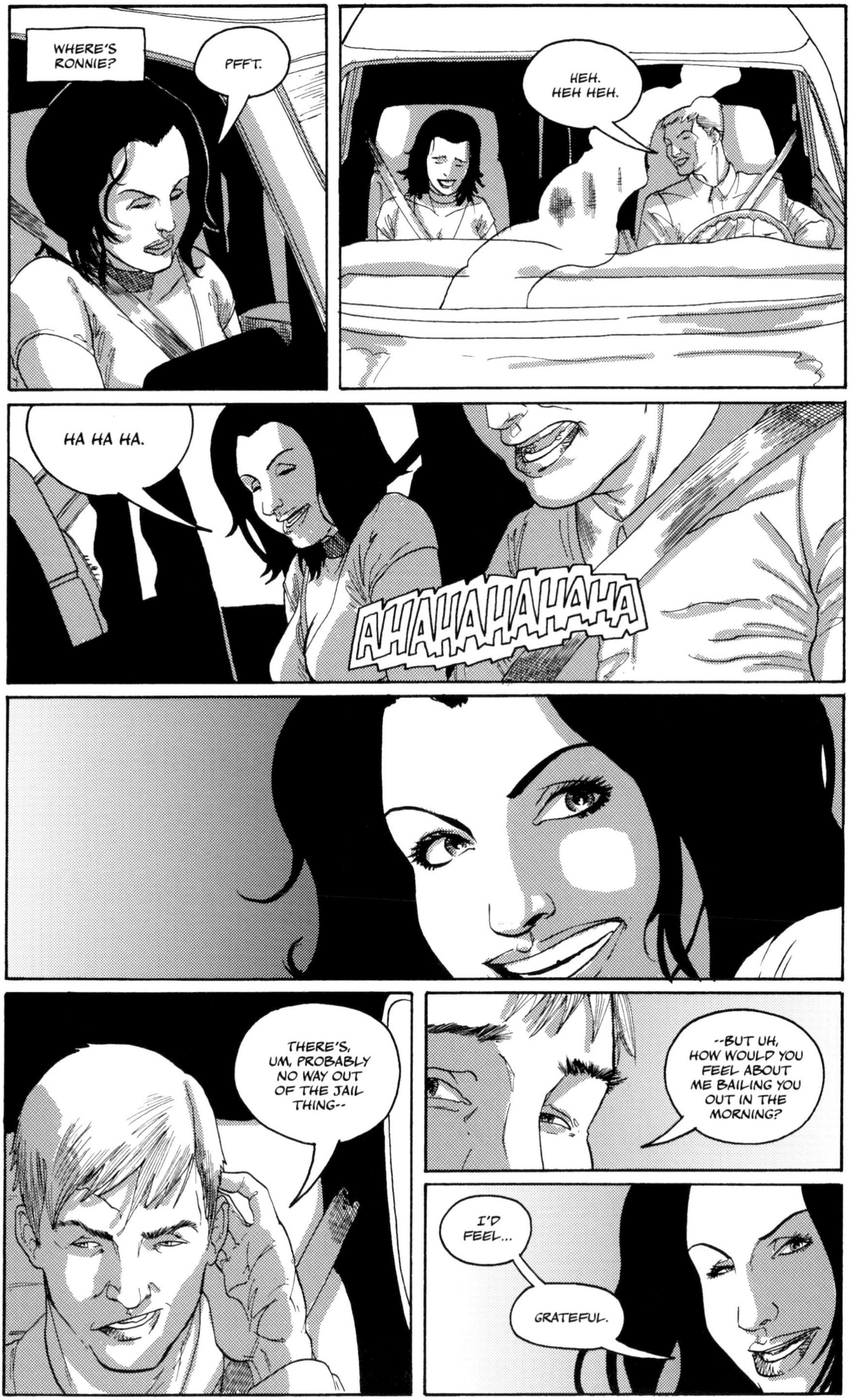
WHERE'S RONNIE?
PFFT.
HEH. HEH HEH.
HA HA HA.
AHAHAHAHAHA
THERE'S, UM, PROBABLY NO WAY OUT OF THE JAIL THING--
--BUT UH, HOW WOULD YOU FEEL ABOUT ME BAILING YOU OUT IN THE MORNING?
I'D FEEL...
GRATEFUL.

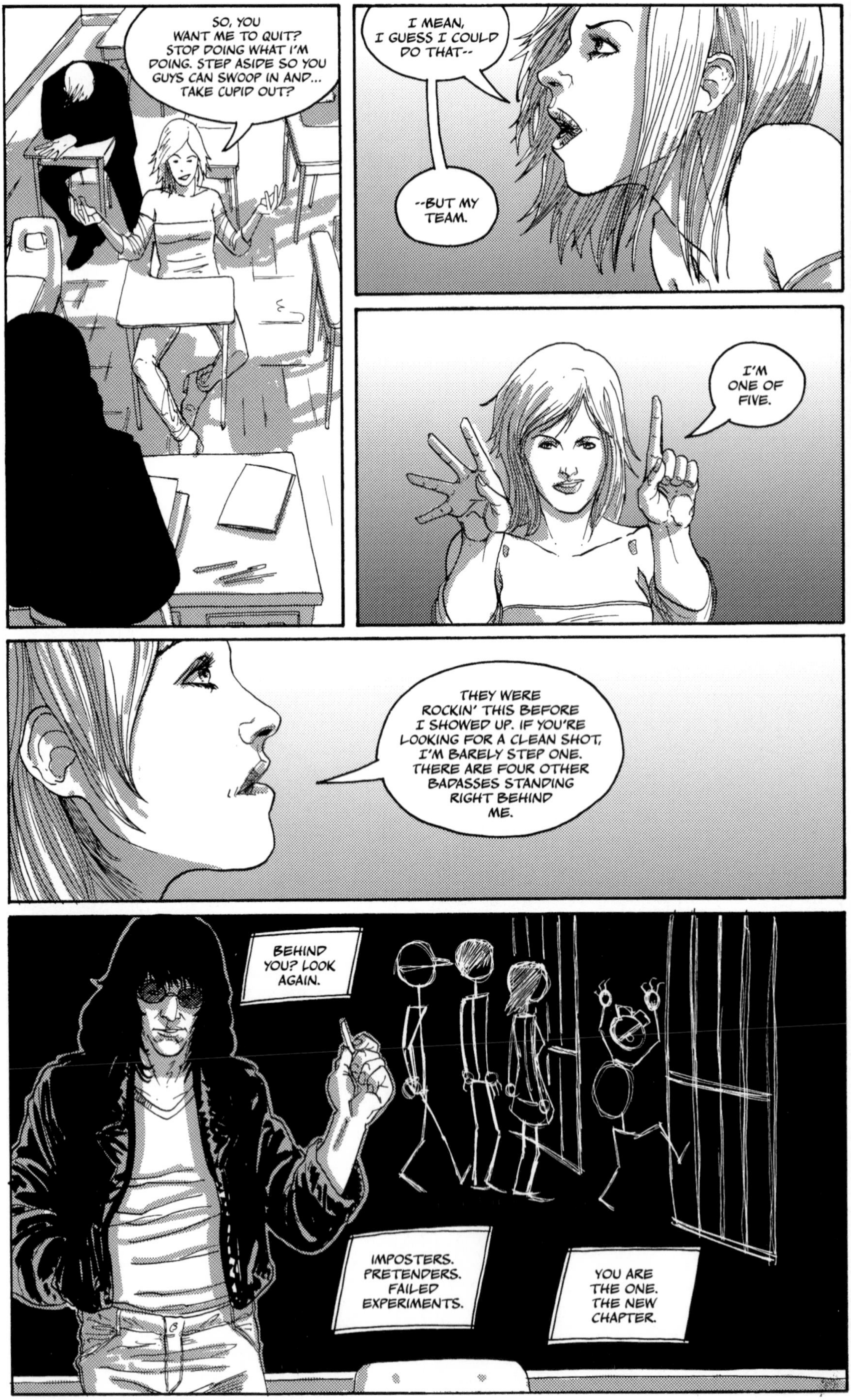

SO, YOU WANT ME TO QUIT? STOP DOING WHAT I'M DOING. STEP ASIDE SO YOU GUYS CAN SWOOP IN AND... TAKE CUPID OUT?
I MEAN, I GUESS I COULD DO THAT--
--BUT MY TEAM.
I'M ONE OF FIVE.
THEY WERE ROCKIN' THIS BEFORE I SHOWED UP. IF YOU'RE LOOKING FOR A CLEAN SHOT, I'M BARELY STEP ONE. THERE ARE FOUR OTHER BADASSES STANDING RIGHT BEHIND ME.
BEHIND YOU? LOOK AGAIN.
IMPOSTERS. PRETENDERS. FAILED EXPERIMENTS.
YOU ARE THE ONE. THE NEW CHAPTER.

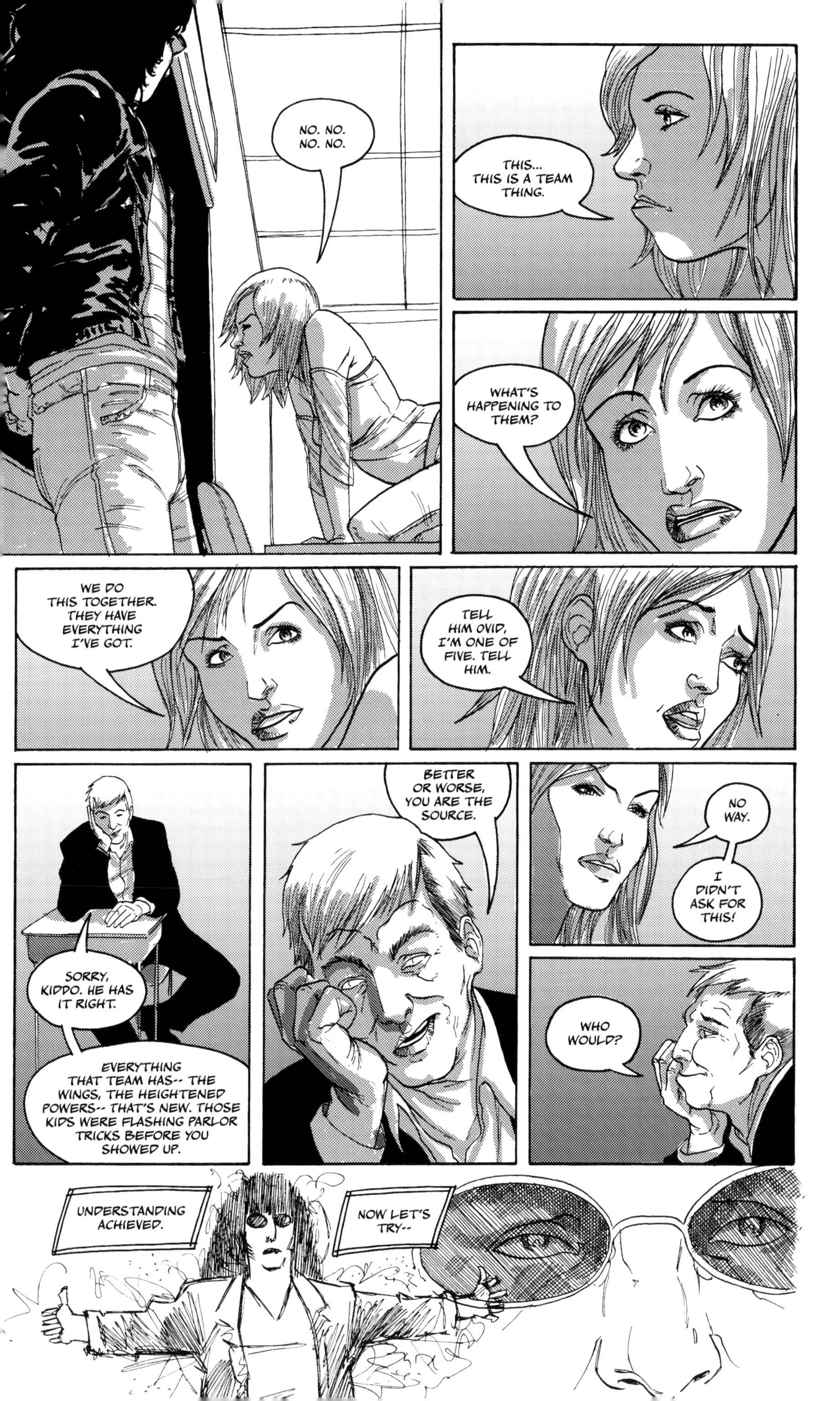
NO. NO. NO. NO.
THIS... THIS IS A TEAM THING.
WHAT'S HAPPENING TO THEM?
WE DO THIS TOGETHER. THEY HAVE EVERYTHING I'VE GOT.
TELL HIM OVID, I'M ONE OF FIVE. TELL HIM.
SORRY, KIDDO. HE HAS IT RIGHT.
EVERYTHING THAT TEAM HAS-- THE WINGS, THE HEIGHTENED POWERS-- THAT'S NEW. THOSE KIDS WERE FLASHING PARLOR TRICKS BEFORE YOU SHOWED UP.
BETTER OR WORSE, YOU ARE THE SOURCE.
NO WAY.
I DIDN'T ASK FOR THIS!
WHO WOULD?
UNDERSTANDING ACHIEVED.
NOW LET'S TRY--

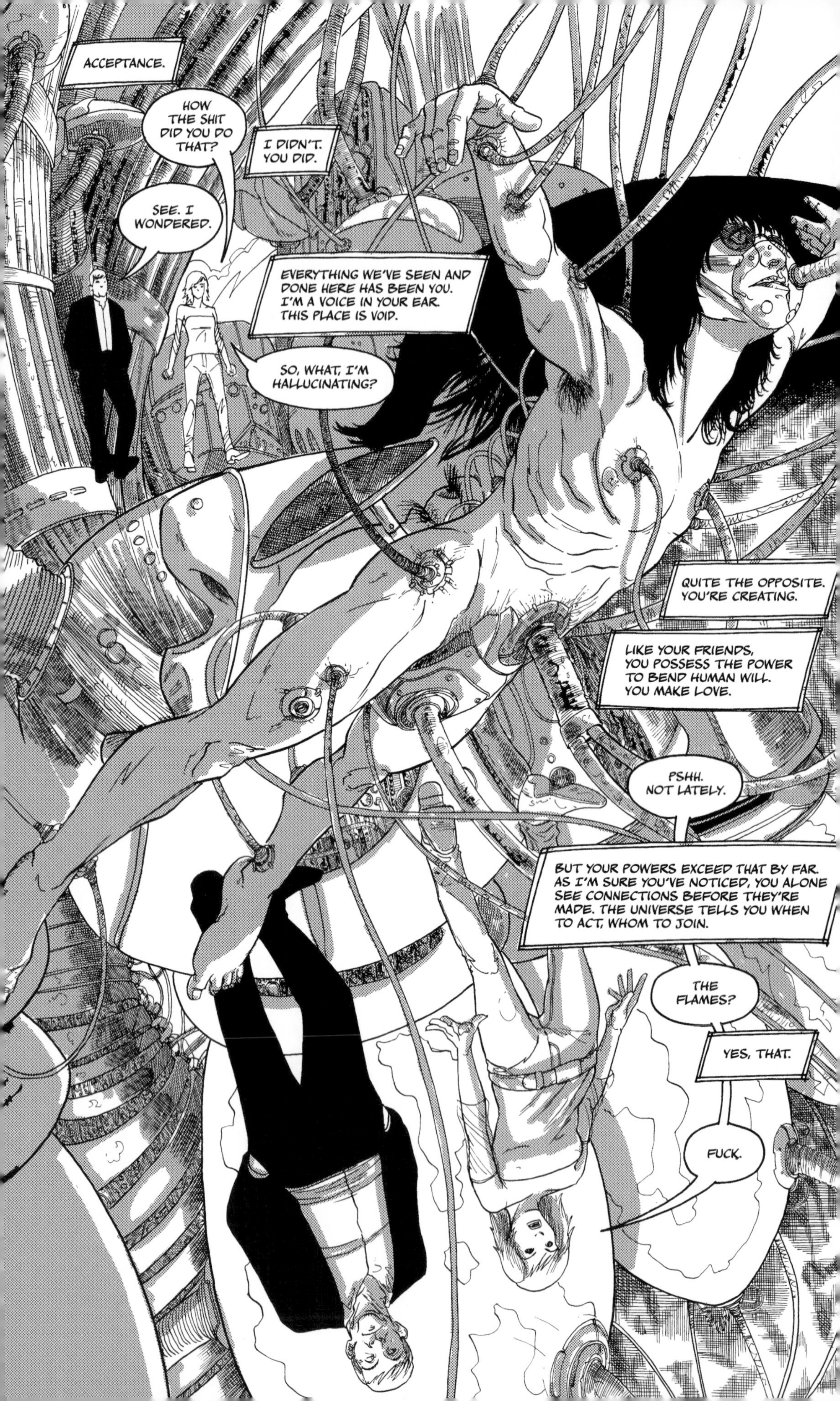
ACCEPTANCE.
HOW THE SHIT DID YOU DO THAT?
I DIDN'T. YOU DID.
SEE. I WONDERED.
EVERYTHING WE'VE SEEN AND DONE HERE HAS BEEN YOU. I'M A VOICE IN YOUR EAR. THIS PLACE IS VOID.
SO, WHAT, I'M HALLUCINATING?
QUITE THE OPPOSITE. YOU'RE CREATING.
LIKE YOUR FRIENDS, YOU POSSESS THE POWER TO BEND HUMAN WILL. YOU MAKE LOVE.
PSHH. NOT LATELY.
BUT YOUR POWERS EXCEED THAT BY FAR. AS I'M SURE YOU'VE NOTICED, YOU ALONE SEE CONNECTIONS BEFORE THEY'RE MADE. THE UNIVERSE TELLS YOU WHEN TO ACT, WHOM TO JOIN.
THE FLAMES?
YES, THAT.
FUCK.

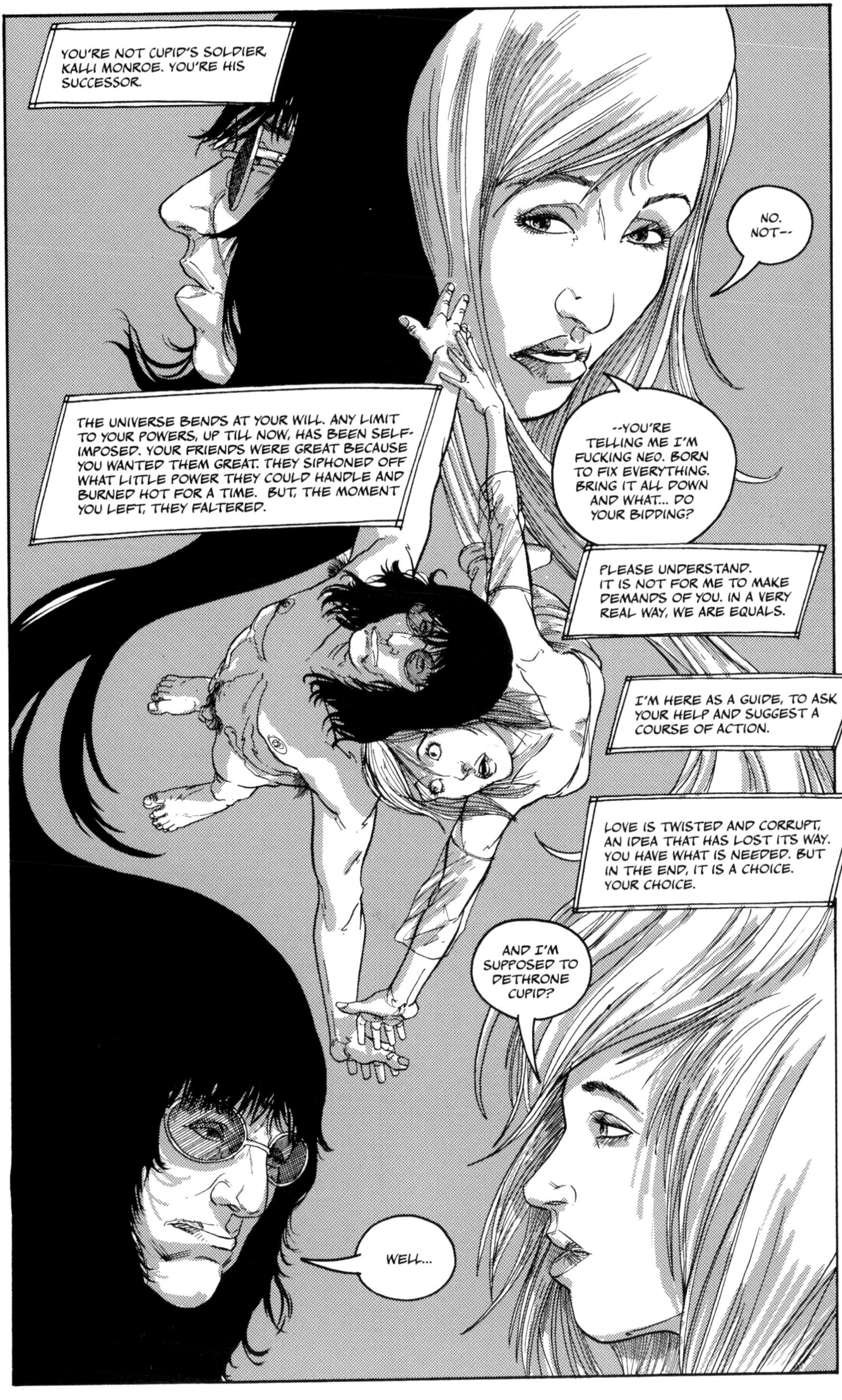
YOU'RE NOT CUPID'S SOLDIER, KALLI MONROE. YOU'RE HIS SUCCESSOR.
NO. NOT--
--YOU'RE TELLING ME I'M FUCKING NEO. BORN TO FIX EVERYTHING. BRING IT ALL DOWN AND WHAT... DO YOUR BIDDING?
THE UNIVERSE BENDS AT YOUR WILL. ANY LIMIT TO YOUR POWERS, UP TILL NOW, HAS BEEN SELF-IMPOSED. YOUR FRIENDS WERE GREAT BECAUSE YOU WANTED THEM GREAT. THEY SIPHONED OFF WHAT LITTLE POWER THEY COULD HANDLE AND BURNED HOT FOR A TIME. BUT, THE MOMENT YOU LEFT, THEY FALTERED.
PLEASE UNDERSTAND. IT IS NOT FOR ME TO MAKE DEMANDS OF YOU. IN A VERY REAL WAY, WE ARE EQUALS.
I'M HERE AS A GUIDE, TO ASK YOUR HELP AND SUGGEST A COURSE OF ACTION.
LOVE IS TWISTED AND CORRUPT, AN IDEA THAT HAS LOST ITS WAY. YOU HAVE WHAT IS NEEDED. BUT IN THE END, IT IS A CHOICE. YOUR CHOICE.
AND I'M SUPPOSED TO DETHRONE CUPID?
WELL...

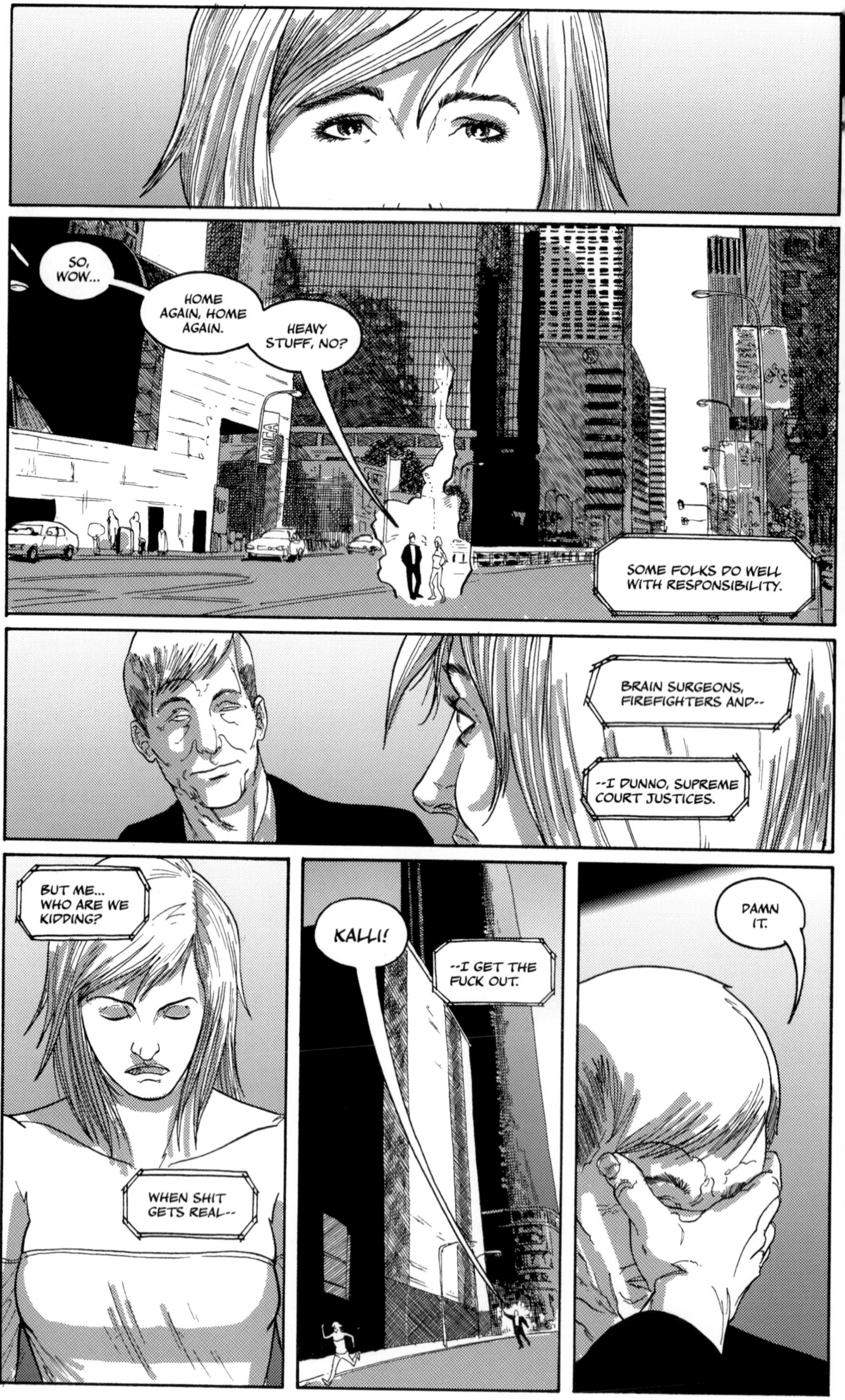
SO, WOW...
HOME AGAIN, HOME AGAIN.
HEAVY STUFF, NO?
SOME FOLKS DO WELL WITH RESPONSIBILITY.
BRAIN SURGEONS, FIREFIGHTERS AND--
--I DUNNO, SUPREME COURT JUSTICES.
BUT ME... WHO ARE WE KIDDING?
WHEN SHIT GETS REAL--
KALLI!
--I GET THE FUCK OUT.
DAMN IT.

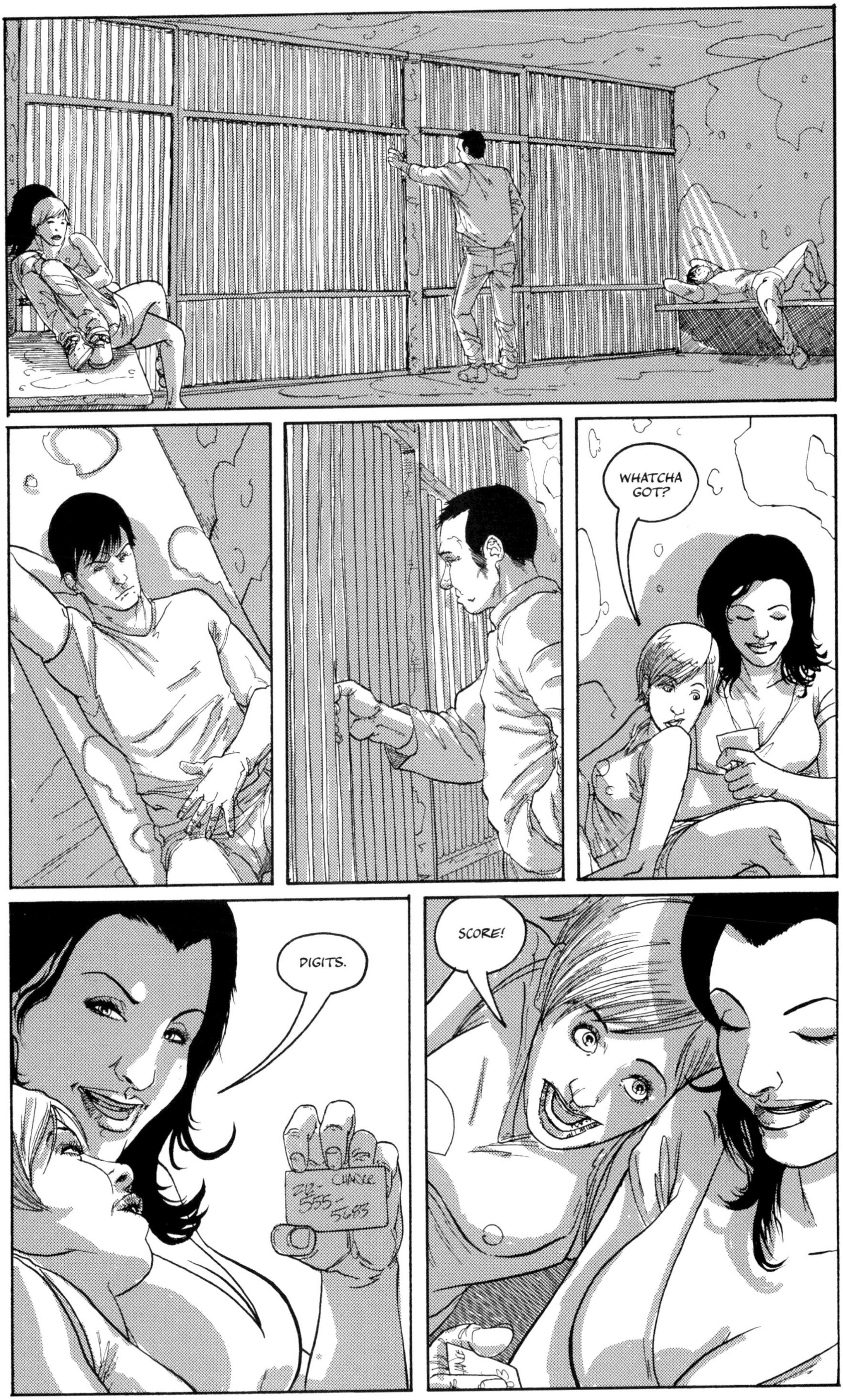
WHATCHA GOT?
DIGITS.
SCORE!

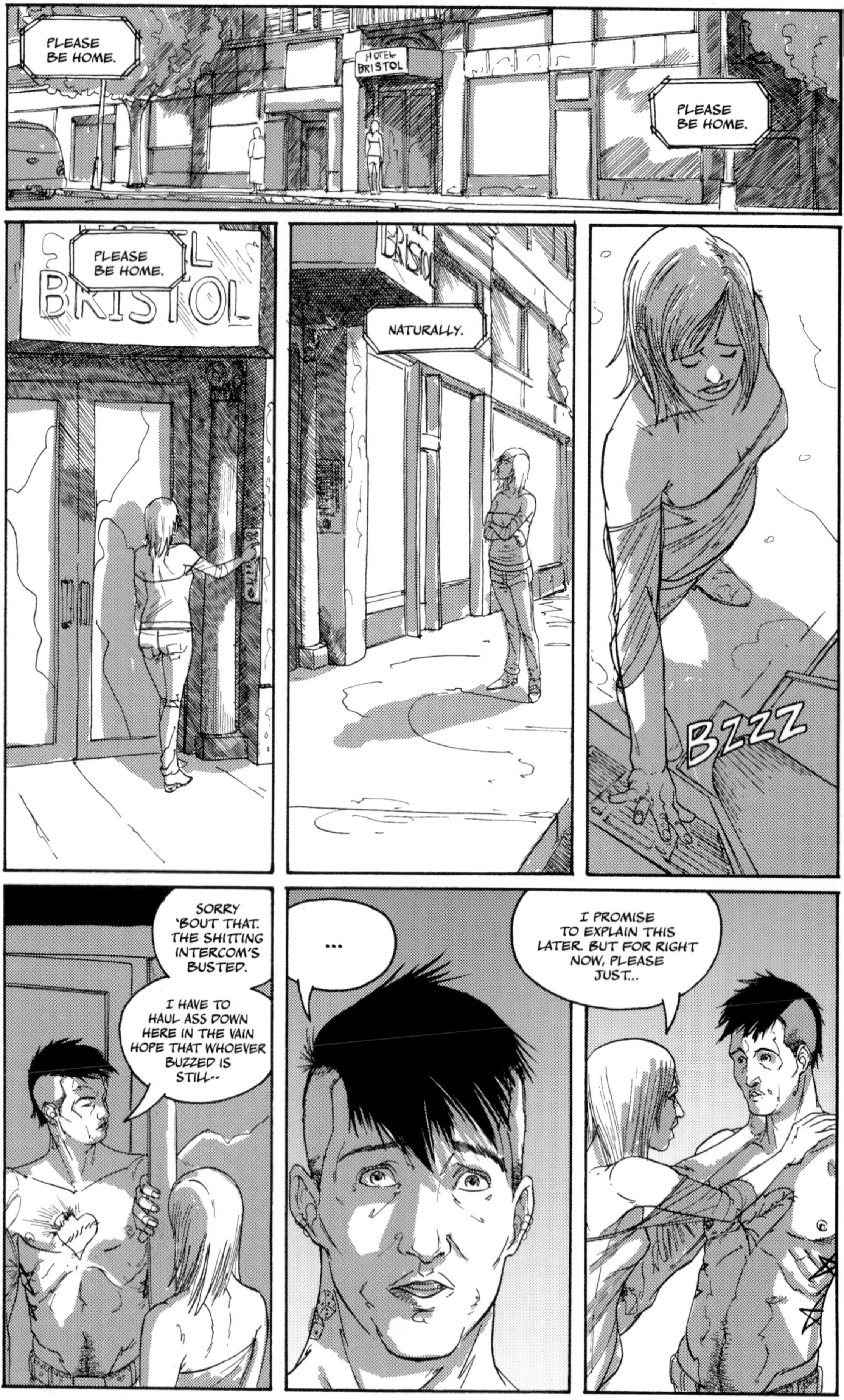
PLEASE BE HOME.
HOTEL BRISTOL
PLEASE BE HOME.
PLEASE BE HOME.
NATURALLY.
BZZZ
SORRY 'BOUT THAT. THE SHITTING INTERCOM'S BUSTED.
I HAVE TO HAUL ASS DOWN HERE IN THE VAIN HOPE THAT WHOEVER BUZZED IS STILL--
...
I PROMISE TO EXPLAIN THIS LATER. BUT FOR RIGHT NOW, PLEASE JUST...

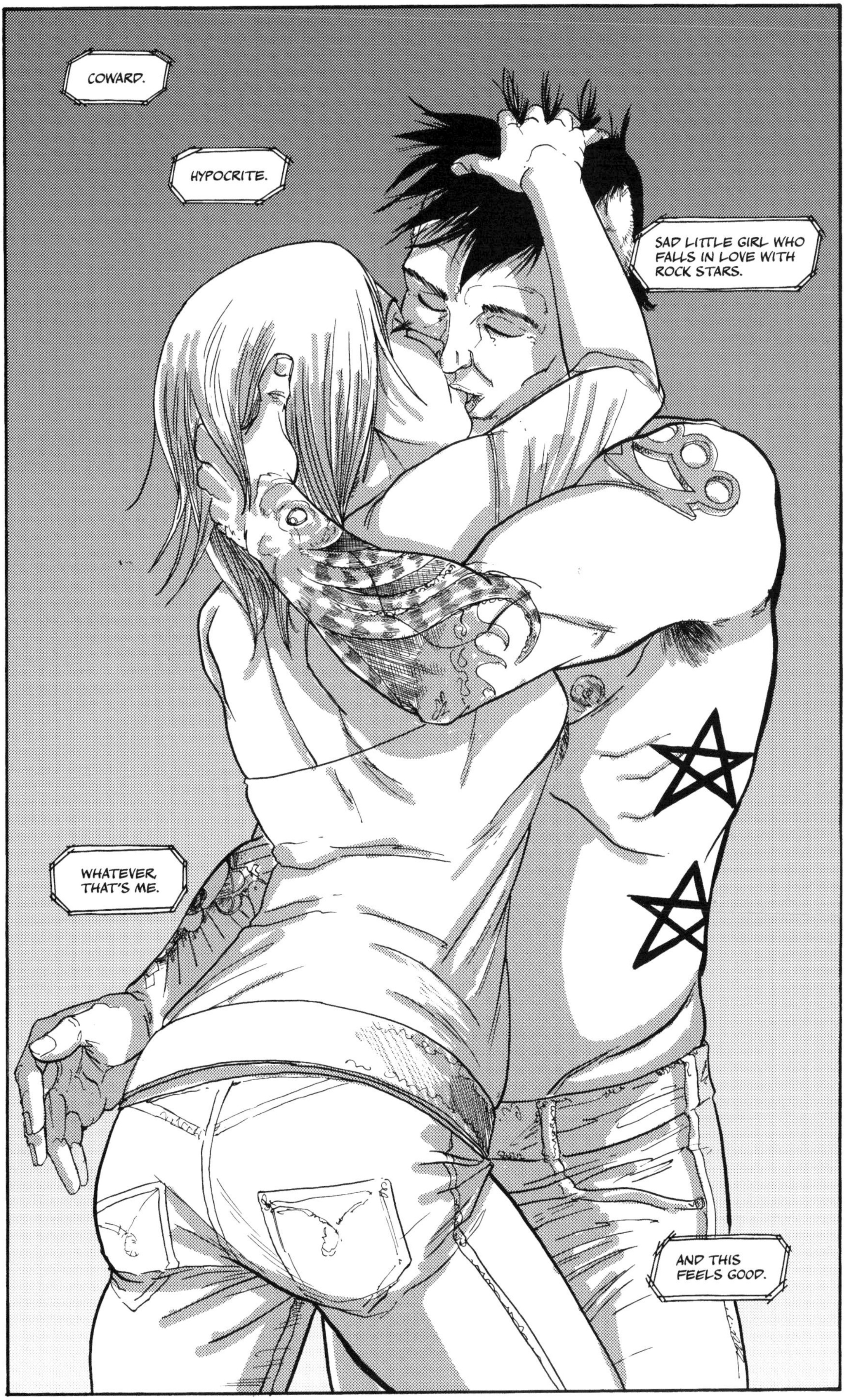
COWARD.
HYPOCRITE.
SAD LITTLE GIRL WHO FALLS IN LOVE WITH ROCK STARS.
WHATEVER. THAT'S ME.
AND THIS FEELS GOOD.

CHAPTER 5

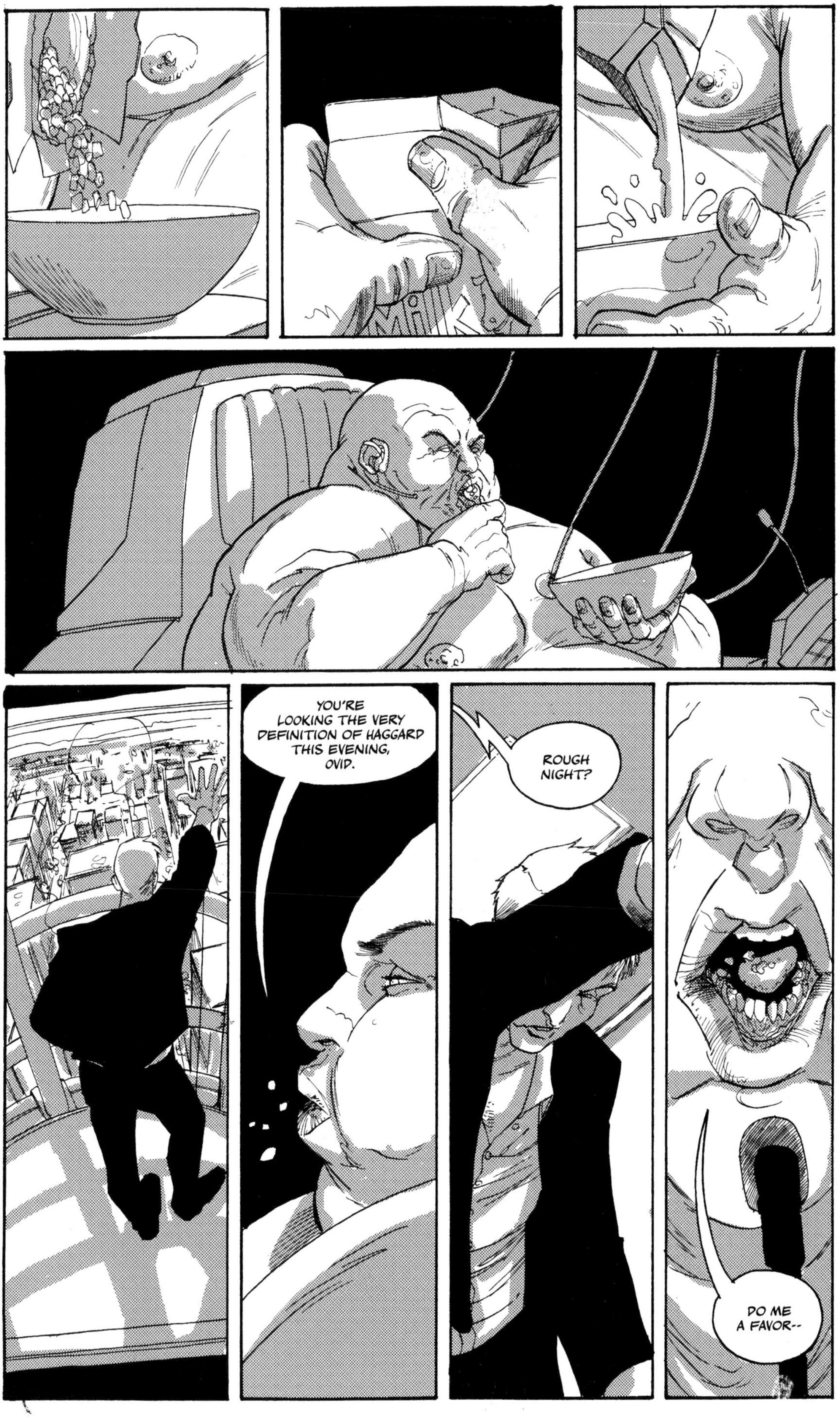
MILK
YOU'RE LOOKING THE VERY DEFINITION OF HAGGARD THIS EVENING, OVID.
ROUGH NIGHT?
DO ME A FAVOR--

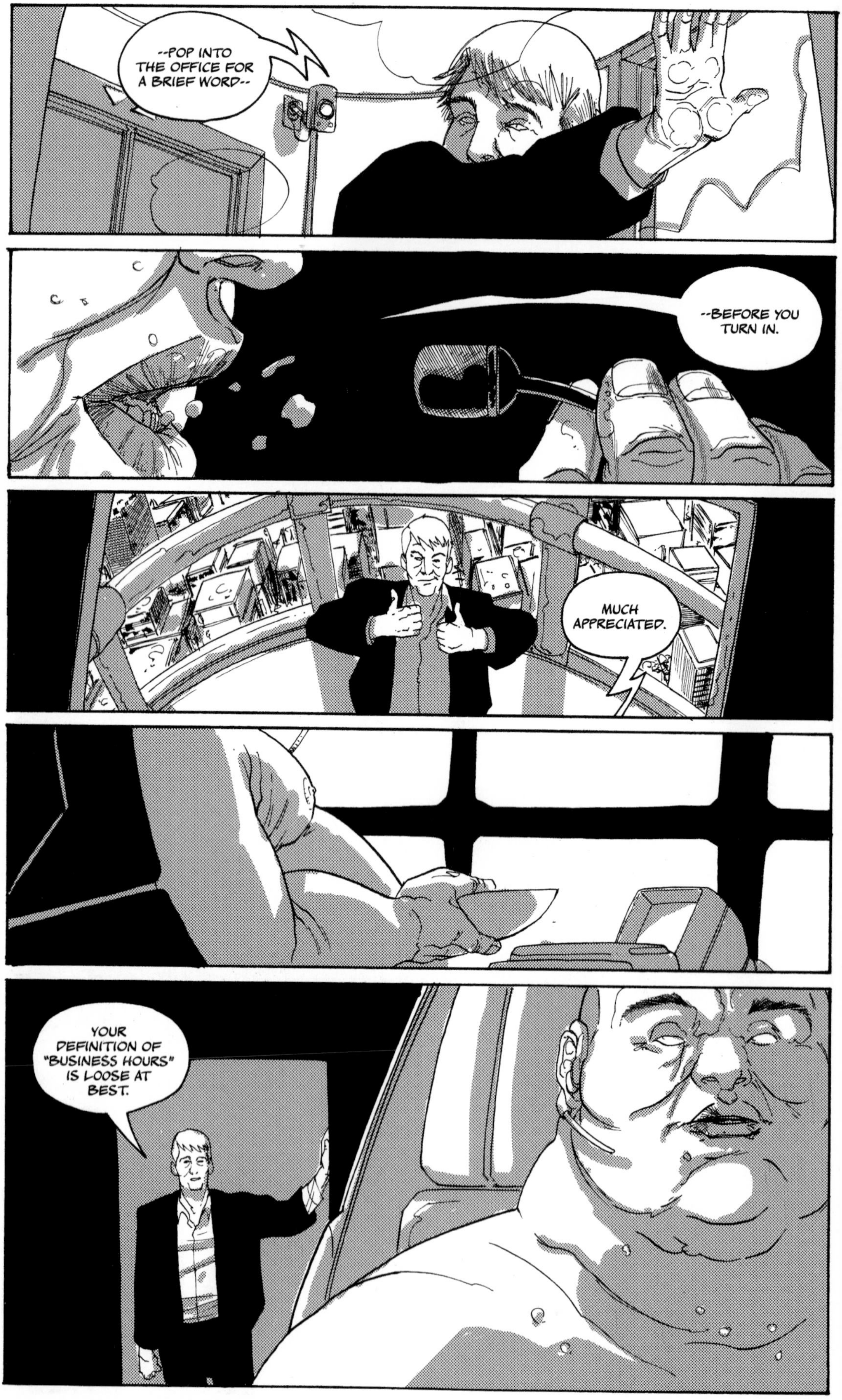
--POP INTO THE OFFICE FOR A BRIEF WORD--
--BEFORE YOU TURN IN.
MUCH APPRECIATED.
YOUR DEFINITION OF "BUSINESS HOURS" IS LOOSE AT BEST.

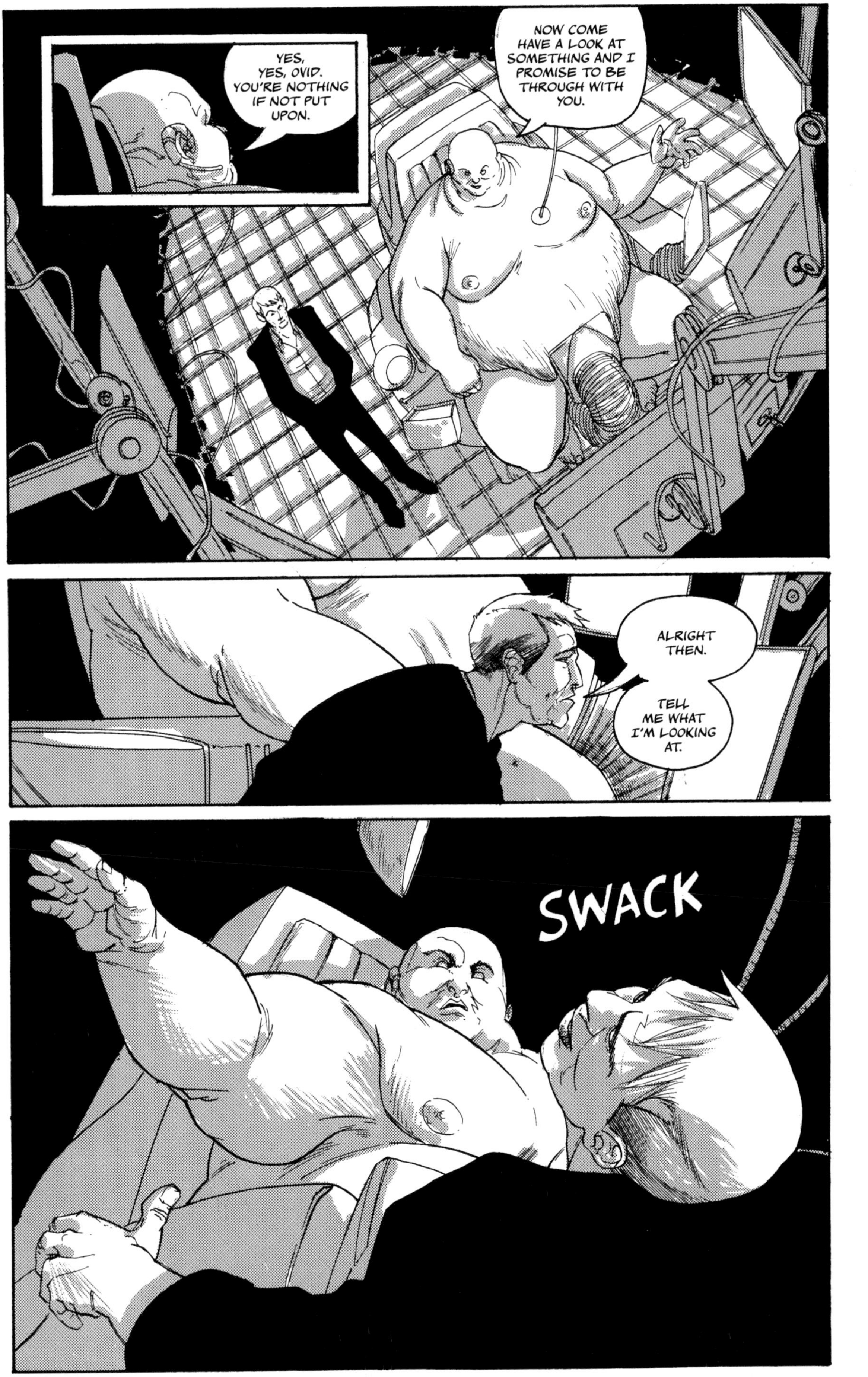
YES, YES, OVID. YOU'RE NOTHING IF NOT PUT UPON.
NOW COME HAVE A LOOK AT SOMETHING AND I PROMISE TO BE THROUGH WITH YOU.
ALRIGHT THEN.
TELL ME WHAT I'M LOOKING AT.
SWACK

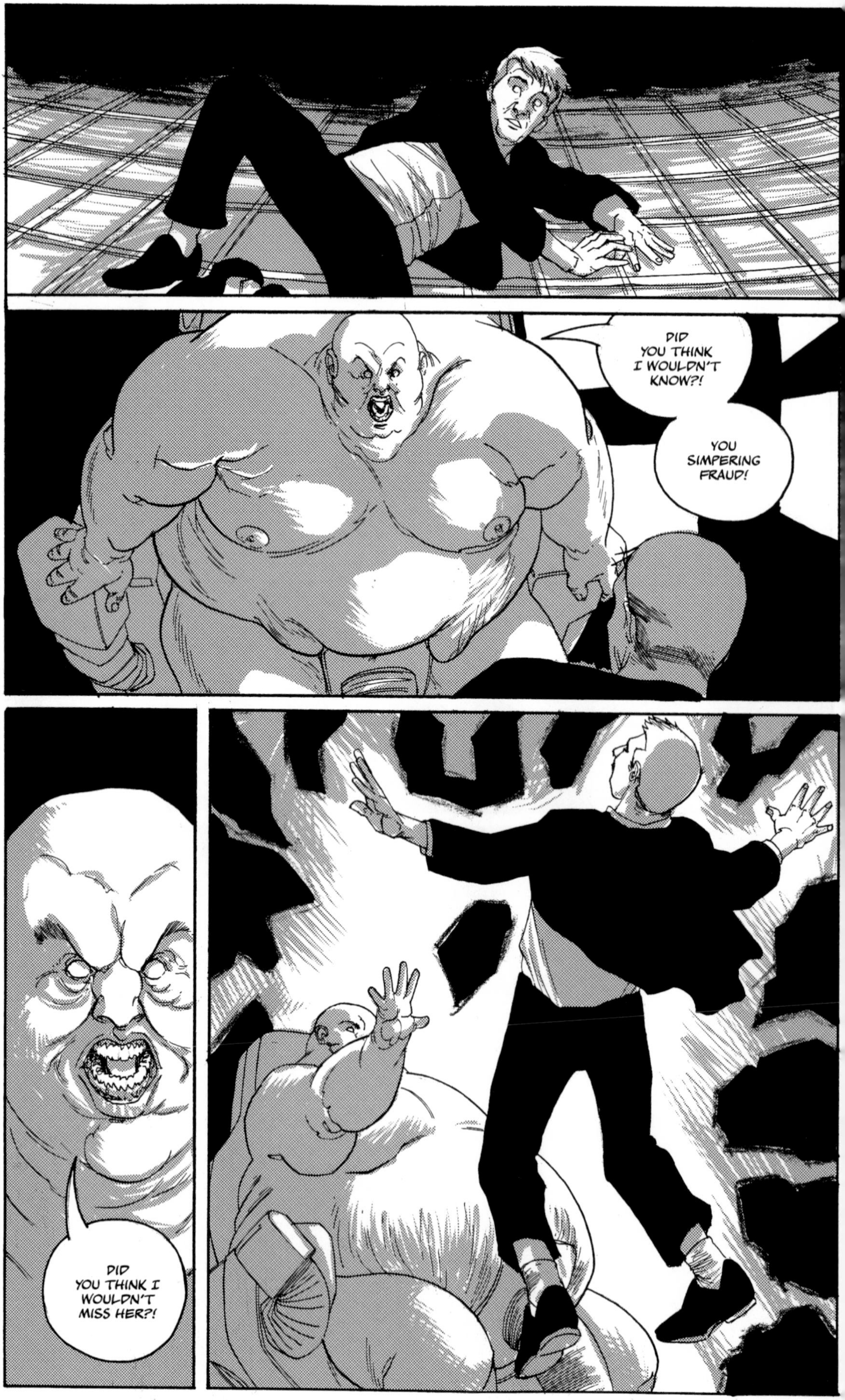
DID YOU THINK I WOULDN'T KNOW?!
YOU SIMPERING FRAUD!
DID YOU THINK I WOULDN'T MISS HER?!

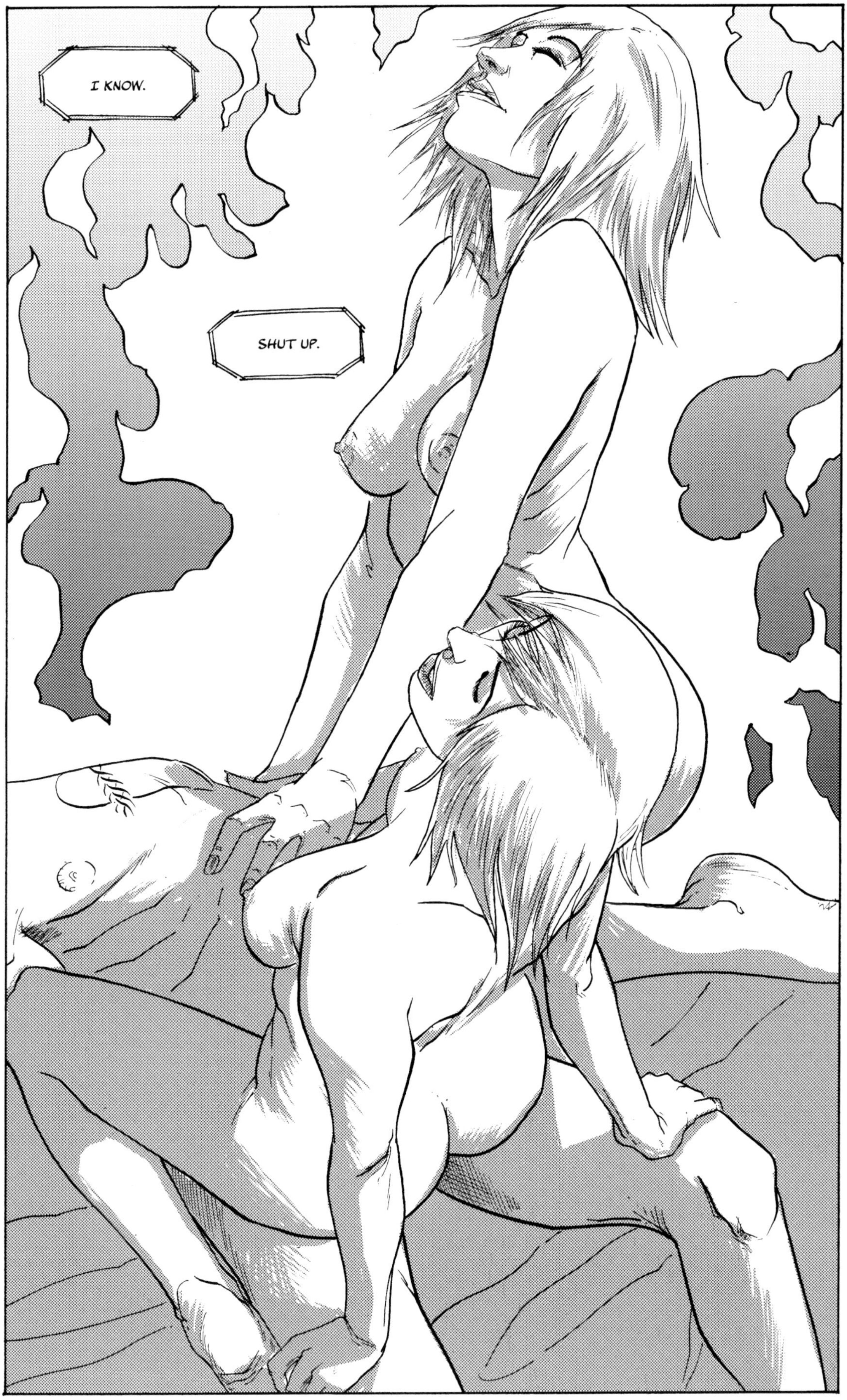
I KNOW.
SHUT UP.

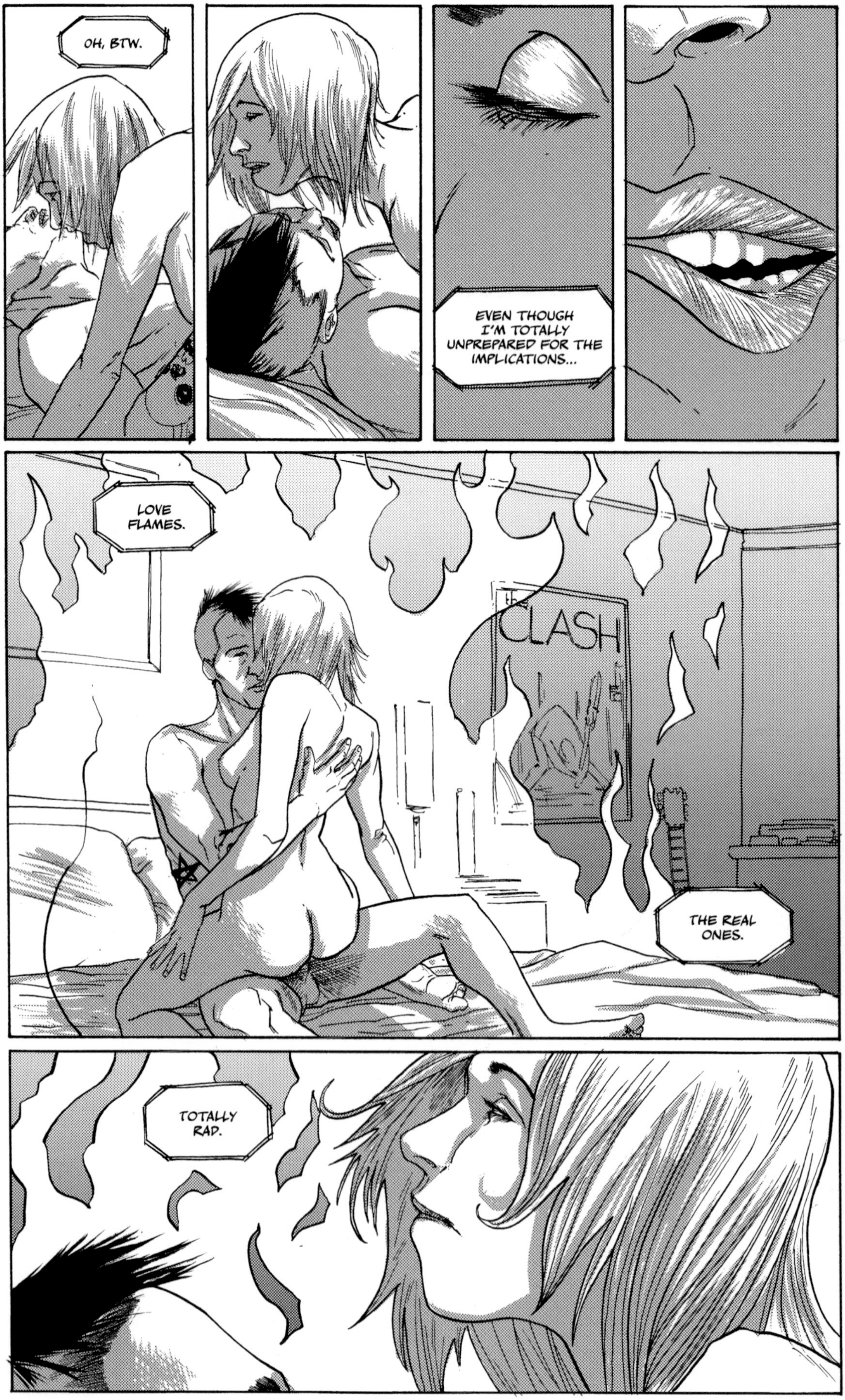
OH, BTW.
EVEN THOUGH I'M TOTALLY UNPREPARED FOR THE IMPLICATIONS...
LOVE FLAMES.
the CLASH
THE REAL ONES.
TOTALLY RAD.

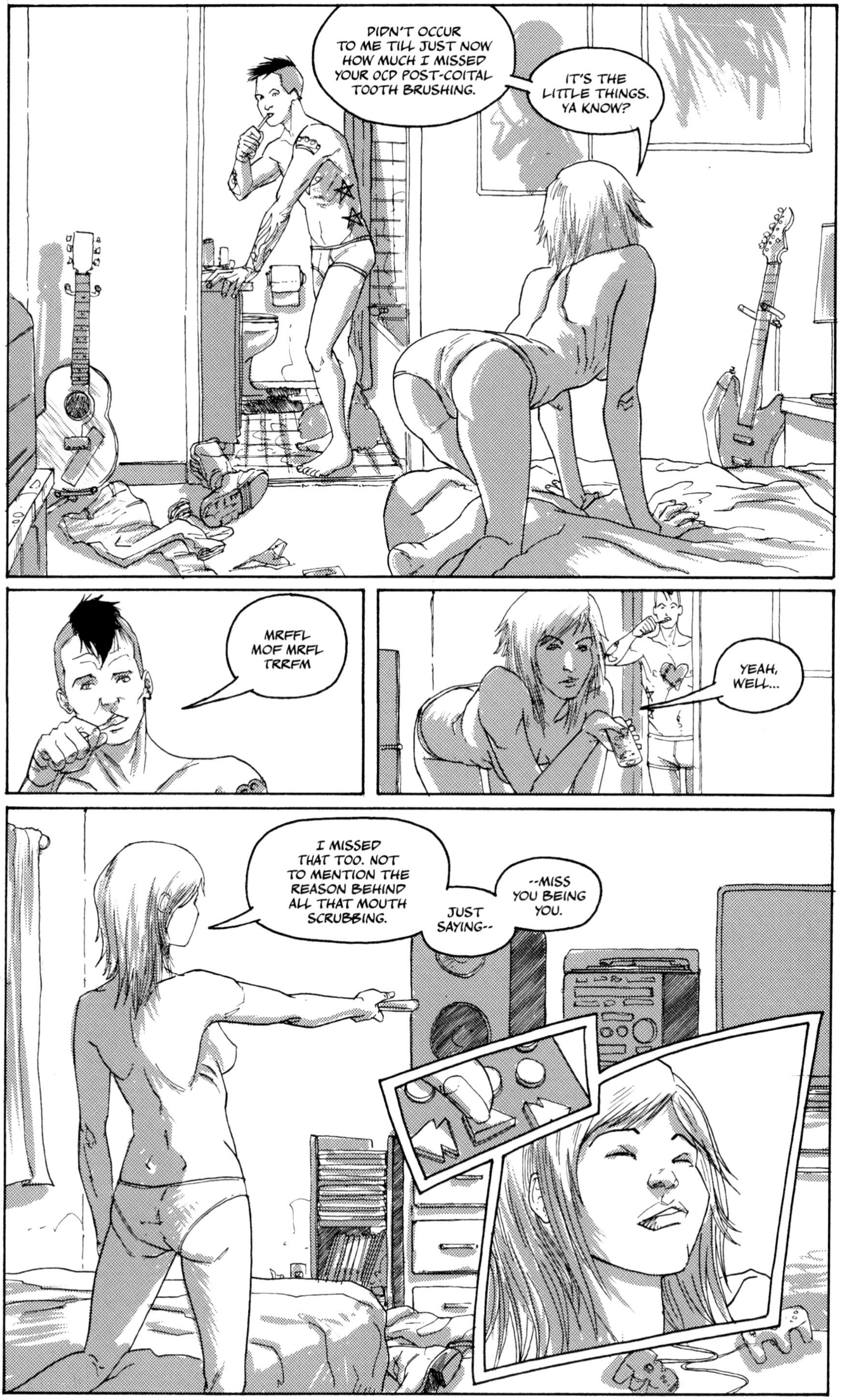
DIDN'T OCCUR TO ME TILL JUST NOW HOW MUCH I MISSED YOUR OCD POST-COITAL TOOTH BRUSHING.
IT'S THE LITTLE THINGS. YA KNOW?
MRFFL MOF MRFL TRRFM
YEAH, WELL...
I MISSED THAT TOO. NOT TO MENTION THE REASON BEHIND ALL THAT MOUTH SCRUBBING.
JUST SAYING--
--MISS YOU BEING YOU.

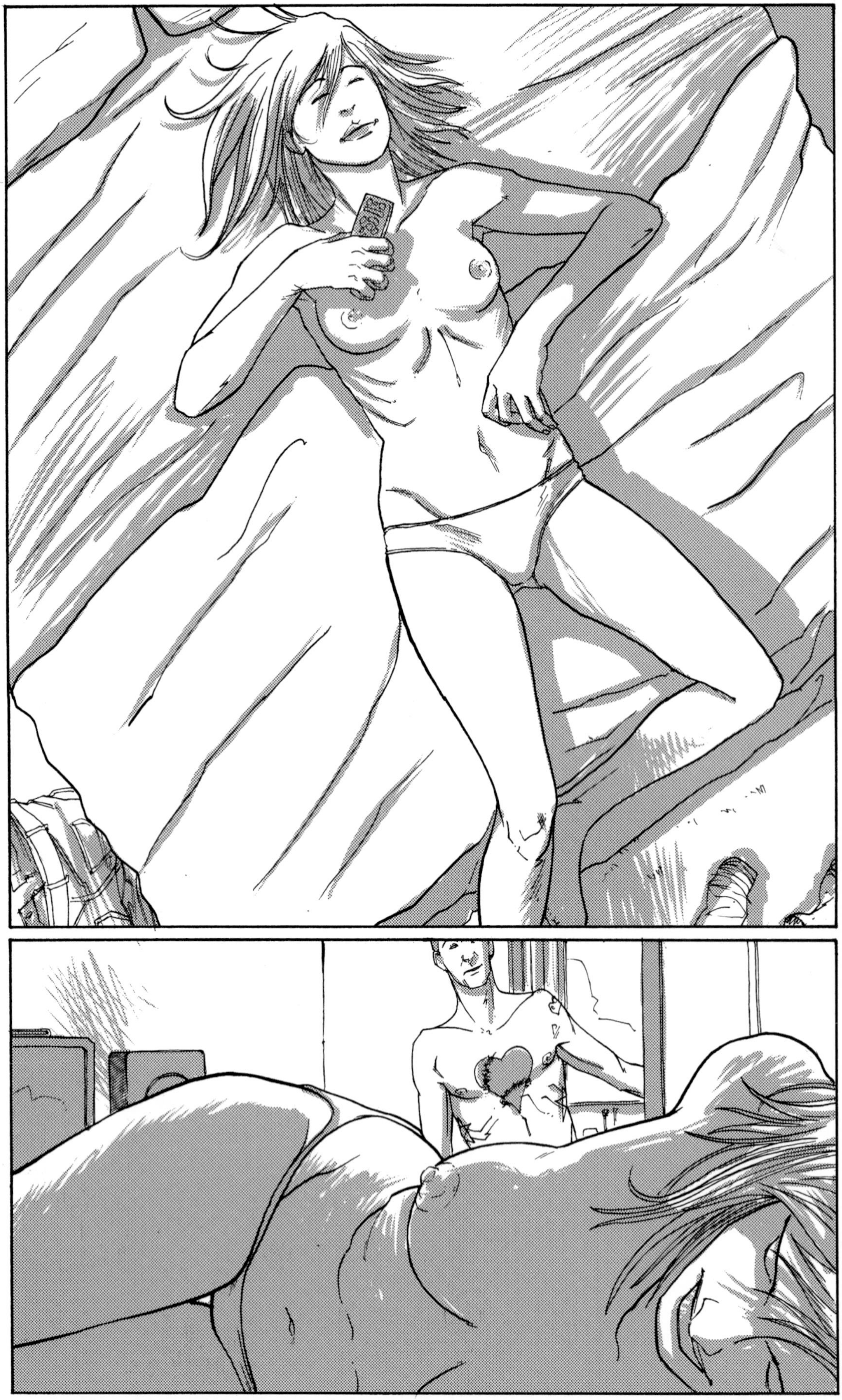

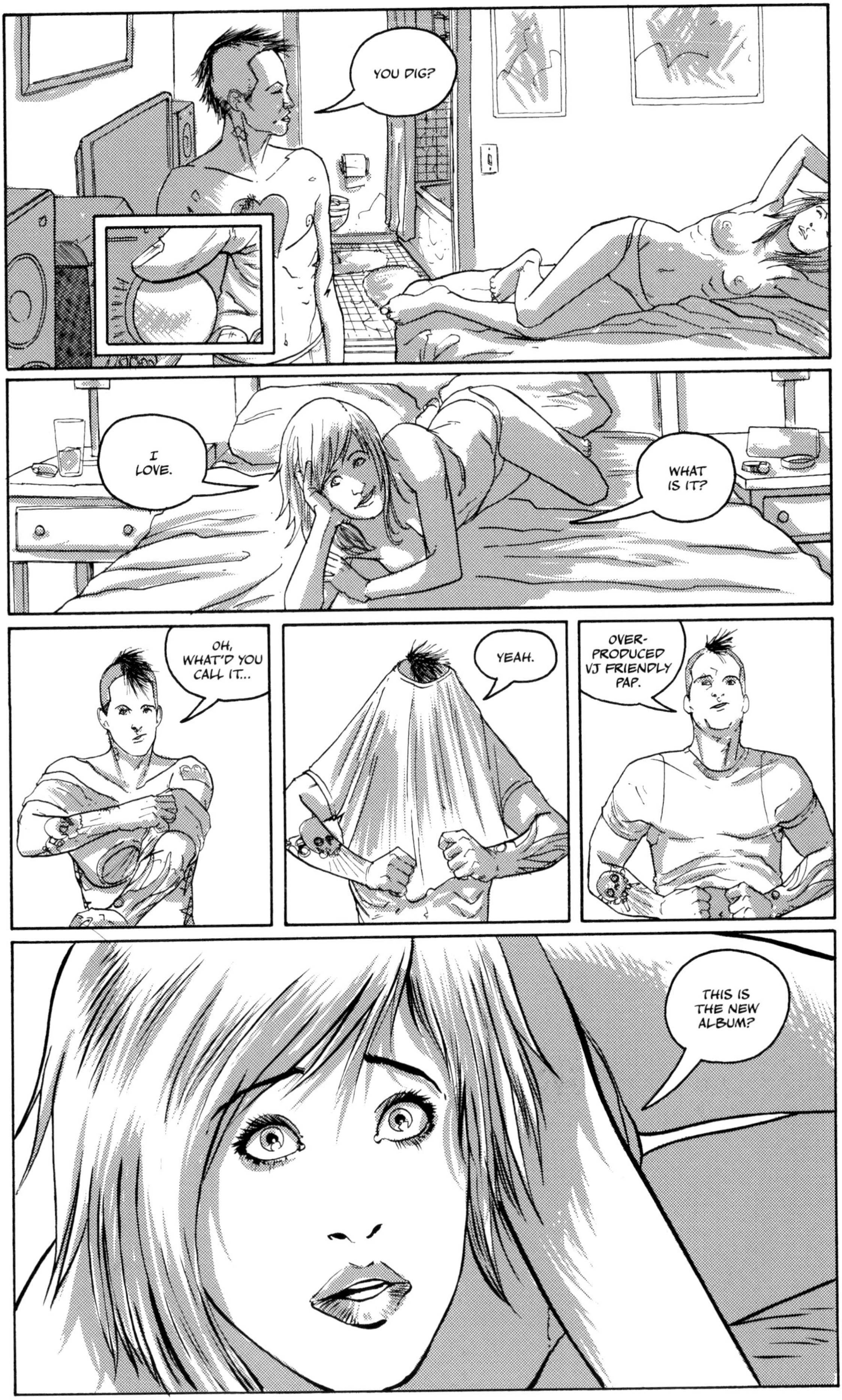
YOU DIG?
I LOVE.
WHAT IS IT?
OH, WHAT'D YOU CALL IT...
YEAH.
OVER-PRODUCED VJ FRIENDLY PAP.
THIS IS THE NEW ALBUM?

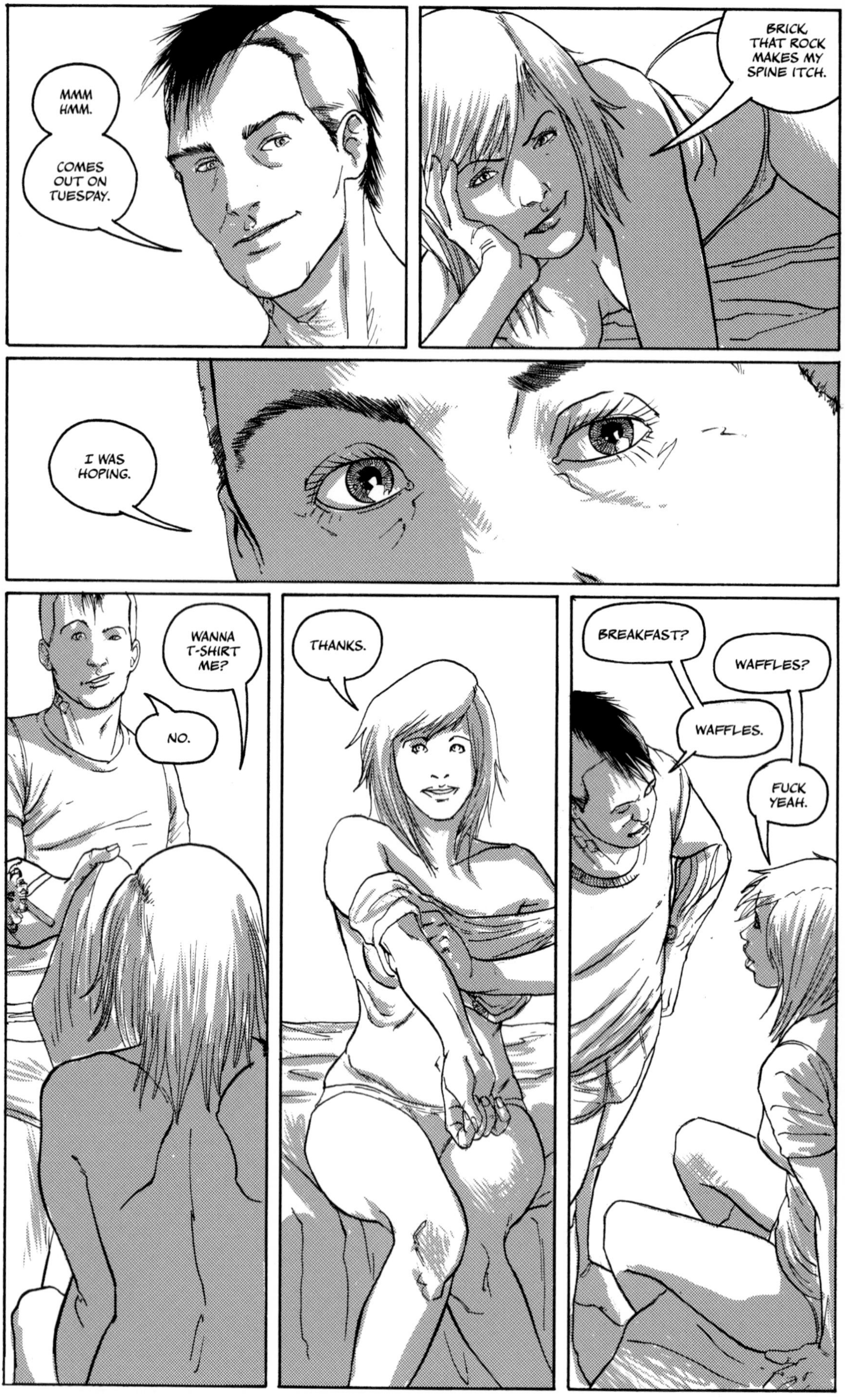
MMM HMM.
COMES OUT ON TUESDAY.
BRICK, THAT ROCK MAKES MY SPINE ITCH.
I WAS HOPING.
WANNA T-SHIRT ME?
NO.
THANKS.
BREAKFAST?
WAFFLES.
WAFFLES?
FUCK YEAH.

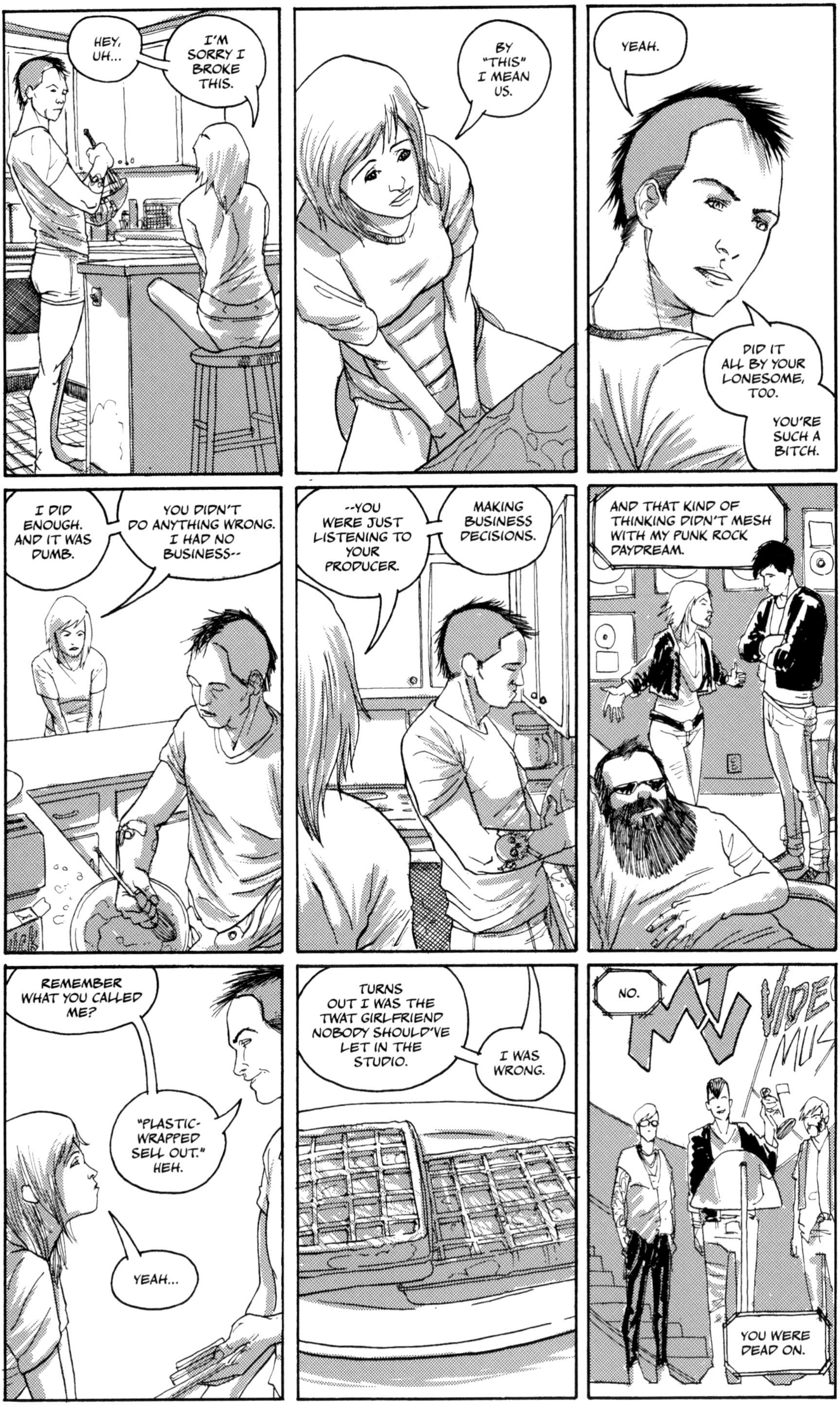

HEY, UH...
I'M SORRY I BROKE THIS.
BY "THIS" I MEAN US.
YEAH.
DID IT ALL BY YOUR LONESOME, TOO.
YOU'RE SUCH A BITCH.
I DID ENOUGH. AND IT WAS DUMB.
YOU DIDN'T DO ANYTHING WRONG. I HAD NO BUSINESS--
--YOU WERE JUST LISTENING TO YOUR PRODUCER.
MAKING BUSINESS DECISIONS.
AND THAT KIND OF THINKING DIDN'T MESH WITH MY PUNK ROCK DAYDREAM.
REMEMBER WHAT YOU CALLED ME?
"PLASTIC-WRAPPED SELL OUT." HEH.
YEAH...
TURNS OUT I WAS THE TWAT GIRLFRIEND NOBODY SHOULD'VE LET IN THE STUDIO.
I WAS WRONG.
NO.
YOU WERE DEAD ON.

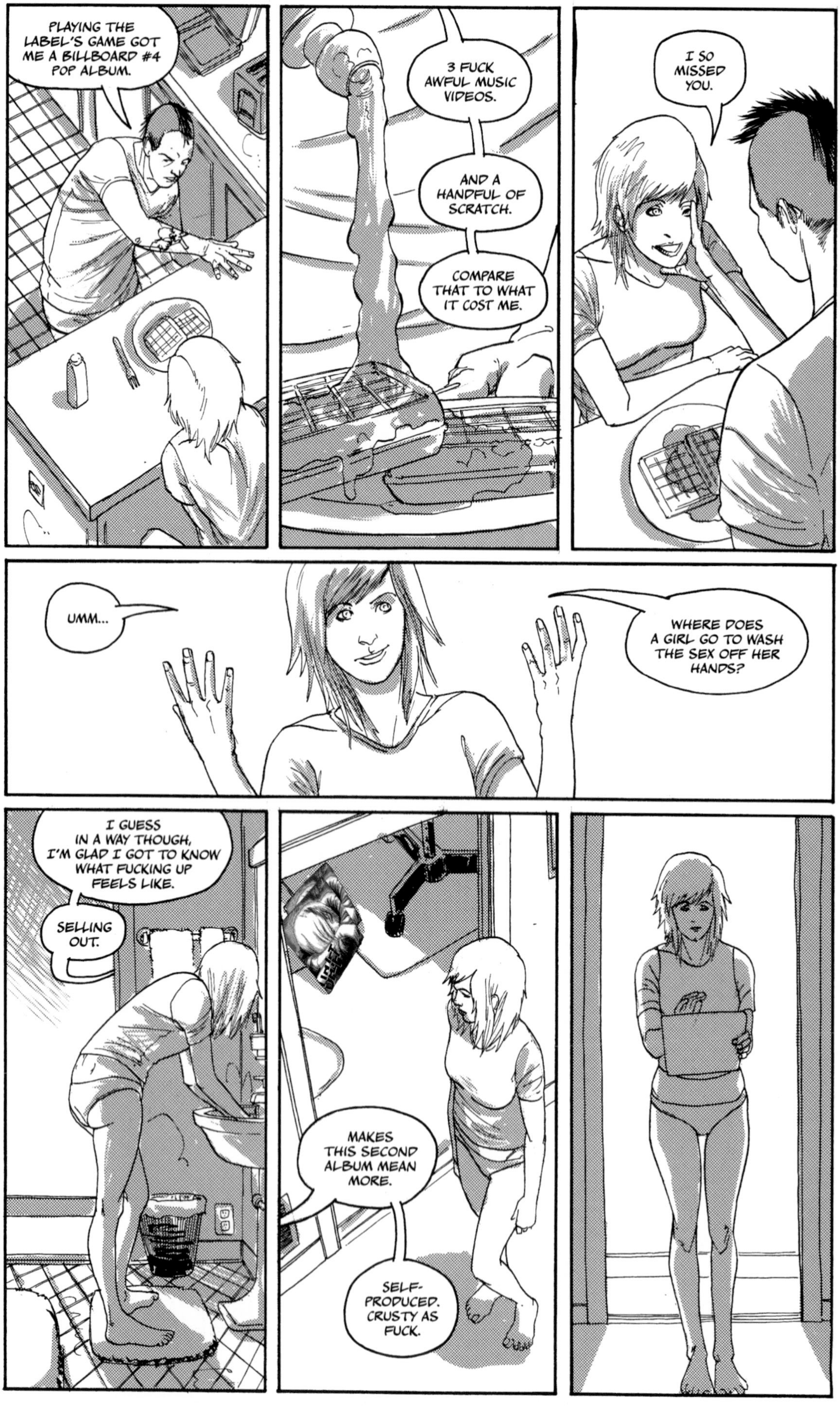

PLAYING THE LABEL'S GAME GOT ME A BILLBOARD #4 POP ALBUM.
3 FUCK AWFUL MUSIC VIDEOS.
AND A HANDFUL OF SCRATCH.
COMPARE THAT TO WHAT IT COST ME.
I SO MISSED YOU.
UMM...
WHERE DOES A GIRL GO TO WASH THE SEX OFF HER HANDS?
I GUESS IN A WAY THOUGH, I'M GLAD I GOT TO KNOW WHAT FUCKING UP FEELS LIKE.
SELLING OUT.
MAKES THIS SECOND ALBUM MEAN MORE.
SELF-PRODUCED. CRUSTY AS FUCK.

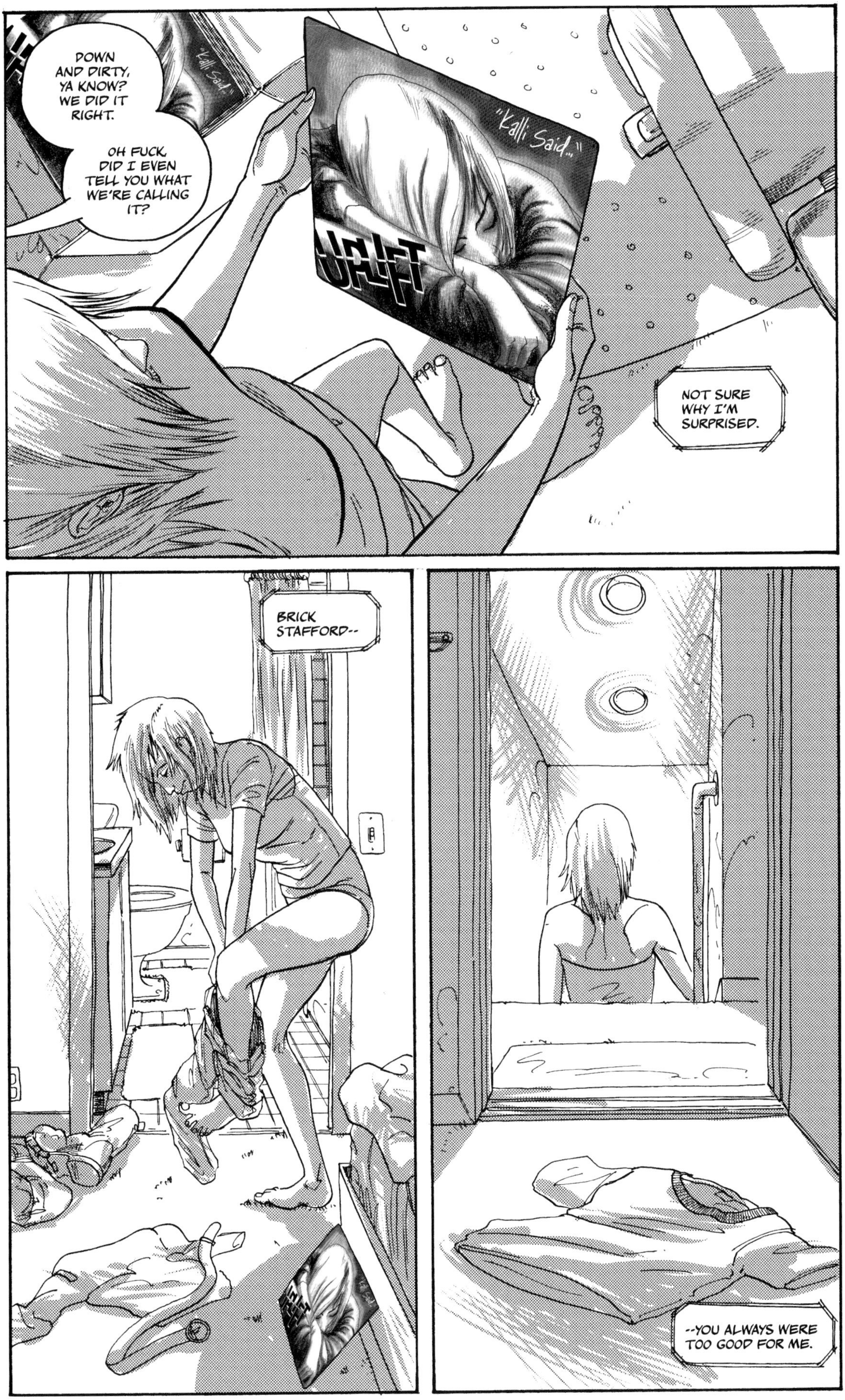
"Kalli Said..."
UPLIFT
DOWN AND DIRTY, YA KNOW? WE DID IT RIGHT.
OH FUCK, DID I EVEN TELL YOU WHAT WE'RE CALLING IT?
NOT SURE WHY I'M SURPRISED.
BRICK STAFFORD--
--YOU ALWAYS WERE TOO GOOD FOR ME.

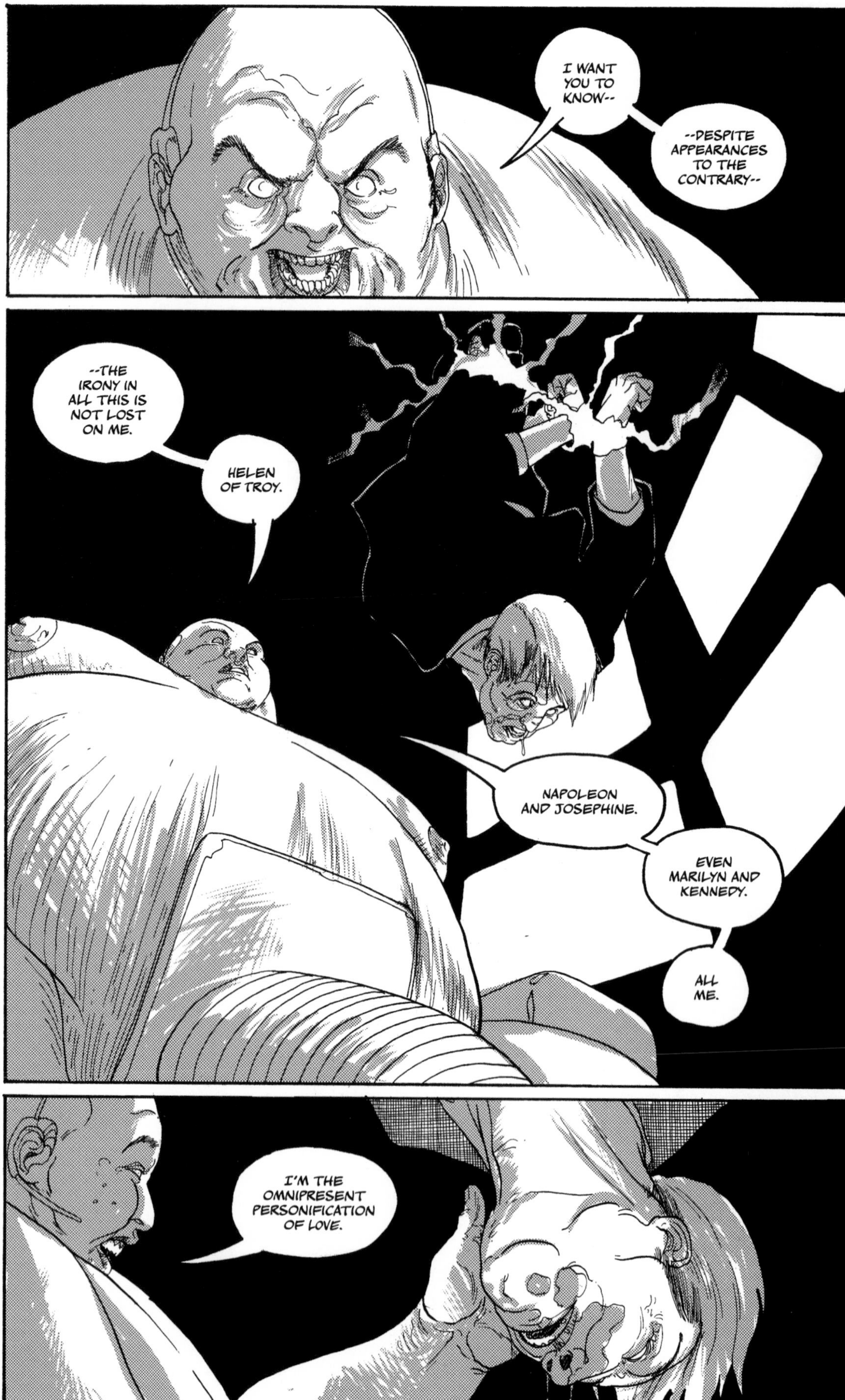
I WANT YOU TO KNOW--
--DESPITE APPEARANCES TO THE CONTRARY--
--THE IRONY IN ALL THIS IS NOT LOST ON ME.
HELEN OF TROY.
NAPOLEON AND JOSEPHINE.
EVEN MARILYN AND KENNEDY.
ALL ME.
I'M THE OMNIPRESENT PERSONIFICATION OF LOVE.

AND WHERE DOES LOVE FIND ITSELF AFTER ALL THESE LIFETIMES?
UTTERLY BLINDSIDED BY WAY OF MISPLACED TRUST.
HOW TERRIBLY CUTE.
WHAT TO DO WITH YOU, OVID?
I COULD EXPEND A GREAT DEAL OF ENERGY MAKING YOU EXPLAIN WHY YOU DECIDED TO BETRAY ME.
WHAT POSSIBLE REASON EVEN A FOOLISH MAN MIGHT HAVE FOR SACRIFICING HIS POSITION OF POWER AND INFLUENCE.
BUT I'VE KNOWN YOU TOO LONG.
AND I KNOW YOU TOO WELL TO WASTE TIME ON SOMETHING SO TRIVIAL.
YOU'RE NOT A MAN WHO ACTS, OVID. NOT OF YOUR OWN ACCORD.
YOU TAKE ORDERS. YOU FOLLOW.
SNAP!
SO FOR NOW, OLD FRIEND, I WON'T CONCERN MYSELF WITH THE MOTIVATIONS OF A SPINELESS PAWN.
I'LL SIMPLY HURT HIM UNTIL HE NAMES HIS MASTER.

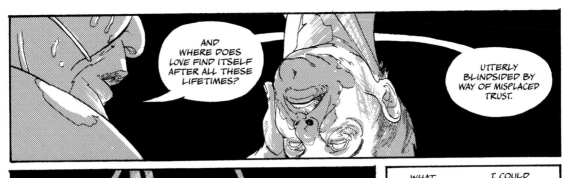

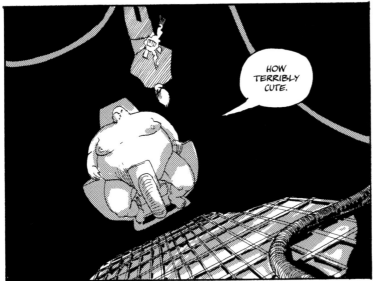

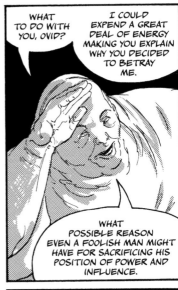

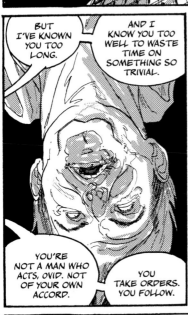

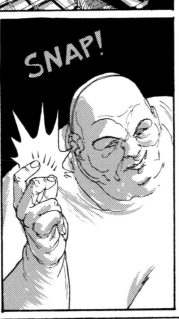

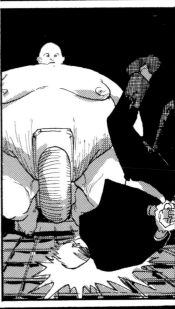

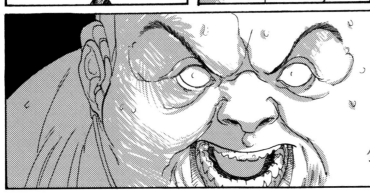

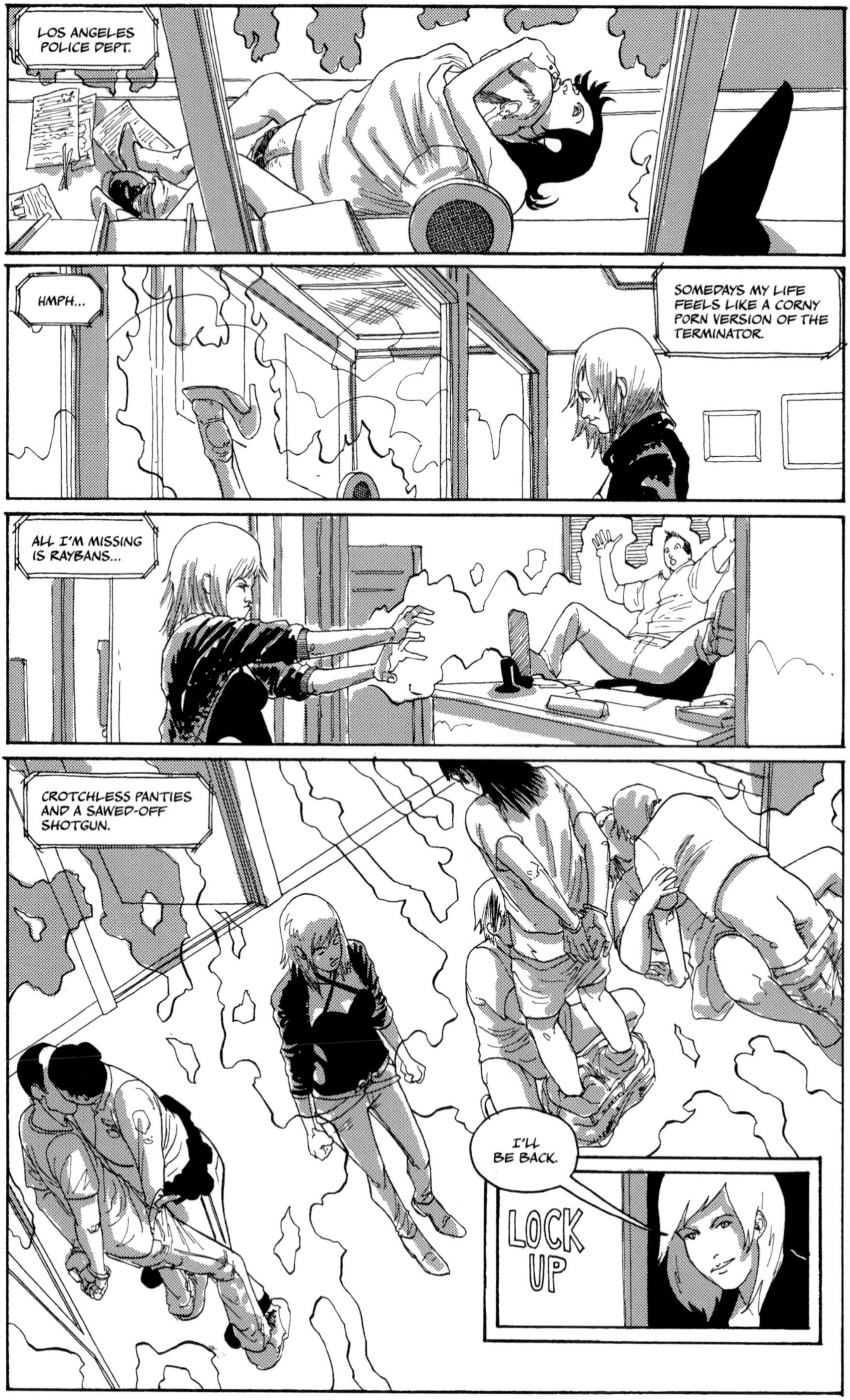
LOS ANGELES POLICE DEPT.
HMPH...
SOMEDAYS MY LIFE FEELS LIKE A CORNY PORN VERSION OF THE TERMINATOR.
ALL I'M MISSING IS RAYBANS...
CROTCHLESS PANTIES AND A SAWED-OFF SHOTGUN.
I'LL BE BACK.
LOCK UP

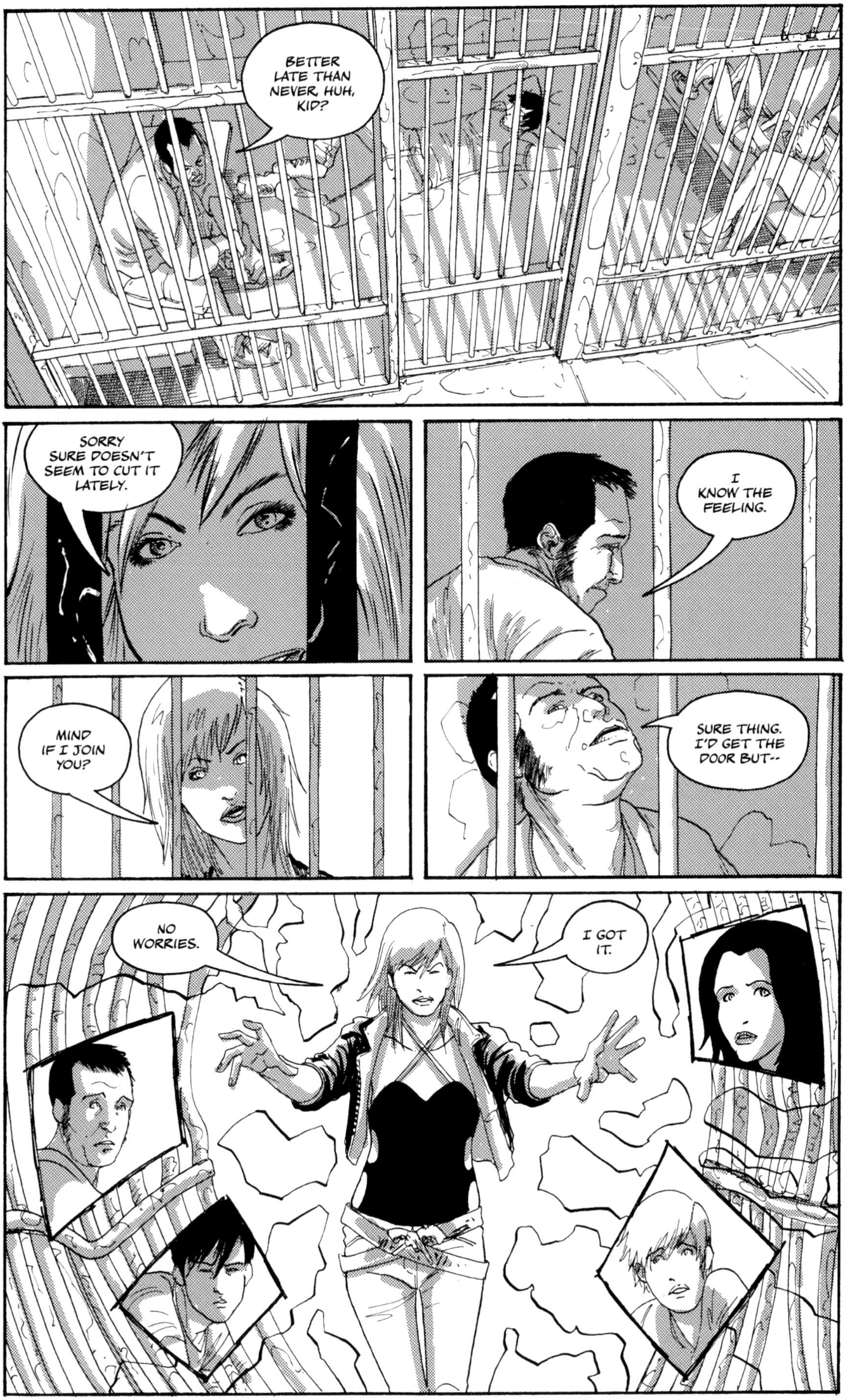
BETTER LATE THAN NEVER, HUH, KID?
SORRY SURE DOESN'T SEEM TO CUT IT LATELY.
I KNOW THE FEELING.
MIND IF I JOIN YOU?
SURE THING. I'D GET THE DOOR BUT--
NO WORRIES.
I GOT IT.

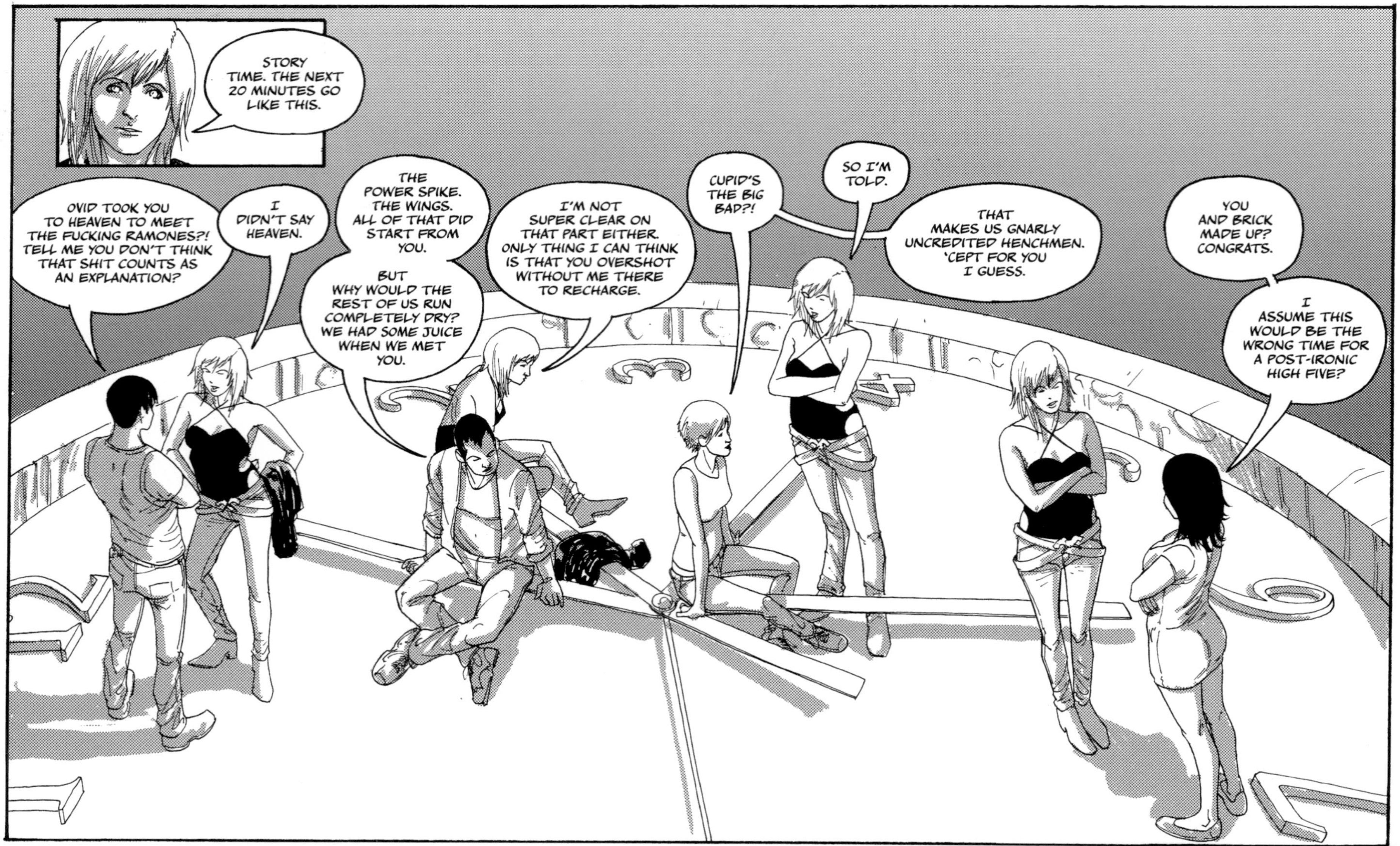
STORY TIME. THE NEXT 20 MINUTES GO LIKE THIS.
OVID TOOK YOU TO HEAVEN TO MEET THE FUCKING RAMONES?! TELL ME YOU DON'T THINK THAT SHIT COUNTS AS AN EXPLANATION?
I DIDN'T SAY HEAVEN.
THE POWER SPIKE. THE WINGS. ALL OF THAT DID START FROM YOU.
BUT WHY WOULD THE REST OF US RUN COMPLETELY DRY? WE HAD SOME JUICE WHEN WE MET YOU.
I'M NOT SUPER CLEAR ON THAT PART EITHER. ONLY THING I CAN THINK IS THAT YOU OVERSHOT WITHOUT ME THERE TO RECHARGE.
CUPID'S THE BIG BAD?!
SO I'M TOLD.
THAT MAKES US GNARLY UNCREDITED HENCHMEN. 'CEPT FOR YOU I GUESS.
YOU AND BRICK MADE UP? CONGRATS.
I ASSUME THIS WOULD BE THE WRONG TIME FOR A POST-IRONIC HIGH FIVE?

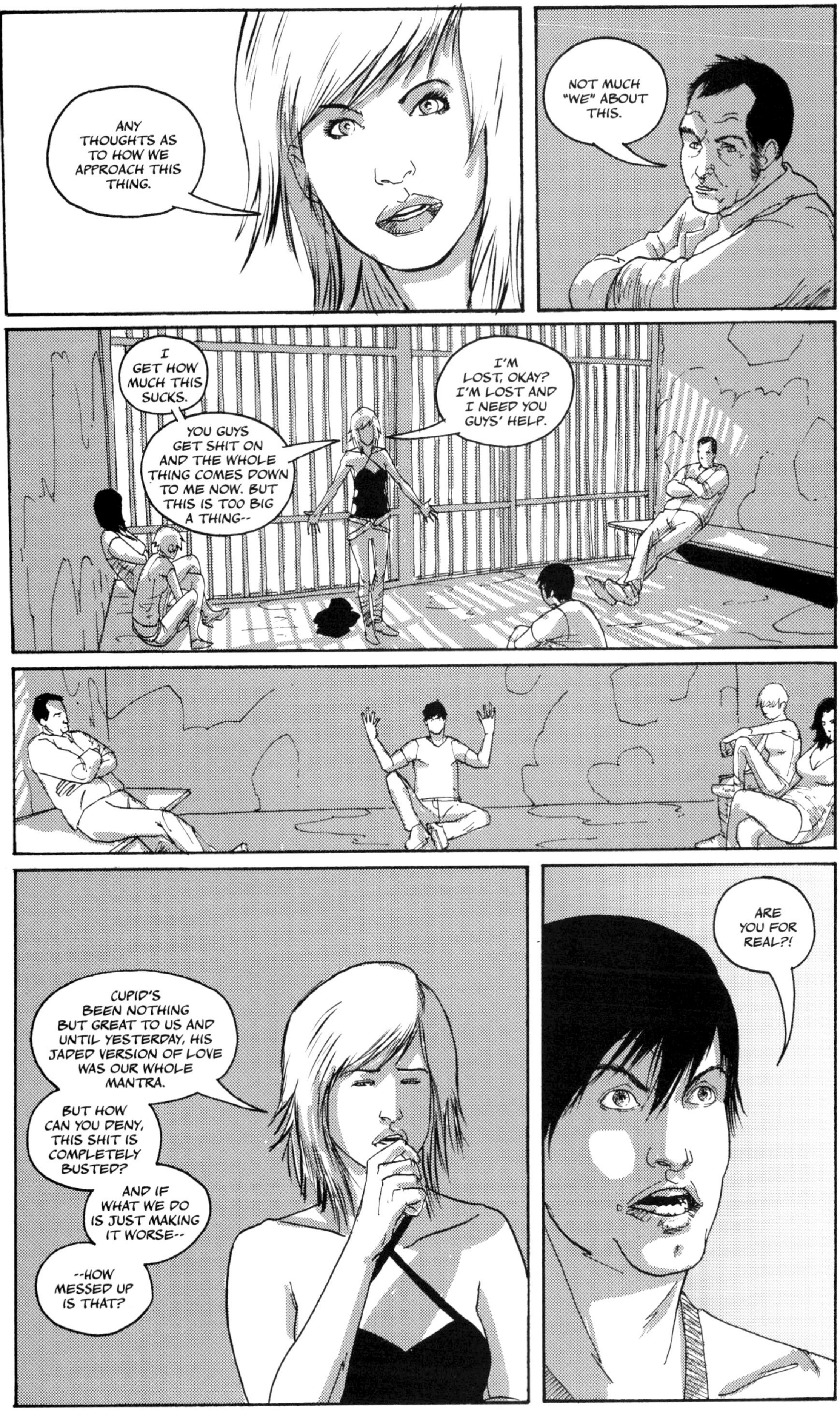
ANY THOUGHTS AS TO HOW WE APPROACH THIS THING.
NOT MUCH "WE" ABOUT THIS.
I GET HOW MUCH THIS SUCKS.
YOU GUYS GET SHIT ON AND THE WHOLE THING COMES DOWN TO ME NOW. BUT THIS IS TOO BIG A THING--
I'M LOST, OKAY? I'M LOST AND I NEED YOU GUYS' HELP.
CUPID'S BEEN NOTHING BUT GREAT TO US AND UNTIL YESTERDAY, HIS JADED VERSION OF LOVE WAS OUR WHOLE MANTRA.
BUT HOW CAN YOU DENY, THIS SHIT IS COMPLETELY BUSTED?
AND IF WHAT WE DO IS JUST MAKING IT WORSE--
--HOW MESSED UP IS THAT?
ARE YOU FOR REAL?!

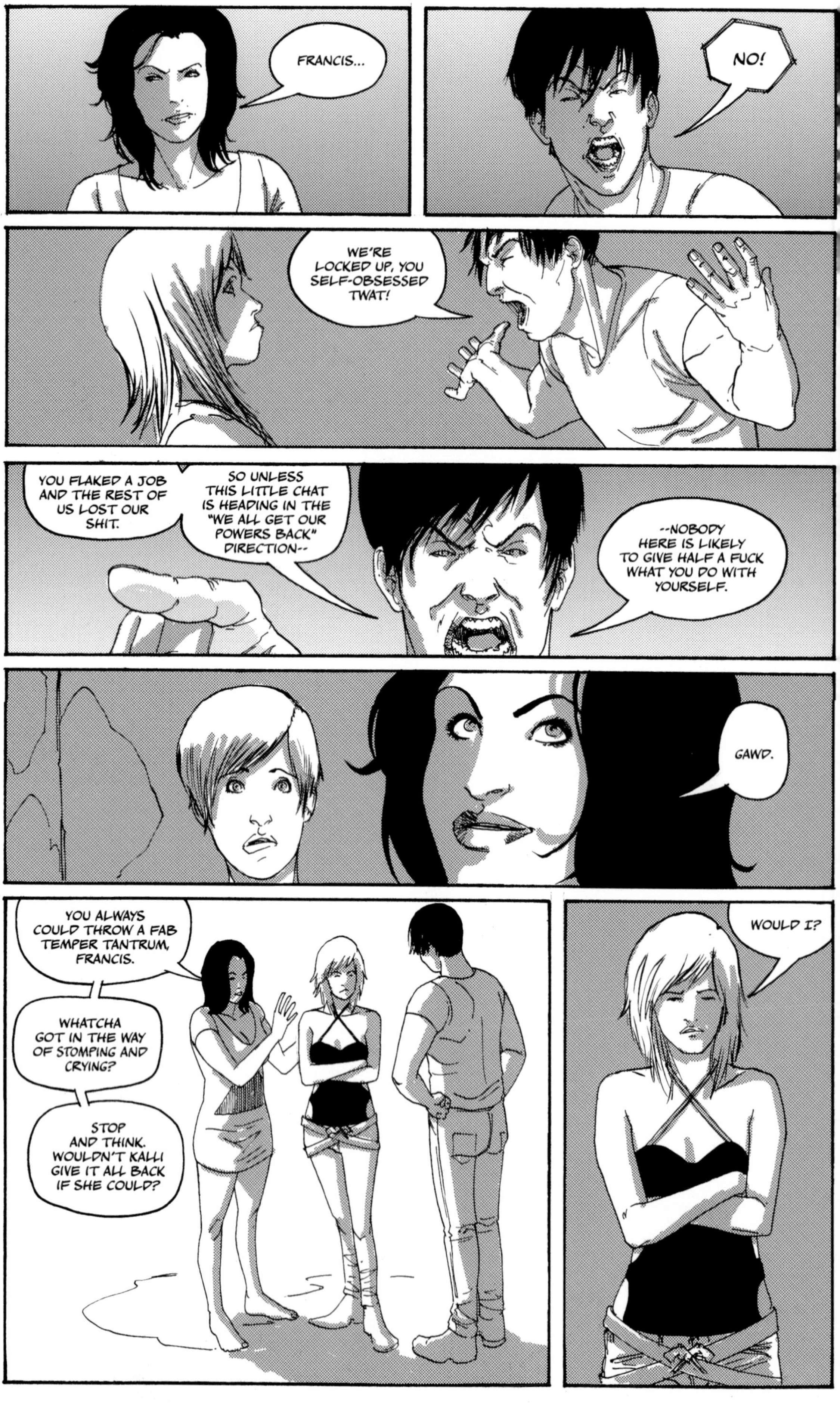
FRANCIS...
NO!
WE'RE LOCKED UP, YOU SELF-OBSESSED TWAT!
YOU FLAKED A JOB AND THE REST OF US LOST OUR SHIT.
SO UNLESS THIS LITTLE CHAT IS HEADING IN THE "WE ALL GET OUR POWERS BACK" DIRECTION--
--NOBODY HERE IS LIKELY TO GIVE HALF A FUCK WHAT YOU DO WITH YOURSELF.
GAWD.
YOU ALWAYS COULD THROW A FAB TEMPER TANTRUM, FRANCIS.
WHATCHA GOT IN THE WAY OF STOMPING AND CRYING?
STOP AND THINK. WOULDN'T KALLI GIVE IT ALL BACK IF SHE COULD?
WOULD I?

WE'RE BADASS LOVE-SLINGING OUTLAWS. I DON'T WANT THAT TO GO AWAY ANY MORE THAN YOU DO. IT'S WHAT MAKES US SPECIAL.

BUT IF WHAT CUPID DOES IS WRONG. IF IT HURTS EVERYONE ELSE, CAN WE REALLY KEEP THAT UP JUST BECAUSE IT FEELS GOOD?

AT SOME POINT DON'T YOU HAVE TO TAKE RESPONSIBILITY FOR SOMETHING?

WAIT!

I JUST BETWEENED THE LINES.

I THINK YOU THINK YOU COULD ENERGIZE OUR BUNNIES. JUST WON'T.

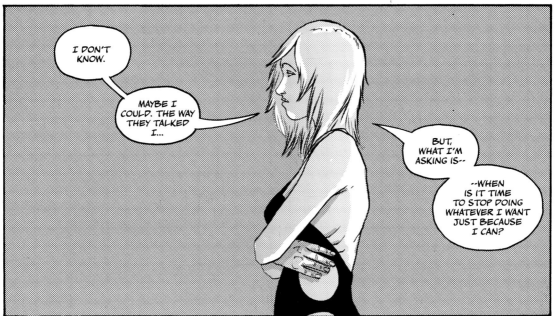

I DON'T KNOW.

MAYBE I COULD. THE WAY THEY TALKED I...

BUT, WHAT I'M ASKING IS--

--WHEN IS IT TIME TO STOP DOING WHATEVER I WANT JUST BECAUSE I CAN?

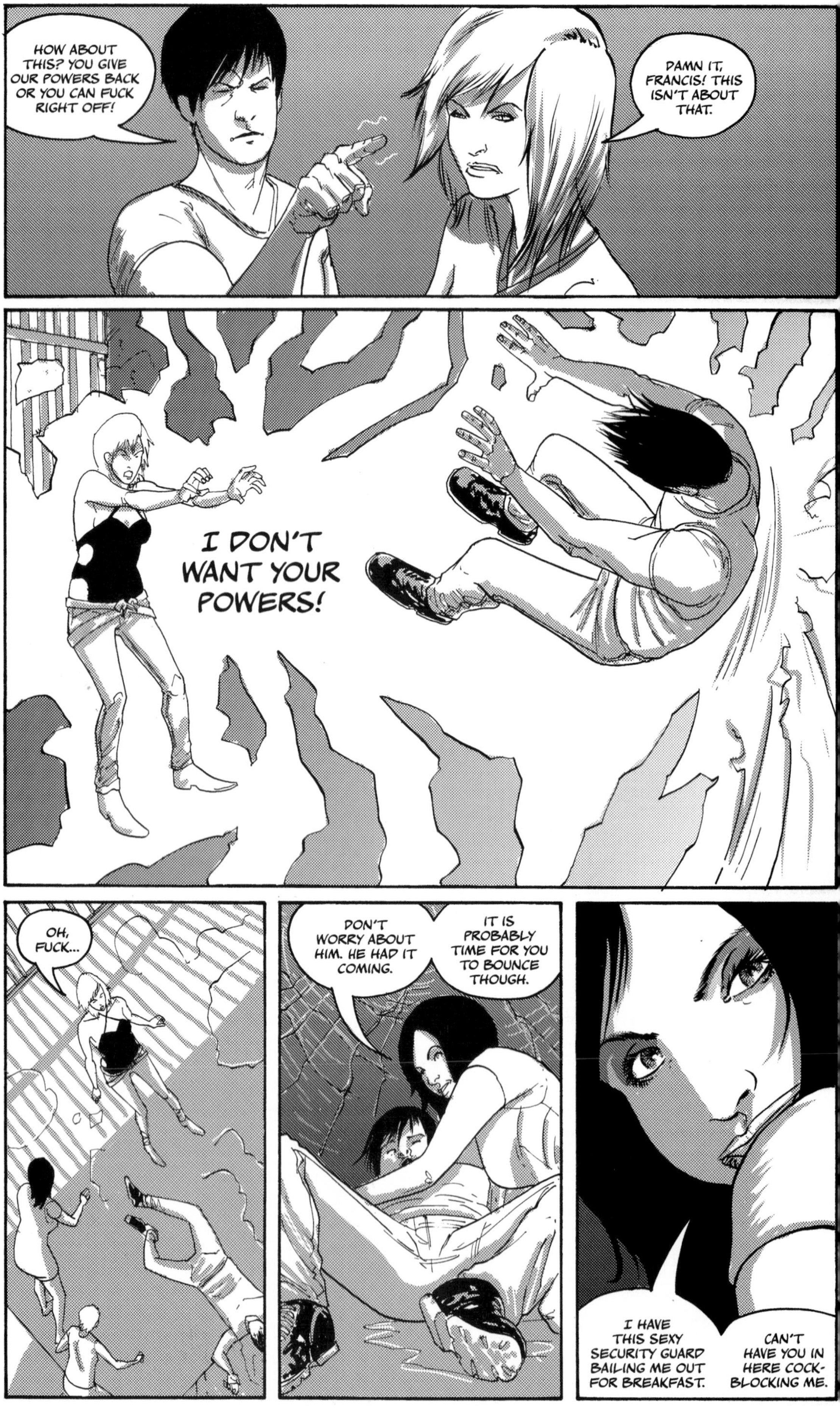

HOW ABOUT THIS? YOU GIVE OUR POWERS BACK OR YOU CAN FUCK RIGHT OFF!
DAMN IT, FRANCIS! THIS ISN'T ABOUT THAT.
I DON'T WANT YOUR POWERS!
OH, FUCK...
DON'T WORRY ABOUT HIM. HE HAD IT COMING.
IT IS PROBABLY TIME FOR YOU TO BOUNCE THOUGH.
I HAVE THIS SEXY SECURITY GUARD BAILING ME OUT FOR BREAKFAST.
CAN'T HAVE YOU IN HERE COCK-BLOCKING ME.

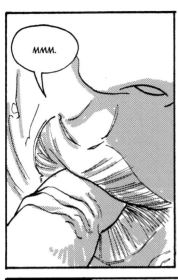

MMM.

THIS IS A TRULY SURPRISING DISPLAY OF FORTITUDE, OVID.

BUT I THINK WE BOTH UNDERSTAND WHERE WE ARE HEADED SO IT'S PROBABLY TIME YOU TELL ME...

WHO IT IS!

THE FACT THAT YOU DON'T ALREADY KNOW--

--DIDN'T SEE THIS COMING--

--JUST LOOK AT YOU.

LOOK WHAT IS LEFT.

HOW COULD THEY NOT MAKE A CHANGE?

THEY?

HOW COULD I ARGUE?

GODS.

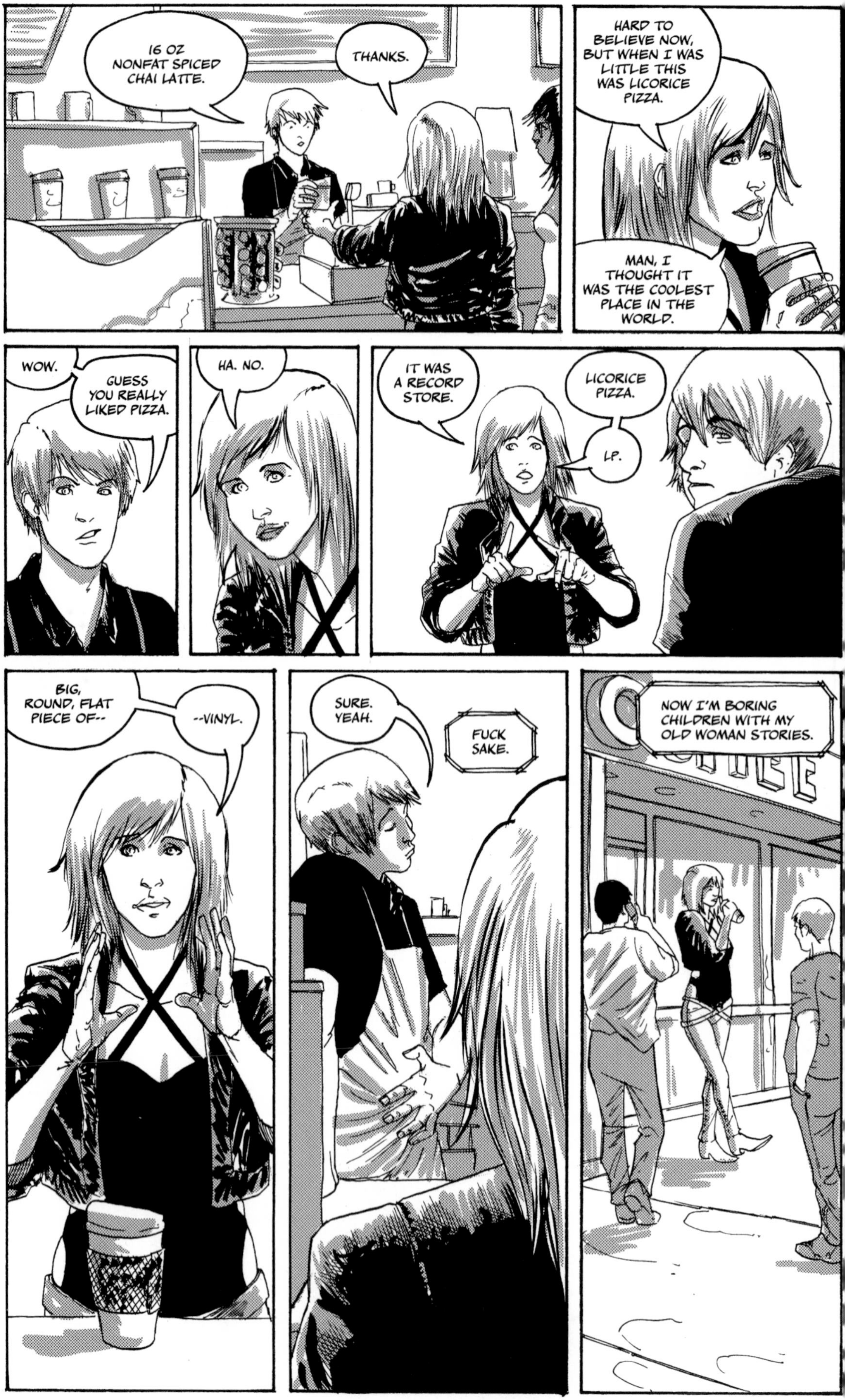
16 OZ NONFAT SPICED CHAI LATTE.
THANKS.
HARD TO BELIEVE NOW, BUT WHEN I WAS LITTLE THIS WAS LICORICE PIZZA.
MAN, I THOUGHT IT WAS THE COOLEST PLACE IN THE WORLD.
WOW.
GUESS YOU REALLY LIKED PIZZA.
HA. NO.
IT WAS A RECORD STORE.
LICORICE PIZZA.
LP.
BIG, ROUND, FLAT PIECE OF--
--VINYL.
SURE. YEAH.
FUCK SAKE.
NOW I'M BORING CHILDREN WITH MY OLD WOMAN STORIES.

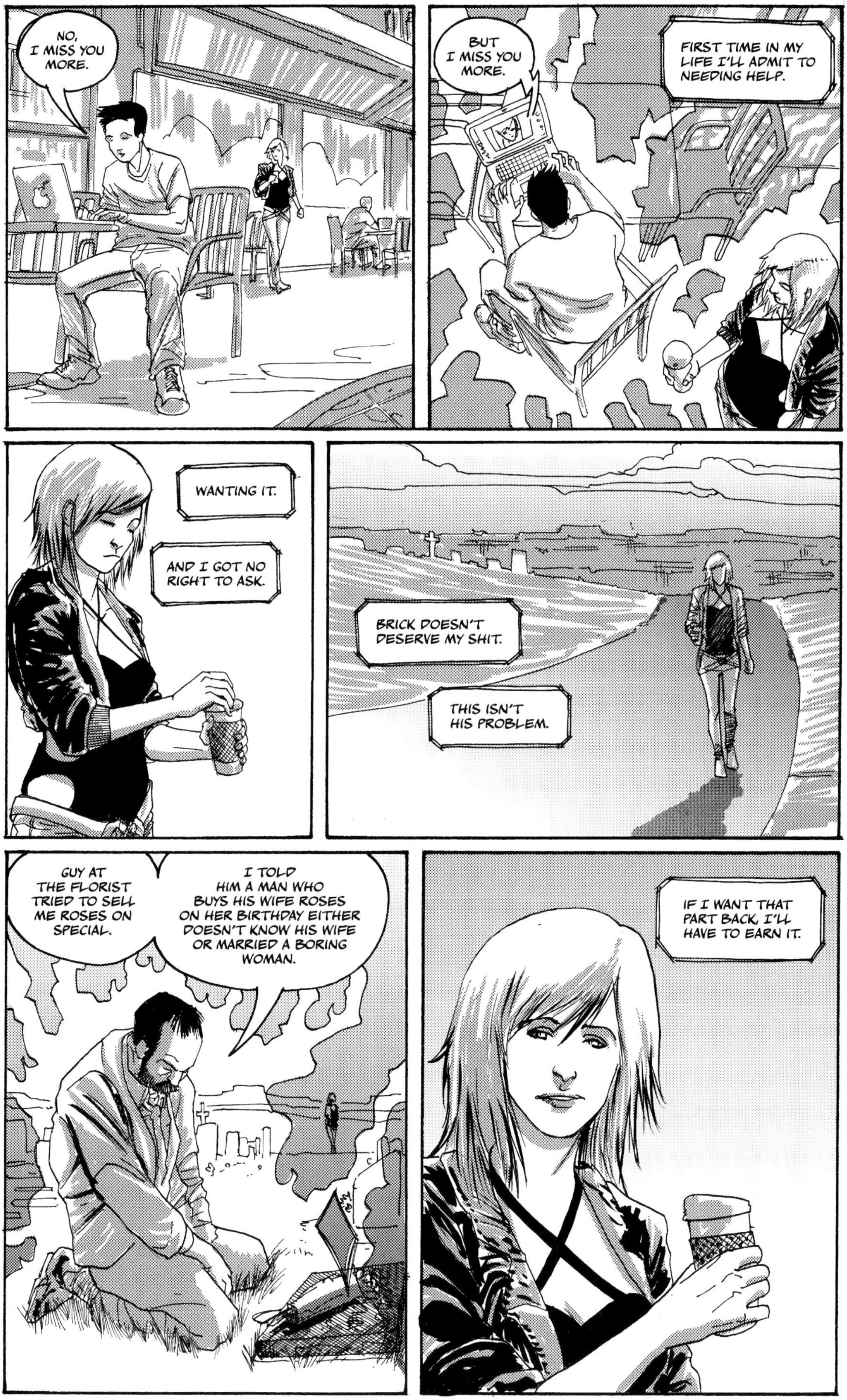
NO, I MISS YOU MORE.
BUT I MISS YOU MORE.
FIRST TIME IN MY LIFE I'LL ADMIT TO NEEDING HELP.
WANTING IT.
AND I GOT NO RIGHT TO ASK.
BRICK DOESN'T DESERVE MY SHIT.
THIS ISN'T HIS PROBLEM.
GUY AT THE FLORIST TRIED TO SELL ME ROSES ON SPECIAL.
I TOLD HIM A MAN WHO BUYS HIS WIFE ROSES ON HER BIRTHDAY EITHER DOESN'T KNOW HIS WIFE OR MARRIED A BORING WOMAN.
IF I WANT THAT PART BACK, I'LL HAVE TO EARN IT.

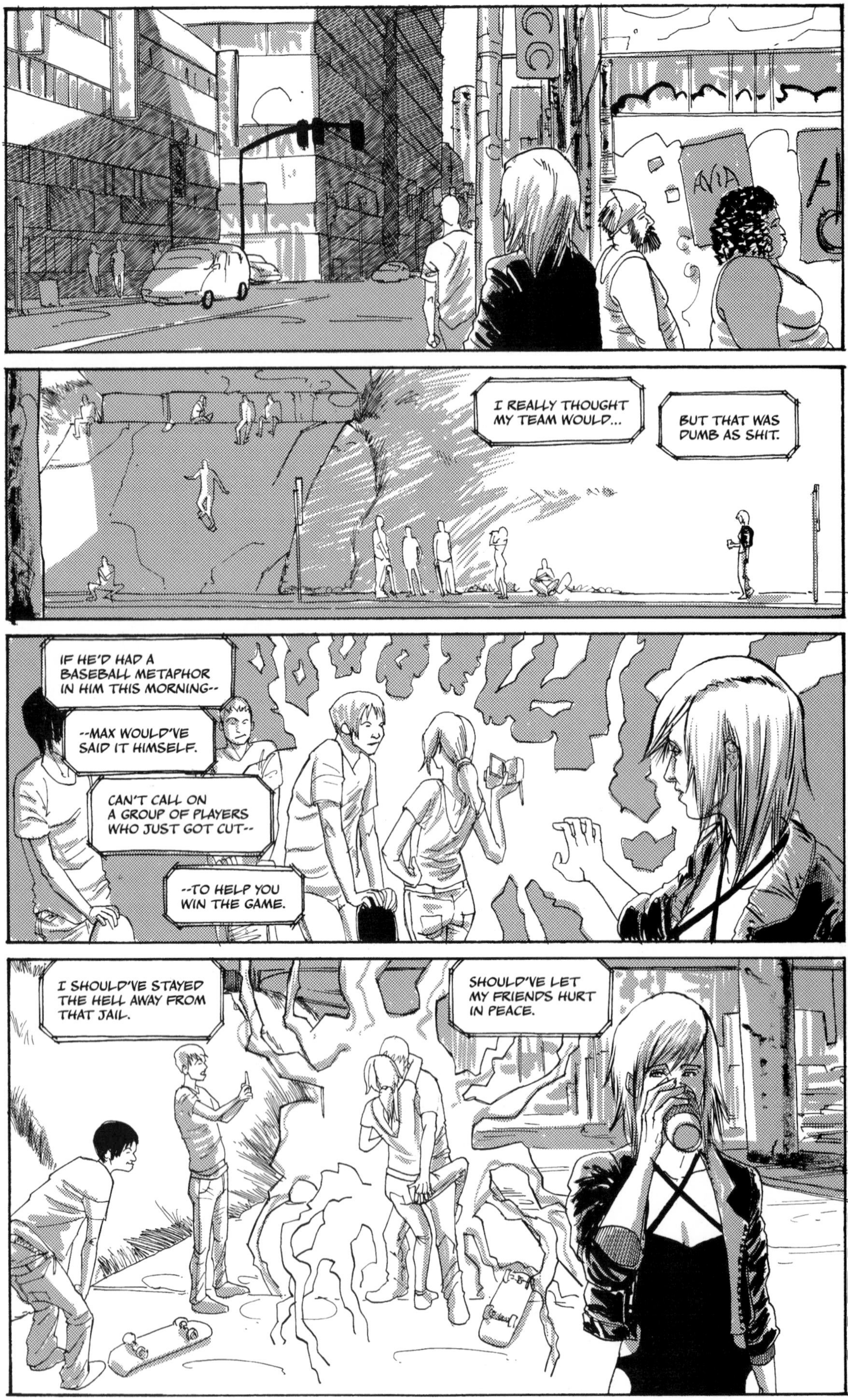

I REALLY THOUGHT MY TEAM WOULD...
BUT THAT WAS DUMB AS SHIT.
IF HE'D HAD A BASEBALL METAPHOR IN HIM THIS MORNING--
--MAX WOULD'VE SAID IT HIMSELF.
CAN'T CALL ON A GROUP OF PLAYERS WHO JUST GOT CUT--
--TO HELP YOU WIN THE GAME.
I SHOULD'VE STAYED THE HELL AWAY FROM THAT JAIL.
SHOULD'VE LET MY FRIENDS HURT IN PEACE.

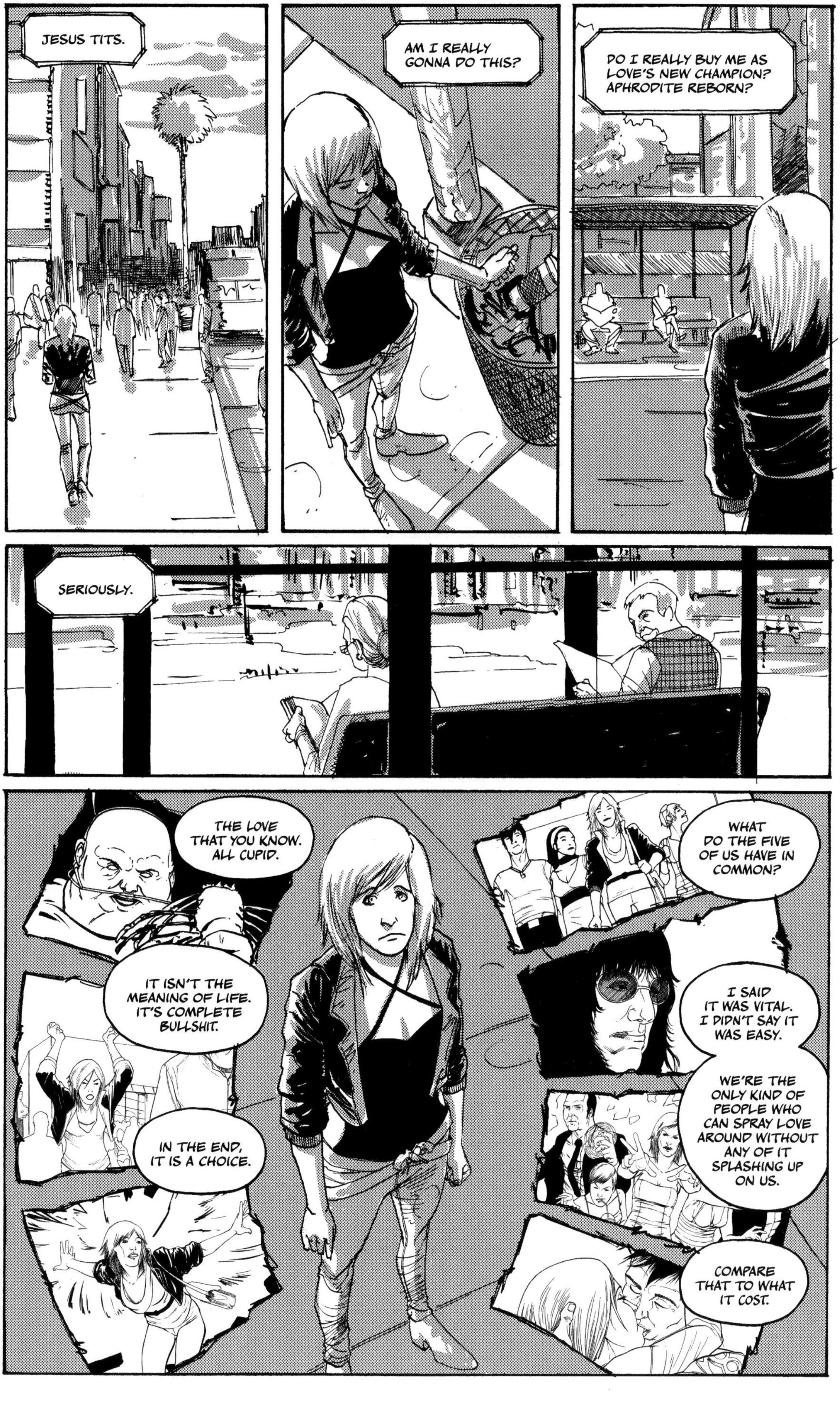
JESUS TITS.
AM I REALLY GONNA DO THIS?
DO I REALLY BUY ME AS LOVE'S NEW CHAMPION? APHRODITE REBORN?
SERIOUSLY.
THE LOVE THAT YOU KNOW. ALL CUPID.
IT ISN'T THE MEANING OF LIFE. IT'S COMPLETE BULLSHIT.
IN THE END, IT IS A CHOICE.
WHAT DO THE FIVE OF US HAVE IN COMMON?
I SAID IT WAS VITAL. I DIDN'T SAY IT WAS EASY.
WE'RE THE ONLY KIND OF PEOPLE WHO CAN SPRAY LOVE AROUND WITHOUT ANY OF IT SPLASHING UP ON US.
COMPARE THAT TO WHAT IT COST.

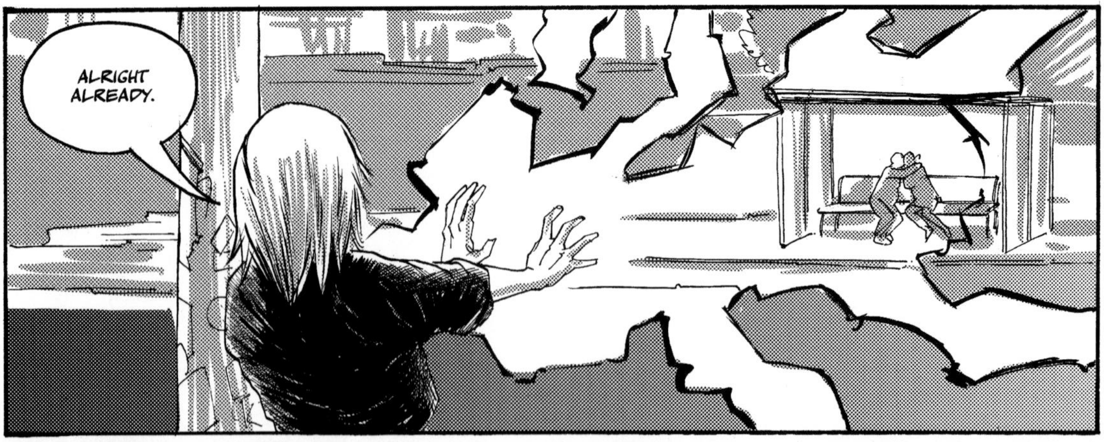
ALRIGHT ALREADY.

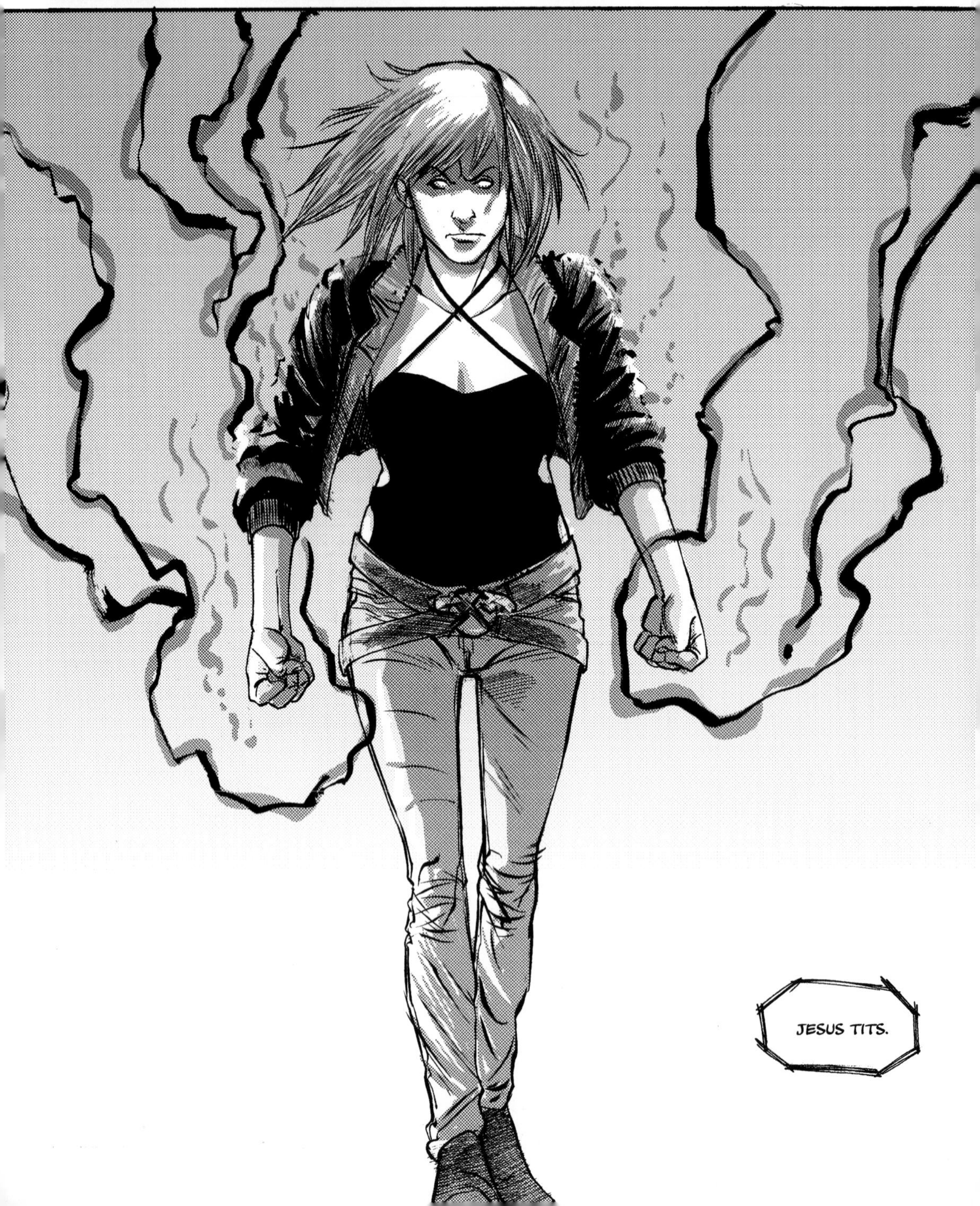
JESUS TITS.

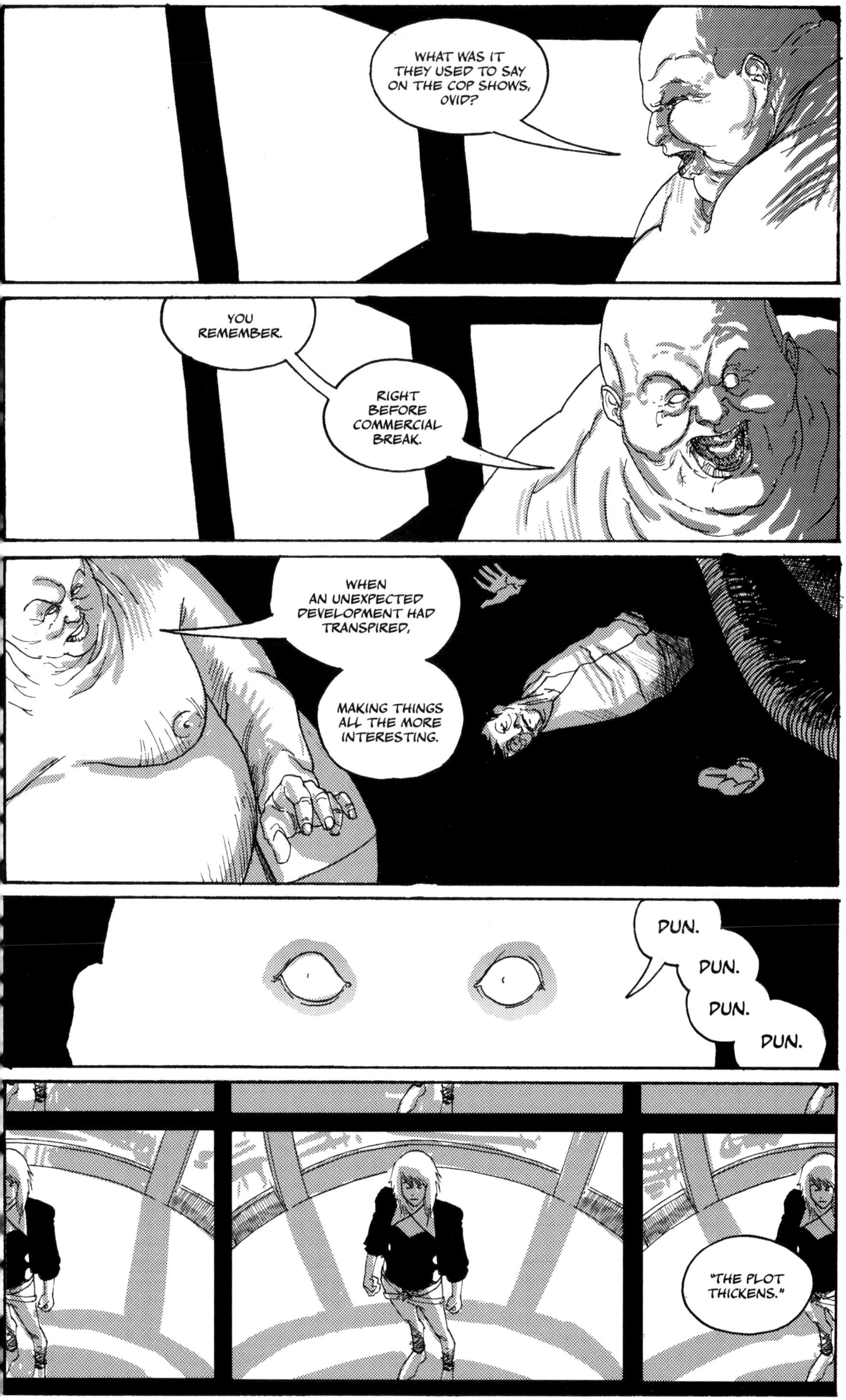
WHAT WAS IT THEY USED TO SAY ON THE COP SHOWS, OVID?
YOU REMEMBER.
RIGHT BEFORE COMMERCIAL BREAK.
WHEN AN UNEXPECTED DEVELOPMENT HAD TRANSPIRED,
MAKING THINGS ALL THE MORE INTERESTING.
DUN.
DUN.
DUN.
DUN.
"THE PLOT THICKENS."

CHAPTER 6

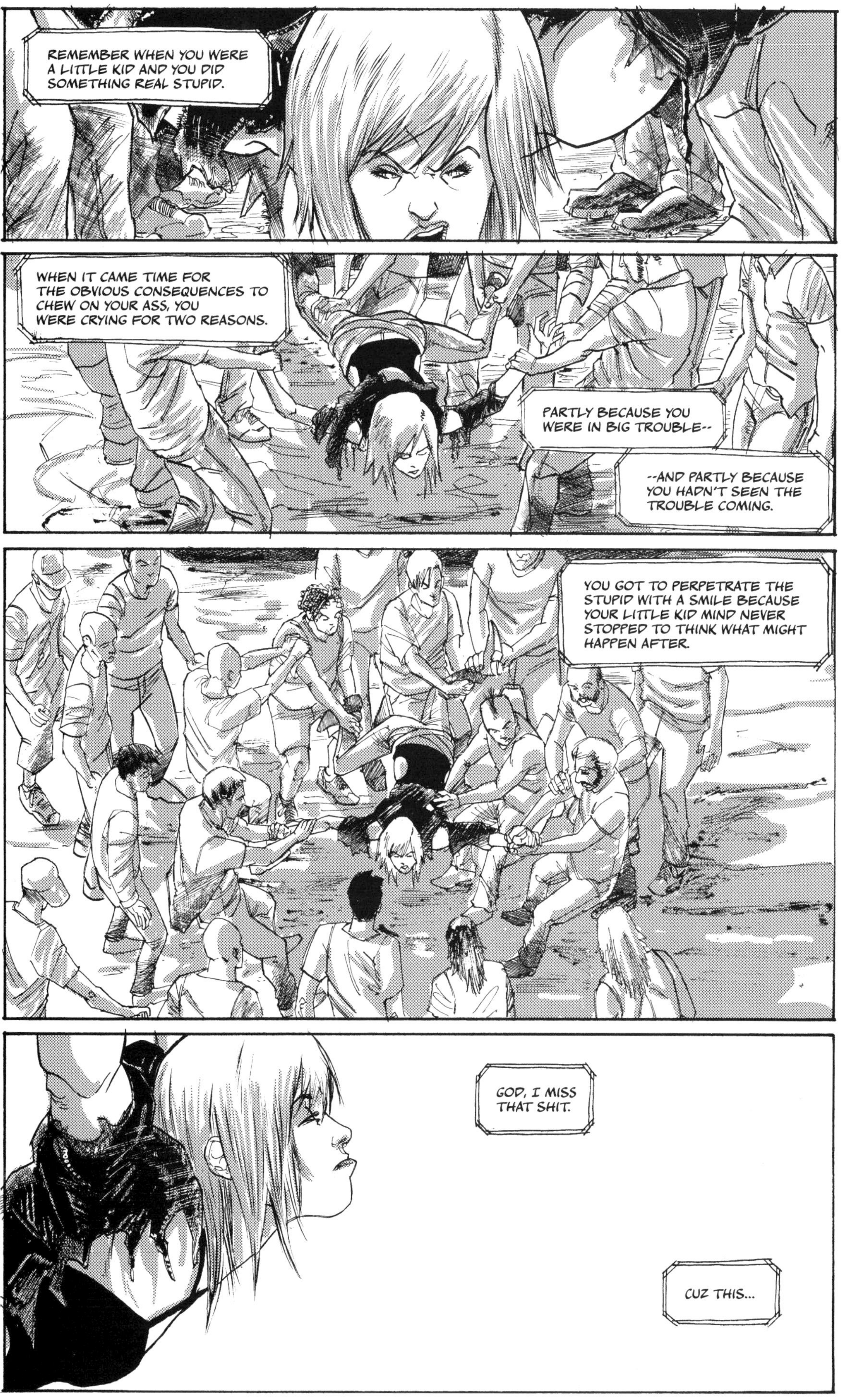
REMEMBER WHEN YOU WERE A LITTLE KID AND YOU DID SOMETHING REAL STUPID.
WHEN IT CAME TIME FOR THE OBVIOUS CONSEQUENCES TO CHEW ON YOUR ASS, YOU WERE CRYING FOR TWO REASONS.
PARTLY BECAUSE YOU WERE IN BIG TROUBLE--
--AND PARTLY BECAUSE YOU HADN'T SEEN THE TROUBLE COMING.
YOU GOT TO PERPETRATE THE STUPID WITH A SMILE BECAUSE YOUR LITTLE KID MIND NEVER STOPPED TO THINK WHAT MIGHT HAPPEN AFTER.
GOD, I MISS THAT SHIT.
CUZ THIS...

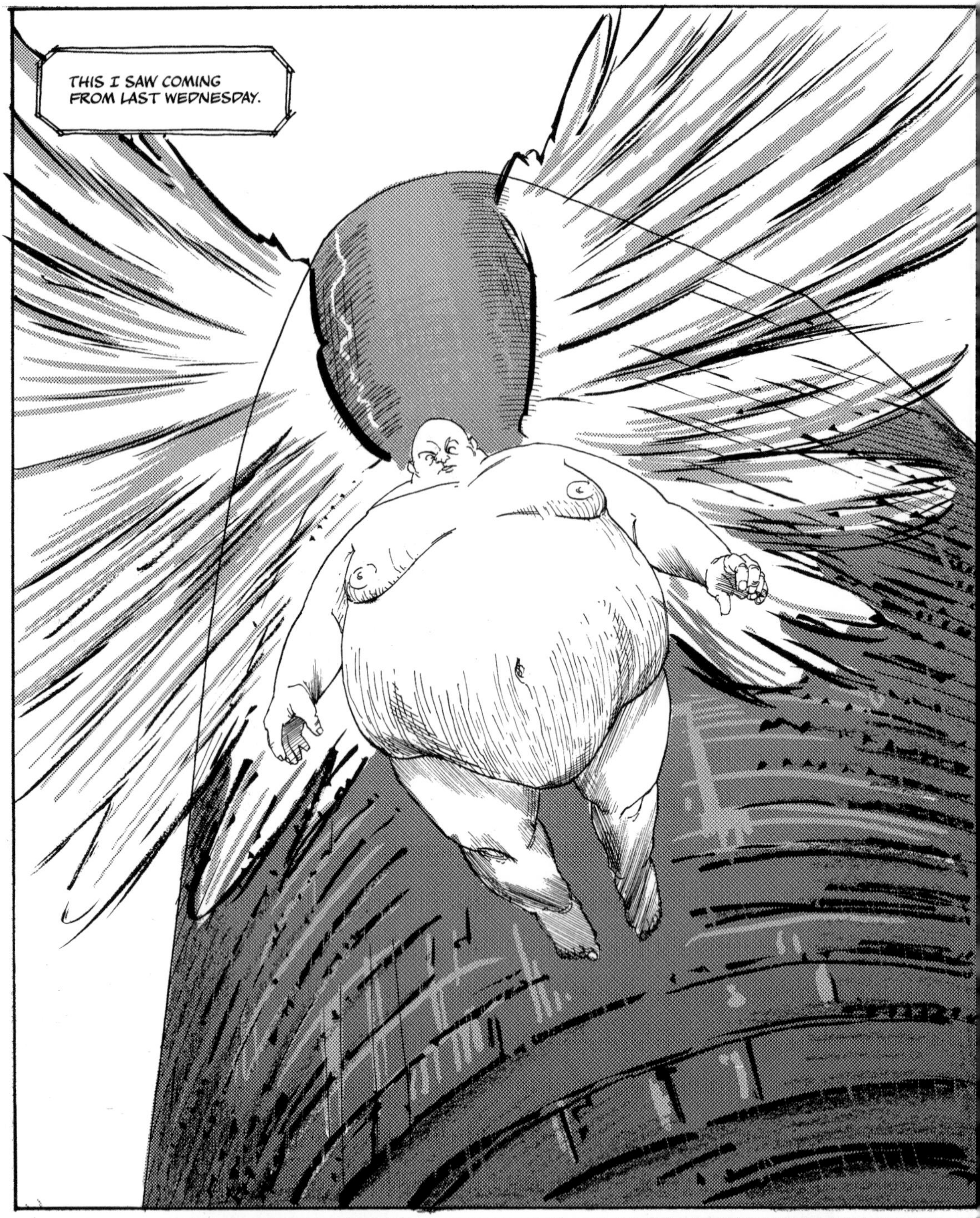
THIS I SAW COMING FROM LAST WEDNESDAY.

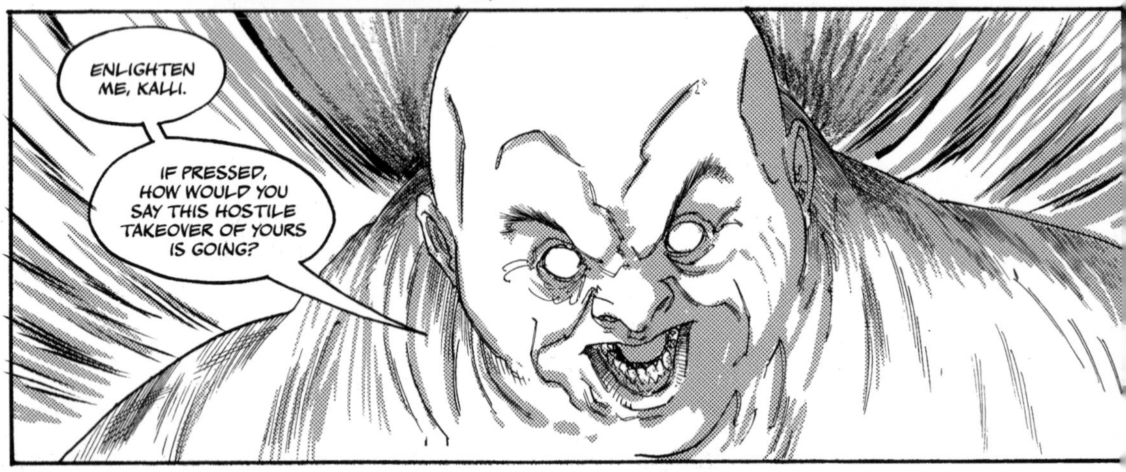
ENLIGHTEN ME, KALLI.
IF PRESSED, HOW WOULD YOU SAY THIS HOSTILE TAKEOVER OF YOURS IS GOING?

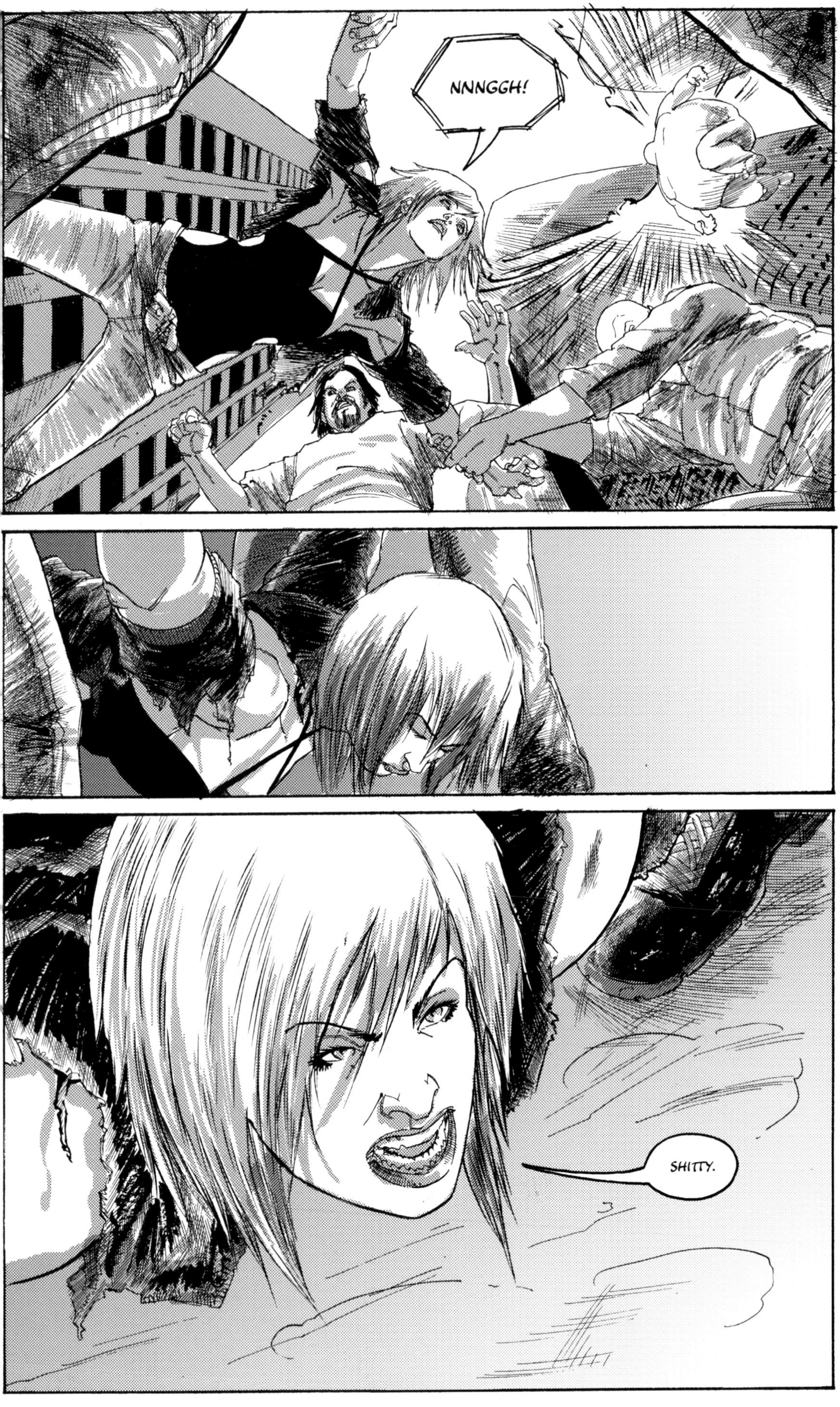
NNNGGH!
SHITTY.

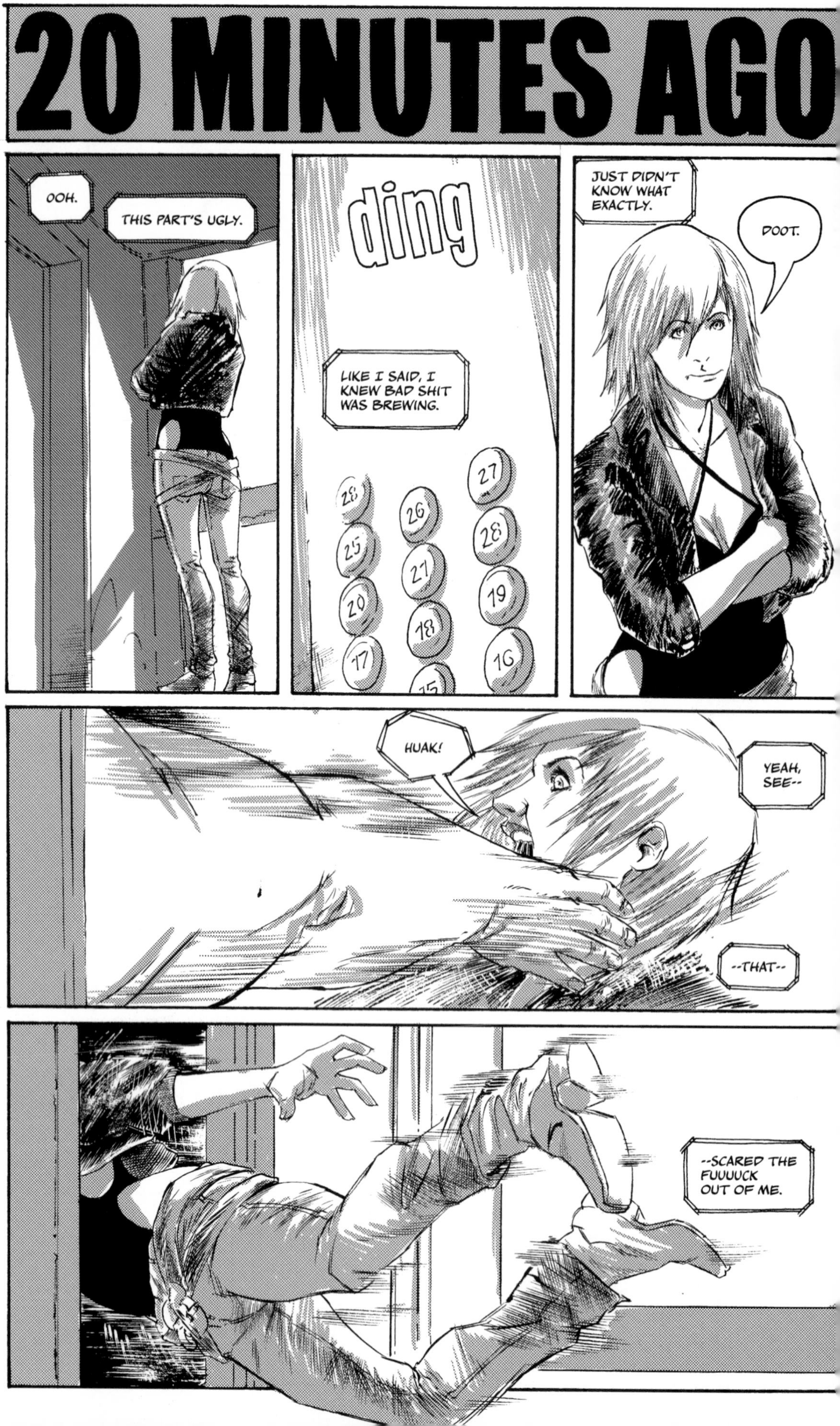
20 MINUTES AGO
OOH.
THIS PART'S UGLY.
ding
LIKE I SAID, I KNEW BAD SHIT WAS BREWING.
28
26
27
25
27
28
20
21
19
18
17
16
JUST DIDN'T KNOW WHAT EXACTLY.
DOOT.
HUAK!
YEAH, SEE--
--THAT--
--SCARED THE FUUUUCK OUT OF ME.

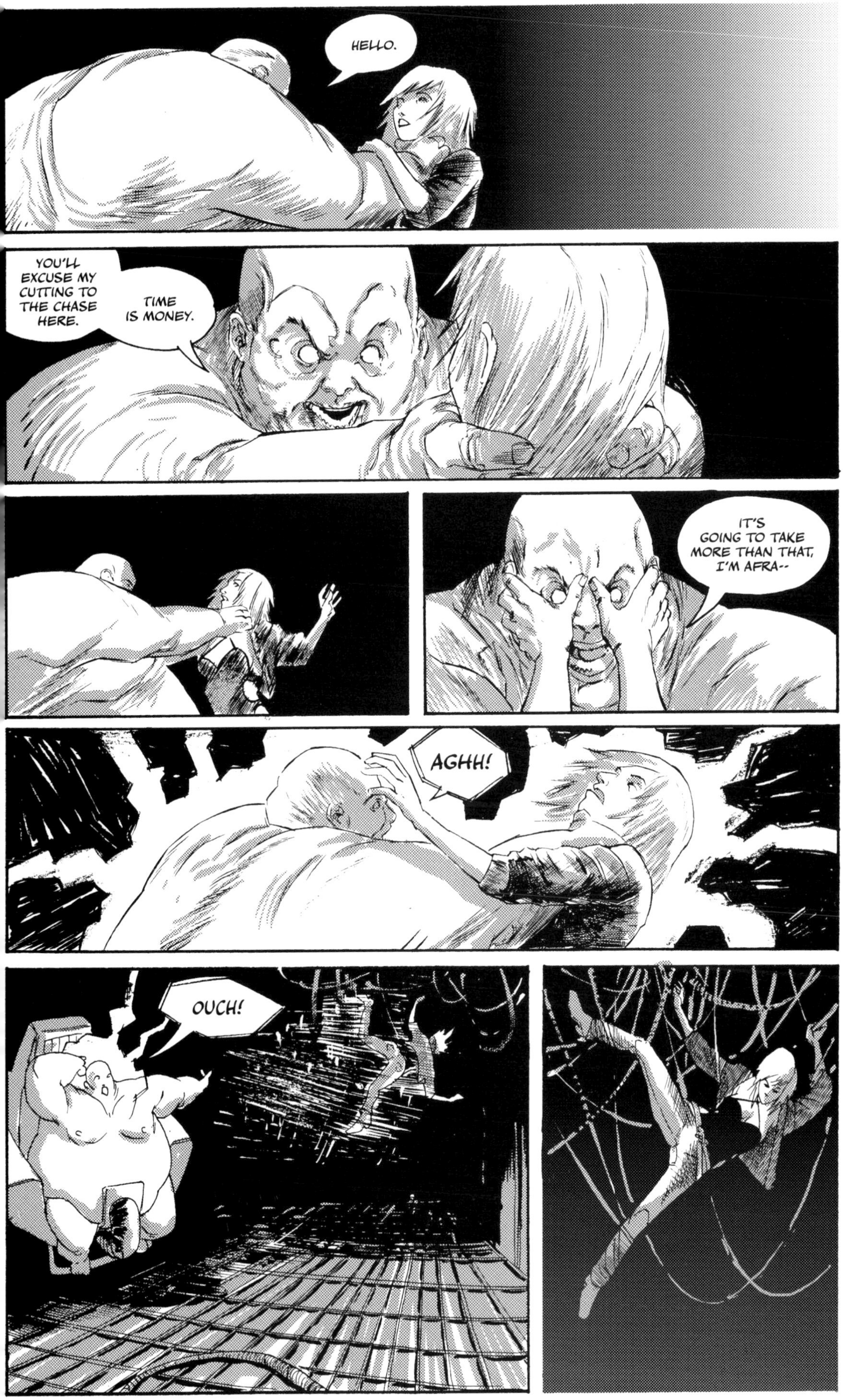
HELLO.
YOU'LL EXCUSE MY CUTTING TO THE CHASE HERE.
TIME IS MONEY.
IT'S GOING TO TAKE MORE THAN THAT, I'M AFRA--
AGHH!
OUCH!

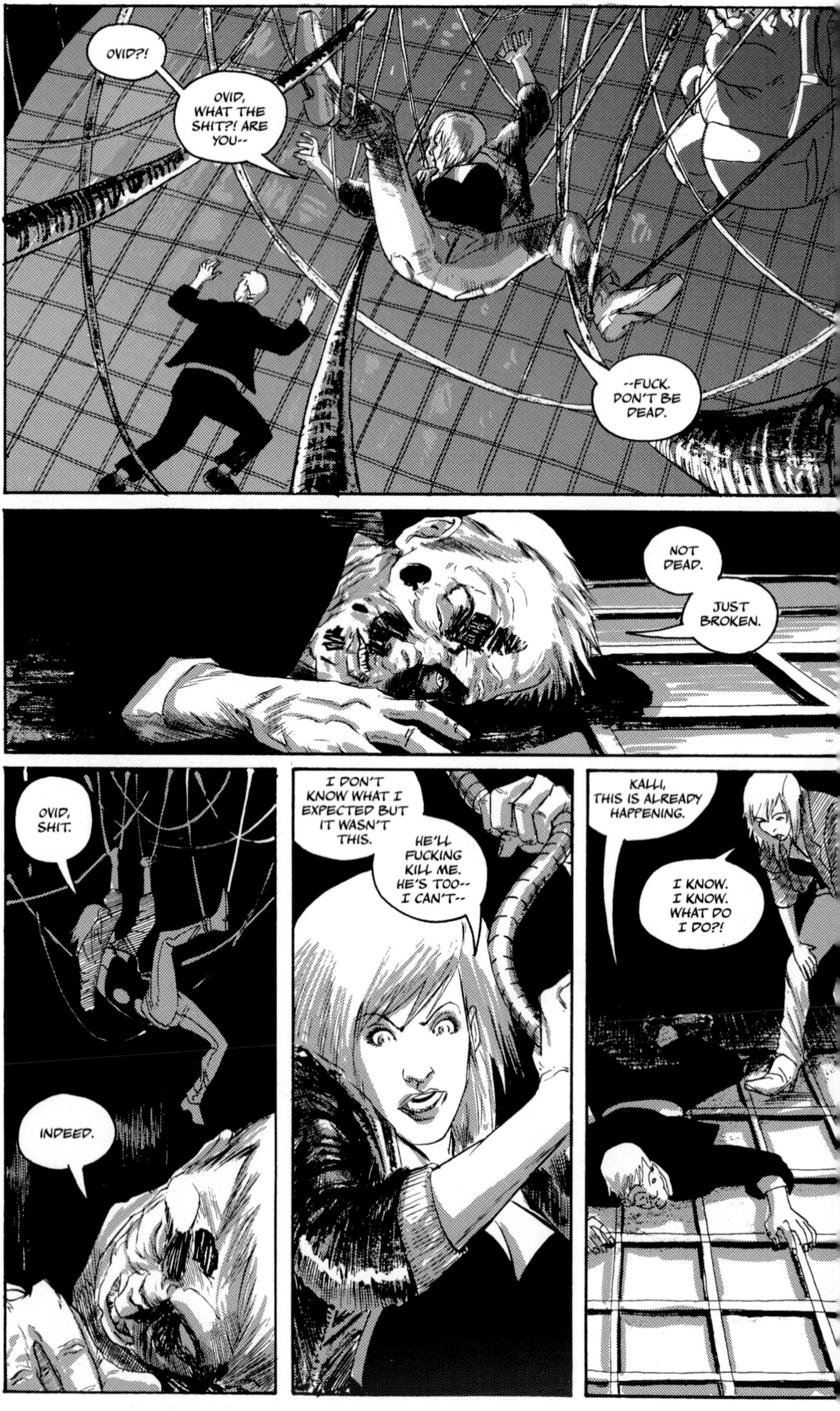
OVID?!
OVID, WHAT THE SHIT?! ARE YOU--
--FUCK. DON'T BE DEAD.
NOT DEAD.
JUST BROKEN.
OVID, SHIT.
INDEED.
I DON'T KNOW WHAT I EXPECTED BUT IT WASN'T THIS.
HE'LL FUCKING KILL ME. HE'S TOO-- I CAN'T--
KALLI, THIS IS ALREADY HAPPENING.
I KNOW. I KNOW. WHAT DO I DO?!

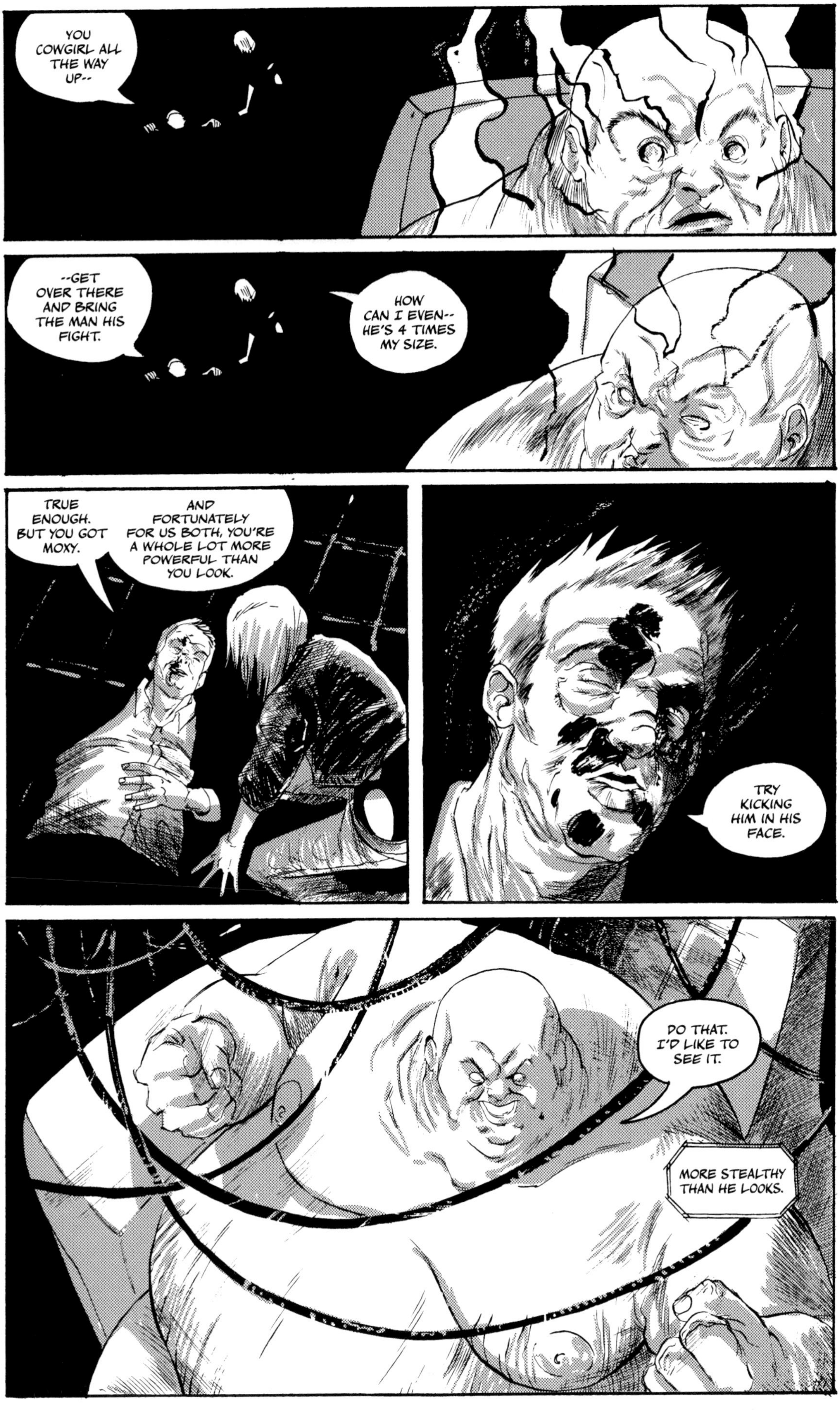
YOU COWGIRL ALL THE WAY UP--
--GET OVER THERE AND BRING THE MAN HIS FIGHT.
HOW CAN I EVEN-- HE'S 4 TIMES MY SIZE.
TRUE ENOUGH. BUT YOU GOT MOXY.
AND FORTUNATELY FOR US BOTH, YOU'RE A WHOLE LOT MORE POWERFUL THAN YOU LOOK.
TRY KICKING HIM IN HIS FACE.
DO THAT. I'D LIKE TO SEE IT.
MORE STEALTHY THAN HE LOOKS.

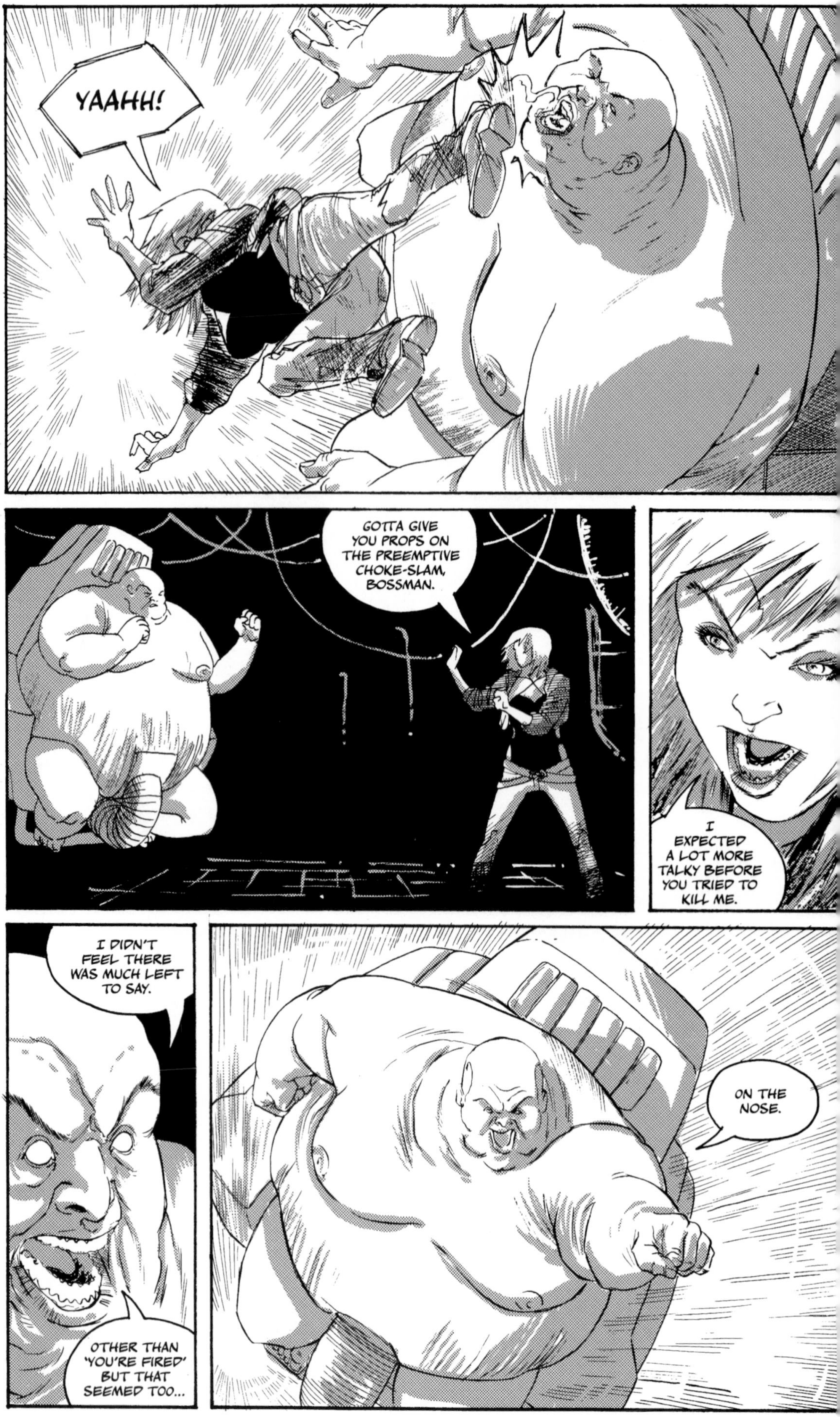
YAAHH!
GOTTA GIVE YOU PROPS ON THE PREEMPTIVE CHOKE-SLAM, BOSSMAN.
I EXPECTED A LOT MORE TALKY BEFORE YOU TRIED TO KILL ME.
I DIDN'T FEEL THERE WAS MUCH LEFT TO SAY.
OTHER THAN 'YOU'RE FIRED' BUT THAT SEEMED TOO...
ON THE NOSE.

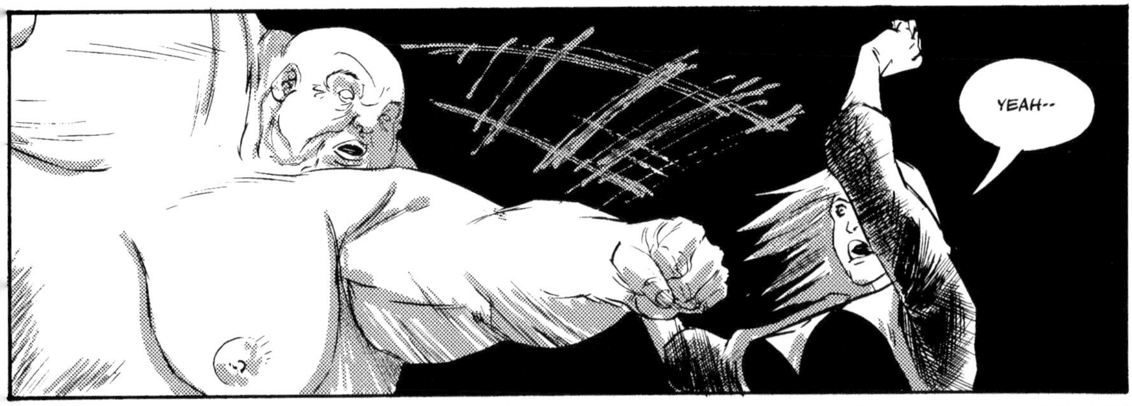
YEAH--

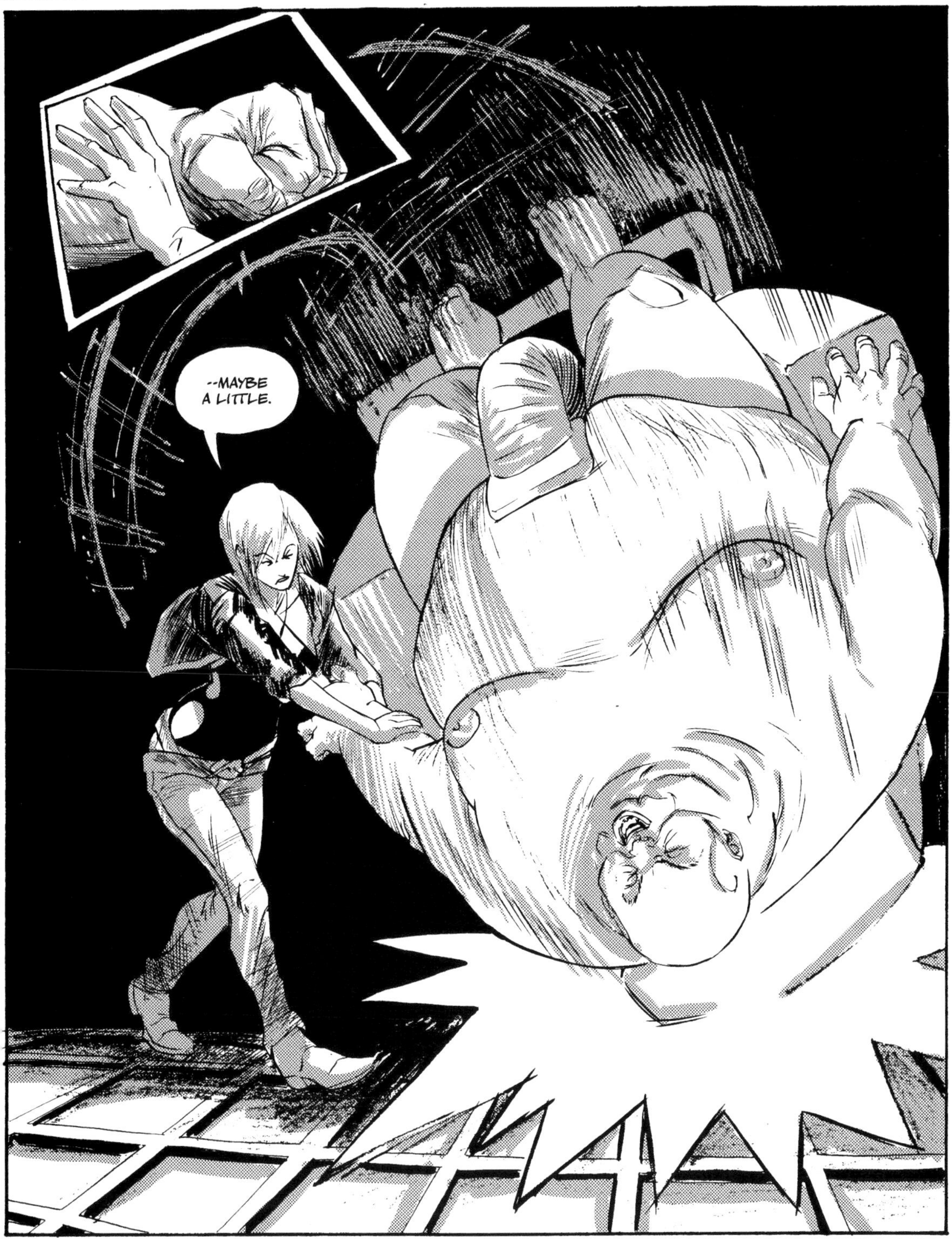
--MAYBE
A LITTLE.

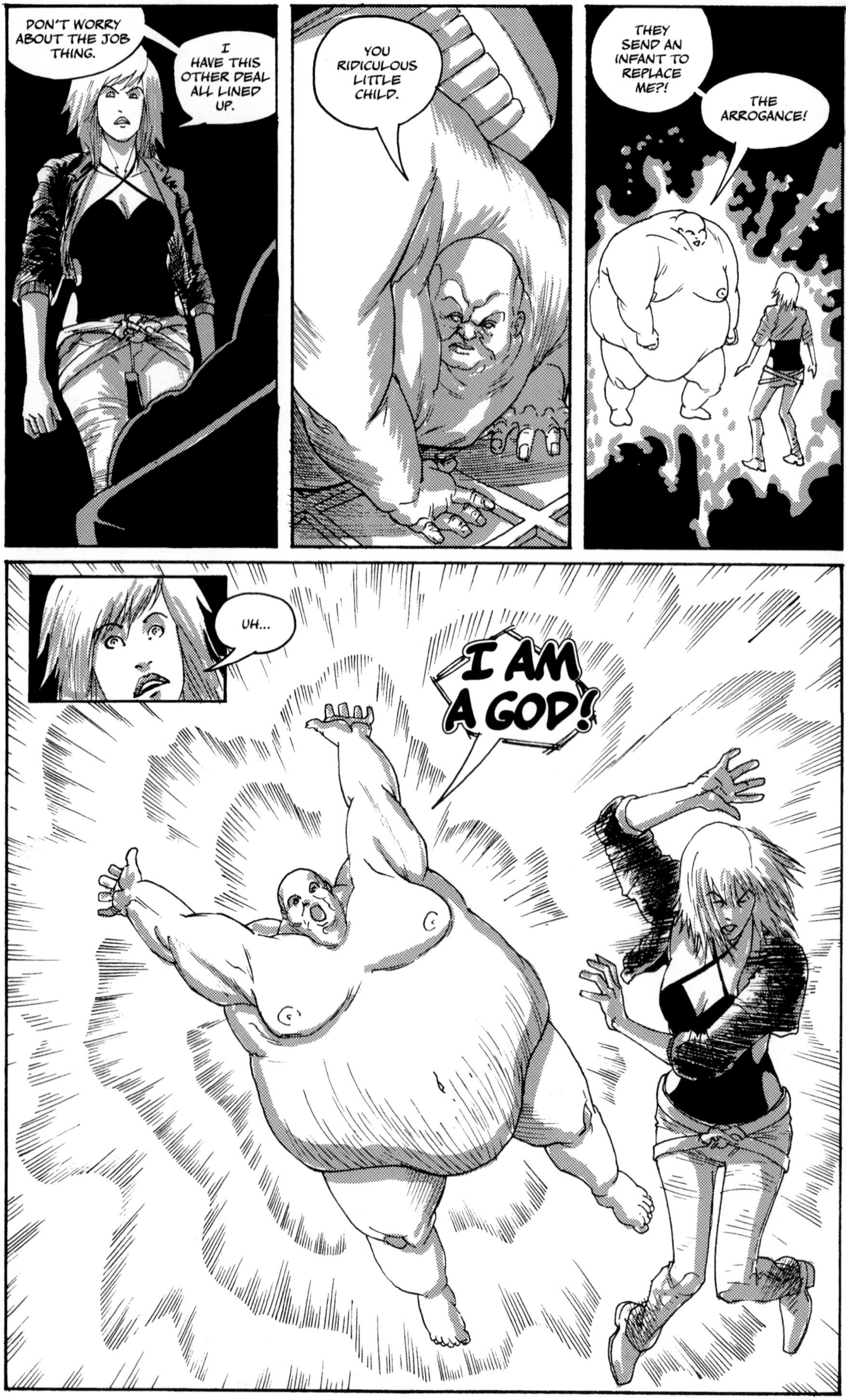
DON'T WORRY ABOUT THE JOB THING.
I HAVE THIS OTHER DEAL ALL LINED UP.
YOU RIDICULOUS LITTLE CHILD.
THEY SEND AN INFANT TO REPLACE ME?!
THE ARROGANCE!
UH...
I AM A GOD!

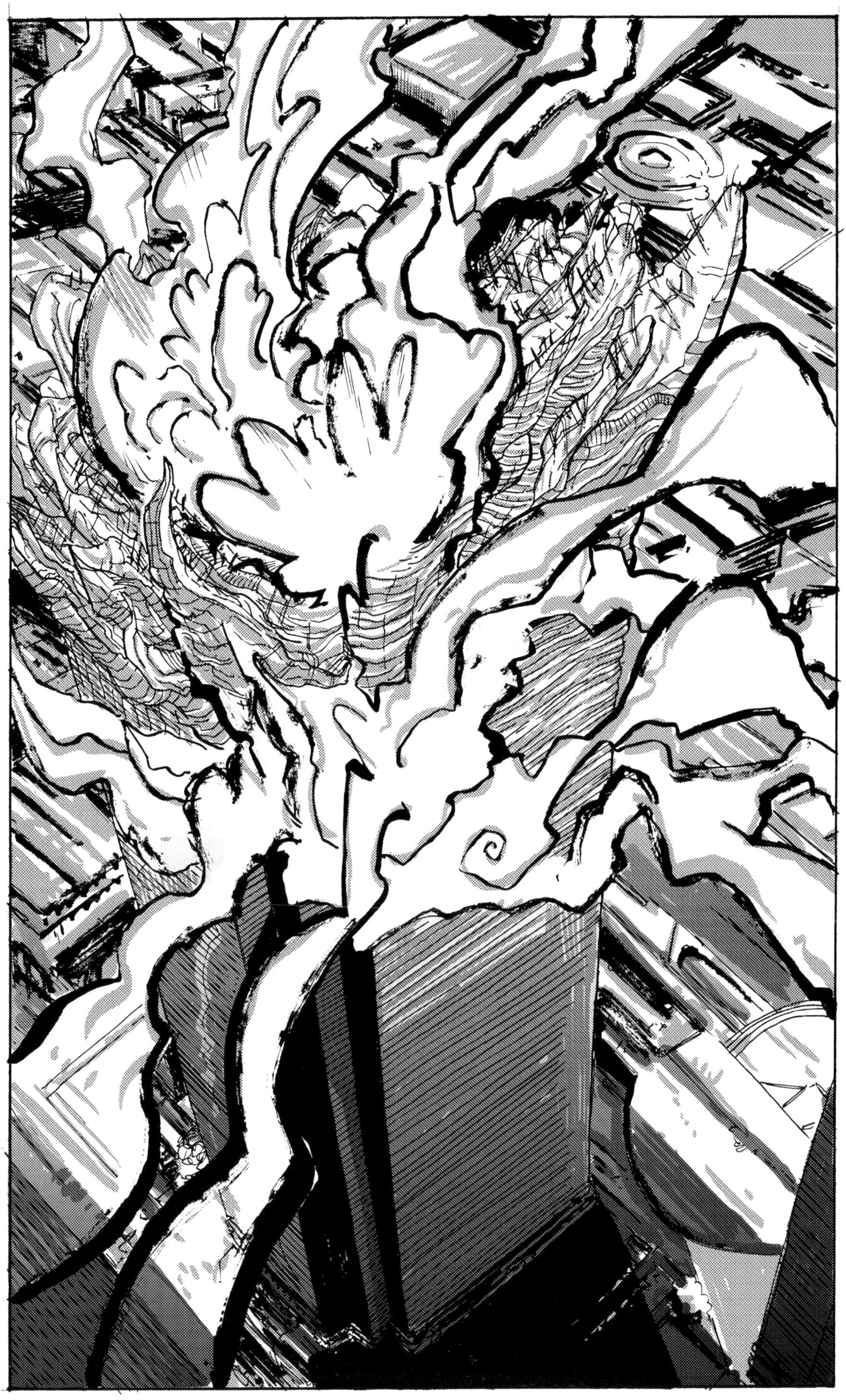

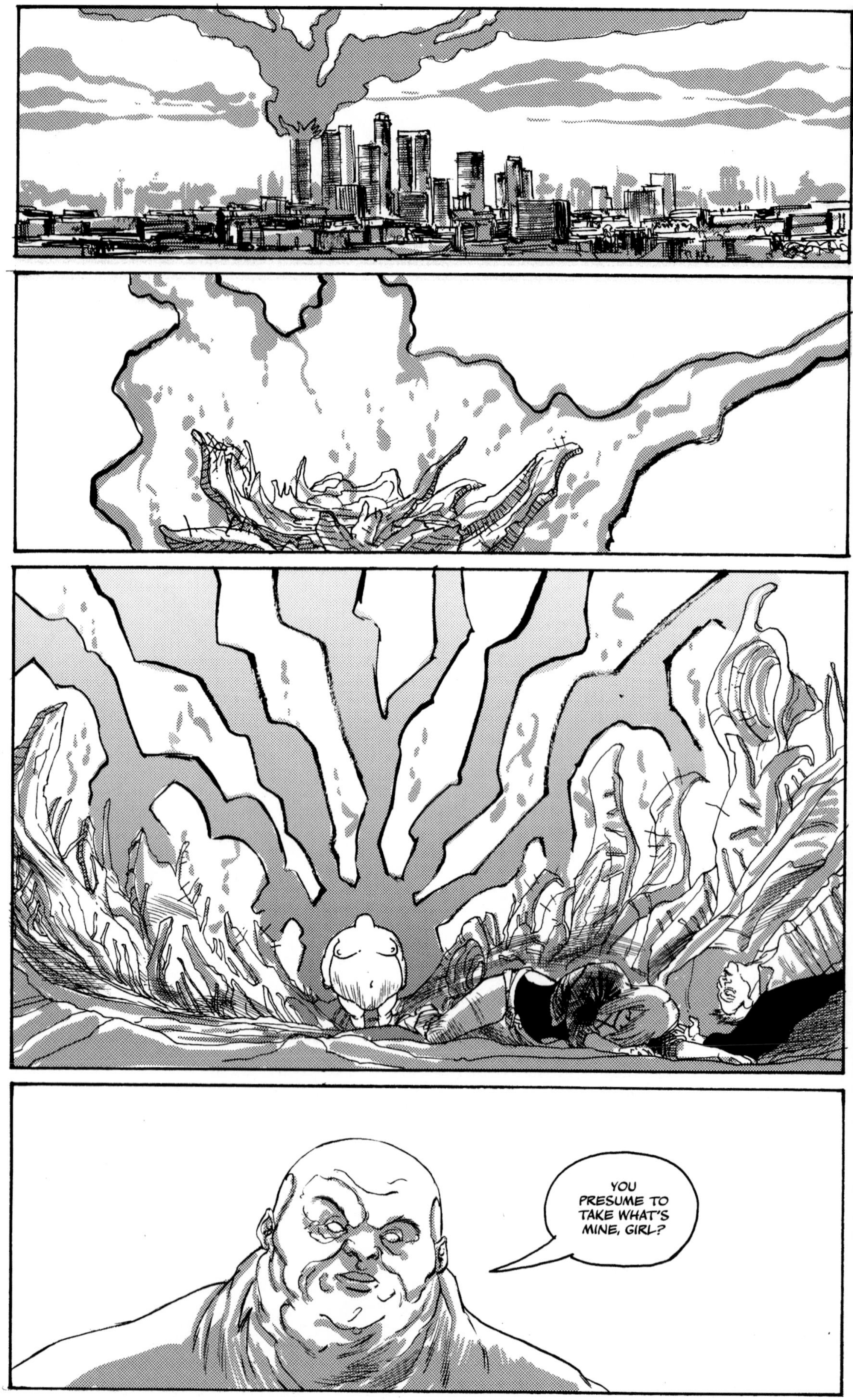
YOU PRESUME TO TAKE WHAT'S MINE, GIRL?

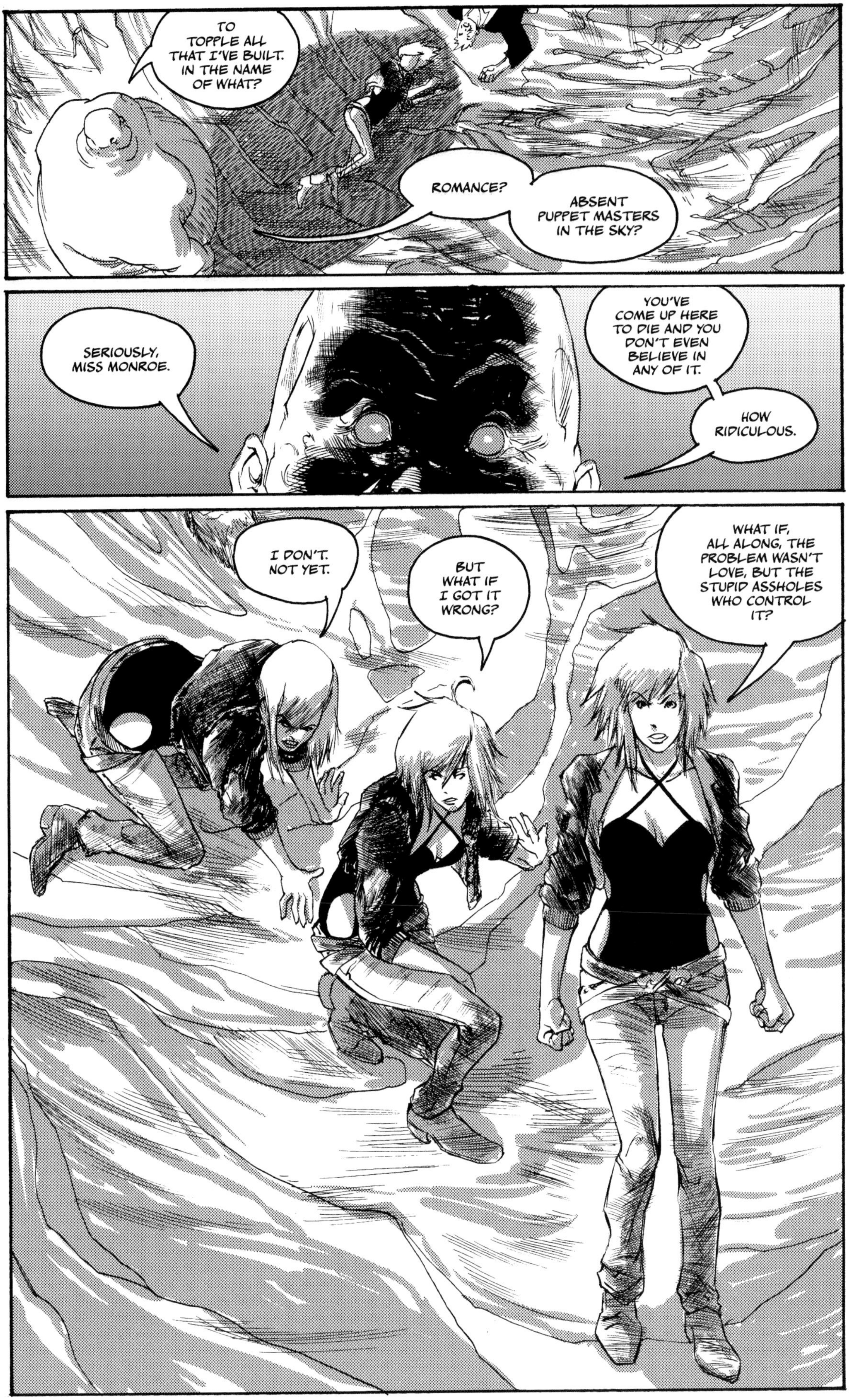

TO TOPPLE ALL THAT I'VE BUILT. IN THE NAME OF WHAT?
ROMANCE?
ABSENT PUPPET MASTERS IN THE SKY?
SERIOUSLY, MISS MONROE.
YOU'VE COME UP HERE TO DIE AND YOU DON'T EVEN BELIEVE IN ANY OF IT.
HOW RIDICULOUS.
I DON'T. NOT YET.
BUT WHAT IF I GOT IT WRONG?
WHAT IF, ALL ALONG, THE PROBLEM WASN'T LOVE, BUT THE STUPID ASSHOLES WHO CONTROL IT?

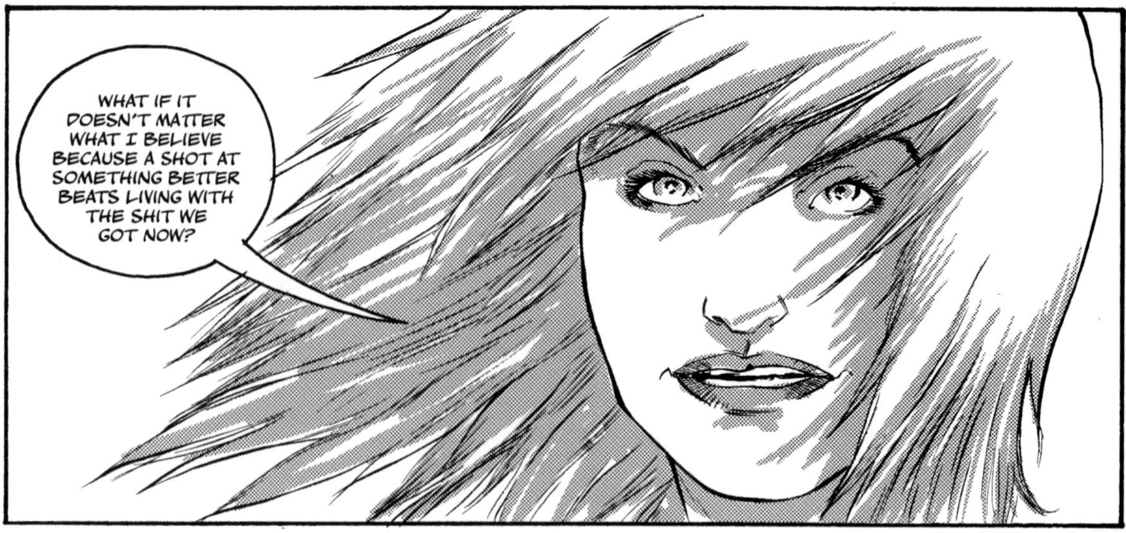
WHAT IF IT DOESN'T MATTER WHAT I BELIEVE BECAUSE A SHOT AT SOMETHING BETTER BEATS LIVING WITH THE SHIT WE GOT NOW?

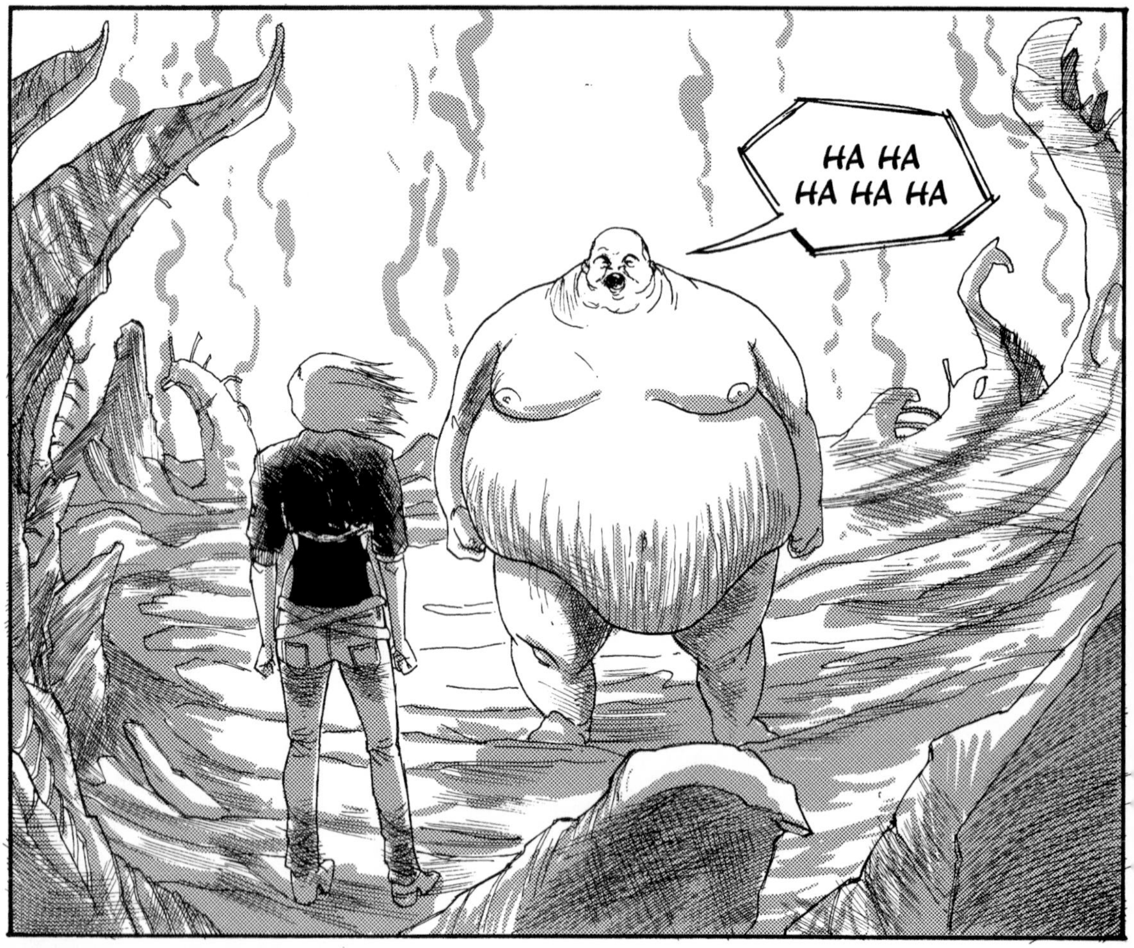
HA HA HA HA HA

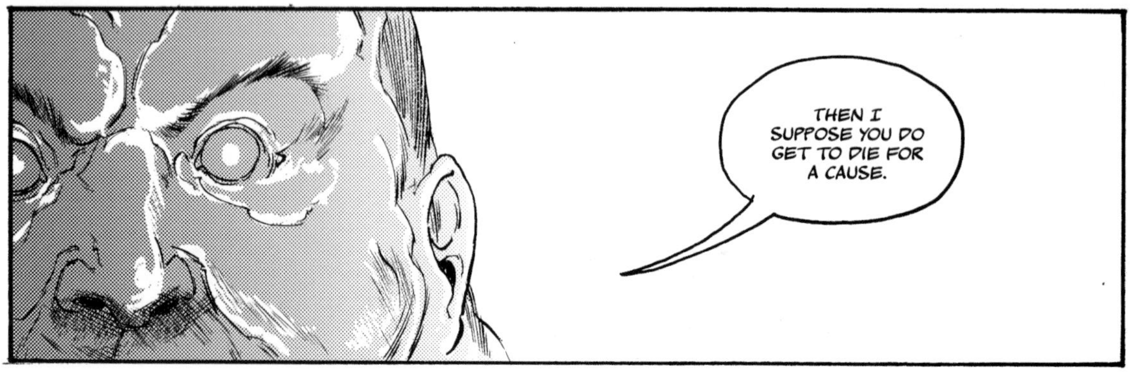
THEN I SUPPOSE YOU DO GET TO DIE FOR A CAUSE.

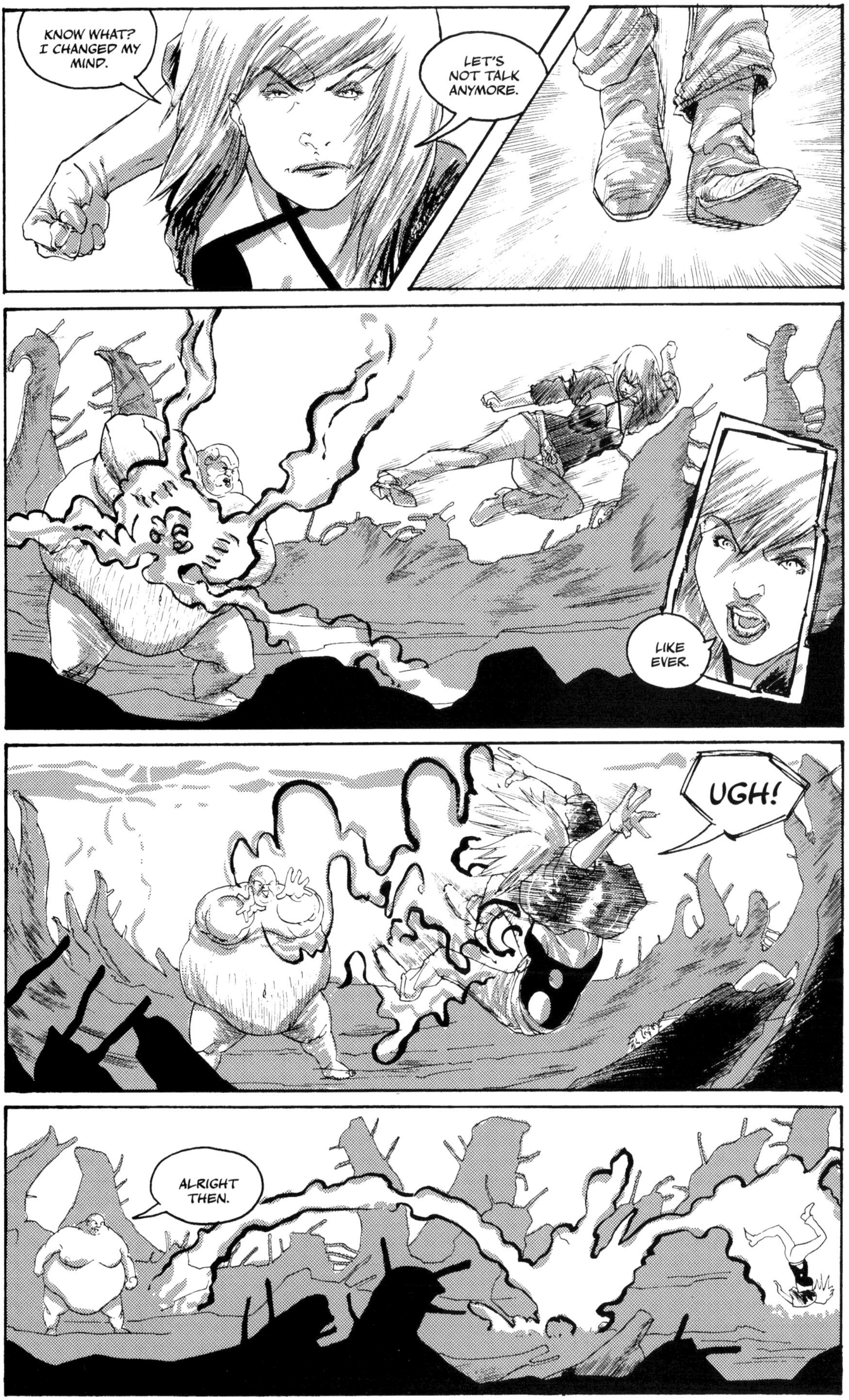
KNOW WHAT? I CHANGED MY MIND.
LET'S NOT TALK ANYMORE.
LIKE EVER.
UGH!
ALRIGHT THEN.

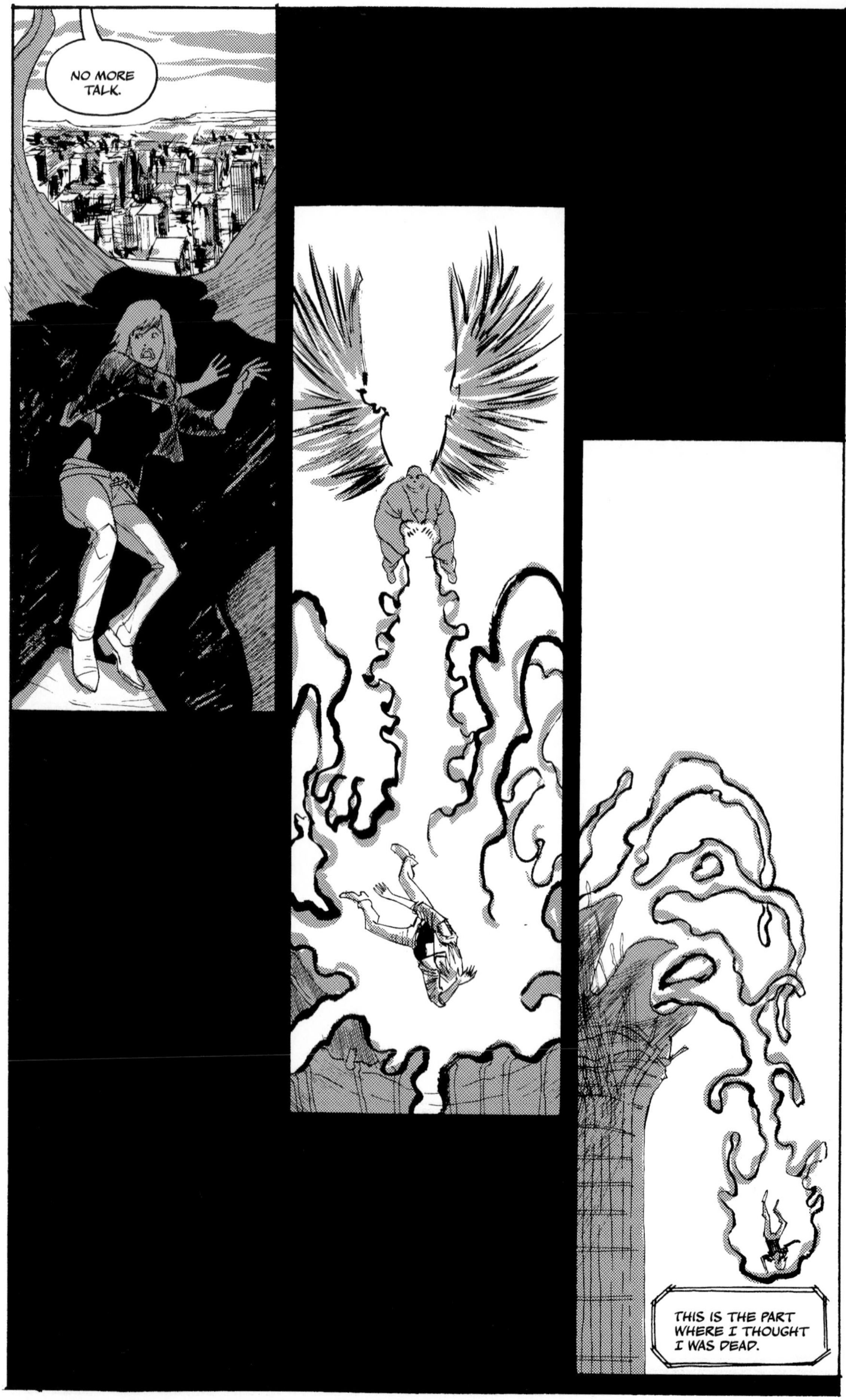
NO MORE TALK.
THIS IS THE PART WHERE I THOUGHT I WAS DEAD.

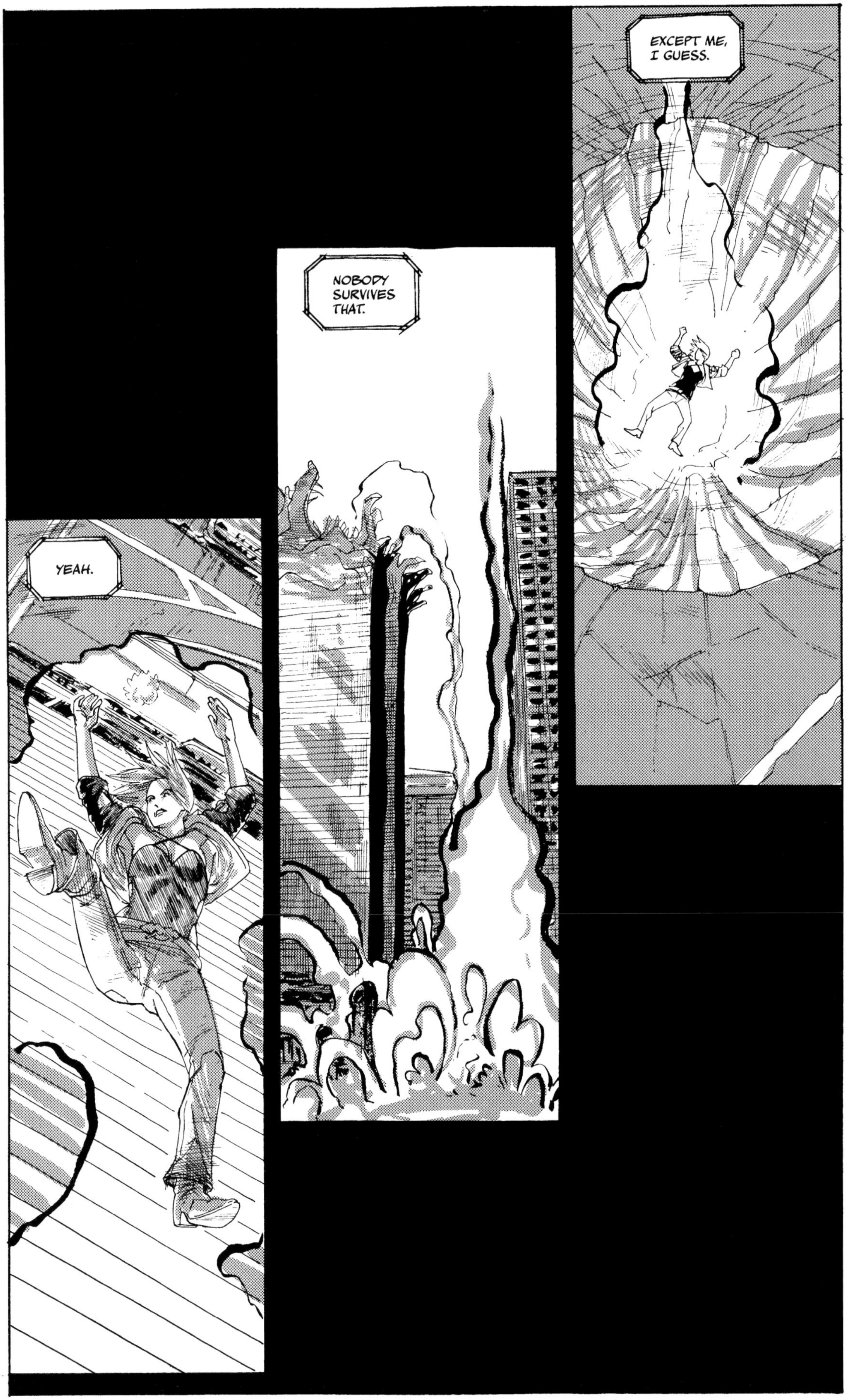
YEAH.
NOBODY SURVIVES THAT.
EXCEPT ME, I GUESS.

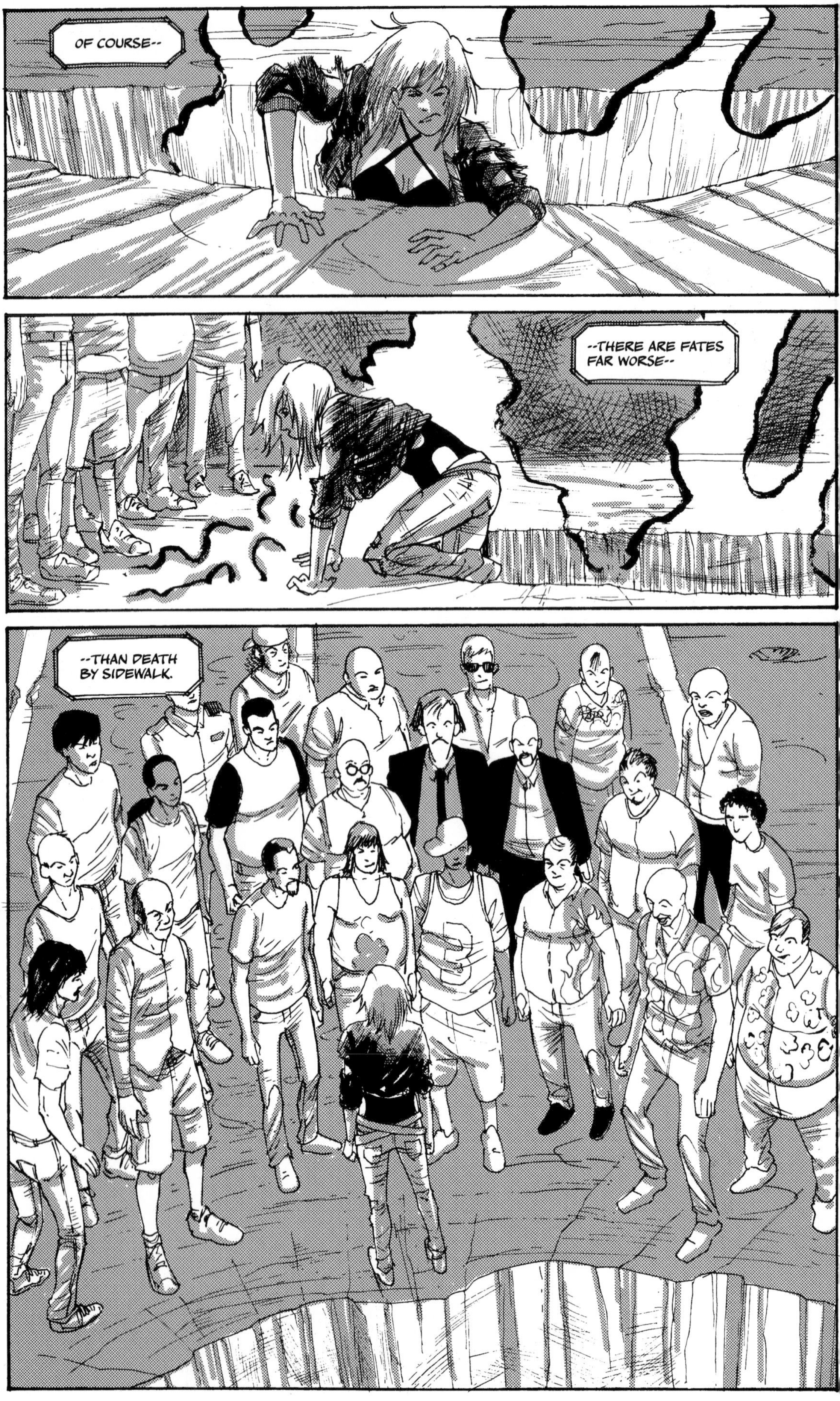
OF COURSE--
--THERE ARE FATES FAR WORSE--
--THAN DEATH BY SIDEWALK.

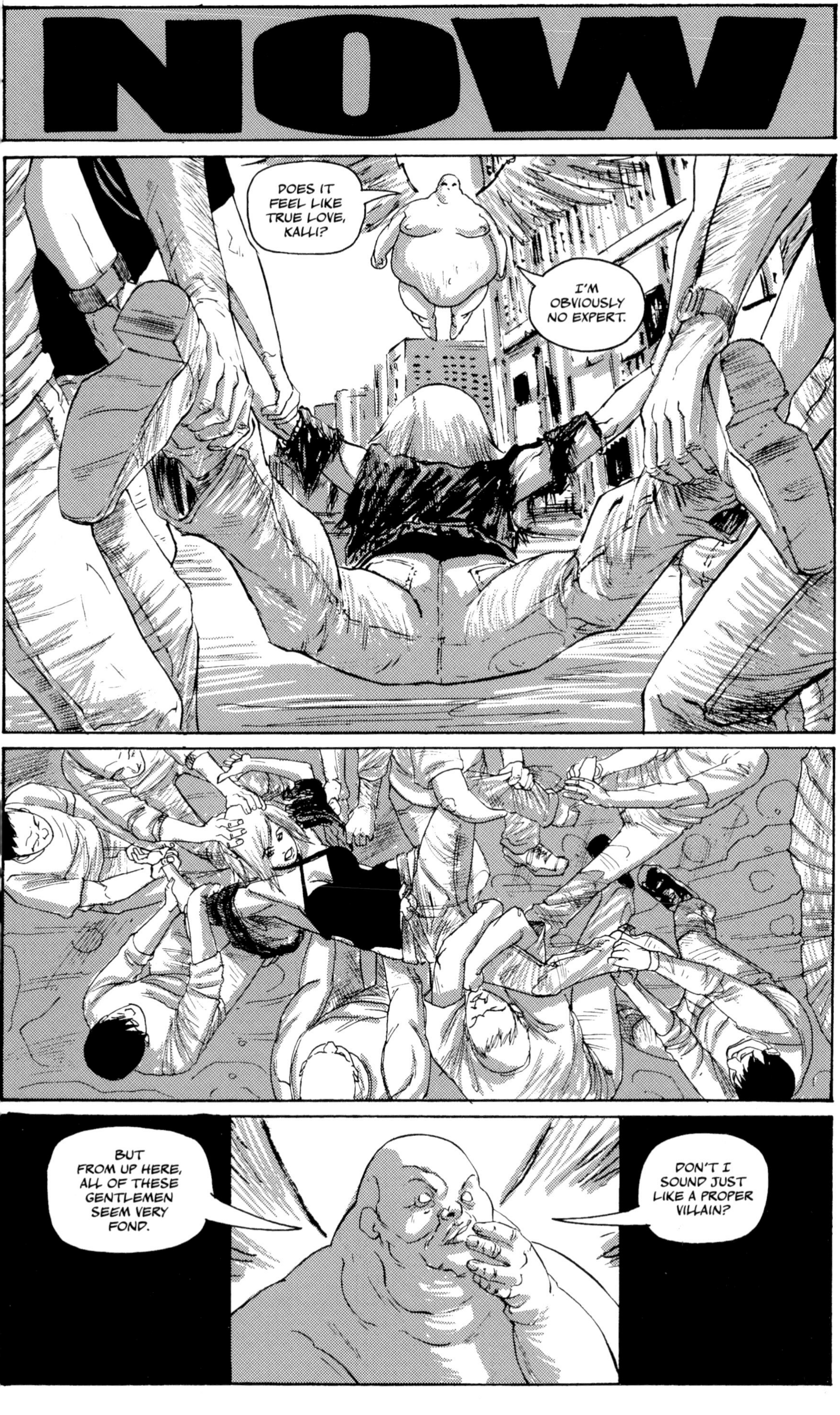
NOW
DOES IT FEEL LIKE TRUE LOVE, KALLI?
I'M OBVIOUSLY NO EXPERT.
BUT FROM UP HERE, ALL OF THESE GENTLEMEN SEEM VERY FOND.
DON'T I SOUND JUST LIKE A PROPER VILLAIN?

FLOATING UP HERE, TRYING TO DECIDE WHETHER TO END YOU MYSELF--

--HERE AND NOW--

--OR TO STAND BACK AND WATCH THESE LUST-CRAZED HOOLIGANS TEAR OFF YOUR SOFT BITS.

YOU KNOW WHAT?

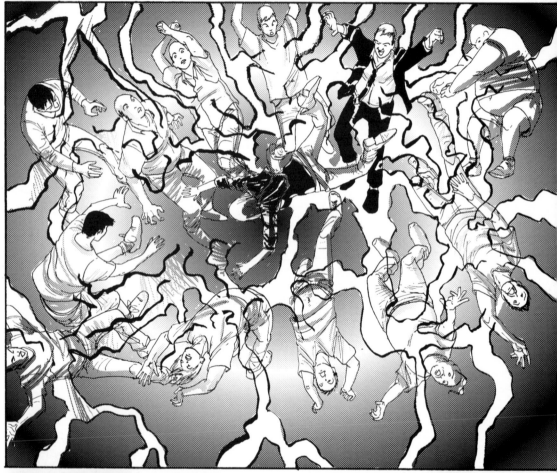

HMPH.

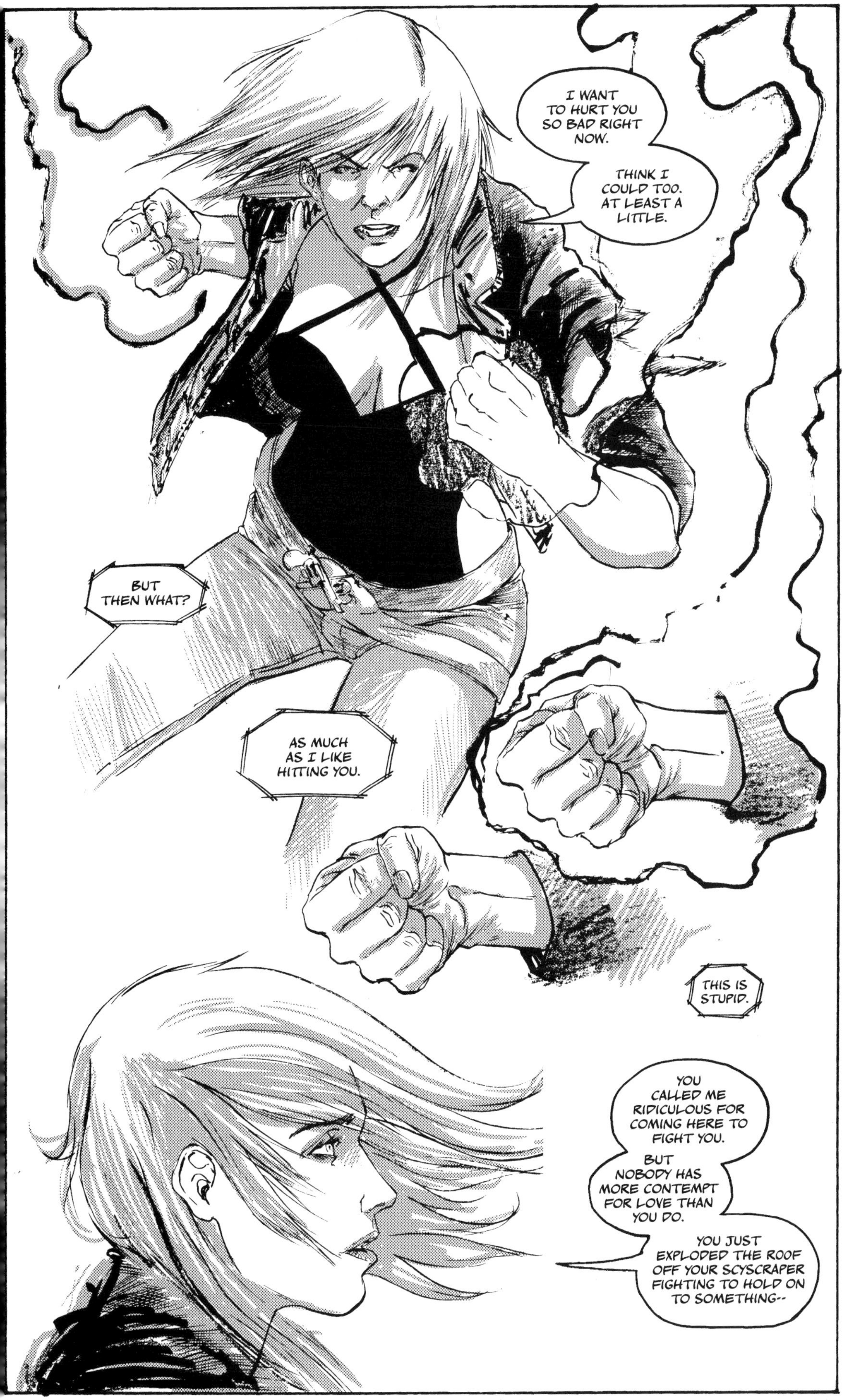
I WANT TO HURT YOU SO BAD RIGHT NOW.
THINK I COULD TOO. AT LEAST A LITTLE.
BUT THEN WHAT?
AS MUCH AS I LIKE HITTING YOU.
THIS IS STUPID.
YOU CALLED ME RIDICULOUS FOR COMING HERE TO FIGHT YOU.
BUT NOBODY HAS MORE CONTEMPT FOR LOVE THAN YOU DO.
YOU JUST EXPLODED THE ROOF OFF YOUR SCYSCRAPER FIGHTING TO HOLD ON TO SOMETHING--

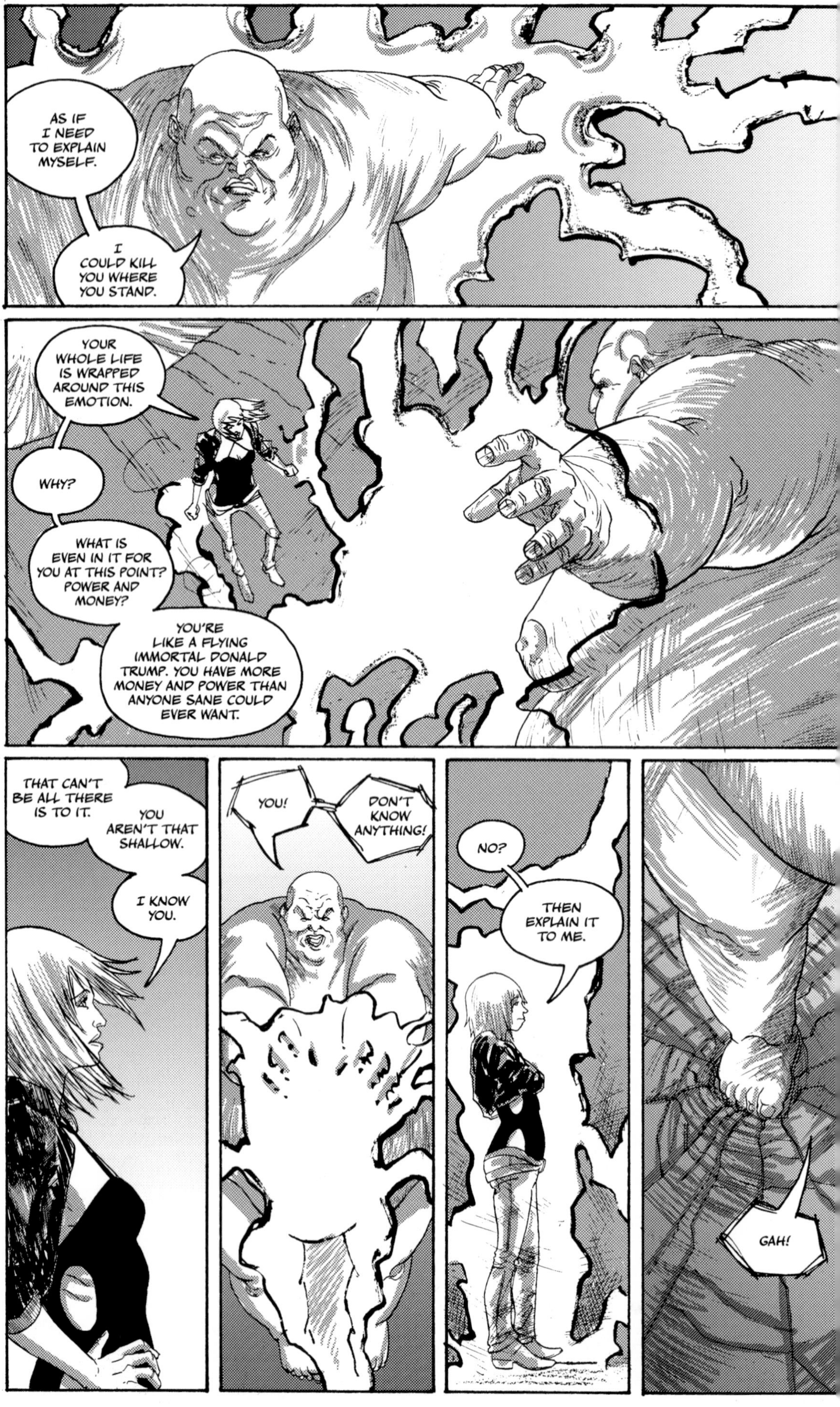
AS IF I NEED TO EXPLAIN MYSELF.
I COULD KILL YOU WHERE YOU STAND.
YOUR WHOLE LIFE IS WRAPPED AROUND THIS EMOTION.
WHY?
WHAT IS EVEN IN IT FOR YOU AT THIS POINT? POWER AND MONEY?
YOU'RE LIKE A FLYING IMMORTAL DONALD TRUMP. YOU HAVE MORE MONEY AND POWER THAN ANYONE SANE COULD EVER WANT.
THAT CAN'T BE ALL THERE IS TO IT.
YOU AREN'T THAT SHALLOW.
I KNOW YOU.
YOU!
DON'T KNOW ANYTHING!
NO?
THEN EXPLAIN IT TO ME.
GAH!

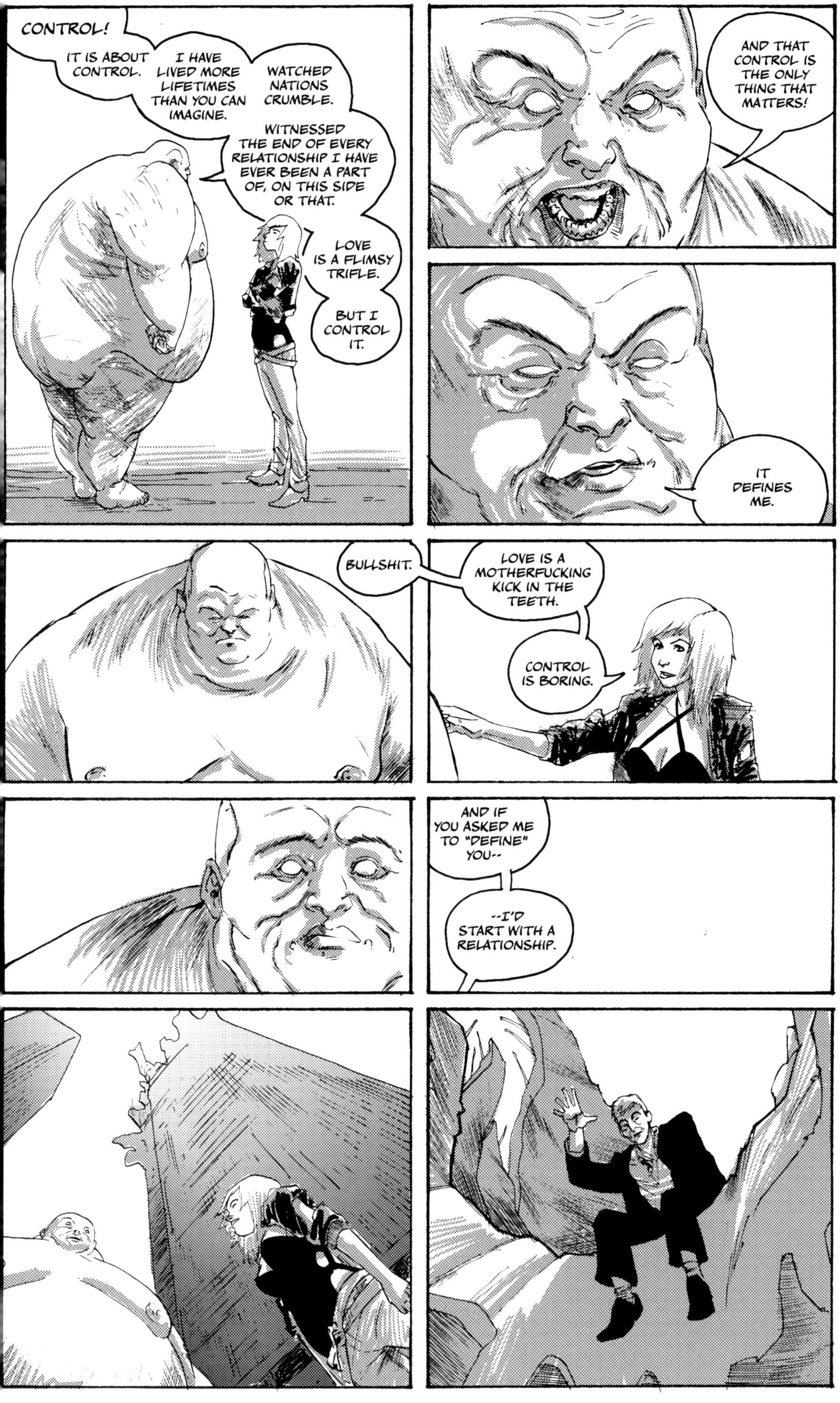
CONTROL!
IT IS ABOUT CONTROL.
I HAVE LIVED MORE LIFETIMES THAN YOU CAN IMAGINE.
WATCHED NATIONS CRUMBLE.
WITNESSED THE END OF EVERY RELATIONSHIP I HAVE EVER BEEN A PART OF, ON THIS SIDE OR THAT.
LOVE IS A FLIMSY TRIFLE.
BUT I CONTROL IT.
AND THAT CONTROL IS THE ONLY THING THAT MATTERS!
IT DEFINES ME.
BULLSHIT.
LOVE IS A MOTHERFUCKING KICK IN THE TEETH.
CONTROL IS BORING.
AND IF YOU ASKED ME TO "DEFINE" YOU--
--I'D START WITH A RELATIONSHIP.

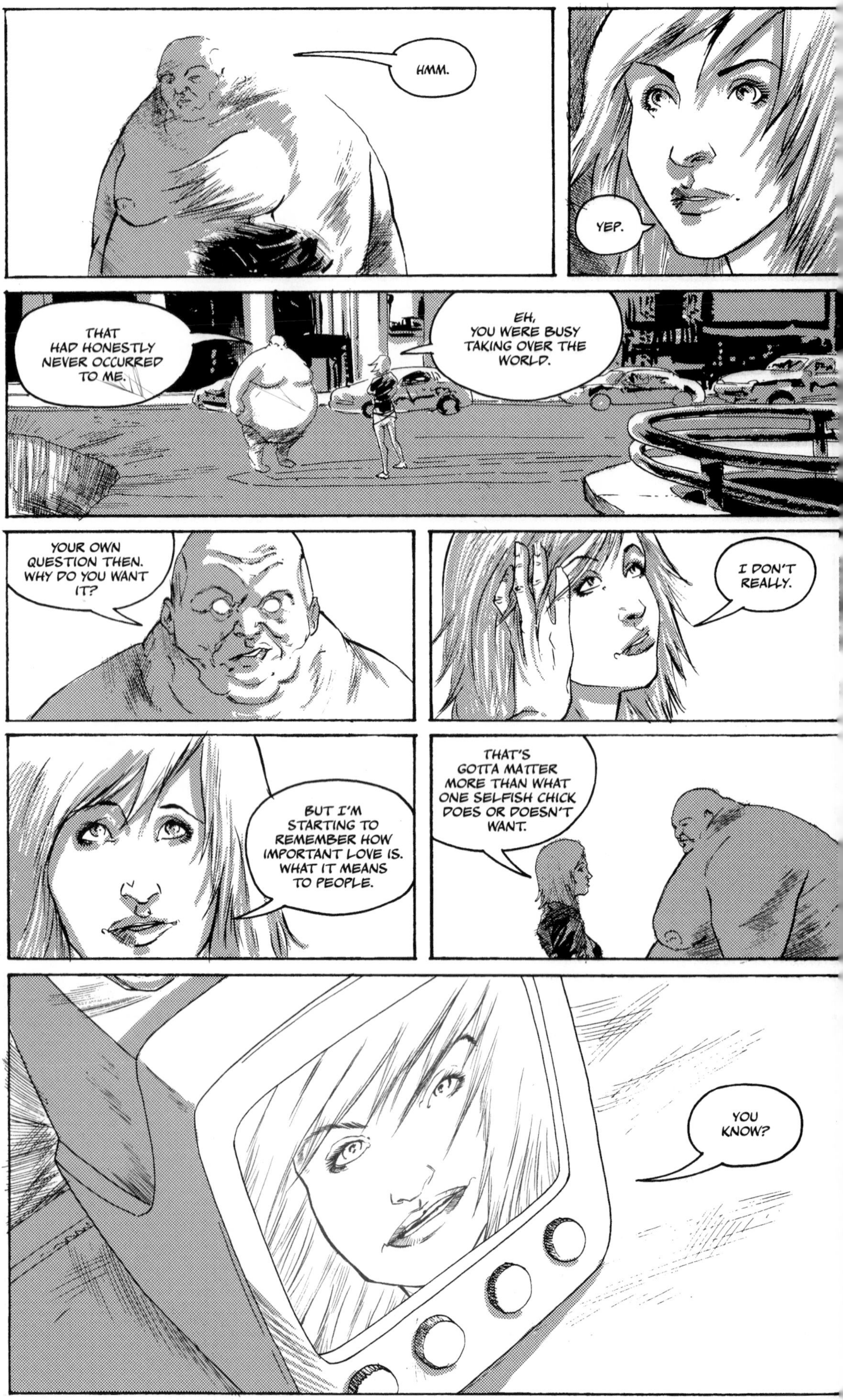
HMM.
YEP.
THAT HAD HONESTLY NEVER OCCURRED TO ME.
EH, YOU WERE BUSY TAKING OVER THE WORLD.
YOUR OWN QUESTION THEN. WHY DO YOU WANT IT?
I DON'T REALLY.
BUT I'M STARTING TO REMEMBER HOW IMPORTANT LOVE IS. WHAT IT MEANS TO PEOPLE.
THAT'S GOTTA MATTER MORE THAN WHAT ONE SELFISH CHICK DOES OR DOESN'T WANT.
YOU KNOW?

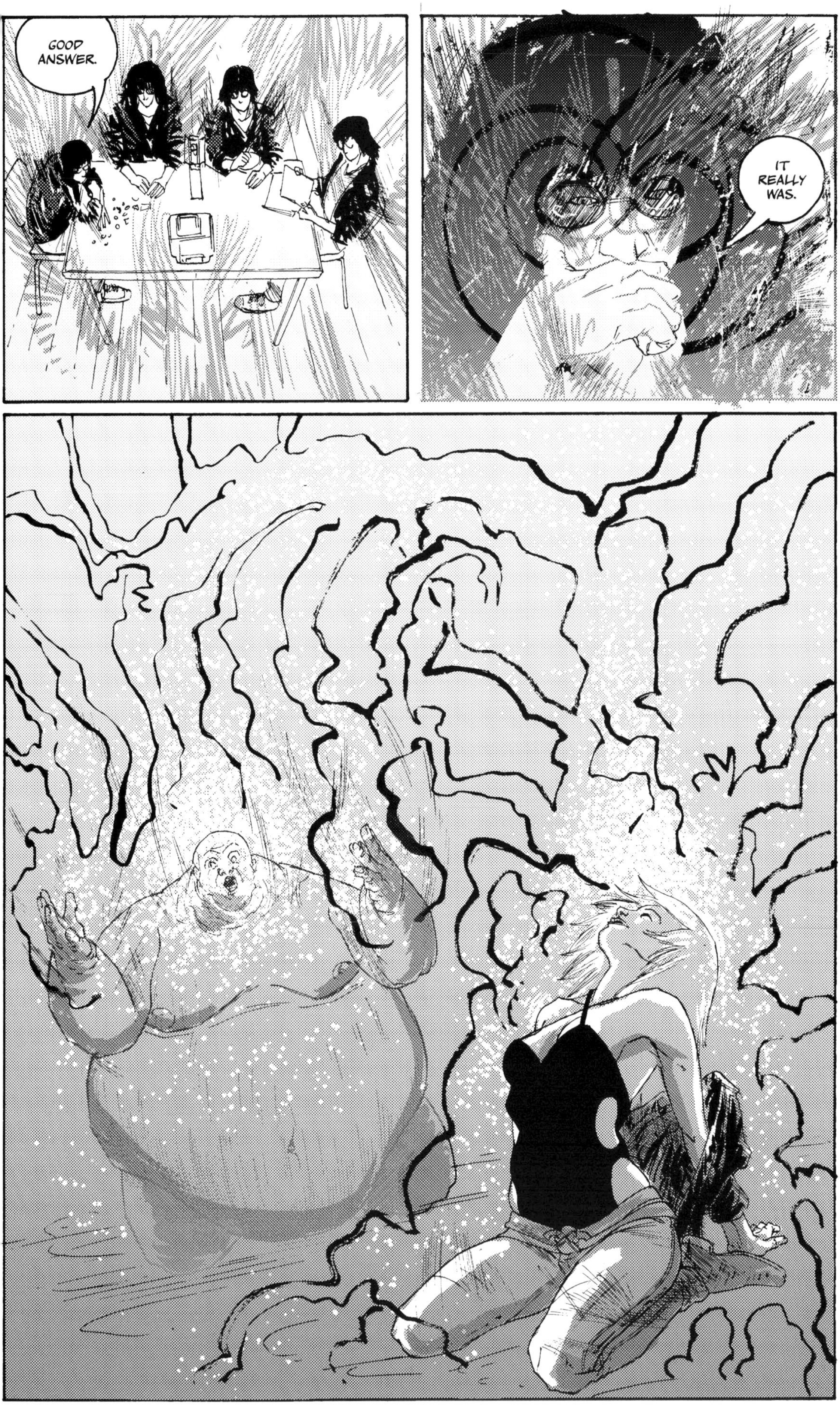
GOOD ANSWER.
IT REALLY WAS.

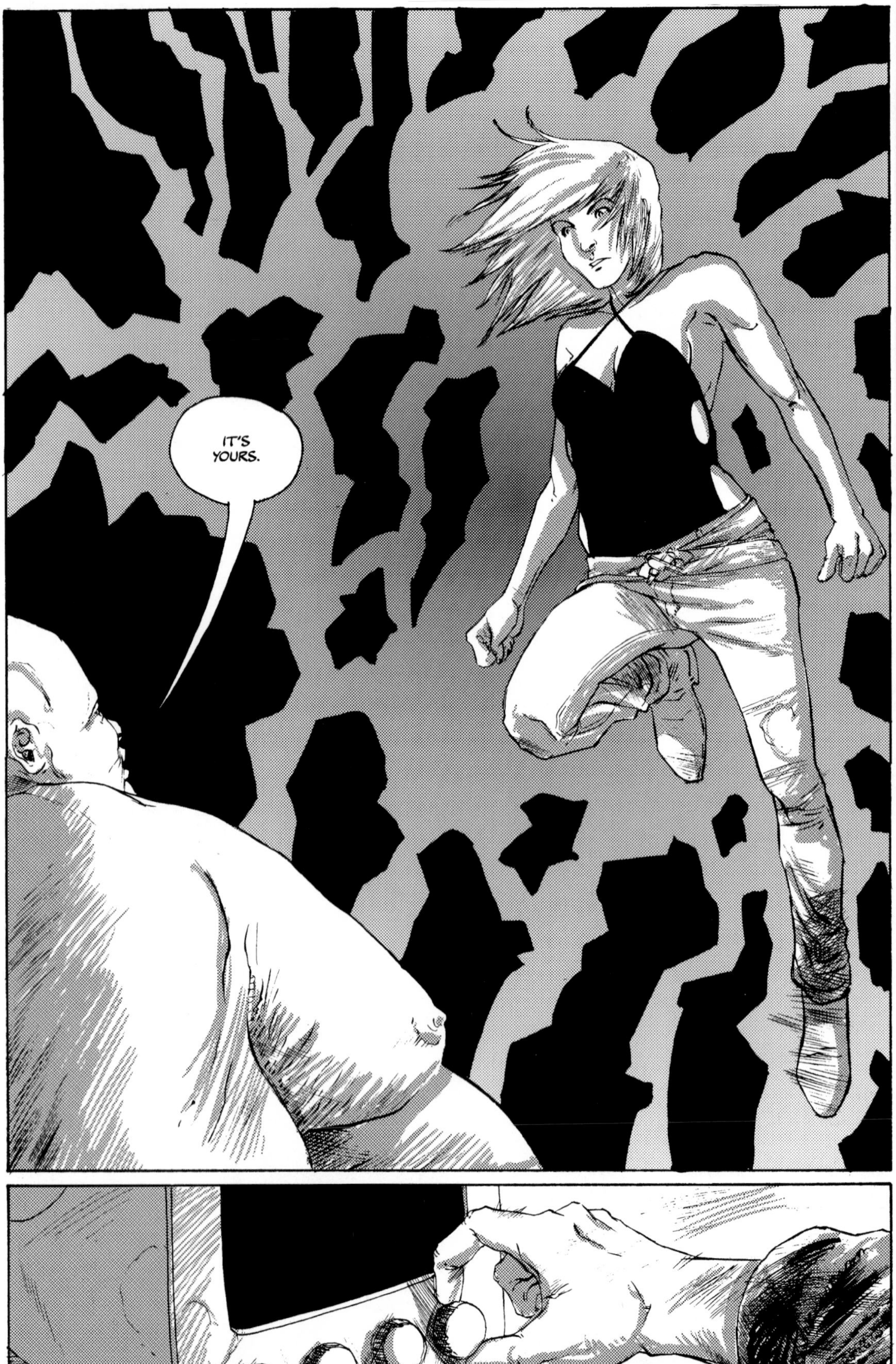
IT'S YOURS.

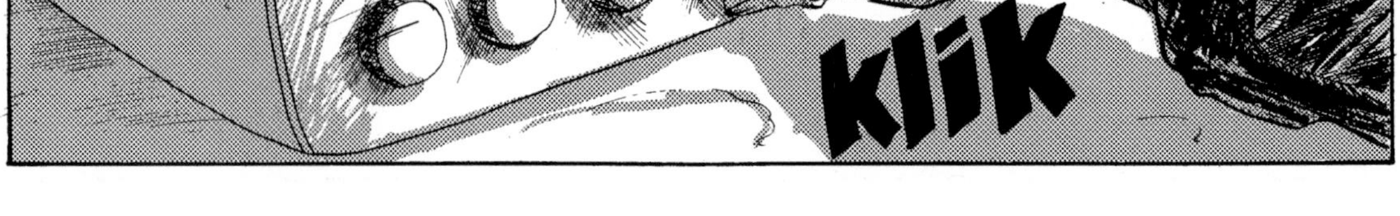
KLIK

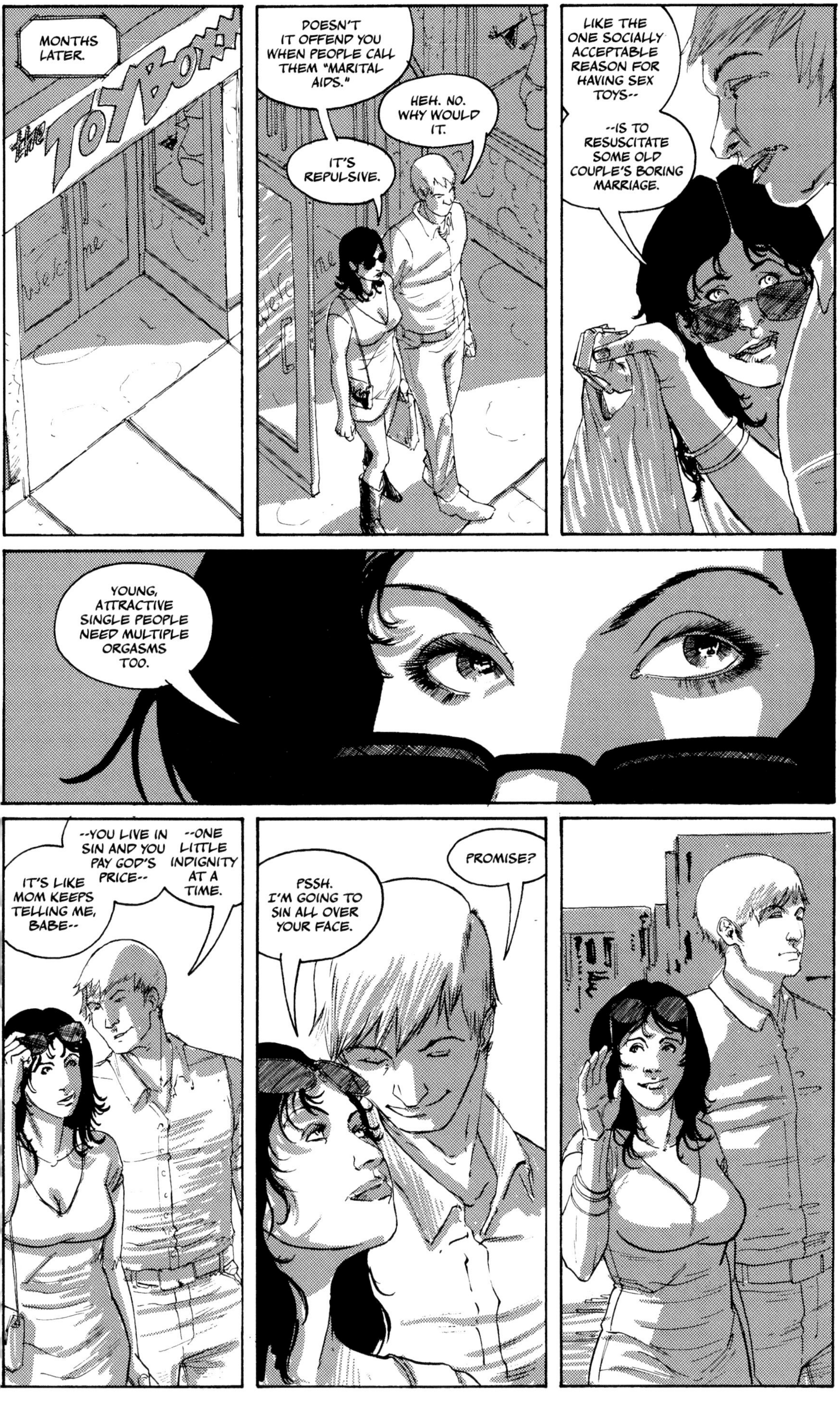
MONTHS LATER.
the TOYBOX
DOESN'T IT OFFEND YOU WHEN PEOPLE CALL THEM "MARITAL AIDS."
HEH. NO. WHY WOULD IT.
IT'S REPULSIVE.
LIKE THE ONE SOCIALLY ACCEPTABLE REASON FOR HAVING SEX TOYS--
--IS TO RESUSCITATE SOME OLD COUPLE'S BORING MARRIAGE.
YOUNG, ATTRACTIVE SINGLE PEOPLE NEED MULTIPLE ORGASMS TOO.
IT'S LIKE MOM KEEPS TELLING ME, BABE--
--YOU LIVE IN SIN AND YOU PAY GOD'S PRICE--
--ONE LITTLE INDIGNITY AT A TIME.
PSSH. I'M GOING TO SIN ALL OVER YOUR FACE.
PROMISE?

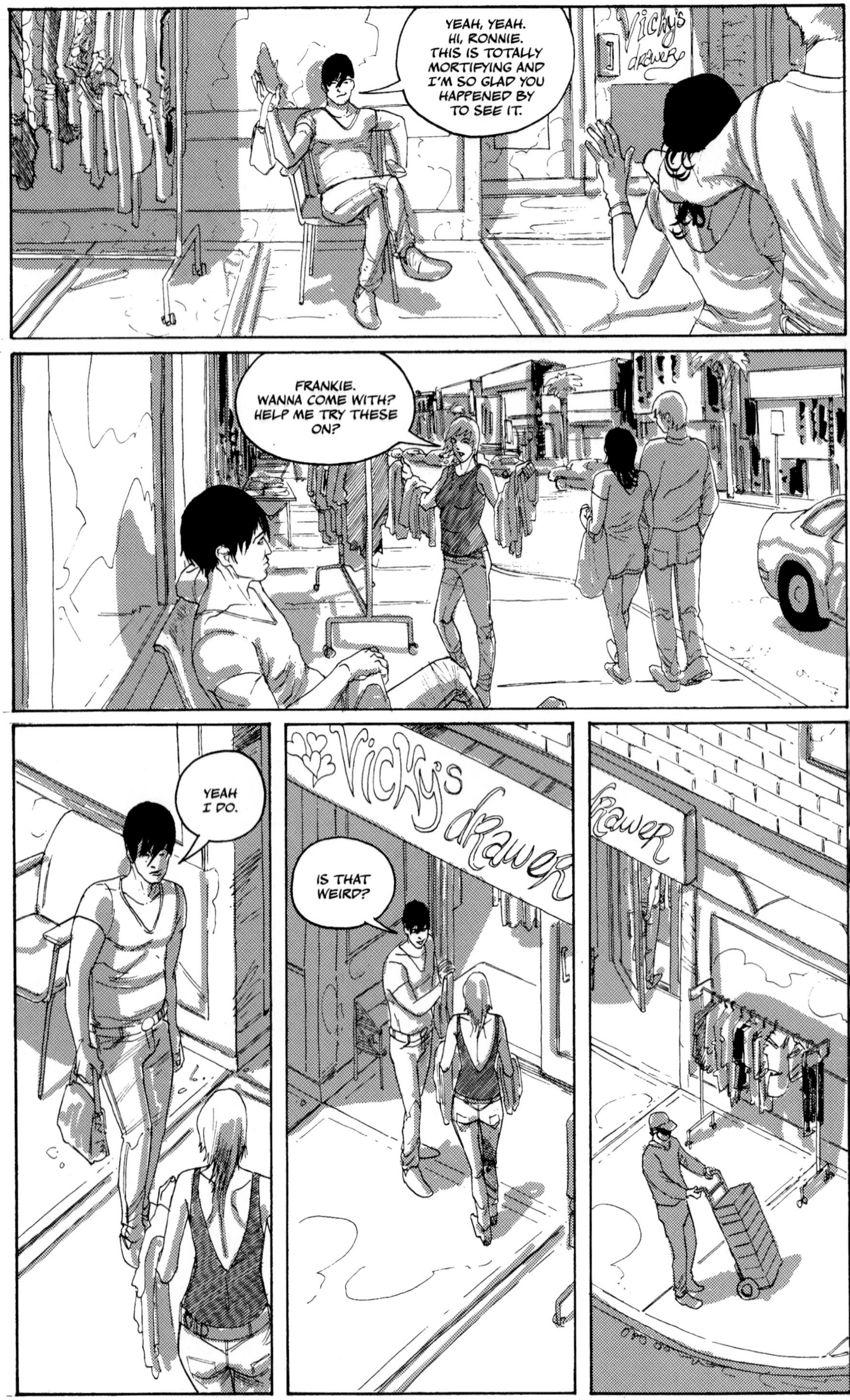

Vicky's drawer
YEAH, YEAH. HI, RONNIE. THIS IS TOTALLY MORTIFYING AND I'M SO GLAD YOU HAPPENED BY TO SEE IT.
FRANKIE. WANNA COME WITH? HELP ME TRY THESE ON?
YEAH I DO.
Vicky's drawer
IS THAT WEIRD?
drawer

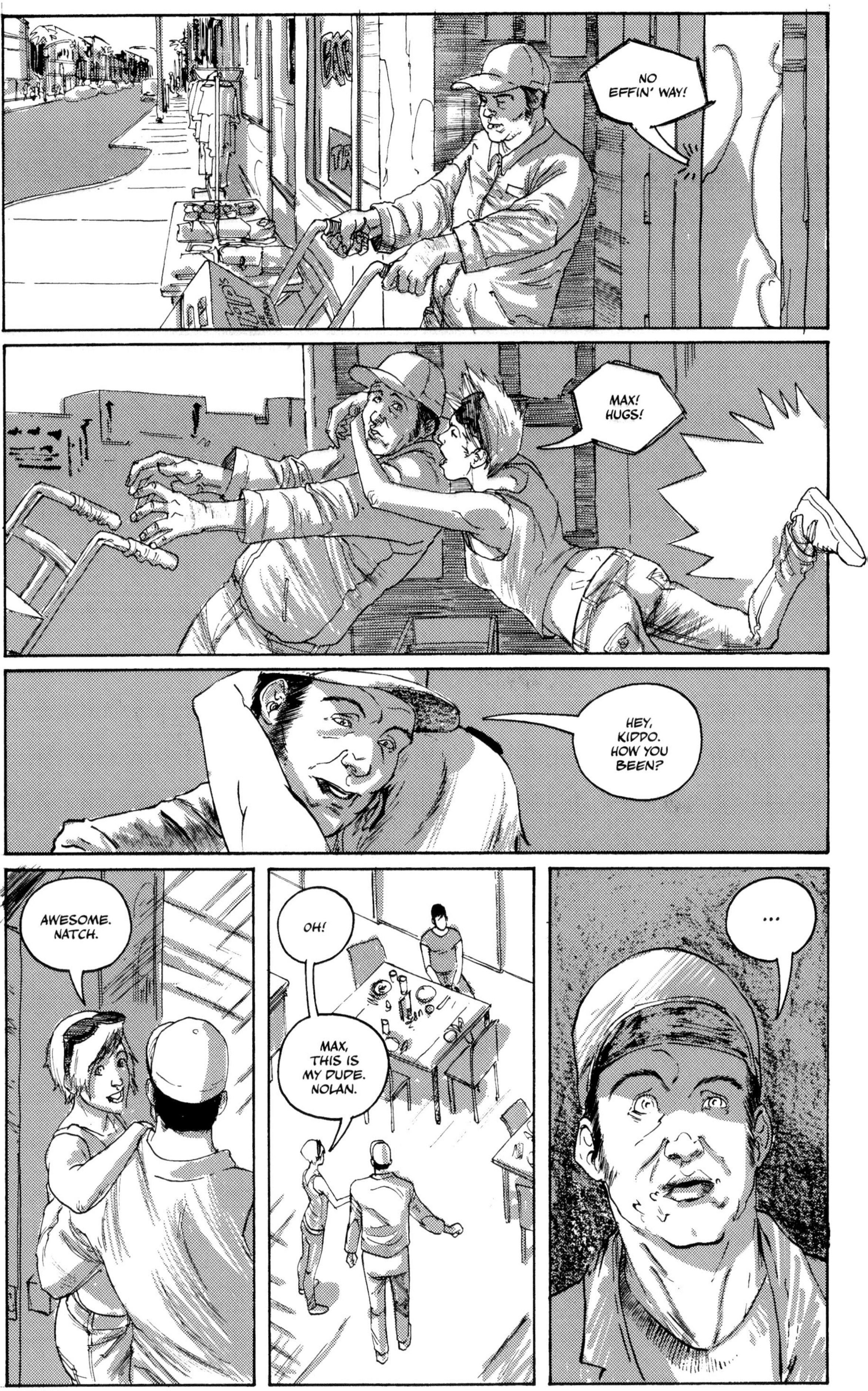
NO EFFIN' WAY!
MAX! HUGS!
HEY, KIDDO. HOW YOU BEEN?
AWESOME. NATCH.
OH!
MAX, THIS IS MY DUDE. NOLAN.
...

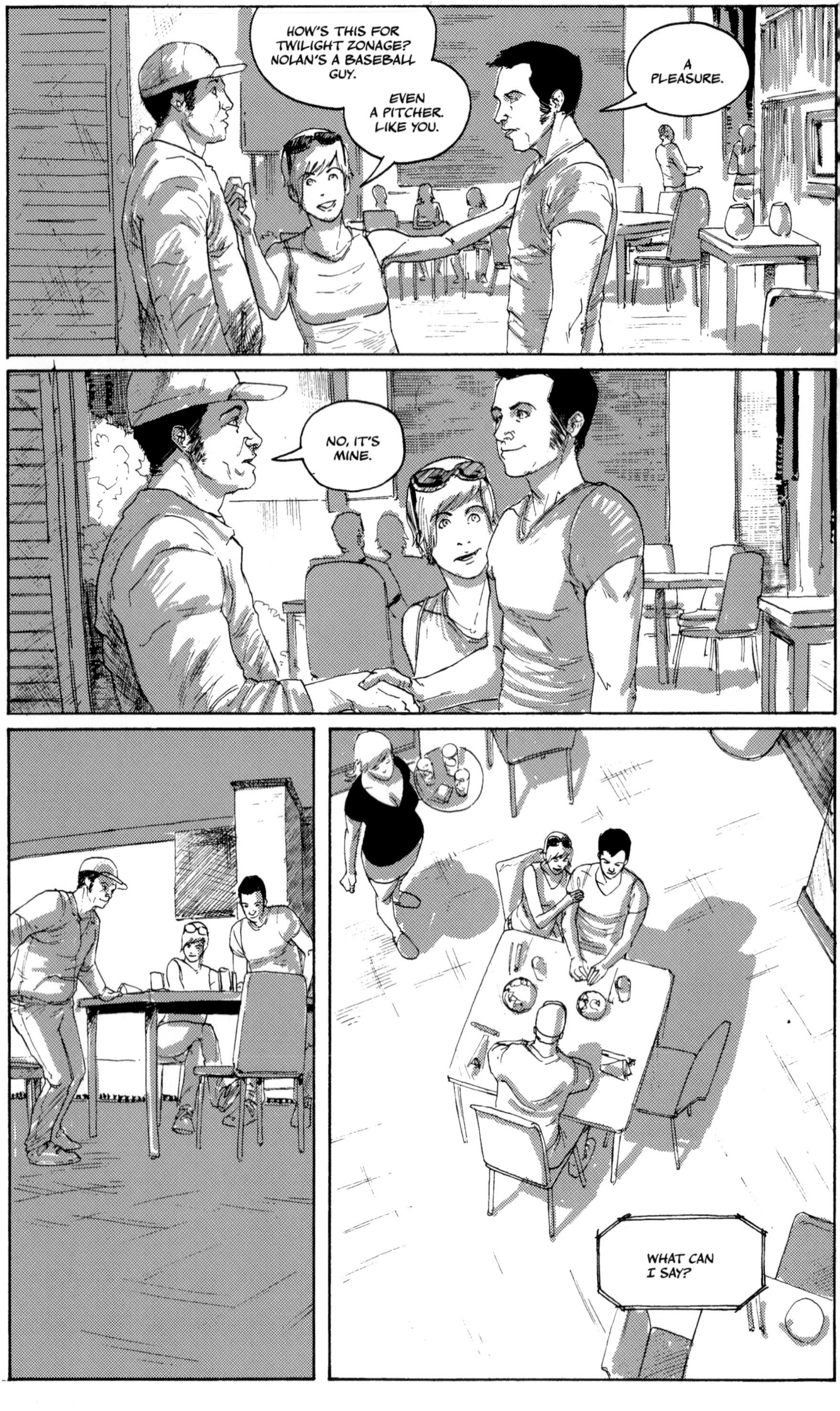
HOW'S THIS FOR TWILIGHT ZONAGE? NOLAN'S A BASEBALL GUY.
EVEN A PITCHER. LIKE YOU.
A PLEASURE.
NO, IT'S MINE.
WHAT CAN I SAY?

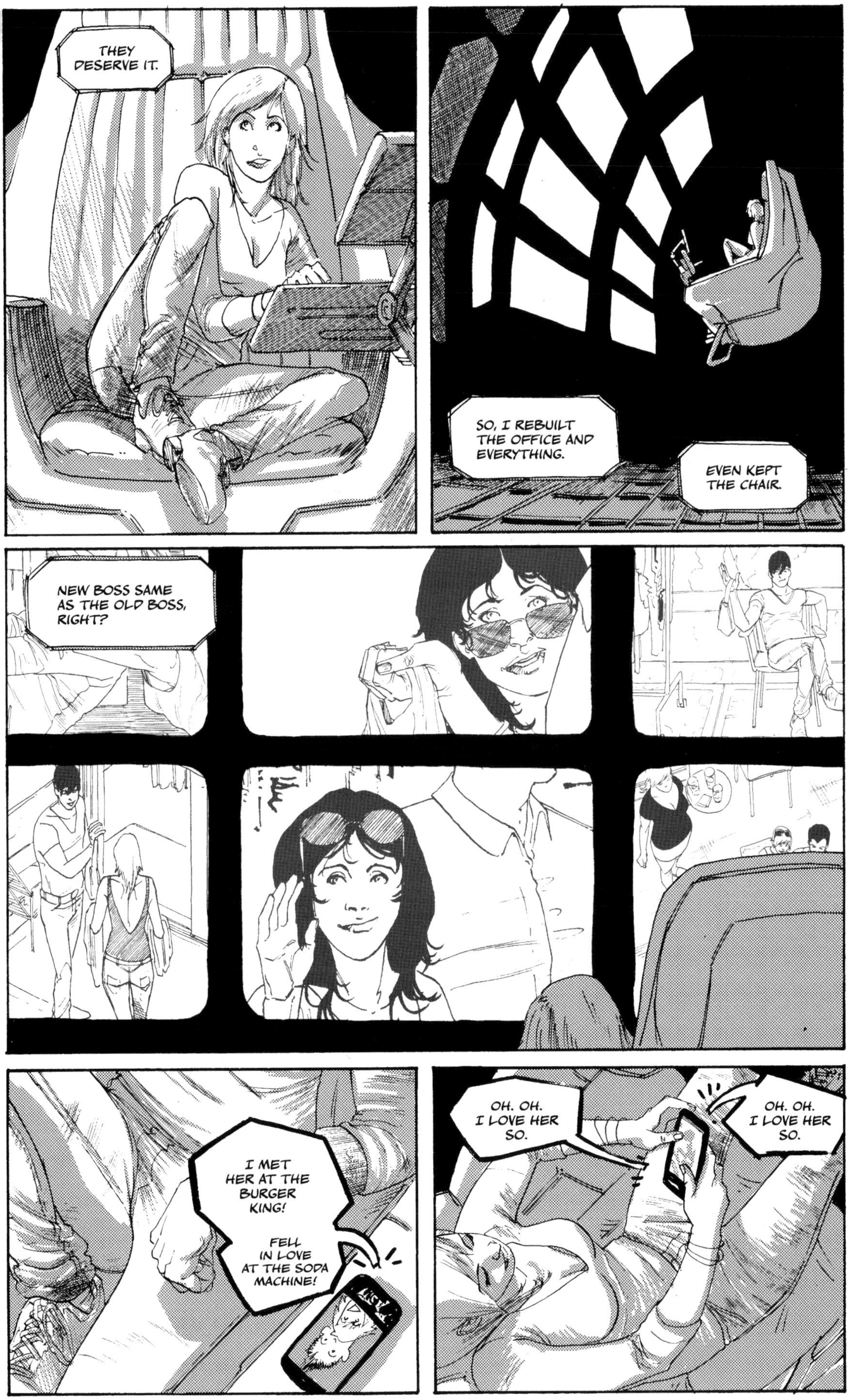
THEY DESERVE IT.
SO, I REBUILT THE OFFICE AND EVERYTHING.
EVEN KEPT THE CHAIR.
NEW BOSS SAME AS THE OLD BOSS, RIGHT?
I MET HER AT THE BURGER KING!
FELL IN LOVE AT THE SODA MACHINE!
OH. OH. I LOVE HER SO.
OH. OH. I LOVE HER SO.

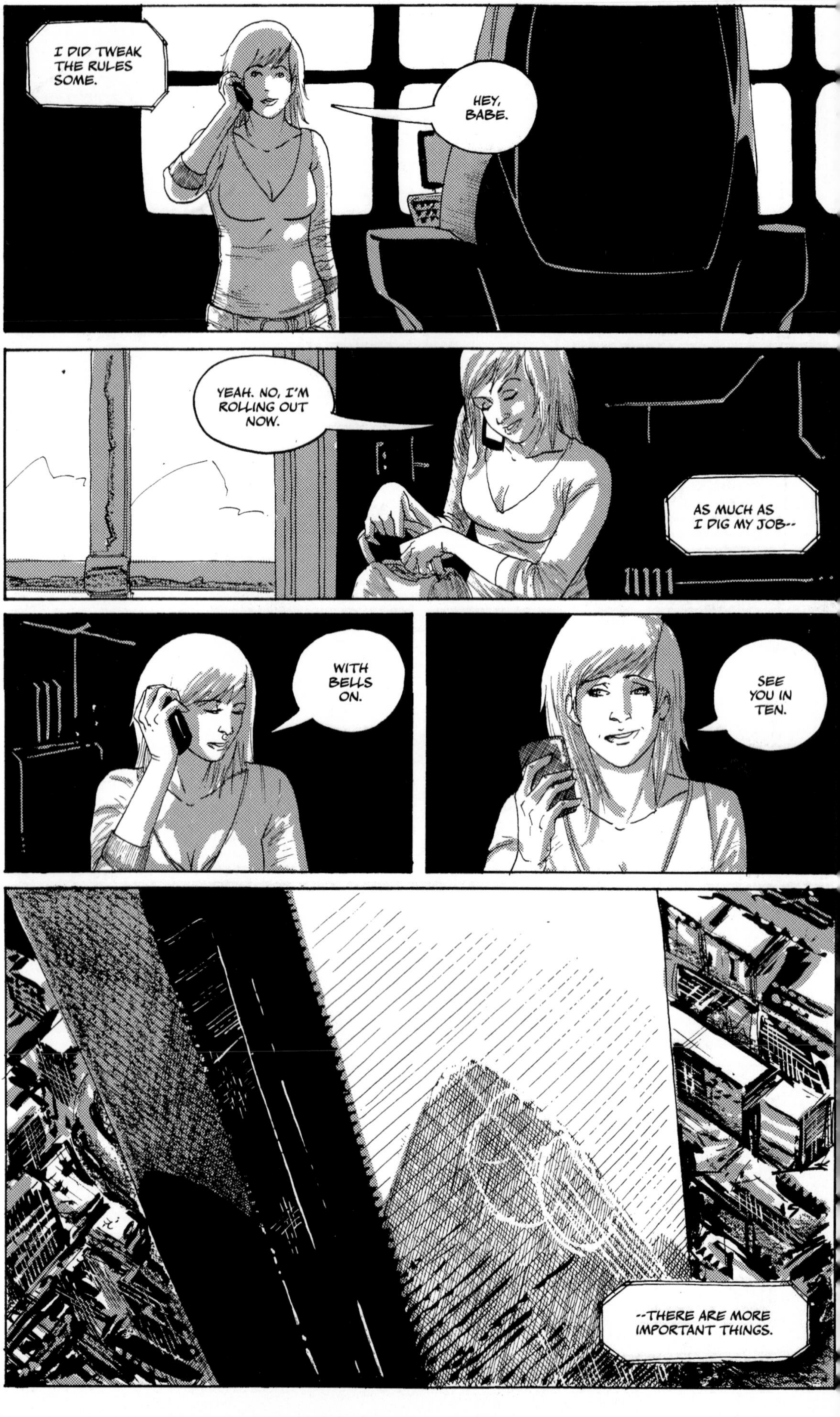

I DID TWEAK THE RULES SOME.
HEY, BABE.
YEAH. NO, I'M ROLLING OUT NOW.
AS MUCH AS I DIG MY JOB--
WITH BELLS ON.
SEE YOU IN TEN.
--THERE ARE MORE IMPORTANT THINGS.

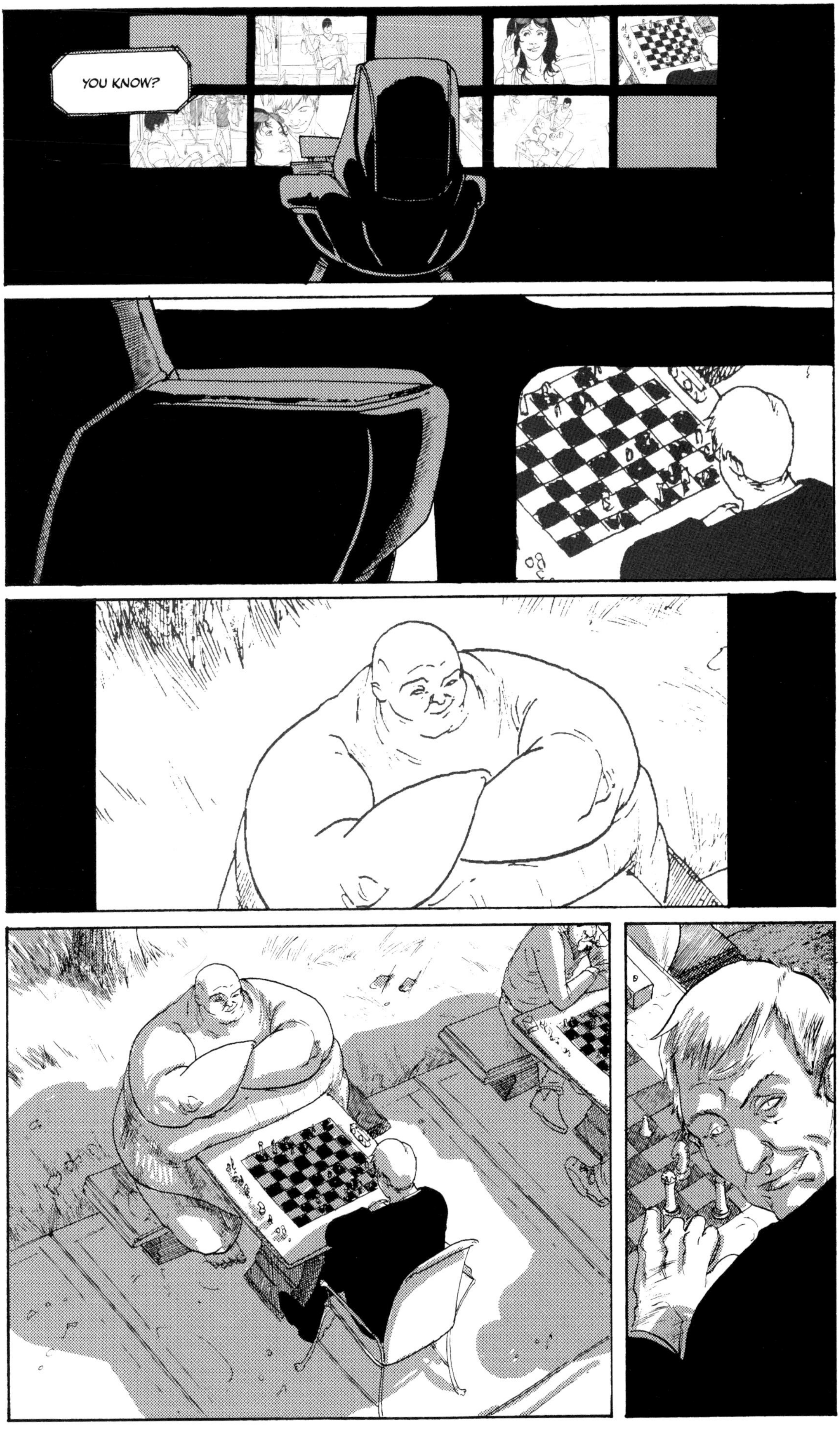
YOU KNOW?